The Fissured Workplace

The Fissured Workplace

Why Work Became So Bad
for So Many and What
Can Be Done to
Improve It

DAVID WEIL

Harvard University Press

Cambridge, Massachusetts
London, England
2014

Library of Congress Cataloging-in-Publication Data

Weil, David, 1961–

The fissured workplace : why work became so bad for so many and
what can be done to improve it / David Weil.

pages   cm

Includes bibliographical references and index.

ISBN 978-0-674-72544-7 (alk. paper)

1. Labor—United States. 2. Industrial relations—United States.
3. Manpower planning—United States. 4. Quality of work life—
United States. I. Title.

HD8066.W44   2014

331.20973—dc23   2013017888

To my family—past, present, and future

Contents

The Fissured Workplace

Vignettes from the Modern Workplace

A maid works at the San Francisco Marriott on Fisherman's Wharf. The hotel property is owned by Host Hotels and Resorts Inc., a lodging real estate company. The maid, however, is evaluated and supervised daily and her hours and payroll managed by Crestline Hotels and Resorts Inc., a national third-party hotel management company. Yet she follows daily procedures (and risks losing her job for failure to accomplish them) regarding cleaning, room set-up, overall pace, and quality standards established by Marriott, whose name the property bears.

A cable installer in Dayton, Ohio, works as an independent contractor (in essence a self-employed business provider), paid on a job-by-job basis by Cascom Inc., a cable installation company. Cascom's primary client is the international media giant Time Warner, which owns cable systems across the United States. The cable installer is paid solely on the basis of the job completed and is entitled to no protections normally afforded employees. Yet all installation contracts are supplied solely by Cascom, which also sets the price for jobs and collects payment for them. The installer must wear a shirt with the Cascom logo and can be removed as a contractor at will for not meeting minimum quotas or quality standards, or at the will of the company.

A recent immigrant to the United States and an aspiring entrepreneur in Boston starts a commercial janitorial service by purchasing a franchise from Coverall, one of the largest U.S. companies in this business. He is owner of the Coverall franchise and works long hours, cleaning clients' businesses, including a Bank of America branch. He receives his clients from Coverall, which sets the price and quality standards, defines the geographic boundaries of his franchise, and loaned him capital to purchase the franchise. The prevailing market rate for janitorial services set by Coverall barely covers the royalties, loan repayment, and other expenses to the franchisor, the gas and car costs for traveling between clients, and compensation for himself and the people who work with him.

A member of a loading dock crew working in Southern California is paid by Premier Warehousing Ventures LLC (PWV)—a company providing temporary workers to other businesses—based on the total time it takes him and members of his crew to load a truck. PWV, in turn, is compensated for the number of trucks loaded by Schneider Logistics, a national logistics and trucking company that manages distribution centers for Walmart. Walmart sets the price, time requirements, and performance standards that are followed by Schneider. Schneider, in turn, structures its contracts with PWV and other labor brokers it uses to provide workers based on those prices and standards and its own profit objectives.

A young Moldovan exchange student works in a Palmyra, Pennsylvania, shipping facility packing chocolates exclusively for the Hershey Company. The job was arranged via the J-1 visa program overseen by the State Department to provide international students with cultural opportunities in the United States via a nonprofit organization, the Council for Educational Travel, USA (CETUSA). CETUSA, in turn, set up summer employment for the student and four hundred others with Exel, a company contracted by Hershey to manage its packing facility. Exel in turn hires a labor contractor, SHS OnSite Solutions, to provide workers, including students holding J-1 visas. Students who paid $6,000 to participate in the exchange program are assigned the 10:00 p.m. to 6:00 a.m. shift in the refrigerated facility and are paid a wage of $8.00 an hour, from which rent and other expenses are deducted, leaving little extra for the "exchange" portion of their experience.

In an earlier era, Marriott, Time Warner, Bank of America, Walmart, and Hershey, as well as other large employers that produced well-known products and services, would likely have directly employed the workers in the above vignettes. Not so now. As major companies have consciously invested in building brands and devoted customers as the cornerstone of their business strategy, they have also shed their role as the direct employer of the people responsible for providing those products and services.

In all of the above cases, the jobs shifted away to be done by separate employers pay low wages; provide limited or often no health care, pension, or other benefits; and offer tenuous job security. Moreover, workers in each case received pay or faced workplace conditions that violated one or more workplace laws. Tudor Ureche, a Moldovan student working in the Hershey packing facility, sent an email to the State Department seeking "help [from] the miserable situation in which I've found myself cought [*sic*]," which included lifting 50–60-pound boxes in a refrigerated facility on the night shift. Pius Awuah, a resident of Lowell, Massachusetts, put his life savings into a Coverall franchise contract that in many respects was simply paying to be an employee (who was then compensated in violation of minimum wages and overtime standards). And Everardo Carrillo and coworkers at a facility operated by Schneider Logistics were paid in violation of the Fair Labor Standards Act and then fired for stepping forward to complain about those working conditions.

The cases are not exceptional, but rather indicative of practices found in the varied industries depicted above as well as in a growing number of other sectors and occupations. Yet these working conditions are not an inevitable result of the nature of those jobs or of amorphous forces like globalization. They result from a fundamental restructuring of employment in many parts of the economy.

The vignettes reveal a transformation in how business organizes work in ways that are invisible to most of us as consumers. We walk into a Marriott and assume that the people who greet us at the front desk or who clean our rooms each day are employees of that venerable brand (as their uniforms imply). We greet the technicians sent to our home to fix our cable, not even questioning whether they work for the media company to whom we pay our bills. In short, we assume that the companies who invest millions of dollars to convince us of the benefits of buying products under their retail nameplate or to purchase the unique services they offer also undertake the operations needed to produce them—including acting as the employer of all the interconnected people who make their businesses possible.

Those assumptions are increasingly wrong. In the late 1980s and early 1990s, many companies, facing increasingly restive capital markets, shed activities deemed peripheral to their core business models: out went janitors, security guards, payroll administrators, and information technology specialists. But then came activities many of us would assume were more central to these well-known businesses: the front desk staff at hotel check-in; the drivers for the package delivery companies who come to our homes or offices; the tower workers who help assure uninterrupted cell phone service promoted in the commercials (and for which we pay a premium). Even the lawyers who handle our business transactions and the consultants who work for well-known accounting companies may now have an arm's-length relationship with those by whom we think they are employed.

By shedding direct employment, lead business enterprises select from among multiple providers of those activities and services formerly done inside the organization, thereby substantially reducing costs and dispatching the many responsibilities connected to being the employer of record. Information and communication technologies have enabled this hidden transformation of work, since they allow lead companies to promulgate and enforce product and quality standards key to their business strategies, thereby maintaining the carefully created reputation of their goods and services and reaping price premiums from their loyal customer base.

The new organization of the workplace also undermines the mechanisms that once led to the workforce sharing part of the value created by their large corporate employers. By shedding employment to other parties, lead companies change a wage-setting problem into a contracting decision. The result is stagnation of real wages for many of the jobs formerly done inside.

Laws originally intended to ensure basic labor standards and to protect workers from health and safety risks now enable these changes by focusing regulatory attention on the wrong parties. Core federal and state laws that regulate employment, often dating back to the first half of the twentieth century, often assume simple and direct employee/employer relationships. They make presumptions about responsibility and liability similar to those we make as customers, presumptions that ignore the transformation that has occurred under the hood of many business enterprises. Traditional approaches to enforcing those laws similarly ignore the myriad new relationships that lie below the surface of the workplace. As a result, the laws crafted to safeguard basic standards, to reduce health and safety risks, and to cushion displacement from injury or economic downturn often fail to do so.

In essence, private strategies and public policies allow major companies to simultaneously profit from the core activities that create value in the eyes of customers and the capital markets and shed the actual production of goods and services. In so doing, they have their cake and eat it too.

How did the workplace fissure? What are the wider impacts? Is continued shedding of employment the inevitable outcome of a modern, flexible economy? Are there ways to assure that workers are treated fairly and responsibly given the continued pressure to fissure employment? These are the central questions explored in this book.

The Fissured Workplace
and Its Consequences

The modern workplace has been profoundly transformed. Employment is no longer the clear relationship between a well-defined employer and a worker. The basic terms of employment—hiring, evaluation, pay, supervision, training, coordination—are now the result of multiple organizations. Responsibility for conditions has become blurred. Like a rock with a fracture that deepens and spreads with time, the workplace over the past three decades has fissured. And fissuring has serious consequences for the bedrock that people depend upon from employment: the share of the economic pie available to workers and their families; their exposure to health and safety and other risks each day at work; and the likelihood that their workplaces comply with the standards set out by law.

The stories opening Part I are not unusual. In 1960 most hotel employees worked for the brand that appeared over the hotel entrance. Today, more than 80% of staff are employed by hotel franchisees and supervised by separate management companies that bear no relation to the brand name of the property where they work. Twenty years ago, workers in the distribution center of a major manufacturer or retailer would be hired, supervised, evaluated, and paid by that company. Today, workers might receive a paycheck from a labor supplier or be managed by the personnel of a logistics company, while their work is governed by the detailed operating standards of the nationally known retailer or consumer brand serviced by the facility. And whereas IBM in its ascendency directly employed workers from designers and engineers to the people on the factory floor producing its computers, Apple can be our economy's most highly valued company while directly employing only 63,000 of the more than 750,000 workers globally responsible for designing, selling, manufacturing, and assembling its products.

A Seismic Shift in the Focus of Employment

During much of the twentieth century, the critical employment relationship was between large businesses and workers. Large businesses with national and international reputations operating at the top of their industries (which will be referred to as "lead businesses" throughout the book) continue to focus on delivering value to their customers and investors. However, most no longer directly employ legions of workers to make products or deliver services. Employment has been actively shed by these market leaders and transferred to a complicated network of smaller business units. Lower-level businesses operate in more highly competitive markets than those of the firms that shifted employment to them.

This creates downward pressure on wages and benefits, murkiness about who bears responsibility for work conditions, and increased likelihood that basic labor standards will be violated. In many cases, fissuring leads simultaneously to a rise in profitability for the lead companies who operate at the top of industries and increasingly precarious working conditions for workers at lower levels.

But the fissured workplace is not simply the result of employers seeking to reduce wages and cut benefits. It represents the intersection of three business strategies, one focused on revenues, one on costs, and one on providing the "glue" to make the overall strategy operate effectively. Its components begin not with employment, but with the demands by capital markets that lead companies focus on core competencies that produce value for investors and consumers. This means building brands, creating innovative products and services, capitalizing on true economies of scale and scope, or coordinating complex supply chains. But focusing on the core also has come to mean shifting activities once considered central to operations to other organizations in order to convert employer-employee relationships into arm's-length market transactions. Finally, fissuring weds these potentially contradictory activities through the glue of the creation, monitoring, and enforcement of standards on product and service delivery, made available through new information and communication technologies and enabled by organizational models like franchising, labor brokers, and third-party management.

The result is businesses and industries wired in fundamentally new ways. Wage setting and supervision shift from core businesses to a myriad of organizations, each operating under the rigorous standards of lead businesses but facing fierce competitive pressures. Although lead businesses set demanding goals and standards, and often detailed work practice requirements for subsidiary companies, the actual liability, oversight, and supervision of the workforce become the problem of one or more other organizations. And by replacing a direct employment relationship with a fissured workplace, employment itself becomes more precarious, with risk shifted onto smaller employers and individual workers, who are often cast in the role of independent businesses in their own right.

Consequences

As the fissured workplace has deepened and spread across the economy, work that once provided middle-class wages and benefits has declined. Jobs that once resided inside lead businesses providing decent earnings and stability now reside with employers who set wages under far more competitive conditions. Where lead companies once shared gains with their internal workforce, fissuring leads to growing inequality in how the value created in the economy is distributed.

Laws that protect workers have not kept pace with the new boundaries of the fissured workplace. Americans' commitment to providing safety and health and decent conditions at the workplace has not changed. But relentless subcontracting can blur responsibility for safety and put workers in harm's way. Outsourcing management to third parties can lead to violation of minimum wage laws. And franchising, an often unrecognized form of fissured employment, can create incentives that simultaneously demand adherence to product quality and create incentives for franchisees to violate laws.

Even the business cycle may be affected by the spread of fissuring. Historically, hiring by large businesses led economic recoveries: as aggregate demand recovered, large firms directly increased employment. Now, employment decisions in many industries are mediated by fissured structures. Not only does this mean that the timing of recoveries may be slowed, since they must flow through multiple layers of fissured relationships; but the composition of jobs added also will reflect those relationships. Seen in this light, it is not surprising that the first jobs to be added following the Great Recession were predominantly at the low end of the wage distribution.

Why Fissure?

Multiple motivations underlie fissuring. In some cases, shedding employment by a lead company to other parties represents what is regarded as a short-term measure to deal with sudden increases in demand.[1] In other cases, fissuring reflects a desire to shift labor costs and liabilities to smaller business entities or to third-party labor intermediaries, such as temporary employment agencies or labor brokers. Employers have incentives to do so for obvious reasons: shifting employment to other parties allows an employer to avoid mandatory social payments (such as unemployment and workers' compensation insurance or payroll taxes) or to shed liability for workplace injuries by deliberately misclassifying workers as independent contractors.[2] Misclassification of this sort is a major problem, particularly in industries like construction and janitorial services.

The fissured workplace does not arise only from pernicious motivations, however. Technologic developments increasingly allow businesses to focus on core competencies while shedding activities not central to the firm's operation. With the falling cost of coordination resulting from new information and communication technologies, productive reconfiguring of the boundaries of companies and entire industries naturally occurs. This is a well-known phenomenon in industries that create intellectual capital, like software, Internet and information technology development, and the creative arts. Decentralized software engineers and game developers need not work in one physical location or even for the same company to develop new apps. In these areas, the fissured workplace reflects the transformation of the production and delivery of intellectual content and in many respects represents a positive development.

More fundamentally, however, the fissured workplace represents a response to pressures from capital markets and is enabled by the falling cost of coordinating business transactions through information and communication technologies. It characterizes the rippling of these forces across industries over time that express themselves in different ways but have common impacts on the situation faced by workers affected by those changes.

Workplace fissuring arises as a consequence of the integration of three distinct strategic elements, the first one focused on revenues (a laser-like focus on core competency), the second focused on costs (shedding employment), and the final one providing the glue to make the overall strategy operate effectively (creating and enforcing standards).

Focusing on Core Competencies

The first element leading to the fissured workplace arises from a broad movement traceable to the late 1970s that urged companies to focus on what mattered most to the business—that is, the company's core competency. Changes in capital markets dramatically increased the pressure brought to bear by investors, lenders, and the capital markets in general on senior management in lead companies to focus their attention on those activities that added greatest value (such as product design, product innovation, cost or quality efficiencies, or other unique strengths) while farming out work to other organizations not central to their core mission. This strategy led companies to focus their key strategies and attention on the development of brands and strong customer identification with the company's goods or services; on building the capacity to introduce new products or designs; or on implementing true economies of scale or scope in production and operation. Activities outside of this core were shifted away. As a result, companies outsourced customer relations to third-party call centers; manufacturers shifted production to networks of subcontractors for subassemblies; and private, public, and nonprofit organizations contracted out everything from cleaning and janitorial services to payroll and human resource functions.

Shedding Employment

By focusing on core competencies, lead businesses in the economy have shed the employment relationship for many activities, and all that comes with it. Shedding the tasks and production activities to other businesses allows lead companies to lower their costs, since externalizing activities to other firms (particularly those operating in more competitive markets) eliminates the need to pay the higher wages and benefits that large enterprises typically provided. It also does away with the need to establish consistency in those human resource policies, since they no longer reside inside the firm. This aspect of fissuring pushes liability for adherence to a range of workplace statutes (and other public policies) outward to other businesses.

Creating and Enforcing Standards

There is an inherent tension between the first two elements of fissured strategies: by shifting the provision of services to other businesses, companies that have created brands may jeopardize them if quality standards are not adhered to closely. Similarly, coordination economies will not persist if the suppliers that one depends on fail to live up to them or to provide the services required in a timely manner. The third element of fissured organizations is, therefore, developing clear, explicit, and detailed standards that provide the blueprint that the enterprises at lower levels must follow. But detailed standards are not enough: the lead organization must also create contracts or develop organizational structures that allow it to monitor such standards and impose real costs if the affiliated companies fail to live up to them.

It is not coincidental, then, that the expansion of the fissured workplace has been accompanied by the creation of many different forms of standard setting and monitoring, among them the promulgation of bar codes, electronic data interchange protocols, product identification, shipment and delivery standards, GPS, and other methods of tracking products through supply chains and monitoring provision of services to customers. At the same time, organizational forms like franchising that were once restricted to a few industries (such as fast-food restaurants) have become omnipresent, spanning sectors from janitorial and landscaping services to home health care.

Having It Both Ways

The fissured workplace gives rise to a basic contradiction in many industries and in the policies of major businesses. In focusing on core competencies, businesses seek to expand their margins and their markets, thereby improving the profitability of their operations. At the same time, by shedding nonessential activities, they seek to push out activities that would be more costly if maintained within the boundaries of the firm (in a variety of apparent and nonapparent ways, as I shall discuss in later chapters). To do the latter while protecting the integrity of the central business model (that is, protecting the brand or the other sources of core competencies), businesses rely on the promulgation and enforcement of myriad standards through a variety of organizational and technological methods. This final piece of the fissured workplace model is fundamental: it explains why many of the forms of fissured work are possible and prevalent now but not in the past, and represents an intrinsic but underacknowledged element of many business models. Consider the following examples taken from standards promulgated in three very different industries:

- *Fast food—Dunkin' Donuts standards for franchisees:* "All Dunkin' Donuts Stores must be developed and operated to our specifications and standards. Uniformity of products sold in Dunkin' Donuts Stores is important, and you have no discretion in the products you sell."[3]
- *Hotel and motel—Microtel brand standards for affiliated properties:* "You operate the Microtel Hotel under the Hotel System . . . We designed the Hotel System for the operation of "super budget" and "hard budget" hotels, and we expect [that] each Microtel Hotel will comply with Hotel System standards to achieve a relatively uniform and standardized package of services and amenities that are offered to guests consistent with the economy budget sector of the hotel industry."[4]
- *Retailing—Saks Fifth Avenue standards for vendors:* "Now that supply chain efficiencies are the key to remaining competitive and satisfying our customers, it has become critical that we develop collaborative partnerships with vendors who have a similar commitment to these technologies. We expect our vendors to support us by shipping their merchandise "floor ready," trading with our required EDI transactions, and following our Transportation, Packing, and Invoicing guidelines."[5]

Each of these examples illustrates both the specificity and the breadth that characterize standards in many modern business systems across major segments of the economy. Competitive strategies that are central to a wide range of industries—including computers, finance, retailing, and service to traditional manufacturing—simply would not be possible to execute without the promulgation and enforcement of stringent standards.

Yet many of the businesses that rely on the close enforcement of such standards create an artificial distance from subordinate organizations when it comes to employment obligations. While a major restaurant brand may set out standards and guidelines that dictate to a minute degree the way that food is prepared, presented, and served, and specify cleaning routines, schedules, and even the products to be used, it would recoil from being held responsible for franchisees' failure to provide overtime pay for workers, for curbing sexual harassment of workers by supervisors, or for reducing exposure to dangerous cleaning materials. Similarly, a lead electronics company in a supply chain may specify all aspects of product quality and production, set a price, and specify delivery standards but blanch at the notion of responsibility for the consequences of those parameters on the ability to pay people the legally required minimum wage.

The failure of public policy makers to fully appreciate the implications of how major sectors of the society organize the production and delivery of services and products means that lead businesses are allowed to have it both ways. Companies can embrace and institute standards and exert enormous control over the activities of subsidiary bodies. But they can also eschew any responsibility for the consequences of that control.

In light of all these factors, the spread of the fissured workplace creates an economy that is wired differently than the traditional model it has gradually replaced. The economic system for much of the twentieth century was dominated by large corporations where economic value creation, power, and employment were concentrated. The fissured economy still is powerfully affected by large businesses with their concentration of value creation and economic power. But employment now has been split off, shifted to a range of secondary players that function in more competitive markets and are separated from the locus of value creation. The consequences for employment and working conditions and the functioning of the economy as a whole are enormous.

Twin-Edged Sword

Lead companies, enabled by changing technology in the economy, have embraced fissured employment in response to market forces. The central cases in this book examine different organizational forms—subcontracting, franchising, third-party management, outsourcing—that bring together the three elements of focusing on the core, shedding employment, and enforcing standards. Those organizational forms have rippled across industries and the economy.

The widespread adoption of new forms of organization in markets is often a sign of a superior method of allocating resources. It signals that a set of outputs (goods and services) can be produced at a lower cost through a new way of organizing production. Economists would be quick to point out that this makes society overall better off: if fewer resources can be used to produce the same bundle of goodies, more resources are released for use elsewhere. The drivers behind the fissured workplace must improve outcomes for someone— why else would they become so pervasive?

There are indeed positive aspects of the reorganization of production for companies, investors, and consumers, and finding new ways to organize production can enhance social welfare. Focusing on core competencies and the benefits of specialization, facilitated by flexible organizational forms, can lead to the development of new and better products available at lower prices. But reorganization can also have real social consequences if the businesses undertaking it do not fully weigh the costs and consequences of their actions.

Fissured Work, Vulnerable Employment

Although the fissured workplace plays out in different ways across industries, its consequences for workplace conditions are similar. By shifting the provision of service or parts of production to other employers, lead businesses create markets for services that are usually very competitive, thereby creating downward pressure on the marginal price for them. This means that the employers competing for that work face significant pressures on the wages and conditions they can offer their workforce, particularly in industries where there is an elastic supply of labor, skill requirements are relatively low, and labor costs represent a significant part of overall costs.

There is abundant evidence that the majority of workers in the United States face an increasingly difficult workplace—and did so even before the Great Recession of 2007–2009. Falling real wages, declining benefits, reduced employment security, and a stifled ability to complain about problems describe a growing part of the employment landscape. Trends in the labor market (particularly in the low-wage segment), studies of workplace compliance, and the findings of government regulators paint a picture of a worsening workplace and more vulnerable workers in recent decades.[6] Consider:

- Real wages for median workers (those at the 50th percentile of the wage distribution) grew by only 0.5% between 2000 and 2012. Median hourly compensation (wages plus benefits) grew by only 4%. Yet productivity (measured as output of goods and services per hour worked) rose by 23% over the same period.
- Fewer and fewer workers have pensions: the proportion of private sector workers with some form of pension fell from 51% in 1979 to 43% in 2009. Of those workers who have them, the vast majority now have defined contribution plans that shift the risk of retirement income onto the worker.[7]
- Among low-wage workers, the U.S. Bureau of Labor Statistics in its 2007 National Compensation Survey reported that only 24% in the bottom quintile of the wage distribution had employer-provided health coverage, compared to 62% of workers in the middle-wage quintile.[8]
- In 2012 the U.S. Department of Labor recovered a record level of back wages from employers—representing the difference between wages workers received and what the law says their employers are responsible for paying.

Many of the industries where researchers in recent years have found high rates of violations of basic labor standards and worsening employment conditions coincide with industries where fissuring is most advanced. These include restaurant and hospitality sectors, janitorial services, many segments of manufacturing, residential construction, and home health care. But fissuring also is present in retailing, telecommunication and IT sectors, hospitals, public schools, auto supply, transportation, and logistics/distribution services. Accounts of fissuring of paralegal and legal jobs, accounting, journalism, and professional services are also increasingly common. In fact, employment fissuring represents an organizational format that has been adopted across many sectors of the economy, assuming many different forms.

There are three reasons we should worry about the social consequences of the fissured workplace. First, it often undermines compliance with basic labor standards. Second, chopping employment into pieces makes production coordination harder and results in a problem economists call externalities that can result in accidents, injuries, and fatalities. Third, there are distributional consequences of the fissured workplace, shifting surplus generated by businesses away from the workforce and to investors.

Obeying the Law

Workplace regulation in the twentieth century saw a progression of legislation beginning with basic protections for children and women from long hours of work in state legislation at the turn of the last century through a long sequence of state and federal legislation, including compensation for workplace accidents and loss of employment; minimum standards for wages and overtime; provision of the right to organize unions and to bargain collectively; protection against discrimination on the basis of race, gender, and age; provision of a safe and healthful work environment; and granting workers leave to care for family medical needs.

Historically, although business groups resisted (often fiercely) passage of these laws, once they were enacted, lead companies in the economy adjusted by creating systems to assure compliance and making those standards and requirements a part of operations and daily practice. Sometimes large employers did so because they were already exceeding the demands of legislation in their internal practices. Large companies, for example, often paid wages to even unskilled workers in excess of the minimum wage or provided pensions or medical leave because of a desire to keep valued workers or to maintain morale and meet standards of fairness inside the firm (which I discuss in Chapter 4). Other times, large businesses complied because they perceived that their scale made them particularly vulnerable to inspections, penalties, or public scrutiny.[9]

By shedding employment to other subordinate businesses, fissured employment altered those incentives. Lead businesses that, for example, shed janitorial and security work to contractors or franchised service providers no longer faced the responsibility for compliance with minimum wage or overtime standards, or even ensuring that payroll, unemployment, or workers' compensation insurance taxes were being paid for those workers. Activities that are shed by lead organizations are often taken up by smaller businesses. Given the competitive markets in which they operate, smaller employers face intense pressure to reduce costs. Noncompliance with a gamut of workplace standards is often the end result.

Some of the highest rates of violations of basic labor standards occur in industries where fissuring is common. In a landmark survey of low-wage work in three major U.S. cities— New York City, Chicago, and Los Angeles— Bernhardt et al. documented high rates of violations of labor standards in a number of low-wage industries. Figure 1.1 presents estimates of the high rates of violation of standards regarding off-the-clock work, overtime pay, and minimum wage requirements in many of the industries discussed above.

Overall, 26% of workers in the three-city sample were paid less than the required minimum wage; 76% of those who worked more than forty hours in the previous week had not been paid the legally required overtime rate; 70% of workers who were asked to come in early or stay after their shift were not paid for that time and were subjected to retaliation by their employers for complaining in some way about work conditions.[10]

Creating External Costs

To understand the second social problem associated with the fissured workplace—externalities—take the classic case of a manufacturer that makes, say, plastic containers. When it does so, it considers all the labor, material, and capital costs it faces in setting its production goals, weighed against the price it thinks it can charge for the containers. If it also creates air and water pollution in the process of making containers but does not face a cost for that

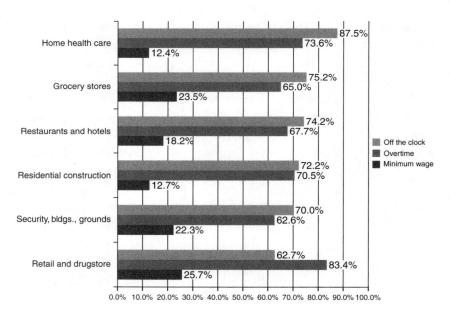

FIGURE 1.1. Labor standards violation rates (percentage in violation) in selected industries. *Source:* Bernhardt, Milkman, et al. 2009.

pollution, it will act as if that cost is zero—in other words, it will ignore the costs of pollution it imposes on society. As a result, its prices will not reflect the total social costs of production, and its market price will be too low. That will lead consumers, responding to the lower price, to consume too many containers, resulting in too much pollution. The pollution externality will leave society worse off than if the container manufacturer, as well as consumers, were forced to include the cost of pollution in their decisions.

Significant externalities arise from fissuring. By fragmenting the employment relationship, certain important decisions that do not directly affect the costs of any of the employers involved fall through the cracks. Complex systems that underlie production require coordination. By carving up employment among many parties, the problem of coordination increases. And when coordination fails, accidents happen. The BP Deepwater Horizon disaster of 2009 is a prime example of this: the U.S. Chemical Safety Board investigative team concluded in the summer of 2012 that a principal cause of that workplace and environmental disaster arose from coordination failure among the three organizations responsible for the drilling. The Chemical Safety Board noted a number of such deficiencies, including those related to the linkages between the hazard assessment systems of BP and its subordinate organization on the Deepwater Horizon, Transocean:

> BP and Transocean hazard assessment systems were inadequate. For example, the bridging document that sought to harmonize safety controls between BP and Transocean was a minimal document that focused only on six personal safety issues such as minimum heights for employing fall protection equipment. The document did not address major accident hazards like the potential for loss of well control.[11]

As a result of this failure of coordination, eleven men died on the rig and billions of dollars of environmental damage were inflicted on Gulf Coast economies and fragile ecosystems. Fissured employment has led to similar outcomes in other industries, from cell tower construction to the logistics industries I examine in detail in Part II.

Dividing the Pie

Finally, the fissured workplace also affects how the economic pie created by companies is divided. A superior form of organization can lower the costs of making goods or delivering services. That potentially can have an impact on three groups: consumers, in the form of prices; investors, in the form of better returns; and workers, in the form of wages and employment.

Large firms employing a wide spectrum of workers—from highly trained engineers and professional managers, to semiskilled production workers, to janitors and groundskeepers—characterized the workplace of the mid-twentieth century. An important consequence of having people with diverse skills and occupations working under one roof was that companies shared the gains received from their market position with the workforce. They did so through how wages were set—in both union and nonunion workplaces. While some businesses shared gains out of corporate beneficence, many did so because of what might be called enlightened self-interest. Because feelings about fairness affect employee morale, fairness considerations have an impact on human resource policies, including wage determination. In particular, perceptions about what one is paid depend in part on what others are paid. If a large company employed executives, secretaries, engineers, mechanics, and janitors, it therefore needed to be cognizant of how the structure of wages was perceived among all those working underneath the common corporate umbrella. As a result, janitors' wages were pulled up because of the wages lead employers paid their factory workers.

Fissured employment fundamentally changes the boundaries of firms—whether through subcontracting, third-party management, or franchising. By shifting work from the lead company outward—imagine the outsourcing of janitorial or security workers—the company transforms wage setting into a pricing problem. As will be seen, this pushes wages down for workers in the businesses now providing services to the lead firm, while lowering the lead business's direct costs. Fissuring results in redistribution away from workers and toward investors. It therefore contributes to the widening income distribution gap.

Mending the Fissured Workplace

An examination of fissured employment puts the question of the boundaries of employment responsibility center stage. Most employment laws in the United States at the state and federal level define "employee" according to stated objectives of the individual statute. This has led to varied—and highly contested—debates on who is or is not an employee. Common law defines an employer as a party who has the right to "direct and control" the performance of an employee as he or she undertakes a set of compensated activities. Courts apply a long list of factors used to determine if such control exists in a given situation, such as control of the work product, determination of the time and place of work, and the provision of tools and materials.[12]

Federal workplace laws define employees and employers. The problem is that each law does so differently. Take two examples. The Fair Labor Standards Act, which sets minimum wage and overtime standards and regulates child labor, defines an employee as "any individual who is employed by an employer" and states that "employ includes to suffer or permit to work." To help clarify this vague definition, courts apply an economic realities test to evaluate the particular employment situation surrounding a worker and an employer. This potentially gives the agency responsible for enforcement the latitude to adjust to changing employment conditions on the ground.[13]

The National Labor Relations Act, the federal statute governing union organizing and collective bargaining, also uses an economic reality test for defining employment. However, a Supreme Court decision in 1944 holding that boys who sold newspapers on the street on commission were in fact Hearst employees despite the company's contention that they were independent contractors led enraged conservatives in Congress to amend the National Labor Relations Act in 1947 to specifically exempt independent contractors.[14] This has led historically to very narrow readings of coverage and application of the act.

The definition of "employee" has become a hotly contested issue in recent years, particularly in regard to the reclassification of employees as independent contractors. Since independent contractors are viewed under law as business entities in their own right, they are exempted from minimum wage and overtime requirements of the Fair Labor Standards Act, workers' compensation, unemployment insurance, Occupational Safety and Health Administration (OSHA) regulations, the National Labor Relations Act, and Social Security.[15]

But as the vignettes opening Part I also make clear, fissured employment further muddies these already murky waters. Although most laws look to the owner of the enterprise as the party ultimately responsible, in many cases the owners are only nominally involved in the setting of employment policies or their implementation. In hotels, for example, the pace and nuances of work

are set by the brand (for example, Hilton); day-to-day human resource functions and oversight of the workforce are handled by an independent hotel
operating company (for example, Tharaldson Lodging); and the employee
may receive her paycheck from a staffing company hired by the hotel operator, rendering the owners of the property little more than the ultimate wallet
from which pay is dispensed.[16] Employment therefore bears little resemblance
to the dyadic relationship often assumed in how we think about and administer our core workplace regulations.

Efforts to address conditions in the workplace arising from fissured employment structures cannot ignore the relationship between organizations at
the top and bottom of those industries. It has long been the case that state
and federal agencies that enforce labor standards face an uphill battle. In the
labor standards area, approximately 8.5 million workplaces are covered by
applicable federal legislation or similar requirements at the state level. There
are a total of 1,000 federal labor standards investigators and an estimated 660
inspectors at the state level to oversee these workplaces. Consequently, the
annual probability of a workplace receiving an investigation is well below 1 in
100, and in industries with deep fissuring as tiny as 1 in 1,000.[17]

The emergence of fissuring further heightens the need to think differently
about how government agencies, as well as labor unions and other worker
advocates, address the problems of precarious employment. An economy dominated by large business organizations with concentrations of employees
operating within their boundaries is difficult to police. An economy where
much of that employment—particularly for workers with lower skills and
market leverage—has been shifted outside of the boundaries of those companies poses even graver questions about the efficacy of the traditional approach
to workplace regulation.

The implications of fissuring go even beyond workplace conditions to more
macro-level outcomes. The productivity of U.S. workers has grown steadily
since 1973, increasing particularly rapidly from the mid-1990s until 2010.
Over the same time period, median hourly compensation stagnated. Yet
some people were indeed doing quite well. While wages stagnated over the
past quarter century, the pay received by top business executives soared. In
1979 the ratio of the pay received by the average CEO in total direct compensation to that of the average production worker was 37.2:1. By 2007 (the year
before the recession) it had grown to 277:1.[18]

As a result of these trends and the fact that the highest-earning households received a large percentage of their income from returns on capital and other nonwage and salary sources, U.S. income distribution has become unequal to an extent not seen since the 1920s. In 2007 the share of national income that went to the top 1% of families hit 23.5%. More strikingly, while the real income of the top 1% grew by 58% between 1993 and 2010, that of the rest of the 99% of families rose by a paltry 6.4%.[19] Although these shifts arise from a complex set of factors, the changing shape of employment and the outward shift of jobs from large companies to smaller ones play a role.

Even our models of the business cycle may be affected by the presence of fissuring. Historically, large businesses led recoveries: as demand returned, large firms directly increased employment. Now, employment decisions in many industries are mediated by fissured structures. Not only does this means that the timing of recoveries may be slowed, since they must "flow through" the fissured relationships; but the composition of jobs added also will reflect those relationships. Seen in this light, it is not surprising that the first jobs to be added following the Great Recession of 2007–2009 were predominantly at the low-wage end of the spectrum, nor that 93% of total income growth during the recovery from 2009 to 2010 went to the top 1% of the income distribution.[20]

Addressing the problems of working conditions, wages, and employment over the next decades will require wrestling with the consequences of the fissured organization and the public's willingness to balance its benefits to some consumers and shareholders against its consequences to those whose workplaces have been fundamentally altered by it. Although the fissured organization raises a raft of new questions and challenges, an understanding of its origins, operation, and implications opens a range of opportunities to address its consequences.

Why Is This Account Different from All Other Accounts?

Contingent work, subcontracting, misclassification, offshoring, and the problems of low-wage work are well-known and abundantly documented phenomena of the past two decades.[21] Coming out of the recession of 1980–1981, many companies in the private sector that had in the post–World War II era provided their workforces with increasing real wages, generous benefit packages, and reasonably secure employment began to introduce practices that broke with these traditions.[22] Many companies began to experiment with contracting out certain services, and, later in that decade, seeking alternative workforces outside of the United States. Through outsourcing, companies seek to minimize labor costs by moving activities formerly undertaken inside the boundaries of an organization to labor markets located outside of the organization.

At the same time, employers replaced jobs that were once full time and permanent with a different type of employment contract with a less clear commitment to longevity or even stable hours. Part-time work, temporary positions, and other "contingent" forms of employment began to pop up in the human resource portfolio of Fortune 500 employers. Independent contracting—where workers left the traditional employment relationship entirely to become (or be classified as) entrepreneurs providing services to former employers—also became increasingly prevalent. Long a practice in industries where individuals possess specialized skills of value to multiple employers, independent contracting popped up in places that previously would have been regarded as traditional employment situations.

Analysts examining these trends associate them with a familiar list of causes: globalization of industries; falling rates of unionization; new technologies and work processes; changing composition of industries; and declining enforcement of workplace policies at the state and federal levels. Together, these changes created pressures for firms to find ways to reduce labor costs and gain flexibility at the workplace. Markets and competition beget contingent work and contracting out.

The concept of fissured employment includes, but is not limited to, these well-known practices. It is also linked to some of the aforementioned environmental changes. But the usual accounts of employment change often do not fully paint the picture of *why* organizations have restructured, and therefore give an incomplete assessment of the implications of these changes for the workplace and the economy. Fissured employment is rooted in part in cost control, but lowering labor costs is only part of the story (and it is motivated by broader aims than many of the above explanations suggest).[23] The fissured workplace reflects a more integrated and comprehensive strategy that businesses have increasingly chosen to take, rooted in considerations of both the revenue and the cost side of the income statement. Facing ever greater pressures from public and private capital markets to improve returns, companies who adopt fissured employment strategies aim to improve profitability by focusing attention and controlling the most profitable aspects of firm value while shedding the actual production of goods or provision of services.

This account of the fissured workplace also examines a wider range of organizational forms than do many accounts of contingent work. Notable among these is franchising—an organizational form once largely restricted to a few industry segments that has now diffused to many other sectors of the economy. Franchising provides a mechanism for a lead company to create a model of business organization that can then be replicated by others, but controlled by a lead company. It creates a mutually advantageous means of sharing the gains of a brand, as well as an ingenious mechanism to push out the difficult task of providing the good or service to other entities with greater incentive to control costs while still selling the product of the lead company. It works, however, because of the franchise agreement, which allows the lead company to create and enforce its definition of the product and limits subordinate units' ability to alter it. The use of franchising as an organizational form has spread from familiar sectors (fast food and hotels) to surprising ones (among them janitorial services and home health care).

The various forms of third-party management used in industries as diverse as hotels, logistics, education, and manufacturing also allow lead companies to shift out the problem of ensuring adherence to core standards while giving the third party manager the incentive to undertake day-to-day operations more vigorously than might a sprawling, geographically dispersed organization. In some cases, third-party managers are brought in to oversee functions that the lead company views as outside its areas of core competency (for example, food service inside a major hospital, or transportation for a school district). In other cases, such as hotels, outside managers are hired to oversee even core functions for the enterprise. In these instances, the model requires that the lead business create and maintain rigorous standards that the third-party manager/operator undertakes and against whose performance it is judged.

Supply chain systems represent an additional organizational form that allows lead firms to implement the fissured model. The increasing scope, depth, and global reach of supply chains that provide products to major manufacturers and retailers create efficiencies for companies like Walmart while reducing their exposure to inventory risk and demand fluctuations (the bane of the retail business). Retail or manufacturing supply chains rely on lead companies promulgating detailed technology, shipping, delivery, and product standards that are adhered to by their supply base. The degree of specificity of those standards and the high stakes attached to their fulfillment are fundamental to the operation of modern supply chain logistics.

Seen in this light, the forces leading to the vulnerable work conditions described at the outset of this chapter are not an inevitable result of the nature of those jobs or industries. *They arise from how those sectors have come to be organized.*

Organization of the Book

This book has three major parts. Chapters 2 and 3 discuss the origins of the modern corporation and how fissuring came to change that stalwart institution of the U.S. economy (Chapter 2). Economists (and other skeptics) often ask, "If something is so advantageous now, why didn't businesses adopt it before?" Chapter 3 answers this question by examining the changes that brought pressure to bear on major businesses to shed employment as well as the technology and standards revolution that enabled them to fissure the workplace. Chapter 4 then examines the crucial issue of how wage setting has changed as a result of the organizational evolution discussed in Part I.

The basic architecture underlying the fissured workplace plays out in distinctive ways in different sectors, with important implications for policies seeking to redress them. Part II therefore explores the major organizational forms resulting in fissured workplaces: subcontracting (Chapter 5), franchising (Chapter 6), and supply chains (Chapter 7). Each chapter examines in depth cases that portray the different mechanisms that underlie each organizational type and their consequences for employers and workers.

Part III takes up the question of how to mend the fissured workplace. Chapter 8 discusses why current workplace laws are poorly suited to dealing with how the employment world actually functions and suggests the kind of legal reforms that could redress this problem. However, mindful of the limitations of legislative solutions to workplace and employment problems, Chapter 9 turns to how government policies under existing laws might—and are—being adapted to deal with fissured employment. Chapter 10 looks at how other workplace institutions—including unions, worker advocates, employer associations, and international monitors—can address the "broken windows" problem arising in fissured workplaces. The book concludes by considering the broader consequences of an economy characterized in major sectors by fissured employment and workplaces and speculates on the future path forward.

Employment in a
Pre-fissured World

During much of the twentieth century, the critical employment relationship was between large businesses and workers in major sectors of the economy. Large employers—General Motors, U.S. Steel, and Alcoa—dominated much of the manufacturing economy. Emerging industries also spawned huge companies: Kodak, IBM, and Xerox grew to be giants in their product markets and in the labor markets from which they drew their workforces. While the service sector operated at a more local level, the national players that did emerge—Hilton and Marriott in hotels, Macy's and Sears in retail—similarly employed thousands.[1]

To understand fissured workplaces, we must go back first to their origins in the modern corporation of the twentieth century. Fissured employment implies that something about the structure of large enterprises is no longer advantageous, leading firms to shift out to other businesses activities that were once regarded as core to the enterprise. This evolution requires an understanding of how large businesses came to dominate industry landscapes in the first place.

Growing Companies, Changing Boundaries

Shifting Retail Boundaries

The emergence of the large corporation of the twentieth century is captured in the business history of the fastest-growing retailer in the United States of its time, one that came to dominate national markets, gained enormous power over its supply network, and created deep concern among the public about its growing clout: A&P. Like a retailer of far greater contemporary repute, A&P grew in scale and scope by internalizing a core set of activities that lowered key costs of providing food to its customers, thereby allowing it to cut its prices and gain market share.[2]

For decades, getting food from farmers and food processors to consumers was handled through a complicated chain of intermediate businesses— wholesalers who would buy products from producers, aggregate them, and move them to other distributors and ultimately to the small stores that would sell them to consumers. Distribution therefore required multiple market transactions (and costs associated with each step).

In the first two decades of the 1900s, consumers relied on local grocery stores. Typically, these stores purchased their supplies from jobbers, small wholesalers who dealt in small quantities of goods. Jobbers, in turn, purchased from larger-scale wholesalers, occasionally directly from manufacturers, or from central produce markets. With an order placed by phone, the jobber saved the local grocer the task of making trips to purchase food or having to hold an inventory of it. A grocery store would draw on many jobbers, since each one carried a relatively narrow line of goods. Because neither the jobber nor the grocer had much shelf or storage space, jobbers delivered their goods multiple times a week.[3]

A&P's key organizational innovation was using scale to dramatically lower the costs of providing food to its customers, largely by internalizing tasks that were traditionally undertaken by jobbers and wholesalers—that is, buying goods from food providers and getting them to small retail groceries. Rather than depending on the warehousing and delivery services of many other intermediate businesses, A&P brought this function inside the walls of the corporation, removing one layer of middlemen (and the costs associated with them), enhancing the opportunity for scale economies, and in particular improving its ability to manage inventory of goods.[4] The fickle nature of consumer demand—even at the turn of the last century—represented a central problem for retailers. As Walmart later would show once again, effective management of inventory costs and risks confers great advantages on a retailer.

A&P's strategy gave the company substantial cost advantages over the small retail stores with which it competed, allowing the company to sell groceries at prices far below those of its competitors. Growth in its market gave it greater clout to negotiate lower prices with food suppliers, further expanding its cost advantages, allowing A&P to grow and capture substantial market share across the country.[5] In so doing, A&P changed the nature of the food retailing industry and the way companies needed to organize themselves to compete. As a result, the boundary of firms in the industry came to incorporate many of the functions that, before A&P's ascendency, would have been undertaken through market transactions.

Defining Enterprise Boundaries

Ronald Coase argued in "The Nature of the Firm" (one of the most famous essays in the history of economics) that the boundaries of a business enterprise could not be understood without thinking about the decision of when work should be done inside versus outside of the organization. Many of the activities of corporations involve the allocation of resources across different activities. This is precisely what markets do. Coase asked, If this is the case, why are organizations superior? His answer was that under certain circumstances, organizations provide a more efficient solution to handling transactions where coordination through a market would be more costly. In a world where the costs of transactions between parties may be significant, many activities become located within the walls of a firm.[6] A&P's model of getting food from producers to a consumer's kitchen lowered costs relative to a long chain of market transactions from producers to wholesale distributors to retail stores.

Oliver Williamson built on the Coasian framework to develop a formal theory of transaction cost economics, viewing the primary purpose and impact of organizations as economizing on transaction costs in the course of producing complicated products and services. In the transaction cost framework pioneered by Williamson, business organizations that make up an industry are neither simply production processes combining capital, labor, and material to produce goods for the market (as traditional economics would lead one to believe) nor organizations untethered from economic forces and able to configure themselves as they wish (as often implied by popular business gurus or some management academics). Over time, competitive forces acting on individual decision makers within organizations pursuing their own objectives lead some functions to end up being done internally, others through various types of relationships (partnerships, franchise agreements, other forms of contracting), and still others through market transactions.[7]

Property rights (or efficient contracts) theorists in the 1980s pushed Coase's and Williamson's questions on the drivers of firm boundaries by asking why parties could not undertake more activities via market relationships by writing contracts that would solve the types of problems that created high transaction costs.[8] Market transactions would be sufficient if two parties could write a "complete contract" that captured the private benefits and costs of two parties (whether business/business, buyer/supplier, or employer/employee) covering all exigencies. But that is often not possible for a variety of reasons. The vagaries and uncertainties of life mean that writing a contract that covers all possible outcomes is simply not possible. Even if it were, many outcomes are not directly observable by one party or the other, making contract terms difficult to enforce. Where one party invests heavily as part of the transaction, making it expensive for it to leave, problematic incentives may arise in relationships, allowing one party to "hold up" the other. And the bigger those problems loom, the higher the incentives need to be in the contract itself to move the contracted party in the right direction. As a result, many forms of contracts are incomplete, making organizational solutions to certain coordination problems necessary. Once again, this means that some activities need to be done inside rather than outside firm boundaries.

Visible Hands and the Origins of the Modern Corporation

Railroads, steamships, and the telegraph transformed the scale of markets in the years following the Civil War. The combination of rapid communication and the slashing of transportation costs meant that potential markets could become national or global. Manufacturers, formerly constrained to filling demand primarily in local markets, now had incentives to dramatically scale up their enterprises.[9]

At the same time, a pre-A&P wave of consolidation had restructured distribution chains, replacing large numbers of unconsolidated wholesalers, which distributed manufactured products through a complicated commission system, with large wholesale channels, which more effectively consolidated demand (a system A&P would displace by further expanding efficiency at the retail end). By consolidating demand more effectively, national markets for goods replaced localized markets, thereby providing a basis for increasing the scale of production.

Technologic innovations created methods of producing existing and new products through more mechanized processes that dramatically reduced their costs and increased the potential size of production runs. Mass production of synthetic dyes and, later, synthetic fibers, plastics, and myriad other chemical products in the 1880s led to dramatic falls in costs per unit and the emergence of huge chemical manufacturers in the United States as well as in Germany and the United Kingdom. The invention of the Bonsack machine in the early 1880s transformed the production of cigarettes, as did new production technologies in the food industry allowing large-scale production of vegetable oils, refining of sugar, and production of food for people and livestock. Manufacturers could harness these new production technologies and more efficient forms of energy to create greater scale advantages, allowing them to benefit from a virtuous circle of growing markets, falling costs arising from scale, greater market share, and further incentives to ratchet down costs through scale.[10]

The melding of technologic innovation with production geared to expanding national and international markets produced astonishing reductions in costs. Adoption of the Bessemer process as the technologic fulcrum of steel production, for example, led the cost of rails produced by Andrew Carnegie's steel mills to fall from about $100 per ton in the early 1870s to a mere $12 per ton in the late 1890s.[11] Similarly, Henry Ford's installation of the assembly line in 1913, coupled with standardization of components and creation of a work organization that broke jobs down to discrete, repeatable, and simple steps, drove the time to assemble a Model T chassis from 12.5 hours to just 1 hour, 33 minutes.[12]

Although economies of scale technically arise from the relation of unit costs to volume, they can only be achieved through the building of organizational capacities. Firms needed to create systems by which to oversee, supervise, and create incentives adequate to the complex task of modern production. The development of modern management was the final innovation to put the above into effect and allow the parts to fit together through organizational and management structures. In particular, the need to coordinate a vast and growing network of railroads or telegraph systems or to assure a stable and consistent flow of materials to achieve high levels of capital utilization in industries such as chemicals required multiple levels of professional managers, supervisors, and specialists in running operations.

Managerial hierarchies first emerged in the railroad industry to coordinate the complex network of trains and telegraphy. They next were adopted in companies like Sears, Roebuck, which took advantage of modern communication and transportation systems to transform the archaic forms of distribution that had long characterized balkanized, small markets.[13] Managerial hierarchies then emerged in those industries where the technology of production created scale economies and competitive advantages, such as in chemicals, petroleum refining, steel production, and machinery manufacturing.

Gaining competitive advantage through scale also provided the basis for firms to expand their product offerings and capitalize on their ability to provide related goods and services to customers. Economies of scope emerge where an enterprise gains a competitive advantage in introducing new products in part because of its dominance in other product areas and its reputation and relationships in distribution. The cost of introducing a new product is therefore far lower for the established firm than it would be for a smaller competitor. Firms like General Foods in food retailing, DuPont in the production of synthetic products, and of course General Motors in the auto industry gained further dominance through broadening product offerings. The result was the basis for a new method of organizing production and distributing goods.[14]

The businesses that became dominant did so through a recipe of (1) investing in production facilities sufficient to capture economies of scale and scope (as determined by technological constraints); (2) investing in national and international marketing and distribution networks; and (3) investing in managerial systems sufficient to coordinate production and distribution as well as by taking advantage of their integration. Those able to do so quickly came to dominate the smaller and less-sophisticated competitors and emerged as the oligopolies and monopolies of the early 1900s. They also grew by employing large numbers of skilled, semiskilled, and unskilled workers to take on the varying tasks of production, distribution, and management under one corporate roof.

Finally, emerging modern corporations like General Motors and DuPont developed a managerial structure that evolved as an apparatus to coordinate the increasingly complex set of operations required of multiproduct, multilocation enterprises with respect to both production and distribution: the multidivisional organization. Some very large businesses had emerged in earlier periods. But with ownership usually concentrated in a single family or at most among several partners, the organization typically looked like a federation of loosely tied businesses (that is, a holding company) with different family members or partners overseeing their piece of the enterprise (usually with considerable autonomy).

The demands of the modern corporation required a level of coordination and integration incompatible with a federation structure. The multidivisional firm still allowed for separate divisions, representing different functional areas (for example, production, inventory, shipment, marketing) or geographic regions. However, a centralized management structure sat on top of these functions, exercising control and final decision authority as well as using streams of data to monitor the activities of subordinate units. Managerial hierarchies reinforced the ultimate control of the top level of the organization, while human resource policies, accounting systems, and performance management provided sufficient incentives to allow delegated authority paired with centralized accountability.[15]

Changing Structures of Business Ownership

The emergence of large-scale enterprises and modern management was accompanied by a second, related development in terms of ownership. The scale of production and the investment capital necessary to underwrite the expansion of the modern enterprise made it impossible for individuals to be the sole source of finance.

New financial markets emerged in response to the need to raise capital on an unparalleled scale. Innovations in financial markets (trusts, dramatically expanded equity markets, and new forms of borrowing through bond markets) moved companies away from a reliance on a small group of family members or an inner set of investors toward new sources of funding and capital structures. This made available capital for investment in machinery well beyond what had previously been the case.[16]

The modern corporation, with its ability to raise capital through issuing equity or taking on debt at a scale impossible for individual owners, created a solution to capital limitations. At the same time, markets developed new mechanisms and instruments to raise capital from investors and move money between different industries with increasing efficiency (as well as creating new opportunities for skullduggery on a much grander scale).

Corporate forms of organization diffused in parallel to the transformation of production and management, reflecting both the capital intensity of industries and the development of managerial sophistication that often accompanied it. Although the original corporate model in the United States goes back to Lowell, Massachusetts, at the turn of the nineteenth century, it spread later in that century from public utilities to railroads, to sectors of manufacturing, and then to banks and insurance sectors.[17]

The fact that more and more large-scale enterprises on the production and distribution sides of the economy drew upon the modern corporation as a source for both accumulating capital and managing enterprises meant a growing divide between those who owned an enterprise and those who operated it. Rather than a single family (or a small number of partners) owning and operating a business, ownership came to be held by a growing number of shareholders, while the complicated task of running the organization became the province of professional managers.

Breaking apart ownership and management created the capacity to vastly increase the scale of operations of corporations by tapping capital from large numbers of investors, accessed through public stock or private capital markets. At the same time, the separation of ownership and control created a variety of puzzles in how to obtain information, create adequate incentives, monitor performance, and make sure that the activities of the hundreds or thousands of people working in multiunit enterprises were aligned with the interests of the owners. Adolph Berle and Gardiner Means, two of the first scholars to carefully document the separation, noted with alarm:

> The explosion of the atom of property destroys the basis of the old assumption that the quest for profits will spur the owner of industrial property to its effective use. It consequently challenges the fundamental economic principle of individual initiative in industry enterprise. It raises for reexamination the question of the motive force back of industry, and the ends for which the modern corporation can be or will be run.[18]

The concentration of economic surplus and power in the modern company, steered by managers operating under weak oversight by dispersed owners, led Berle and Means to forecast that corporations would soon exert an influence over the economic landscape rivaling that of the political power of the state: "The future may see the economic organism, now typified by the corporation, not only on an equal plane with the state, but possibly even superseding it as the dominant form of organization."[19]

Large corporations indeed came to dominate manufacturing, communications, food production, and retailing in the first half of the twentieth century. Production and distribution scale and the evolution of sophisticated organizational structures helped propel that growth, focused on building and expanding particular product lines, brands, and areas of competitive strength. Alfred P. Sloan, the CEO who built General Motors, is best known for transforming it from a loose confederation of automobile companies acquired during the period of industry consolidation into an integrated, multiproduct automotive giant. But Sloan also believed in staying focused on automobiles. When the opportunity arose for GM to produce ethyl gasoline, a higher-performance fuel, he and other executives rejected the idea, since it was a "chemical product rather than a mechanical one" and required an entirely different distribution mechanism.[20]

But as the century continued, some companies chose to radically expand their scope along with their size and to move far beyond their original area of competitive strength. By the 1960s executives operating with less restrictive attitudes about business scope than Sloan's acquired or engaged in mergers with companies often from businesses far afield of their own. A bevy of sprawling conglomerate corporations resulted, including companies like Beatrice (which then owned such diverse entities as Playtex, a manufacturer of bras, and Avis, a car rental company); Litton Industries (which, along with being a major defense manufacturer and shipbuilder, diversified into manufacturing office equipment and microwave ovens, operating restaurants, and distributing packaged foods); and ITT Corporation (which began in 1920 as a telegraph and telephone company but ballooned in the 1960s into a conglomerate by purchasing over three hundred companies, including the Sheraton Hotel chain and Continental Bread). Eleven of the top twenty-five acquiring companies at the height of this "go-go" era were classified as conglomerates, and that group acquired more than five hundred companies between 1961 and 1968.[21]

Defenders of conglomerate merger and acquisition activity argued that diversification allowed large companies to create their own internal capital markets where corporate resources could be efficiently allocated to a wide range of business sectors.[22] Other business analysts, however, viewed the trend with alarm, citing conglomerate acquisitions as a prime example of the consequences of the gulf between ownership and management. Conglomerates reflected senior executive decisions to grow simply for the sake of growing and perpetuating the organization.

Whether through a strategy of growth focused on established product lines or through a conglomerate strategy, major companies in the postwar era pursued stability over risk taking, as reflected in follow-the-leader pricing policies (stabilized through the dominance of U.S. corporations in many industries), long-term pricing and contract agreements for key inputs with suppliers, and ever-more-refined demand management through advertising and marketing. This conception of the self-perpetuating, planned, and ever-growing corporate entity was best (and most mordantly) described by John Kenneth Galbraith:

> The firm must be large enough to carry large capital commitments to modern technology. It must also be large enough to control its markets. But the present view also explains what the older explanations don't explain . . . The size of General Motors is in the service not of monopoly or the economies of scale but of planning. And for the planning—control of supply, control of demand, provision of capital, minimization of risk—there is no clear upper limit to the desirable size. It could be that the bigger the better. The corporate form accommodates to this need. Quite clearly it allows the firm to be very, very large.[23]

The Development of Internal Labor Markets

An important piece of the management task facing corporations in the first half of the 1900s was hiring, training, evaluating, and compensating the thousands of people working within them. Just as ad hoc methods for managing resource flow were no longer possible given the scale of operations, finding systematic means to handle complex human resource functions became essential for the functioning of the organization. Collective bargaining and the development of sophisticated industrial relations functions in corporations became one track of development given the emergence of labor unions in the manufacturing sector in the 1930s and expansion of unions in other areas. Large nonunion corporations developed their own sophisticated policies to handle these functions along different lines.

These parallel developments in union and nonunion workplaces led to what Peter Doeringer and Michael Piore deemed internal labor markets: the system created inside major businesses that set policies for wages, employment practices, and other features of the workplace. Although their framework originally described internal labor market features common in large, union enterprises, Doeringer and Piore—and the many who followed their work—drew attention to the fact that workplaces in the enterprises dominating the economy were governed by administrative rules and procedures responsible for wage determination systems not affected directly by supply and demand conditions in local labor markets, but rather by the institutional practices that emerged within the firm.[24]

A key characteristic of those rules was their rigidity with respect to "external" labor markets surrounding (and in some cases connected to) them. Thus, while internal labor markets included ports of entry into the external labor market that were susceptible to fluctuations in supply and demand, the internal structures, and movement within them, were less connected to those external conditions, and movement into and out of them was governed by organizational rules.

The conditions that created significant advantages for the growth of large-scale enterprises, modern management practices, and divisional organizational structures also were well served by internal labor markets governed by rules that increased skill acquisition, stable methods of advancement, and employee loyalty. For employees, once on the inside of an internal labor market—whether entering as a production worker in a steel plant, a maintenance worker at a large food manufacturer, or a junior executive at a chemical company—one could look forward to certainty in employment, an established profile of wage or salary increases over time, and fairly clear expectations of what was required to retain employment and advance in the organization (again, whether that meant on the factory floor or in the corporate hierarchy).

For employers, internal labor markets meant stability in the supply of a labor force with the requisite skills to undertake the various activities necessary to produce steel, chemicals, or hotel services. By creating limited ports of entry, employers achieved some degree of market power in setting wages and salaries for their workforce, given the benefits created by maintaining a long-term attachment to the firm (a form of "velvet handcuffs").[25] Incentives within the system were well aligned: employee loyalty was rewarded with continuing employment and a rising profile of compensation. Employers secured a workforce capable of producing the output and services for stable but growing markets.[26]

The growth of broad and deep internal labor markets occurred in both unionized and nonunionized sectors in the post–World War II era. In the union sector, labor agreements in the automobile, steel, and rubber industries built these arrangements into elaborate job classification systems that were negotiated and administered through the collective bargaining process. These core collective agreements set the bargaining standards that were then adopted in other industries (in some cases where such detailed job classifications were less well suited, but still readily adopted).[27]

Complex internal labor markets developed among large corporations in the nonunion sector as well. In companies like Kodak, IBM, and Aetna, formal systems for promotion, job posting, evaluation, and compensation developed to handle the same problem facing union employers managing a large workforce and providing incentives to align their interests with those of the company. Rapid growth in existing and new markets, expanding product lines, and the increasing complexity created by coordinating a large organization raised the need to find methods of promoting from within a company, finding mechanisms for resolving disputes, and making sure that compensation, review, and disciplinary policies led to the retention of good employees.[28]

Departments related to administering the human resource policies for the workforce also grew during this period. In 1955 a little fewer than 30% of a representative sample of large firms had personnel / human resource management offices. By 1965 about 35% had such offices. Bolstered by the need to comply with new workplace laws governing pensions, occupational health and safety (including the Occupational Health and Safety Act), discrimination, and affirmative action passed in the later 1960s and the first half of the 1970s, the number of firms with human resource offices grew quickly: by 1975 the proportion with such departments reached just under 50%, and by 1985 it hit 70%.[29]

Large firms with internal labor markets were not only characterized by explicit human resource policies administered by departments and personnel specialists. Workers in large enterprises in the 1970s and 1980s—regardless of union status—tended to be paid more than otherwise comparable workers in small enterprises and to receive better benefits and face more desirable working conditions than workers of comparable ability, productivity, and even "collar color."[30] These large-firm wage effects began to shrink (although not disappear) only in the 1990s.[31]

Internal labor markets also brought expanded benefits to workers, particularly in large firms. This is reflected in the declining share of total employee compensation (wages plus benefits like pensions and health coverage, as well as legally required benefits like workers' compensation) accounted for by wages. In 1951 wages represented about 83% of total compensation among a survey of large companies in the private sector. By 1961 that shrank to 78%, and by 1971 to 74%. By 1979 wages represented only 70% of compensation received by workers in large firms.[32]

Like wages, increases in overall benefit coverage particularly reflected the policies of the largest companies in the economy. In 1979 the share of employees with pension coverage rose from 21% among firms with 1–24 workers to 48% in firms with 25–99 workers and to 71% in firms with 100–499 workers; it reached 89% among firms with 1,000 or more employees. Similarly, group health coverage rose from 34% in firms with fewer than 24 workers to 76% in those with 100–499 workers and topped out at 86% in the largest firms, those with more than 1,000 employees.[33]

The Great Unraveling

The late 1940s through the late 1970s marked an era when conditions were quite favorable for a large segment of middle-class workers in the United States employed in the kind of enterprises discussed above. There were, of course, large numbers of employees—particularly concentrated in minority, geographically isolated, or immigrant communities—who worked under precarious labor market conditions.[34] Yet workers in the thriving manufacturing sector of the U.S. economy—auto, steel, rubber, food—enjoyed rising wages, a growing scope and quality of benefits (including health care and pensions), and access to representation through unions.

Employers in those industries operated in product markets very different from those we have come to associate with the manufacturing sector in industrialized nations. Companies had pricing power, increasing demand for their products domestically and abroad, and access to capital for expansion. Competition often operated on nonprice dimensions, leading firms to try to maintain or expand market share through advertising and ever-increasing product line offerings and by seeking new consumers in other parts of the world. This created a very stable environment for setting compensation, benefits, and other workplace policies. In fact, given the potential downside that attacking labor entailed in the form of potential strikes and other forms of production disruption, achieving labor peace as part of a larger strategy of expansion made good sense for the bottom line.[35]

One of the most vibrant times of labor movement growth coincided with this period. Beginning with the passage of the National Labor Relations Act in 1935, the number of workers and the percentage of the workforce in unions grew rapidly, from about 7%t of total employment at the time the act was passed to a high of almost 35% in 1954.[36] In particular, unions in the manufacturing and construction sectors reached their apogee, as did collective bargaining agreements covering wages, benefits, and workplace conditions.

The relatively uninterrupted ascent in the post–World War II era of core manufacturing industries—as well as of emerging industries like business computing, telecommunications, construction, and financial services—allowed creation of human resource policies that provided steady training and mechanisms for advancement. Centralized corporate personnel, benefits, and labor relations departments were developed to administer complex health and pension plans and to deal with unions in dispute resolution.

The system of labor relations and sophisticated internal labor markets was therefore built on product and capital markets characterized by relative stability. What began to emerge in the 1970s under the pressures of inflation and overheated macroeconomic demand, along with global competition in core sectors of the U.S. economy, shook the basis of those systems. As these features of the environment changed dramatically, basic firm strategies, including those related to the workplace, were challenged.[37]

* * *

By the 1970s, lead companies across many sectors of the United States economy, among them General Motors, Hilton, IBM, Boeing, and Sears, had developed large workforces deployed across thousands of workplaces to carry out their core service, manufacturing, research and development, distribution, or retail roles. Large headquarters and division offices undertook strategic activities like marketing, product testing and research, and logistics, supported by finance, human resources, labor relations, accounting, IT, and other functions.

In large U.S. retail stores, manufacturing facilities, hotel properties, and other organizational units, employees tasked with core activities—building cars, helping customers at front desks, working in warehouse operations, or developing new computer hardware—worked alongside those providing support functions—janitors, maintenance staff, security personnel, and administrative employees. Elaborate internal labor market systems set wages, benefits, and other personnel policies, knitting together the very diverse set of people operating under the corporate umbrella.[38]

As a whole, the system reflected a distinctive solution to the complex coordination challenges facing firms and markets. But just as A&P's upheaval of retail distribution signaled new ways of coordinating economic activities, fundamental changes in the costs of coordination—an explosion in computing speed and memory, the creation of technologies like bar codes, GPS, and electronic sensors, and the promulgation of standards for sharing the resulting torrent of information—would lead to seismic shifts in what businesses chose to do inside or outside their walls in the closing two decades of the twentieth century.

Why Fissure?

The large corporation of days of yore came with distinctive borders around its perimeter, with most employment located inside firm walls. The large business of today looks more like a small solar system, with a lead firm at its center and smaller workplaces orbiting around it. Some of those orbiting bodies have their own small moons moving about them. But as they move farther away from the lead organization, the profit margins they can achieve diminish, with consequent impacts on their workforces.

It would seem that businesses would always have an incentive to shift out activities that were not core to their profitability to other firms if such activities could be done at lower cost externally. What changed that made this practice so much more pervasive? One of the unsatisfactory aspects of many analyses of contingent employment, precarious work, and the rise of workforce vulnerability generally is that they provide lists of usual suspects for the problems, but an incomplete account of why those factors together have led to the growing adoption of these practices. Although it is true, for example, that more industries are now exposed to international competition, simply asserting this fact does not mean that companies are in a better position to contract out work.

For an answer we must return to the business history described in Chapter 2: if the modern corporation that dominated the economic scene during of much of the twentieth century reflected adaptations to the market and technological forces acting on leading enterprises of the era, the decision to shed many of those activities to other business entities implies a change in both the forces acting on those companies and the technologies and organizational forms available to them to undertake business. In fact, that is exactly what happened.

The fissured workplace reflects two interrelated changes that led companies to shed more and more employment as they faced intensifying pressure to focus on their core competencies. First, capital markets demanded it, reflective of changes in how those markets operate and the standards to which they held (and hold) businesses seeking financing. Berle's and Mean's concern that the separation of ownership from management insulated the modern corporation from scrutiny was replaced by a concern that the harsh stewardship of capital markets caused corporations to focus too strenuously on the short term. Changes in the financial sector created powerful incentives for lead firms to redraw the very boundaries of the corporation.

Second, technological changes created new ways of designing and monitoring the work of other parties, inside or outside the corporation. This enabled companies to shed activities while still ensuring that subordinate businesses adhered to detailed and explicit performance standards. Over the past three decades, it has become far less expensive to contract with other organizations—or create new organizational forms—to undertake activities that are part of producing goods or providing services. That alters the calculus of what should be done inside or outside enterprise boundaries. As a result, lead companies can simultaneously focus attention on a core set of activities (and direct employment relationships) as demanded by capital markets and shed more and more of the actual work done by the enterprise. We look at both changes in this chapter.

Demanding Capital

In chronicling the rise of the modern corporation, Adolph Berle and Gardiner Means in the early 1930s worried about the social consequences of the divorce of ownership and control. John Kenneth Galbraith thirty years later expected this schism to lead to managerial dominance of the economic landscape, as corporate leaders and their minions sought stability and persistence of their positions, leading to business and cultural malaise. Mainstream economists, at the same time, worried that the principal/agent problem inherent in the separation would lead businesses to become fat and lazy, unresponsive to the need to create value for their shareholders and not willing to make the changes necessary for the United States to compete with emerging countries, particularly Japan.

These concerns look almost quaint now. Economists began to raise very different concerns a few years later, when they began emphasizing the disciplining effects of capital markets and the role of management in maximizing a business's value to shareholders, who are the residual claimants to what was produced by the firm.[1] The efficient market model of financial markets holds that the value of shares reflects the market's take on a company's underlying value and future prospects. Because capital markets are highly competitive, managers whose actions stray appreciably from those of owners—regardless of how diffuse those owners are—will quickly be reined in by the falling value of shares and the demand by shareholders to replace incompetent (or self-interested) managers with others more capable of obtaining full value from the business.[2] Major changes in financial markets have been the subject of many books, particularly in the wake of the Great Recession, and will not be recounted in detail here.[3] But a synopsis of the transformation of several critical pieces helps explain the growing demands placed on companies by public and private capital.

Institutional Investors

Sophisticated institutional investors who steer trillions of dollars into and out of private and public companies played a crucial role in disciplining the behavior of managers and keeping their attention focused on returns. One critical impetus arose from changes in the way households save for retirement. In 1980 about 58% of wage and salary workers with pensions had defined benefit pension plans, while less than 10% had defined contribution plans (with the remaining workers having a mix of both). By 2011 the balance had dramatically shifted, so that less than 10% of workers with pensions had defined benefit plans, while more than 60% had defined contribution plans.[4] The impact of this shift is significant: defined contribution plans require the recipients to invest money that has been contributed by the employer in stocks, bonds, and other assets that will one day fund (hopefully) their retirement.

The rise of defined contribution pensions—401(k) accounts—and the growth of IRAs (another replacement for traditional defined benefit plans) led to a huge infusion of household financial capital to be managed. In 1980, 3% of household financial assets in the United States were held in investment companies; by 2011 that share stood at 23%. A large portion of the capital held in 401(k)s and IRAs was managed through mutual funds, leading to an explosion in the assets held by those institutions.[5] In 1980 mutual funds were a backwater among investments, holding about $134 billion in financial assets. By 2011 mutual funds held $11.6 trillion in assets.[6]

Mutual funds are major investors in U.S.-issued stocks, holding 25% of outstanding stock at the end of 2011.[7] The management of assets in mutual funds is concentrated: in 2011 the largest five companies managed 40% of total net assets (versus 34% in 1990), the top ten managed 53%, and the top twenty-five managed 73%.[8] A small number of companies—BlackRock, Fidelity, Vanguard, T. Rowe Price—stand at the pinnacle of companies holding and moving capital assets. BlackRock, which managed $3.5 trillion in assets in 2011, owned at least 5% of the shares of more than 1,800 U.S. corporations. Similarly, Fidelity owned at least 5% of 677 companies and Vanguard owned 5% of 524. This made BlackRock the largest shareholder in one in five U.S. corporations, and Fidelity and Vanguard the largest owners in about one in ten U.S. corporations.[9]

The scale of assets managed by companies like BlackRock, Vanguard, and Fidelity, the fungibility of those assets, and the large number of alternative investments available to fund managers together breed little patience for low performance for stocks of a given risk level. Institutional investors increased the volatility in ownership of companies and the sensitivity of managers to changes in company valuations.[10] For example, mutual funds seldom buy and hold stocks, but rather buy and sell them frequently. In 2011 average weighted stock turnover in fund portfolios was 52% each year (a number somewhat below the almost forty-year average turnover rate of 58%).[11] Money flowing into publicly traded companies from mutual funds is therefore "impatient" and moves frequently in search of better returns for a given level of risk.[12] Other institutional investors, such as public pension systems like CALPERS, hedge funds, and insurance companies, utilize the growing range of instruments for investment and therefore play directly (through their clout in the market) and indirectly (through their daily trading activity) an equally aggressive role in the life of the companies held (or potentially held) by them.[13]

The Private Equity Model

The rise of private equity firms also played a growing role in forcing restructuring of leading businesses.[14] The number and value of deals from private equity firms expanded dramatically in the years before the 2008 recession. In 2001 there were only 20 deals, accounting for $335 billion of invested capital. By 2005 the number had grown to 171 deals, with a total of $1.077 trillion of capital invested, with the trend peaking in 2007 with 607 deals and $1.5 trillion in invested capital. Funds focused on buyouts make up about two-thirds of private equity capital, although given that private equity money is then heavily leveraged with capital borrowed by acquired companies (see below), the amount of money used in private equity buyout deals was probably well over $3 trillion in 2011.[15]

The methods employed by companies like BlackStone Group, KKR and Company, and Bain Capital involve not only the buying and selling of other companies, but a more direct role in the operations of those enterprises once acquired. In a typical deal, the private equity partners (who are designated "general partners") bring in investment capital from a set of limited partners, usually investors like pension funds, academic endowments, and wealthy individuals. The capital becomes the basis for a fund to acquire a portfolio of properties and companies. The general partners receive fees of usually 2% of the invested funds from the limited partners, as well as earning 20% of profits from the acquisitions once a hurdle rate for the limited partners has been achieved.

Using the investment funds, the private equity firms acquire a set of target companies that are viewed as undervalued by the market. Similar to leveraged buyouts in an earlier era, the private equity investors use only a portion of the investment funds to acquire the companies.[16] The remaining capital (far larger than the amount from the private equity investors) is borrowed through short-term (and high-interest) financing on the books of the acquired company from investment banks, other hedge funds, and other lenders.[17] At the end of the investment period for the fund, the value of the portfolio of companies is tallied and profits distributed to the fund's partners.

Profits for the group arise because the now heavily leveraged companies in the private equity portfolio face intense pressure to undertake radical restructuring, in part through the policies instituted by the new ownership group. Ownership conveys the right to take whatever steps—selling off of business units; restructuring those that are not sold; shedding particular activities— are deemed necessary to increase the value of the acquired companies so that they can eventually be sold at a profit. This creates a very high-powered and direct means of restructuring companies.[18]

Executive Compensation and Firm Performance

The demands of investors on companies to improve performance were further sharpened by the growth of incentive-based pay systems for CEOs and other senior executives. Performance-based pay flows from the property rights perspective of incentive design. If the owners of companies really seek to increase their returns, they should fashion contracts with top managers to give the latter the incentives to do so (rather than allow them to pursue their own interests at the expense of investors as forecast by Berle and Means).[19]

Executive compensation for CEOs of the fifty largest firms in the United States was relatively modest, holding steady around the $1 million mark (in 2000 dollars), from the late 1930s all the way until the early 1970s. Beginning in the 1970s, however, the pay of top executives began to rise dramatically, crossing a particularly steep inflection point in the 1990s, when median pay for executives soared. Among the top fifty firms, median CEO compensation (in 2000 constant dollars) increased from $1.2 million in the 1970s to $1.8 million in the 1980s, and then jumped to $4.1 million in the 1990s. For the period 2000 to 2005 real median compensation among this group of CEOs hit $9.2 million.[20]

This rapid rise in compensation reflected the shift to performance-based pay linked to stock prices and options in major companies. Salary and bonuses represented 100% of compensation for CEOs in the largest fifty firms in the United States from 1936 to 1950. In the 1960s, salary and bonuses still accounted for 87% of all compensation. However, in the 1980s, compensation in the form of salary and bonuses fell to 74%, dropping further, to 53% of compensation, in the 1990s. By the time stocks, options, and compensation peaked in the period between 2000 and 2005, top CEOs earned only 40% of their compensation from salary and bonuses, while 23% came from stocks and long-term incentive plans (largely restricted stock) and 37% from options.[21]

As academic studies and news exposés revealed, while rewards did accompany upside results, executives also seemed to be well compensated even when stock prices went in the wrong direction (sometimes drastically so). One reason is that performance-based compensation policies (and the academic literature that justified them) generally assume an "arm's-length model of bargaining" between the CEO and top executives on one hand and the board of directors on the other in setting up incentive schemes. The reality, as researchers like Lucian Bebchuk and Jesse Fried demonstrated, is far different; there are a variety of reasons that the relationship between executives and directors is far more intertwined than suggested by the arm's-length model often assumed in corporate governance.[22]

As a result of both the intended performance effects and the hidden self-dealing built into many compensation systems, executive compensation dramatically increased the earning of top corporate leaders relative to others. The ratio between the pay received by the average CEO in total direct compensation and that of the average production worker went from 37.2:1 in 1979 to an astounding 277:1 in 2007. The effects of the recession knocked the ratio back to a "mere" 185:1 in 2009.[23]

Capital markets were not fazed by the trends in executive compensation. In fact, investors widely applauded the companies for adopting these pay schemes. But they did because of the policies CEOs and other business leaders instituted in pursuit of higher valuations.

• • •

Today, one would be hard pressed to argue that the distance between ownership and control allows the creation of the "planned society" and the new industrial state forecasted by Galbraith. While there is still intense debate about whether the end result of capital markets remains efficient or myopic, few would disagree that management of corporate enterprises faced enormous pressure beginning in the mid-1970s as U.S. dominance in many core manufacturing industries faded and capital markets became more fluid.[24] In response, the lead companies subjected to this pressure began to change strategies significantly, putting in motion policies that would fissure employment.

The Pursuit of Core Competency and Its Consequences

A new and clear message emanated from public capital markets and private equity companies, reaching a crescendo by the late 1980s and early 1990s. It was echoed in articles and books by academics in business schools as well as by an army of consultants in new and established consulting companies. The message was simple: firms should focus their attention and their resources on a set of core competencies that represented distinctive capabilities and sources of comparative advantage in the markets in which they competed. Anything that did not directly support those core competencies would be carefully evaluated as to whether it should (1) remain part of the business at all; (2) be restructured to be done more efficiently internally; or (3) be outsourced to some other party that could provide the necessary activity externally at lower cost. In essence, the message was, Find your distinctive niche and stick to it. Then shed everything else.

The idea of core competency begs the question of what is "core" to a firm. Most proponents stressed that it was not about particular services, products, or functions by which companies gained current success, but about the underlying skills, knowledge sets, or business platforms that consistently produced those successful products or services. For a components provider in the automobile industry, core competency meant consistently developing and refining new products for transmissions rather than production excellence per se. For a hotel company, core competency reflected the ability to consistently provide a certain kind of customer experience for a type of business traveler, rather than owning and running a particular property in an important city. For a retailer, it meant the ability to manage inventory risk while offering customers a broader selection of products at its stores.[25] In an article often cited for its articulation of the concept, Prahalad and Hamel wrote: "During the 1980s, top executives were judged on their ability to restructure, declutter, and delayer their corporations. In the 1990s, they'll be judged on their ability to identify, cultivate, and exploit the core competencies that make growth possible—indeed, they'll have to rethink the concept of the corporation itself."[26]

The idea of core competency pushes executives to not define their business in terms of current products or strategic business units. Even firms in concentrated industries face competition: assuming that the profitability of a current set of products assures long-term success ignores these competitive pressures. In the popular conception of a core competency, a company needs to be able to recreate the reasons for its current success over time if it is to remain profitable (and in the good graces of its investors). That is what gives it long-term advantages over competitors, such as an ability to create and bring to market distinctive new products; to deliver consistent, high-quality services in multiple markets; or to consistently drive down the costs of making its products.

The business history of Apple Inc. is illustrative. The company's soaring profitability over the past decade arises not from its products per se but from its capacity to design, engineer, and market high-quality digital products at the cutting edge of its consumer base's tastes. Its decision to focus on product design, marketing, and retailing rather than on manufacturing goes back to the days of the Apple II (the company's earliest successful line of home computers, introduced in 1977). An estimated 70% of the manufacturing of the Apple II series was outsourced to other companies. In addition, Apple outsourced parts of marketing, printing, and even design aspects to other companies.[27]

Reliance on outsourcing remained a basic part of strategy spanning 1986–1997, the troubled period when Apple's founder, Steve Jobs, was ousted from the company. With Jobs's return as CEO in 1997, Apple struck out in new directions with the introduction of the iPod and the corresponding iTune stores (2001), iPhone (2007), and iPad (2010), digital products that came to eclipse its computer lines. Apple maintained its focus on design, new product development, and retailing (including through its own Apple stores). At the same time, it further expanded its outsourcing of manufacturing. When asked by President Barack Obama in February 2011 at a dinner meeting of Silicon Valley executives what it would take to make Apple products in the United States, Jobs crisply replied, "Those jobs aren't coming back." By 2012 the company directly employed 63,000 workers (primarily in its design and engineering staffs as well as in its retail operations), while relying on an estimated 750,000 workers worldwide outside the company to manufacture, assemble, and distribute its products.[28] Investors were delighted by the outcomes of the strategy that decoupled the tasks of creating new products from manufacturing them: Apple's stock price went from $7 in 2003 to over $600 in 2012.

The search for core competencies—and the demand to produce results for investors that demonstrated success in defining them and implementing changes reflecting them—has been ongoing ever since. While the results have been defined and play out in different ways over time, three broad phases of activity can be articulated. First, the search for core competency led to the dismantling of conglomerate corporations generally. But it also meant selling off business units in more narrowly focused companies, a particular focus of new private equity owners and buyout specialists.

Second, companies sought to shed activities necessary for ongoing operations but judged peripheral to core activities. This meant a set of headquarters functions at large companies that had often become extensive in prior periods of rapid growth, such as human resources, accounting and finance, and, more recently, information technology (IT). Likewise, it meant shedding many activities at the front lines of companies—whether in manufacturing plants, store outlets, or service delivery units—that were necessary to ongoing operations but not central to the core business, such as maintenance and janitorial services or security.

In more recent times, the demand for focus has led businesses to shed activities that are part of the core competency itself. Even the elements that make up a core competency are not immune from being shifted outward to other parties.

Goodbye, Conglomerates

Between 1962 and 1969, 22% of Fortune 500 companies were acquired in mergers. A group of huge conglomerate companies selling a wide and frequently incoherent range of products and brands emerged from this binge. Creating conglomerate companies was controversial even at the time of their growth. The Federal Trade Commission deemed conglomerate accounting that masked the profitability of individual product lines "a tool of deception."[29] The actual performance of many conglomerates undercut arguments about the economies of scale arising from centralized management of diverse business units ("good management is the same for any business") or superior access to capital that being part of the conglomerate conferred. Instead, unhappy shareholders of public companies and private equity investors began to question the results of broad acquisition strategies.[30]

Weakening macroeconomic conditions and declining stock prices created further pressure on conglomerate companies by the late 1960s to demonstrate to investors the value of the highly diversified enterprises. Corporate raiders attacked them as unwieldy and underperforming behemoths. By acquiring the companies through corporate takeover and selling off the loosely related (or unrelated) units, investors could extract value through the improved performance of units closer to the core business, and also benefit by selling the other units to external investors who could gain greater value from them. The dismantling of the conglomerate in this view would reveal that its pieces were worth more than the firm as a whole.[31]

The rise and demise of Beatrice Foods is instructive.[32] The company was founded as the Beatrice Creamery Company in Beatrice, Nebraska, in 1894, beginning as a grading operation for other dairy producers but quickly becoming a butter producer and creamery with its own label and product line. It grew by perfecting methods of packaging and distribution. By the early part of the 1900s, the company distributed products, and by 1930 it had moved its headquarters to what was then the hub of the U.S. food industry, Chicago, where the company produced 30 million gallons of milk and 10 million gallons of ice cream annually. It continued to grow in the next decades through acquisition of other creameries and expansion of its own production, responding to growing post–World War II demand for food. Beginning in the 1950s, Beatrice began to expand into related areas of food by acquiring other branded companies and changing its name to the more expansive Beatrice Foods, eventually acquiring well-known companies and food brands like Hunt's (catsup), Tropicana (orange juice), Wesson (cooking oil), La Choy (packaged Chinese food), and Orville Redenbacher's (popcorn). Acquisitions began to change shape in the 1970s when it purchased brands and companies like Jolly Rancher and Good & Plenty (candy), Culligan (water treatment), Avis (rental cars), Playtex (undergarments), Samsonite (luggage), and Airstream (trailers).[33]

Kohlberg Kravis and Roberts (later KKR), a major private equity company specializing in leveraged buyouts, understood what many in the public did not: that Beatrice had acquired well over a hundred major and valuable national brands. It purchased Beatrice for $8.7 billion in 1986 and began over the next four years to sell off the welter of brands and companies under its umbrella. The final units still operating under the Beatrice name were sold to ConAgra in 1990.

By the late 1980s, the flagship conglomerate companies of the 1960s had been dismantled through the actions of private equity companies like Kohlberg Kravis Roberts, corporate raiders like T. Boone Pickens, and leveraged buyout machers like Michael Milliken. But breaking apart conglomerated behemoths like Beatrice represented only the start of efforts to focus on core competencies. Along with and following divestment of peripheral business units, the insistent effort to shed turned inward.

Cutting the Corporate Periphery

Headquarters offices of companies and divisions blossomed in size and scope during much of the twentieth century. In time, the large range of support activities, spanning accounting, human resources, and information technology, came under increasing scrutiny as potential sources of cost reduction. These activities, it was argued, could be more efficiently undertaken by outside entities with greater experience and cost advantages in their provision.

Personnel, benefits, labor relations, and human resource departments had been fast-growing areas in corporate and divisional offices. The growth of unions in the middle part of the century led firms covered by collective bargaining agreements to create larger bureaucracies to deal with labor relations and compensation policies. Later, passage of laws on safety and health, discrimination, and fringe benefits required additional expertise. Over time, the offices gravitated away from a sole focus on compliance toward the broader function of human resource policies as a source of potential efficiency for the company, and in some cases as a source of strategic advantage.[34]

Yet because these departments were almost always cost centers rather than profit centers, they became an early target of outsourcing. Payroll represented the first function to be outsourced under the personnel/human resource umbrella, in part because of the potential efficiencies of undertaking these relatively standardized functions. Given the specific legal requirements of state and federal policies, the common platform of many payroll procedures, and the potential scale advantages of developing software systems to handle large payroll requirements, companies like Automatic Data Processing (ADP), Paychex Inc., and Ceridian Corporation grew quickly. These companies handle payroll and benefit functions.[35]

The scope of human resource activities being outsourced, however, soon broadened to include design, development, and implementation of benefit plans and workforce diversity programs. The complexity of some areas of legal compliance also led businesses to shift this work outward, particularly in rapidly changing areas of law. By the early years of the twenty-first century, the human resource outsourcing industry was estimated to have annual revenues of $21.7 billion, which accounted for more than 8% of all human resource spending. Contractors offered services in most areas of human resource policy, and major companies in a variety of sectors drew on their services. For example, in 1998 BP entered a seven-year deal to outsource compensation, benefits, payroll, organizational development, performance management, employee development, training, recruitment, and relocation to Exult, a small start-up company. As the outsourcing arrangement progressed over the period, an estimated 40% of BP's internal human resource staff was cut.[36]

Exult and the series of companies that later acquired it signed similarly large deals with Bank of America, International Paper, Prudential Financial, and many others.[37]

Information technology activities in corporate offices became another common target for shifting outward. As with outsourcing payroll, companies seeking to trim overhead costs are attracted to the potential cost savings arising by bidding out IT activities to a competitive market with multiple vendors of similar services. An added impetus arises from the rapidly evolving nature of IT requirements and capacities: because of the pace of IT change, a company (even a large one) is challenged to keep abreast of software, hardware, and increasingly Internet-based innovations. For companies where IT is not central to the business model, contracting out provides access to the forefront of new services that may be applicable (at a comparable or lower cost than creating these capacities internally).

Even though outsourcing IT began only in the 1990s, by 1998, 38% of surveyed companies had shed some of their IT activities to outside vendors.[38] As was the case with human resources, the first IT activities to be shed were routine functions that were fairly standardized across companies or new services with which the organization had little prior experience. These included data center operations, application maintenance, and network management.[39] Because of the idiosyncratic nature of other IT work, the scope of outsourcing widened more slowly to IT functions serving more core activities such as marketing (through web design and maintenance), user support, and application development. But recent surveys indicate that expansion to these more customized areas is proceeding, facilitated by companies providing high-security cloud-based servers.[40]

Cutting the Workplace Periphery

In the past, major employers hired landscaping crews, janitors and maintenance staffs, and security providers to keep facilities clean, well maintained, and looking presentable to employees, customers, and the public. But just as departments like payroll, publications, human resources, and information technology showed up as cost centers rather than profit centers, these activities were not directly related to making products or delivering services. Given the rising pressure to focus on core competencies, janitorial and maintenance services were some of the early activities to be pushed out of large businesses.

The logic was clear: Why should a major company pay its own employees to mop floors, clean bathrooms, vacuum rugs, and mow lawns when a myriad of outside companies were willing to offer those services? The incentives at some companies were further sharpened by the fact that some of these activities were unionized (particularly facility security services) even in workplaces where other employees were not covered by collective bargaining.

These activities were also relatively self-contained, lowering the costs of shifting them out to other service providers once the decision to shed them had been made. And as more of these activities moved outward, new competitive markets for service provision grew. The competition in the new markets to provide janitorial and security services intensified, lowering prevailing prices and further benefiting lead companies.[41]

In some cases, lead companies hired other big companies for those services, for example ABM Industries, a $3.5 billion maintenance, security, and janitorial company. Those large companies often hired and trained their own employees to provide cleaning services. This was particularly true if maintenance services included specialized activities requiring a trained workforce, such as when cleaning required particular techniques or capabilities.

In other cases, companies hired third parties to coordinate maintenance for them, such as cleaning of company headquarters or landscaping of the grounds. In turn, those companies, acting much like general contractors in the construction industry, hired other, smaller businesses to undertake pieces of the contract. In some cases, different floors of the same company might be cleaned by separate cleaning contractors. Work and employment could be split even more as contractors further subcontracted the work.[42]

Franchising also began to expand in the outsourced cleaning industry. Janitorial service providers usually do their work after hours with no direct supervision from the customer. Assuring customers that cleaners will both meet quality standards and be trustworthy custodians of facilities after hours creates opportunities for branding janitorial services. A new industry formed for providing branded services to medium and large business users via franchised janitorial services.

Whether to specialty maintenance companies, to subcontracting networks, or to franchised enterprises, the shifting out of peripheral activities is significant. By 2000 an estimated 45% of janitors worked under contracting arrangements, and more than 70% of guards were employed as contractors.[43]

Cutting Deeper

As the pressure to focus continued, business units within many corporations sought further ways to shed activities and reduce costs while protecting the parts of the business central to profitability. Management scholars and consultants promoted the idea of streamlining business processes that had, over time, become encumbered, slow, and wasteful. Companies had allowed many operations to become flabby, in this view, and were weighed down by internal processes that were often redundant, inefficient, quality-plagued, and unproductive. To compete more effectively, companies needed to strip their business practices to the core, analyze what the critical features of them should be, and rebuild them accordingly.

"Reengineering" was an influential approach in this area first articulated by Hammer and Champy and then taken up by other business scholars and by management consultants; it involved taking apart the components of processes by which businesses made products or provided services. Through a rigorous examination of these pieces, the production process could be reengineered in order to reduce waste, increase throughput, speed up delivery processes, and improve productivity. In so doing, companies would be able to better provide their products at lower cost.[44]

One example of the ever-deepening effort to shed activities from the core of companies occurred in logistics and distribution. Moving intermediate products between different stages of production or out to retailers or customers is an intrinsic part of production. Changes in retailing discussed below have made logistics even more important. Auto parts suppliers providing components to car companies operating under lean production principles often must be ready to deliver parts in relatively short time spans requiring efficient logistic operations. Modern lean retailers similarly demand rapid replenishment of products and sophisticated logistic operations.

Nonetheless, manufacturers, agricultural companies, and retailers began to shift distribution operations outward. In the 1980s this began by having trucking companies take over more of the basic transportation activities formerly done by their own in-house transportation fleets. In the 1990s companies like DHL began to offer expanded services for clients in packaging, sorting, and labeling for internal and external operations. By the early years of the twenty-first century, integration of information technology with distribution activities allowed providers like UPS and Schneider Logistics to manage particular transportation operations such as product returns. Most recently, logistic operations have come to entail taking on the responsibility for the entire logistic activities of major companies.[45]

As in other cases, the first stage of shedding activities was fairly straightforward and standardized. Logistics providers can achieve lower costs by higher-capacity utilization of distribution facilities, by allocating those distribution facilities more efficiently, by more efficient transportation routing, and by other economies arising from providing services to multiple customers at once. They can also more effectively smooth the ups and downs of logistic needs across companies facing different demand patterns. As a result, transportation and distribution activities moved outward fairly quickly as the market for such services developed and the financial benefits of using them became apparent to many companies.[46]

If such economies arose in logistics, why not move up the production process to manufacturing or procurement? If an outside business could provide janitorial and landscaping services to hotels, why not find other providers to clean rooms, or to run the kitchens of chain restaurants? The logic of shedding activities could potentially be applied deeper and deeper into the core operations of businesses—as long as the crown jewels of core competency were not compromised.

Dangers of Shifting Too Much

The benefits and costs of shedding corporate, divisional, and facility-level activities to other companies become more complex as the activities go deeper into the core competency of the lead company. Businesses face significant risks if outsourced functions interact with decisions central to core competency or require nuanced understandings of customers, markets, or other external factors. For example, companies have found that shifting away major human resource and IT functions can backfire if it impinges upon the development of key staff positions in the case of personnel or undermines building strategic data systems or services in regard to IT. The problem is intensified if business functions are hard to bring back in-house once outsourced.

Shifting out core production activities came to the manufacturing sector in the late 1980s. In a detailed study of the use of temporary employment agencies at an automotive supply company, Erickcek, Houseman, and Kalleberg found that four of the five auto supply plants they studied used temporary agencies, with two of the plants relying on them for more than 20% of their production employment.[47] In a period of rapid growth, the company chose to rely on lower-paid temporary workers alongside a relatively high-paid non-union workforce.

However, the strategy was not without its problems. The extensive use of temporary workers impacted the quality of the supplier's products. As the share of workers from temporary agencies increased beyond one-quarter of the workforce, this problem became particularly acute. The human resource director described the tension between plant managers concerned about quality and executives concerned about lowering costs:

> And . . . quality is starting to have problems . . . and now it's like, "We've got to get this temporary ratio back down." We'll start edging back down to 20, and . . . then the goal becomes 15 percent . . . and now there's always this discussion, "Well, it's more cost-effective to have the temporaries." So it doesn't seem to be an initiative with the executives to get that ratio down. So even though they talk about it, we are never going to get this high rate down.[48]

In the end, the human resources director notes that the cost advantage concerns raised by senior executives prevailed and that the plant settled at operating "within 20 to 25 percent . . . But we are in this constant state of denial, yet that number still stays up there and . . . the vice president of human resources is . . . [saying], "We've got to get it down."

The auto supplier story reveals a tension created by fissuring, relating to what is called a principal/agent dilemma. Because the interests and objectives of subordinate providers of fissured activities are different than those of the lead business, the incentives of the business doing the work of the lead company may undermine some of the latter's objectives. In pursuit of its own profits, an independent provider of a service may choose to compromise quality, use lower-skilled employees, or be more likely to violate workplace laws than the lead company. The more misaligned the incentives of the secondary provider are relative to those of the lead company, the bigger the problem.

Shedding activities to other organizations creates a second problem. By shifting employment to another party and paying for services provided, the lead employer is less able to monitor performance, since those doing the work are now potentially hidden within another organization. Once again, this problem can be addressed in part by how the lead company carves up the work to be done, ensuring that the performance is as observable as possible. If so, the lead company will be able to detect if it is getting the performance it needs, and the market forces created by secondary businesses jockeying to be providers of the service will push toward pricing linked to performance (which is the point). However, if performance is not easily observed, other mechanisms must be devised to provide better information if the strategy is to succeed.

A third problem arises when shifting out activities to others creates the threat of "holdups." Engaging outside parties to undertake important activities for the lead company risks allowing those outsiders to use their potential leverage to withhold those activities to capture some of the benefits that arise from fissuring. This problem becomes particularly vexing if the subordinate unit has significant ability to advance its internal agenda over that of the primary organization, such as through the control of skill.

A central task for successful fissuring is to strategically shift out work so that the lead firm remains in what Red Barber, the famed announcer for the Brooklyn Dodgers, called "the cat-bird's seat." That is, make sure the subordinate players have limited power to stray from the central objectives of the lead company. For example, one way to limit the potential for holdup is to have many potential businesses available to provide the fissured activity. The more competitive the market for those services, the less able any one company will be to demand to share more of the benefits from fissuring.[49]

The fissured workplace therefore does not reflect an either/or strategy, but rather a careful balancing act. On one hand, the lead organization wants to protect and enhance the core competencies driving its profit model. On the other, it wants to shift work to other parties to the extent possible. But here is where balance is crucial. Shifting too much work out or selecting the wrong party to do that work can undermine the crown jewels arising from the core competencies of central concern to customers and investors. One needs a glue to hold the two pieces together.

New Technology and the Falling Cost of Coordination

The corporation of the twentieth century had a set of organizational arrangements to solve the boundary problems of firms and markets, built on the communication technologies, monitoring and coordination mechanisms, and systems of contracts of that era. The revolution in computing power (and the impact of Moore's Law, which says that the number of transistors on integrated circuits doubles every eighteen to twenty-four months) has lowered the costs of acquiring information in regard to selection and monitoring.[50] The expansion and ubiquity of communication provided by the Internet and digital communication systems similarly lower the cost of acquiring and sharing information relevant to these purposes.

The development of complementary technologies that allow low-cost collection and instantaneous transmission of data—everything from bar codes and scanners (2-D and now 3-D), small, even microscopic, wireless sensor technologies of all varieties including motes, and geo-coded transponders— creates unparalleled (a.k.a. scary) capabilities to track detailed information at minute levels of time and geographic specificity. Together, these technologies enable new relationships in all aspects of how businesses, markets, and their boundaries are configured.

A final form of cost reduction developed alongside the above-mentioned high-tech forms is more low-tech in nature. A variety of new organizational methods of contracting came into their own in the 1980s going forward that lowered the costs of shifting work out. The most striking of these was franchising. Although traditional franchising arose much earlier as a unique business form to enable distribution in a small number of industries, its application to fast food and later to other sectors (what is called business-format franchising) transformed it into a malleable way of structuring business relationships. The development of new forms of contracting and the establishment of law and experience around it lowered the cost of applying the fissured idea to new industries and relationships.[51]

Fissured workplaces could not have spread absent the falling cost of gathering information and undertaking monitoring in light of developments in the digital world. Two examples illustrate the implications of information and communication technologies in this way.

Falling Information Costs in Trucking

Running a trucking business inherently raises the problem of costly information. The work requires hiring individuals to transport valuable goods from one place to another, unmonitored for much of the time between when they are loaded on and taken out of the vehicle. Not only is the cargo valuable, but so is the vehicle used to move it. Along with the security of the goods, delivering them on time is also a key outcome for the end customer and the trucking business. So the trucking company faces the problem of both selecting good drivers and monitoring them as they drive and deliver the goods.

Falling information and communication technologies gave rise to a solution: onboard computing (OBC). OBC allows truckers to find the best routes for travel and to avoid potential delays. More importantly (from the perspective of companies), it allows trucking firms to know where drivers are at any time. The arrival of OBC and the falling costs of information associated with it should therefore lead trucking companies to realign their relationships with truckers. Baker and Hubbard, in a series of papers on the impacts of OBC on organizational structure and outcomes, point out that OBC can affect trucking companies in two ways. On one hand, it lowers the direct costs of monitoring truckers, allowing the company to watch drivers more closely. This might induce companies to keep truckers as direct employees, because they can use ongoing information to keep truckers on schedule and prevent unauthorized detours or stops (and also to detect costly behavior like speeding on highways or even falling asleep at the wheel).[52]

However, OBC also reduces the cost of coordinating drivers, since it provides real-time information on location. With lower costs of coordination, if a company could assure that its packages would move from point A to point B on time but could secure those services more inexpensively through, say, treating the truck driver as an independent operator outside of the pay structure of the large firm, so much the better. This increases the lead company's ability and interest in contracting out trucking activities rather than doing them on an in-house basis.[53] The OBC example also points out that fissuring, as enabled by falling information costs, is not simply a yes/no decision but still involves a balancing of the first two elements of the recipe, albeit with a greater tip toward shifting that work outward given the lower costs.

Falling Information Costs in Retailing

As in trucking, the technologies that allowed for the lean retailing revolution require a rebalancing of the benefits and costs of contracting. In this case, the key technologies are bar codes, scanners, and electronic data interchange (EDI), along with the falling costs of computers, allowing use of abundant real-time sales data. On one hand, these technologies lower the cost of monitoring the performance of suppliers and could push toward greater backward integration by retail firms. In this sense, digital information systems helped solve Ford's problems of overly ambitious backward integration in the 1930s by improving the lead company's ability to watch key suppliers.

On the other hand, as with trucking, the digital technologies allow better coordination of suppliers. This means that the retailer, as the coordinator with the principal economies of scale in distribution, can take greater advantage of its logistics competency, while leaving the provision of goods to manufacturers who have scale advantages in production. So the retailer coordinates the system (increasingly not with its own trucks, but using subcontracted trucks under close scrutiny) but keeps the production activity safely ensconced with the supplier. Enhanced monitoring allows it to carefully scrutinize performance. Along with the availability of multiple suppliers in increasingly global supply chains, the advantage remains on the side of the lead retailer, lowering holdup and associated dangers.

What the Glue Must Do

For fissuring to be successful, the lead company must design and deploy mechanisms that assure that the businesses in orbit around it operate in a way compatible with its core strategies.[54] Importantly, the chosen organizational mechanisms must ensure that the secondary players do not undermine the basis of the lead company's core competency (for example, brand image, product quality, coordination economies).[55] Easier said than done.

The principal/agent problem—that is, the difficulty faced by one party (the principal) of using another party (the agent) to undertake work on its behalf—arises because information is costly. First, it is costly for the principal to gather information about the agents in selecting across them: some agents may have qualities that might undermine the objectives of the principal. If the characteristics of the agent are particularly hard (costly) to see, the agents who approach the principal first might be the ones who in fact the principal wants to avoid. This issue, called *adverse selection,* can be alleviated the more the principal can make informed decisions about the agents it chooses.[56]

The second problem arises from the cost of observing the agent once hired. Many of the activities that the principal wants the agent to undertake are hard to observe directly (our discussion of employment picked up this problem in regard to setting wages). The harder (or, once again, more costly) it is to observe and monitor the agent, the more its actions may diverge from what the principal wants.[57]

To play its crucial role as glue to assure that subsidiary businesses undertake the activities shed by the lead organization without undermining outcomes central to its core competencies, the lead company must promulgate and communicate standards and see that they are followed. This requires significant investment by the lead organization beyond simply listing what it wants its subordinates to do. Specifically, standards and accompanying policies must accomplish three things:

1. Provide clear and explicit guidance on what is expected. This is the nub of standards promulgated by many lead organizations in different forms.
2. Provide a system of monitoring and auditing to ensure that those standards are followed.
3. Provide for significant penalties in the face of failure to meet goals.

Of course, the problem of incomplete contracts remains even given explicit standards: there will never be sufficient pages in a manual or enough lawyers to craft them to cover every exigency that might arise to assure that the core values of a company are protected while shifting work to others. But the contract systems that have emerged, and the organizational forms that have grown around them, clearly try to do so to the extent possible and significantly curtail the principal/agent problems that may arise. Examining the three elements of standards reveals how serious companies are about keeping the core elements of fissuring from undermining one another.

Explicit Standards: What We Expect

The glue for fissured employment rests on explicit and detailed standards crafted by lead businesses and followed by all subsidiary organizations. The competitive importance of standards, as well as their detailed content, has been overlooked in much of the literature dealing with incomplete contracting.[58] One reason is that standards reflect core competencies and reveal strategic—and proprietary—aspects of the lead business. They are therefore jealously guarded and difficult to obtain. I present many different examples of standards in reviewing "fissured forms" in Part II. But several examples illustrate their general nature.

The information technologies and related systems underlying lean retailers dramatically reduce the amount of time between purchase of goods and provision to customers. But this technology platform also alters the relationship between retailers and their complex network of suppliers, in particular by specifying in great detail the logistical arrangements required for delivering and replenishing products.

Saks Fifth Avenue, a publicly held department store catering to upper-end customers, has adopted lean retailing principles as part of its core competency. It depends on its vendors to comply with rigorous delivery standards and provides them with a standards manual with clear guidelines on their interaction. The manual covers issues ranging from methods of payment and order shipment protocols to the consequences of failing to meet standards. The preamble to the manual makes the importance of standards to Saks's core competency very clear:

> Saks Fifth Avenue is committed to supporting the Universal Product Code (UPC), Electronic Data Interchange (EDI), and the GS1 US standards. We believe that by implementing these technologies and guidelines, we can expedite our merchandise flow to the selling floor, manage our inventories better, increase sales, and enhance customer service. This in turn allows us to continue to build a more successful and mutually profitable partnership with our vendors.[59]

The Saks Fifth Avenue vendor standards manual makes the importance of vendor adoption of these standards very clear in its opening pages. For example, it provides explicit instructions on the preparation of cartons, orders, labeling, and packing for all products shipped to it in order to "utilize available technology to implement efficiencies and improved management within the supply chain while expediting our merchandise to the selling floor and enhancing our service to our customer." To achieve this objective, the standards specify that the vendor's shipments must be accurate and received 100% "floor ready," without any merchandise preparation required by the retailer.

This in turn entails adoption of a complex set of requirements around using the correct hangers and other display materials (ten pages on such matters, including detailed pictures) and labels (eight pages on these matters).

Subcontracted work for lead businesses in technical fields requires similar attention to detail. These businesses require not only specific terms about when and how the particular subcontracted work is to be conducted, but exacting terms about the quality, pace, and technical standards to be achieved. AT&T, for example, provides a detailed task matrix for subcontractors that undertake maintenance activities on the company's cell towers, specifying not only the particular work expected of the contractor, but also the role of AT&T and subordinate organizations in monitoring that work.

With branding as their defining core competency, fast-food restaurants insist that franchisees adhere rigidly to standards regarding products, service, and physical facilities. The preliminary documents prospective franchisees receive make the centrality of standards in the operation of the business explicit. The Dunkin' Donuts standard franchise agreement is typical (and blunt) in its statement of this principle: "All Dunkin' Donuts Stores must be developed and operated to our specifications and standards. Uniformity of products sold in Dunkin' Donuts Stores is important, and you have no discretion in the products you sell."[60] Taco Bell's franchise agreement similarly states that the franchisee

> shall faithfully, completely, and continuously perform, fulfill, observe and follow all instructions, requirements, standards, specifications, systems and procedures contained therein [the company's franchise operations manual]; including those dealing with the selection, purchase, storage, preparation, packaging, service and sale (including menu content and presentation) of all food and beverage products, and the maintenance and report of Restaurant buildings, grounds, furnishings, fixtures, and equipment, as well as those relating to employee uniforms and dress, accounting, bookkeeping, record retention and other business systems, procedures and operations.[61]

All fast-food franchises provide detailed standards setting out the terms for prospective franchisees and an even more detailed operating manual once franchisees have joined the chain.[62] Table 3.1 gives excerpts from several fast-food franchise agreements, illustrating the detailed standards incorporated in them as well as the requirement that franchisees adhere closely to them.

Table 3.1 Franchise agreement statements regarding compliance with brand standards: Fast-food industry, selected examples

Eating/drinking brand	Excerpt from franchise agreement
Dairy Queen	Your operating agreement is a contract between you, ADQ and us. You are a part of the national and international franchise system of DQ Grill & Chill and Dairy Queen franchisees and sub-licensees, and you must adhere to various system standards of quality and uniformity that ADQ establishes and modifies periodically, as well as standards and requirements that we establish and modify periodically. You will use ADQ's nationally recognized trademarks and service marks that are approved for your concept; have access to the distinctive operational and management attributes of the DQ system; participate in ADQ's national and regional sales promotion programs; and receive the benefits of association with a nationally recognized franchise system, including various forms of training, opening and operational assistance (see Item 11).[1]
Dunkin' Donuts	If you sign a franchise agreement, you will operate a franchised *Dunkin' Donuts* Store. Under our franchise agreement, we grant our franchisees the right (and they accept the obligation) to operate a *Dunkin' Donuts* Store, selling doughnuts, coffee, bagels, muffins, compatible bakery products, croissants, pizzas, snacks and other sandwiches and beverages that we approve. We may periodically make changes to the systems, menu, standards, and facility, signage, equipment and fixture requirements. You may have to make additional investments in the franchised business periodically during the term of the franchise if those kinds of changes are made or if your store's equipment or facilities wear out or become obsolete, or for other reasons (for example, as may be needed to comply with a change in the system standards or code changes). All *Dunkin' Donuts* Stores must be developed and operated to our specifications and standards. Uniformity of products sold in *Dunkin' Donuts* Stores is important, and you have no discretion in the products you sell. The franchise agreement is limited to a single, specific location and we have the right to operate or franchise or license others who may compete with you for the same customers . . . The distinguishing characteristics of the *Dunkin' Donuts* System include, for example, distinctive exterior and interior design, decor, color and identification schemes and furnishings; special menu items; standards, specifications and procedures for operations, manufacturing, distribution and delivery; quality of products and services offered; management programs; training and assistance; and marketing, advertising and promotional programs, all of which we may change, supplement, and further develop.[2]

(continued)

Table 3.1   (continued)

Eating/drinking brand	Excerpt from franchise agreement
Einstein Bros. Bagels	Restaurants are characterized by our system (the "System"). Some of the features of our System are a specially-designed building or facility, with specially developed equipment, equipment layouts, signage, distinctive interior and exterior design and accessories, products, procedures for operations; quality and uniformity of products and services offered; procedures for management and inventory control; training and assistance; and advertising and promotional programs. We may periodically change and improve parts of the System . . . You must operate your Restaurant in accordance with our standards and procedures, as set out in our Confidential Operating Manual (the "Manual"). We will lend you a copy of the Manual for the duration of the Franchise Agreement. In addition, we will grant you the right to use our marks, including the mark "Einstein Bros." and any other trade names and marks that we designate in writing for use with the System (the "Proprietary Marks").[3]
KFC	KFC outlets must be built to specifications approved by KFCC. The KFC Operating Standards Library (the "Standards Library") explains the required standards for preparing products to be sold at the KFC outlet and operating the outlet (see Standards Library—Table of Contents attached as Exhibit I). The KFC outlets are characterized by a unique system which includes special recipes and menu items; distinctive design, décor, color scheme and furnishings; standards, specifications and procedures for operations; procedures for quality control; training and assistance; and advertising and promotional programs (the "System").[4]
Long John Silver's	LJS Restaurants offer a limited menu featuring fish, seafood, chicken and related items. The Restaurants are designed to serve food promptly and offer dine-in, take-out and in a significant number of Restaurants, drive-thru service. Your Restaurant must be built to LSJ's specifications and operated in accordance with LJS's standards.[5]
Pizza Hut	A broad spectrum of the general public patronizes Restaurants as a source of high-quality pizza and related products and services. A unique system characterizes Restaurants that consists of special recipes, seasonings, and menu items; distinctive design, décor, color scheme, and furnishings; standards, specifications, and procedures for operations; procedures for quality control; training and assistance programs; and advertising and promotional programs (the "System"). A variety of trademarks, service marks, slogans, logos, and emblems that PHI designates for use in connection with the System (the "Pizza Hut Marks") identify the System. PHI has operated Pizza Hut "Red Roof" restaurants since 1958, when PHI opened its first restaurant.

Table 3.1 (continued)

Eating/drinking brand	Excerpt from franchise agreement
	PHI has granted franchises for Pizza Hut "Red Roof" restaurants since 1959. PHI has operated Pizza Hut "Delivery" restaurants and PHI has allowed its franchisees to engage in delivery of pizzas since 1984. PHI has operated Pizza Hut "Express" restaurants (a concept not offered under this disclosure document) since 1987.[6]
Taco Bell	You must operate your facilities according to methods, standards, and procedures (the "System") that Taco Bell provides in minute detail. The System is Taco Bell's sole property and is embodied in the Franchise Operations Manual, commonly referred to as the Answer System (the "Manual"). Taco Bell will furnish you with Books 1, 2, 3 and 5 of the Answer System at no cost and you may order, at your option and expense, Books 4 and 6, all of which are also currently available in cd format. The Manual is incorporated by reference into and is part of the Franchise Agreement, and has the same force and effect as other provisions of the Agreement. Taco Bell may choose to provide the Manual to you via electronic access to a confidential website, in which case Taco Bell will notify you that all or part of the Manual is posted on the website. You agree that it is your responsibility to provide access to the website to those of your employees (but no other persons) for whom the website is intended by Taco Bell. Your failure to follow the System as described in the Manual is a breach of the Franchise Agreement.[7]

1. American Dairy Queen Corporation: Dairy Queen Franchise Disclosure Document, April 17, 2009. Filed and accessed through the California franchising database, http://134.186.208 .233/caleasi/Pub/Exsearch.htm.

2. Dunkin' Donuts Franchising LLC: Dunkin' Donuts Franchise Disclosure Document, March 28, 2008. Accessed through BlueMauMau.org, http://www.bluemaumau.org/ufocs_free _and_without_a_salesman_attached.

3. Einstein and Noah Corporation: Einstein Bros. Restaurant Franchise Disclosure Document, December 20, 2005. Accessed through FREEFranchiseDocs.com, http://www.freefranchisedocs .com/einstein-and-noah-corporation-UFOC.html.

4. KFC Corporation: KFC Franchise Disclosure Document, March 24, 2009. Filed and accessed through the California franchising database, http://134.186.208.233/caleasi/Pub/Exsearch.htm.

5. Long John Silver's Inc.: Long John Silver's Franchise Disclosure Document, March 24, 2009. Filed and accessed through the California franchising database, http://134.186.208.233/caleasi/Pub /Exsearch.htm.

6. Pizza Hut Inc.: Pizza Hut Franchise Disclosure Document, March 25, 2009. Filed and accessed through the California franchising database, http://134.186.208.233/caleasi/Pub/Exsearch .htm.

7. Taco Bell Corporation: Taco Bell Franchise Disclosure Document, March 24, 2009. Filed and accessed through the California franchising database, http://134.186.208.233/caleasi /Pub/Exsearch.htm.

Monitoring and Auditing: Do What We Ask

In order to ascertain if the businesses undertaking the work are doing what the lead organization intends, the contracts, standards manuals, and franchise agreements provide for explicit forms of ongoing monitoring. These are usually a combination of self-audits and audits (sometimes surprise inspections or, in the case of franchising, customer visits by undercover staff of the franchisor) undertaken by the lead organization or on their behalf by third parties.

Saks Fifth Avenue conducts accuracy and financial audits on vendor shipments as they arrive at distribution centers. This allows the company to validate shipment accuracy "by comparing and verifying the electronic information transmitted in your ASN [advanced ship notice] in conjunction with the associated GS1-128 label (at store, style, color, size, size, quantity level) or on your invoice against the physical units of the contents of your cartons." It also uses a random audit process to create for each vendor a performance index gauging its accuracy level; vendors are ranked in tiers, from "platinum" (best) to "targeted level" (worst).

Subcontracted relationships in many of the agreements reviewed in Part II usually include an escalating level of audits, based on the degree of quality, deadlines, or other compliance issues. Typical is a contract between a major telecommunications carrier (Cingular) and its subcontractors used to undertake ongoing maintenance work; it includes an escalating system of audits, increasing as the number of quality problems increases. Under the audit system, Cingular

> will audit 15% of all Sites awarded in a market at Vendor's expense . . . If greater than 1% of the initial 15% of individual Sites audited per market have Major Defects, then Cingular may request an additional 5% of Sites be audited in that market at Vendor's sole expense.[63]

Franchising agreements similarly provide for the usually unrestricted right of the franchisor to conduct inspections. The Taco Bell agreement, for example, states:

> The Company shall have the right at any time and from time to time without notice to have its representatives enter the Restaurant premises for the

purpose of inspecting the condition thereof and the operation of the Restaurant for compliance with the standards, specifications, requirements and instructions contained in this Agreement and in the Manual, and for any other reasonable purpose connected with the operation of the Restaurant.[64]

In addition to surprise inspections of facilities, chains in the eating and drinking industry also use "secret shoppers" to gauge adherence with service standards.

Penalties and Other Consequences

A system of standards is ultimately only as strong as the potential costs they impose on those who are required to follow them. Though they take different forms and escalate with varying tolerance for noncompliance and quality infractions, the standards underlying fissured employment all include significant consequences for failing to live up to them. These take two principal forms. First are fees or penalties related to specific failure to meet standards, which may begin with warnings and proceed to fees related to the costs (to the lead organization) imposed by the infraction, a fee deemed a form of liquidated damages, or a penalty simply intended to impose a cost (but not directly related to the quality or service infraction).

For example, the Saks Fifth Avenue vendor agreement grants Saks the right to

> refuse and/or return all goods which do not meet our purchase order specifications of style, size, color, quantity and/or quality (including unauthorized substitutions); or which are shipped before the ship date, or after the cancel date, or without valid purchase order numbers or without valid department numbers . . . To cancel a purchase order, in whole or in part, in the event the goods are not shipped in accordance with the terms and conditions hereof . . . To cancel a purchase order, in whole or in part, in the event the goods are shipped after the cancel date, time being of the essence.[65]

The manual presents an extensive list of "offset charges and codes" that indicates the "expense offset" that will be charged to the company for being out of compliance with standards specified in the manual. For example, if a vendor includes more than one purchase order in a carton, it will be charged $5 per carton or $150 per shipment, whichever is greater. Ticketing a product with the wrong retail price is assessed at $25 per shipment plus $.05 per unit with the wrong price. A late advanced ship notice costs $5 per carton (with no stated upper limit). Saks reserves the right to either deduct total charges from its payment to the vendor for the products or "demand direct payment of expense offset fees . . . specified in the Vendor Standards Manual." These offsets can become quite costly, as can those associated with having the order returned for failure to hit the delivery window.

The telecommunications contract frames penalties (in the form of liquidated damages) specifically around the importance of time: "SUPPLIER recognizes the importance of meeting Delivery Dates and agrees to the following liquidated damage provisions and procedures." If a contractor fails to meet a deadline after the parties have attempted to resolve a delay, the carrier is given the right to cancel the order and to recover liquidated damages specified in the contract. The damages are "the greater of either (a) 15% of the price of Delayed Materials and/or Services or (b) a specified $ amount for each day of delay."

The second type of penalty, which is even more costly, is the loss of the contract, supply relationship, or franchise. The right to revoke the agreement is usually explicit and places a great deal of power in the hands of the lead organization. In the telecommunications case, Cingular (the carrier) states in its terms with subcontractors that "CINGULAR may Terminate the Agreement, or any Order in whole or in any part, at any time, for its own convenience and without cause, without any charge, liability or obligation whatsoever upon written notice to SUPPLIER."[66]

In franchising, agreements usually require the franchisee to correct any failure to meet standards found in the course of inspections. If the franchisee fails to correct the problem, the franchisor retains the right to fix the deficiency itself and charge the franchisee for the cost of doing so. Pizza Hut's franchise agreement includes the right to close an outlet where a failure to meet standards potentially threatens the health and safety of either employees or customers.[67] The ultimate penalty for failing to live up to standards is loss of the franchise itself and the associated investments of the franchisee. Given the size of these investments, they are an area of significant tension and litigation. But as I explore in Chapter 6, the franchisor retains significant authority to terminate franchisees.[68]

Coming Full Circle: Capital Market Responses to Shedding Employment

Financial markets increasingly drive companies under their exacting scrutiny to focus on shareholder value. This leads them to shed business units and products no longer viewed as core and to prune away remaining activities even in the core that might be viewed as peripheral. Several recent studies provide evidence underscoring the connection between capital market pressure and employment restructuring.

Employment Impacts of Private Equity Activity

Based on a study of 3,200 firms that were targeted by private equity firms between 1980 and 2005 and the 150,000 establishments connected to them, Steven Davis et al. estimate the impact of private equity buyouts on employment growth and destruction relative to a control sample of similar firms and establishments that were not acquired. The study finds that establishments controlled by the targets of private equity had employment declines of 3% over the two years following the buyout and 6% over five years relative to the control sample. The authors note that "these results say that pre-existing employment positions are at greater risk of loss in the wake of private equity buyouts." The employment declines are particularly large in cases where publicly held companies are acquired and taken private by the private equity firms.[69]

However, the study also finds employment increases at new establishments of the target firm opened after acquisition. When those increases are included, overall net relative job losses at target firms are less than 1%. Nonetheless, the net employment impacts at targeted firms in public-to-private buyouts remain high: over 10% net loss two years following the transaction.[70]

A companion study by the same research team examined productivity effects in manufacturing firms targeted by private equity.[71] They found higher labor productivity growth in establishments targeted by private equity than in a control set of firms, attributable to shrinking or closing less productive establishments in the targeted firms. This is consistent with the shedding process described in this chapter. The study does not provide direct evidence on the types of jobs that are being eliminated in the period following acquisitions or on the types of new jobs created later. However, the aggregate net employment changes and productivity effects found in the studies are consistent with a story where targeted firms eliminate jobs in business units, product areas, or functions no longer judged as core by the private equity owners, and expand, later on, in only those job areas directly related to their core activities.[72]

Stock Market Effects of Downsizing

In June 2012 Dan Akerson, the CEO of General Motors, announced a series of new policies to cut employment at its European and Canadian operations while streamlining its global product development functions "as key priorities to boost the automaker's lackluster stock price."[73] GM's share price increased in the days after the announcement was made.

If financial markets increasingly push companies to pare activities and focus on core competencies, one would expect to find evidence of a relationship between such employment reductions and increases in the share prices of publicly held companies. In the middle part of the past century, when large companies directly employed large and diverse workforces, a layoff would be perceived by investors as a sign of retrenchment by that company in light of an anticipated downturn in demand and therefore a need for employment reductions. Reduced employment spelled trouble for a company and its investors, and stock prices would fall in the wake of that news.

But the reaction of stock markets to employment reduction announcements began to change in the 1990s, as reflected in research by Hank Farber and Kevin Hallock.[74] They show that the stated reason for major layoffs has changed over time. As one would expect, companies cite factors directly related to slumps in demand following business cycle trends, although those reasons were cited less frequently during recessions in the early 1990s and 2000 than in the 1970s and 1980s. Reorganizations were more commonly cited as reasons for layoffs in recent years, particularly in the 1990s and during the recession in the early years of the twenty-first century. Cost control issues were also cited more frequently as causes for layoffs, being invoked in about 6.5% of all job announcements in the 1970s, 10% in the 1980s, and 17% in the 1990s.

But the most striking findings concern the effects of job loss press releases on changes in stock prices before and after the announcement.[75] Share prices responded negatively following job loss announcements in the 1970s and 1980s. However, stock prices actually rose on average following job loss announcements in the 1990s and were not significantly affected by layoff announcements in the first decade of the twenty-first century. The fact that capital markets responded less negatively, and in some of Hallock's and Farber's estimates positively, to announcements of layoffs implies that mass layoffs in recent decades are viewed very differently than they were in the era of large employers. Rather than seeing them as signs of weakening positions, investors seem to view layoffs at worst as routine corporate activities and even positively as a signal that executives have decided to redraw the lines of what will and will not be done by the company going forward.

Wage Determination in a Fissured Workplace

Compelled by capital markets and enabled by technology and new organizational forms, companies in a growing number of industries transformed the way they organized themselves to undertake business. The movement of activities from inside to outside the boundaries of a company alters employment and, as discussed in Chapter 3, leads to both a deepening and a spreading of the fissured workplace. The consequences for employment are profound.

Chapter 2 described how complicated internal labor markets emerged in large businesses of the twentieth century. How does shifting activities to other parties alter the nature of employment? The answers are subtle and fundamental, and are often missed by analysts who cast outsourcing, subcontracting, and even misclassification as tactics solely instituted to dodge legal obligations or by proponents who defend those practices as inherently a positive reflection of the modern, flexible business organization.

The story of why shifting employment outward has deeper advantages is somewhat complicated. Before exploring it further, let's cut to the chase. For any successful company, profits are shared among two groups: workers, in the form of better wages and benefits, and investors, in the form of higher returns. In the markets described in Chapter 2, where lead companies directly employed many workers, workers received a significant share of the profitability in terms of both wages and benefits. Fissuring changes how gains are shared in a fundamental way: by shifting work out, lead firms no longer face a wage determination problem for that work, but rather a pricing problem in selecting between companies vying for it. That change is critical because it results in fewer gains going to the workers who undertake those activities. It instead shifts those gains to investors. To see why, we must delve into the factors that drive wage setting.

Round Up the Usual Suspects

In virtually any market situation, businesses face incentives to lower costs. The more intense the competition, the greater is that pressure. Although the changes in capital markets sharpened that pressure, it would be folly to forget its ongoing presence in markets.

It is therefore almost axiomatic that businesses will seek methods to reduce labor costs. Unit labor costs are driven by two factors: the price of labor (a.k.a. wages and benefits) and the amount of output produced per each unit of labor input (a.k.a. productivity). To the extent that shifting employment to other firms through practices like outsourcing reduces labor costs without compromising product or service integrity, one would expect a movement in that direction.

Many discussions of elements of fissuring—the increasing use of contracting and outsourcing and contingent work arrangements—focus on motivations driven by reducing labor costs. One important example is the long-term effort by businesses to avoid unionization. Unions raise wages, increase benefits, reduce management authority to unilaterally dismiss workers, and increase scrutiny of compliance with workplace regulations. The National Labor Relations Act precludes employers from simply closing down workplaces solely because of the presence of unions, or threatening to do so if a union is elected.[1] But shedding employment can provide more subtle ways to shift away from a highly unionized workforce or move work to forms of employment that are both legally and strategically difficult for unions to organize, at least historically (as we shall see through a number of cases in Part II).

A second explanation is the desire to shift a wide range of required social insurance benefits like unemployment insurance and workers' compensation premiums as well as private benefits like insurance and retirement to other parties. Socially required and privately provided benefits make the cost to employers of hiring workers far greater than wages or salaries. Wages and salaries comprise 69.4% of employer costs per hours worked in the United States for all workers. An additional 7.8% of employer costs are related to federally required benefits (Social Security, Medicare, and federal unemployment insurance) as well as state benefits (unemployment insurance and workers' compensation). Privately provided benefits for insurance (health, life, disability) and retirement average an additional 13.5%.[2]

To the extent that institutions like temporary agencies or smaller companies doing subcontracted work for a lead business comply with the law, required social payments should be captured in the price those subordinate labor providers charge. Part III will document many instances, however, where compliance is far from complete among subordinate employers to lead businesses due to employee misclassification, pay systems that subvert legal requirements such as overtime, or because workers are paid under the table in cash.

Even given payment of legally required benefits, subordinate businesses may provide fewer—or no—benefits in the area of insurance or retirement, lowering the costs to the lead businesses that may draw on them. For example, the federal laws regulating employee benefits require that if a benefit like health care is offered to one worker, it must be offered to all workers. By shifting out employment to another business (such as a temporary agency that does not provide its workforce with health benefits) the company can lower the de facto cost of hiring additional workers.[3]

A third incentive for shedding employment arises from the desire to minimize liability. With employment comes responsibility for outcomes like workplace injuries, illnesses, and fatalities as well as for discrimination, harassment, and unjust dismissal. If shedding employment shifts liabilities to other parties, it lowers expected costs to lead businesses. Liability is indeed an important element of the story of fissuring, and I explore it in detail in Chapter 8.

All of the above explanations can reduce labor costs and the risks associated with employment. But attributing the dramatic rise in shedding employment solely to them does not adequately explain how lead businesses balance the benefits of lower costs from shedding employment against the benefits of continuing to use workers from inside their company, and why the fissured workplace has spread and deepened.

There is something more subtle afoot. It requires thinking about wage determination in large companies.

Large Firms, Monopsony Power, and Wage Determination

> The most autocratic and unfettered employer spontaneously
> adopts Standard Rates for classes of workmen, just as the large
> shopkeeper fixes his prices, not according to the haggling capacity of
> particular customers, but by a definite percentage on cost.
>
> —Sidney and Beatrice Webb (1897)

The large employers that dominated business in much of the twentieth century were in a different position than employers in traditional labor market
models. The extreme case occurs in a company town where a single employer
essentially provides the only jobs in the labor market. Such an employer (or
monopsonist) faces the entire labor supply, and must pay higher wages if it
wishes to increase the number of people employed.[4] For a unitary employer
paying the same wage rate to workers for a similar job, the cost of an additional
hired worker not only reflects the wage for that worker, but also the incremen-
tal costs for all employees who have already been hired for that job because the
company pays all workers at the same wage as that paid to the last worker
hired. As a result, the employer hires fewer workers and pays a lower wage than
would occur in a competitive labor market with multiple employers.[5]

Company towns are rare, but an employer need not rule over a coal town
to wield some level of monopsony power.[6] A common source of employer
power in a labor market arises from information problems. A labor market
works by matching workers' job preferences with employers' demand for workers. That makes information a critical lubricant in the operation of a labor
market. Pure labor market models (which assume that markets function like
a freewheeling bourse) assume that such information costs are minimal. Employer suitors quickly find their employee mates.

But information is not costless, nor is it held equally by all the parties in
a labor market. In practice, a worker's search for a job is limited by time,
knowledge, and geographic preferences. Large employers have more robust
information because of their size, sophistication, and economies of scale in
acquiring it. Workers, however, face "search frictions" in the labor market
because of limited information on employment options as well as family,
social, and other geographic ties that restrict their willingness to move.

Information asymmetries and search frictions create some degree of monopsony power, meaning that large employers set wages rather than simply accepting the going rate in the labor market. This gives them greater latitude in establishing compensation policies, although the employer's policies still must reflect the supply of workers and their contribution to the production of the firm.[7]

Some level of monopsony control and discretion in setting wages underlies the compensation and human resource policies set by major companies across the economy. As the social scientists Beatrice and Sidney Webb pointed out at the turn of the twentieth century, large employers that dominated the economy and the labor market required unified personnel and pay policies and internal labor markets for a variety of reasons: to take advantage of administrative efficiencies, to create consistency in corporate policies, and to reduce exposure to violations of laws.[8]

There is an extensive literature that seeks to square the general existence of elaborate internal labor markets and findings like wage premiums in large firms with the operation of competitive labor markets. One view argues that these phenomena are not incompatible with the functioning of competitive labor markets, but simply reflect the complexity of labor as an input in production—an input whose productivity changes over the course of employment. Walter Oi explains wage policies in many large firms as outgrowths of the quasi–fixed-cost nature of labor, where the hiring of workers requires firms to invest in search and training costs, irrespective of how long a worker stays with the company. This fixed element of compensation gives employers incentives to create compensation systems that allow them to recover these costs through ensuring longer-term attachments (via higher wages or changing earnings profiles over time) as provided by many internal labor market policies. In a related vein, Becker explains the features of compensation systems as methods to create sufficient incentives for firms to invest in workers and to collect on their investment in job-specific human capital over the course of employment. Personnel policies lead firms to pay workers somewhat above their marginal productivity early in their tenure, when they are learning a job, and to pay them below their marginal productivity later on, when their job-specific skills have less value on the external market, leading firms to recapture their investment while giving workers an incentive to stay on in later periods.[9]

Another set of theories explains internal labor markets and "implicit contract" theory, where risk-neutral employers strike agreements with risk-averse workers that smooth wages over time, accommodating both parties in the process. These arrangements have some of the characteristics of internal labor markets (for example, job classifications or grades and wages linked to internal practices) but arise from underlying supply and demand features.

A third view explains internal labor markets as the methods by which firms overcome the day-to-day holdup problems, given that the employment contract between workers and employers is inherently incomplete—that is, it cannot adequately commit to language the complicated and changing nature of what the employer wishes the worker to do. As a result, a combination of explicit and implicit contract devices arises to prevent either party from cheating the other. In this view, the overall employment relationship creates value that the parties then must figure out a way to share in the course of ongoing employment. These contracts reflect both conditions in the external labor markets and relative bargaining power within the firm.[10]

None of these explanations, however, recognizes a basic aspect of the workplace: it brings together large groups of people, and people by nature are deeply social beings. Workers operating under one roof communicate and quickly discover a lot about their co-workers. This includes whether the person sitting in the next cubicle is being paid more for doing the same job. Paying individuals who do similar jobs different wages could have deleterious consequences on productivity, increase turnover, or even inspire a union-organizing drive. Unified personnel policies and simplified compensation structures for workers with varying levels of productivity play a fundamental role in reducing frictions among workers.

Fairness and Wage Determination

Fairness matters. In contrast to assumptions of traditional economics that individuals maximize gains solely for themselves, a large empirical literature from psychology, decision science, and more recently behavioral economics reveals that people care not only about their own gains but also about those of others. In fact, people frequently gauge the magnitude of their own benefits relative to those of others. And they are often willing to sacrifice some of their own gains because of equally important beliefs about fairness.

The "ultimatum game" is one of the best demonstrations of the importance of fairness in human interactions and has been extensively tested experimentally and in the field. The game is simple: two people are told there is a pot of money (say $10) to be split between them. One player gets the right to decide how to split it. The second player can accept or reject the first player's decision. If the second player rejects it, no one receives anything. If people were completely self-interested, the expected result would be clear: the first player would keep almost everything and leave a few crumbs (coins) for the second player. Since the second player is still better off with a little (for example, $.50) than before the game started, he or she should accept any non-zero offer.

But that is not how the game turns out. The typical person in the second player position will reject lowball offers (looking across studies, offers below 20% of the pot of money are usually rejected)—even at the expense of walking away with nothing. Equally important, first players seem to understand this in advance, because they typically offer the second player between 40% and 50% of the pot.[11] The results, which have been replicated many times in many different forms, attest to the importance of fairness, because they are based on one-round (nonrepeat) games where the incentives are high for the proposer to take as much as possible and for the responder to accept any offer. When ultimatum games are played in multiple-round scenarios, the incentives to share that pot only become higher.

Fairness perceptions affect all kinds of real-world interactions and relationships. Relationships are an intrinsic part of the workplace, and fairness perceptions are therefore basic to how decisions are made within it. The factors driving wage setting arise not just from an employer's consideration of the additional output a worker might provide if given a higher wage, but on the worker's perceptions of the fairness of that wage. For example, Daniel Kahneman, one of the pioneers of behavioral economics, showed that people's perception of the fairness of a wage cut depends on why they feel it was done: cuts driven by increases in unemployment (and therefore more people looking for work) are viewed as unfair; a company that cuts wages because it is on the brink of bankruptcy is judged more favorably. Like the proposer in the ultimatum game, managers seem to understand this and seldom cut nominal wages in practice.[12]

Similarly, fairness considerations about compensation depend not only on how much I think I deserve to be paid on an absolute basis (given my experience, education, skills), but also on what I am paid relative to others. Who are relevant comparison groups? It depends on where I am when making the appraisal. If I am looking for a job, my assessment is based on what I see in the labor market—as predicted by traditional economic theory. My sources of information may be incomplete, but I will be looking at comparable jobs in my search.[13] The acceptability of a wage offer will bounce up and down with the overall conditions in the labor market.

Once I am inside an organization, however, the wage level that becomes relevant to me focuses on other workers in my company. Just as, in experiments, how two people split their joint gains matters as much (or more) than their absolute gains, once inside an employer's organization, I care more about what the person in the next cubicle is being paid than about what someone across the street doing the same type of work is being paid by a different employer.[14] "Referent wages" are important not only in terms of others doing work similar to mine, but also for those I perceive as at higher and lower levels of the organization. In order to understand why large employers adopted the wage and internal labor markets used in previous decades and why they have moved toward fissuring, we need to probe two kinds of fairness notions as they apply to wages: horizontal equity (how people think about different pay rates for similar work) and vertical equity (how they think about different pay rates for different types of work).

Horizontal Equity and Pay Policy

The Webbs' observation is most apparent in the area of horizontal equity: Am I being paid the same as other people who are similar to me? The need to address fairness concerns within a type of job that pushes for a common rate is balanced against the desire to provide incentives for improved performance and quality. If an employer can track performance relatively easily, the pay policy may have a component related to performance. The more that performance is observable and has important consequences for a firm, the greater the incentive to design policies that link the two. But there will still be a benefit that the design applies equally to all workers in that grade.[15]

One method for doing so is compensating workers on the basis of a piece rate—paying a standard rate linked to output, thereby allowing higher-productivity workers to earn more than lower-productivity workers even if they are sitting beside each other.[16]

Piece rates have always been found in a relatively limited set of industries (agriculture, garment production, and some manufacturing), and not those one would associate with large employers with labor market power. Even beyond piece rate systems, there are far fewer incentive pay systems than one would expect given what would seem the benefits of linking pay and performance. In large nonunion companies, for example, Fred Foulkes noted in 1980 that "while merit pay plans are common in the entirely nonunion companies studied, for a variety of reasons they are frequently not administered as the stated policies would have one believe. Instead, the principles of seniority, automatic progression, and equal treatment seem to be given much weight."[17] Bewley documents a similar reluctance to embrace merit pay systems two decades later. Why is that the case?

The most common reason cited is that it is very difficult to actually observe performance in many job situations.[18] First, many outcomes in workplaces arise not from individual activities but from teamwork. It is often hard to observe individual contributions to team outcomes. Second, it may be that the nature of production may lead to outcomes affected (positively and negatively) by other factors not in control of individuals. A bad sales day in a resort town may be the result of unmotivated sales people, a bad patch of weather, or a longer-term economic downturn. Third, even if performance impacts can be measured, to do so is costly. It becomes even more costly as an organization grows in size or complexity.[19] Fourth, employers usually care about not one, but multiple outcomes, creating difficulties in creating an incentive scheme that aligns with different (and sometimes competing) objectives.[20]

But once again, that the practice of paying for performance is not more widespread reflects underlying perceptions of fairness. Incentive pay schemes assume that individuals work hard only if they are given incentives to expend effort. But the experimental evidence suggests that people expend more than minimal effort at a task if they believe they are being paid fairly for it. Higher pay elicits higher effort among fairness-minded individuals ("that's why you are paying me more"). In a "repeated game" situation, this behavior is further reinforced—you treated me fairly in the past, so I will exert more effort next time, and know you will pay me fairly in the next round. Even in cases where a significant number of fellow workers are "self-maximizers" who look out only for themselves, the presence of even a small number of more altruistic workers can lead employers to set wages at higher levels out of deference to fairness.[21]

As a result, large employers historically fudged horizontal compensation problems by creating consistent pay for people in comparable positions in a company, even if their performance varied. The vast majority of businesses (78%) interviewed in Bewley's study of compensation policies cited "internal harmony and morale" as the main reason why internal pay equity was important.[22] Labor market studies show that wages within firms vary far less than one would expect given the existence of considerable differences in productivity across workers.[23] Firms move toward a single-wage policy for workers of similarly observable skill/ability because of the negative consequences arising from having multiple rates for workers who otherwise seem similar.

A very common method of achieving fairness ends while providing some incentives linked to performance is seniority. Seniority pay provides a steady increase in pay with tenure in a firm. Assuming that retention is a signal of meeting at least minimum performance standards, if workers improve their performance over time, compensation moves with it. If I can expect my pay to rise over time, in a manner similar to that of my coworkers, I will judge the system as fair, and the employer will gain benefits (and share them in the form of higher wages) from my improved performance over time.[24]

Vertical Equity and Compensation

Workers' contentment with their wages, however, arises not only from what they are paid relative to others in a comparable job or place in the organization, but also from how they are paid relative to those above and below them in the organization. In particular, experimental and empirical evidence points to the fact that people look "up" in judging their pay, asking, What is my pay relative to the jobs at the next rung in my organization? If the pay of the group just above me is too high—or if the gap widens over time—I may be less and less happy with the pay I receive, regardless of its absolute level.

Psychologists have long known that people care more about a small loss in income than about an equal gain in income.[25] This effect—called loss aversion—means that perceptions of being adversely affected by a change in a current situation will make people feel worse than a comparable improvement in position makes them feel better. In a workplace context, loss aversion means that if a worker's pay situation changes in a way that is judged unfair, it will have larger effects than if the situation changes in a way that is judged as improving fairness.

Wage comparisons across different occupations or jobs can have this effect. Imagine that I have a job I view as "better" (for example, requiring more skill or savvy) than another job at my workplace. One day, I find out what people in that job are paid. I will be more upset to find out that I am being paid relatively *less* than someone holding that job than I would be happy to find out I am being paid *more* (by the same amount) than the same person. This behavior also suggests I will tend to look up rather than down in the wage structure in assessing whether I am being paid fairly. A janitor in a car factory will be more attuned to the wage paid to the assembly worker whose station he cleans than to that of the groundskeeper maintaining the lawn outside.

In a large organization, vertical equity issues like these can be particularly vexing. Unionized workplaces in traditional manufacturing solved this problem through collectively bargained deals that linked these grades—often providing for upward ratcheting of the whole wage system (leaving relative wages intact) over time. The collectively bargained contract creates a transparent set of expectations of what is fair (in part because it reflects the preferences of the workforce, at least as represented by the union's negotiating committee).

Large nonunion workplaces also must accommodate the demands of vertical equity in setting compensation policies, even though unfettered by collective bargaining. Higher wages in part reflect an effort to avoid unionization, but also to avoid the kind of internal frictions described above.[26] In his studies of wage policies, Bewley also found that nonunion executives justified formal internal pay structures on the basis of equity.[27] Although they acknowledged that differences in pay between grades proved useful as incentives, 69% of the businesses interviewed cited "internal equity, internal harmony, fairness, and good morale" as the principal justification.[28]

A repercussion of the need to satisfy vertical equity demand is that a large employer might end up paying workers at lower ends of the wage system a higher wage than it might prefer in order to preserve internal labor market peace. As we shall see, a number of studies show this to be precisely what happens in wage setting.

Take My Workers—Please!

Taking horizontal and vertical equity concerns together leads to a prediction that large firms might end up paying more for jobs at different levels of the organization to solve these problems than would occur on the outside. This aspect of wage determination explains the large-employer wage premium discussed in Chapter 2.

The basic monopsony model assumes that an employer will set a single wage rate for workers of a particular type (that is, skill or occupation) rather than follow what is called in a monopoly situation a price discrimination policy (that is, charging different prices to different consumers). The need to set a single wage for the workplace has the effect of pushing up the cost to the employer of hiring more workers of a given type, since the additional cost of one more worker requires paying him or her more, as well as more for all who are already employed at that type of work.[29]

In principle, an employer with monopsony power could compensate workers according to their individual contribution to production (or "marginal product," the additional output per worker) if it pursued a varied wage policy. But this goes against the fairness grain and, as we have seen, has never been a common form of compensation. Wage discrimination (à la price discrimination) is rarely seen in large firms despite the benefits it could confer. As long as workers are under one roof, the problems presented by horizontal and vertical equity remain.

But what if the large employer could wage discriminate by changing the boundaries of the firm itself? What if, instead of facing a wage determination problem for a large and varied workforce, it creates a situation of setting prices for work to be done by other parties external to the enterprise? If multiple businesses compete vigorously with one another to obtain that firm's business, each small firm would offer its workers wages to perform work for the lead firm. Under this setup, the large employer (or now former employer) receives a price for the contractors' services or production rather than being required to directly set and pay wages to the individual workers who actually undertake the work.

As such, the larger employer creates competition for work among different purveyors and pays them based on its assessment of their contribution. Less-efficient producers could be paid less than more-efficient producers. In this way, the lead organization faces a schedule of *prices for services* rather than *wages for labor,* leaving the task of compensation to the individual providers of the service or product. In effect, the lead firm devolves its employment activity to a network of smaller providers. In so doing, it creates a mechanism—a competitive market for services that in the past was handled internally through direct employment—in the form of a network of service providers.

By shifting employment to smaller organizations external to the enterprise that operate in competitive markets, the lead firm creates a mechanism whereby workers will receive a wage close to the additional value they create. At the same time, this avoids the problem of having workers with very different wages operating under one roof. The lead firm captures the difference between the individual additional productivity of each worker and what would be the prevailing single wage rate if it set one.

As a result, two workers on the same project may effectively end up being paid very different wages, closer to something reflecting their individual marginal productivity than would be the case if they were in the direct employ of the parent organization.[30] Such a mechanism would benefit the employer over the case where it set a single wage rate for workers with similar job titles but variation in productivity, or in cases where an employer's wage policy affects the market as a whole.

A related argument for shifting work outward arises from the problems created by vertical equity expectations in internal labor markets. Even if workers have differing skill levels and job assignments, vertical equity norms in firms may lead large employers to pay lower-skill workers higher wages because of the presence of higher-paid workers whose compensation becomes a referent wage within the internal labor market.[31] Shifting those lower-skilled jobs outward can solve this problem.

Setting Wages by Setting Prices

Imagine that the DW Hotel (or, to be more upscale, simply the DW) directly hired all of its workers—from landscapers, to maids, to valets, to front desk personnel. Horizontal equity would require comparable pay for those in a grade—and maybe even across the properties in a metropolitan area (particularly if the workforce moved among properties). Vertical equity would require considering the pay of maids and valets in setting the pay of landscapers and considering the wages of managers in setting the pay of desk personnel. The DW would be required to create and administer a comprehensive pay and human resources policy.

But what if the DW focuses its attention on its reputation (its core competency) and no longer sees the actual administration of hotels as central to its business strategy? This would allow it to cut loose the messy process of hotel operations to other organizations—particularly organizations that might bid against one another for the right to undertake that activity. Now the DW could transform the production of hotel services into a market, with different entities competing for pieces of the business. Each provider would offer its services—which once would have been undertaken directly by the DW—for a price.

As a result, the DW would create competition for work among different purveyors and pay them a price based on its assessment of their contribution. Less-efficient producers could be paid less than more-efficient producers. In this way, the DW faces a schedule of prices for services (for example, management of its workforce) rather than wages for labor, leaving the complex task of compensation to the individual providers of the service or product.[32] In effect, the lead enterprise devolves its employment activity to a network of smaller providers. In so doing, it creates a mechanism—a competitive market for services that in the past were handled internally through direct employment—in the form of a network of service providers.

By shifting employment to smaller organizations operating in competitive markets, a large employer creates a mechanism to pay workers closer to the additional value they create but avoids the problem of having workers with very different wages operating under one roof. In so doing, the employer captures the difference between the individual additional productivity of each worker and what would be the prevailing single wage rate if it set one.[33]

Businesses at the top of supply chains split off employment so that they can focus their attention on more profitable activities connected to the revenue side of their income statement, leaving the manufacture of products or the provision of service to be fissured off. This has important implications for how the profitability of those companies is shared between different parties. Recall that in the former, integrated model of large employers, firms ended up sharing part of their gains with the workforce in the form of higher pay to deal with internal perceptions of fairness. That meant less to share with consumers in the form of lower prices and with investors in the form of higher returns.

With fissuring, the fairness problems are less acute and wages can be pushed downward. That means more gains to be passed on to consumers as lower prices or better returns for investors. In those fissured structures where a firm's core competency has attracted a particularly devoted customer base through branding or the ongoing introduction of cool new products, the reduced wage costs will flow particularly toward investors.[34] Shifting work outward allows redistribution of gains upward.

Paying Janitors and Guards Inside and Outside the Walls

As noted in Chapter 3, janitors and security guards were in the vanguard of fissuring. By 2000 about 45% of janitors worked under contracting arrangements, and more than 70% of guards were employed as contractors.[35] Shifting janitors and security guards from inside to outside the walls of lead businesses has had significant impacts on pay for workers in those occupations.

The impact of shedding janitorial jobs in otherwise higher-wage companies is borne out in several studies of contracting out among janitorial workers. Using a statistical model to predict the factors that increase the likelihood of contracting out specific types of jobs, Abraham and Taylor demonstrate that the higher the typical wage for the workforce at an establishment, the more likely that establishment will contract out its janitorial work. They also show that establishments that do any contracting out of janitorial workers tend to shift out the function entirely.[36]

Wages and benefits for workers employed directly versus contracted out can be compared given the significant number of people in both groups. Using statistical models that control for both observed characteristics of the workers and the places in which they work, several studies directly compare the wages and benefits for these occupations. Berlinski found that janitors who worked as contractors earned 15% less than those working in-house, and contracted security guards earned 17% less than comparable in-house guards. Dube and Kaplan found similar impacts of contracting, with a "wage penalty" for working as a contractor of 4%–7% for janitors and 8%–24% for security guards.[37] The latter study also found that contractors in both occupations are much less likely to receive health benefits: about 60% of in-house guards received health benefits versus 38% of contract guards; similarly, 49% of in-house janitors received some health coverage versus 24% of contracted janitors.[38]

These results therefore suggest that otherwise comparable workers doing janitorial or security work in comparable places are paid very differently.[39] It is worth reiterating the distributional implications of this finding: by "solving" the problem posed by the Webbs at the outset of this chapter by shifting work outward, lead companies have redistributed part of the profits once shared with the workforce because of fairness concerns to consumers and particularly to investors.[40] And as we shall see in detail in Part II, companies have devised a number of different organizational methods to do so beyond the contracting/outsourcing used in the case of janitors and security guards.

In a series of articles about the use of subcontracted janitors to clean major supermarkets and retail establishments in Southern California, Nancy Cleeland describes in more evocative terms the consequences of fissuring for janitors. One story focused on a man who worked the midnight shift seven nights a week. His duties required

> stripping, waxing, and buffing the floors . . . He says he earns far less than the minimum wage, and just laughs when asked about overtime pay for his 56-hour weeks. Strong chemicals make his nose bleed, burn his fingers and eat the soles of his cheap sneakers . . . Not only are many janitors earning subminimum wages—about $550 to $750 twice a month for 56-hour weeks—they are also untaxed.

None of the janitors interviewed by Cleeland could name the company employing them—only the person who paid them with personal checks.[41]

The Social Consequences of Fissured Employment

The fissured workplace is not simply another term for subcontracting, outsourcing, or offshoring. Nor does it solely arise from lead companies seeking to avoid payment of private or socially required benefits. Rather, the fissured workplace reflects a fundamental restructuring of business organizations. Employment decisions arise from a careful and ongoing balancing act by lead companies and the subsequent behaviors of the many smaller companies operating beneath them.

What makes sense from a private calculus of balancing the benefits and costs of shedding business functions and employment relationships may differ from what is socially desirable. The economic concept of an externality—the failure of private parties to fully weigh the social costs of their actions—can be usefully applied here. A major retailer or telecommunication company may decide that it can reduce its costs and exposure to liability by contracting out work to another party (who in turn breaks the task into several additional layers of contractors) and still maintain quality, technical requirements, or brand reliability through some of the mechanisms described above. But if the consequence of the decision to shed activities is to reduce the labor force's pay, protections, benefits, and access to longer-term career opportunities, the social costs of those actions are borne by others.

The integrated elements underlying the fissured workplace help explain why trends like wage stagnation have been so persistent and noncompliance with workplace laws increasingly common in many parts of the economy. They help explain why work has become so much worse for so many, even as the share of national income going to reward investors (and the very top of the income distribution) has increased. Part II provides a deeper look at how the fissured workplace has played out and its public consequences in a variety of industries and organizational forms.

The Forms and Consequences of the Fissured Workplace

In his book *The Big Squeeze,* New York Times reporter Steven Greenhouse recounts a cavalcade of woes facing people in their daily work life. Drawing on hundreds of interviews, Greenhouse summarizes the worsening conditions at the workplace faced by millions of workers:

> One of the least examined but most important trends taking place in the United States today is the broad decline in the status and treatment of American workers—white-collar and blue-collar workers, middle-class and low-end workers—that began nearly three decades ago, gradually gathered momentum, and hit with full force soon after the turn of this century. A profound shift has left a broad swath of the American workforce on a lower plane than in decades past, with health coverage, pension benefits, job security, workloads, stress levels, and often wages growing worse for millions of workers.[1]

The book recounts case after case of eroding wages and benefits and the often egregious violation of basic labor standards, abrupt termination of long-standing and loyal employees, flagrant discrimination, and abusive behavior by supervisors.

Scholars and popular writers alike have documented for more than a decade the fact that working conditions in the United States—and those in many other industrialized nations—have declined. Even before the onset of the Great Recession in December 2007, a growing part of the U.S. workforce became increasingly vulnerable to a range of economic, health and safety, and social risks. These troubling conditions have been examined in considerable detail in a number of recent studies.[2]

Part I discussed the origins, causes, and dynamics that have led to the fissured workplace. The strategy pursued by lead businesses in many industries is to pursue core areas of value creation while shedding activities—and employment—to other, subsidiary, business entities. Lead businesses balance the pursuit of core competencies against the effort to shed activities to other organizations via a variety of mechanisms that provide a means of assuring that subordinate organizations adhere to quality, technical, time, and brand standards.

Part II looks at subcontracting, franchising, and supply chain structures: three organizational mechanisms used to ensure this balance that result in fissured workplaces and their connection to worsening conditions as described by Greenhouse and others. Table II.1 presents examples of these three forms that lead to fissured workplaces and examples of each from a variety of industries, ranging from some of the oldest (mining) to the newest (cell phones). Although the occupations that fissuring affects are concentrated at the low-wage end of the labor market (janitors, warehousing, home health aides, fast food), the practice increasingly includes mid-level employees (machine operators, cell tower workers, customer service providers) and even highly skilled workers (journalists and lawyers).

In subcontracting, the lead firm contracts out activities to separate parties. Once shed, these activities are typically further broken apart into subcontracting to other parties, resulting in cascading levels of employment. In contrast, under franchising, the lead business keeps overall control of management of the brand but creates an organizational structure that allows separate business entities—franchisees—to carry out the activities. Finally, in supply chain structures, the lead company plays the key role of coordinator of complicated networks of subsidiary organizations that together provide goods or services.[3]

Each lead business is orbited by successive tiers of business enterprises (described in each row of Table II.1). The nature of the relationship between each tier is specified in the types of contracts or agreements between the respective businesses. For example, the cellular tower industry begins with major cell carriers like AT&T and Verizon who contract with "turfers," large companies who act as lead contractors. Turfers, in turn, contract the actual work to a next tier, and often several tiers, with small subcontractors providing maintenance services on specific towers. Each subcontracting tier operates for the one above it through bidding systems and highly detailed contracts specifying terms of work.

In a franchised industry like fast foods, the tiers are linked through detailed franchise agreements that specify business operations central to the brand and expectations by the parties on maintaining it. Supply chain structures like retailing rely on standards specifying how each tier will coordinate with others, usually through the adoption of standards regarding both product characteristics and logistics.

The agreements underlying subcontracting, franchising, and supply chains—and the market relationships that arise around them—differ in form but have similar impacts on the pressures facing each tier's bottom line. Since labor is usually a significant component of cost, the tiered structure and the glue that holds it together have consequences for employment conditions. When shifting employment outward to other businesses in more competitive settings operating in low-wage labor markets, the incentive for skirting workplace standards can be significant. The rise of labor standards violations—from failure to pay minimum wages or overtime to requiring employees to work off the clock—reflect this problem.

As discussed in Chapter 4, shifting activities outside of lead companies to successive tiers also means a change in the wage-setting process. When janitors were direct employees of manufacturers, hotels, or financial institutions, the higher wages earned by others inside company walls pulled up the wage levels of janitors. Once janitorial activities shift to other businesses in orbiting tiers, those job referents become irrelevant to wage setting. Janitorial wages move closer to those prevailing in the more narrow market of other contractors of cleaning services or of franchised janitorial service providers. The downward pressure on wages and associated benefits intensifies with each cascading tier of fissured employment depicted in Table II.1.

Finally, the tiered organization of fissured workplaces can create coordination failures, particularly where it is superimposed on complicated production processes. When the steps of production are broken into activities overseen by different business organizations, the actions of workers of one employer are more likely to create risks for the workforce of another. This has been a long-standing problem in construction. As more and more places of work are

Table II.1 Three organizational forms resulting in fissured workplaces (selected examples in parentheses)

Industry	Lead business	1st tier	2nd tier	3rd tier	4th tier
Subcontractor model					
Coal mining	Mine controlling business (Massey Energy)	Mine operators (Performance Coal Co.)	Contract operators (Black Diamond Construction Inc.)		
Cellular phones	Cell phone carriers (AT&T)	Turfing managers (Nsoro)	Lead subcontractor (WesTower)	Second-level subcontractor (ALT Inc.)	Third-level subcontractor
Logistics operations	Retailer or manufacturer (Walmart; Hershey)	Logistics provider (Schneider Logistics)	Temporary help company (PWV)	Second-level temp. agency (Rogers-Premier)	
Cable services	Media provider (Time Warner)	Regional cable turfer (Cascom)	Installers as independent contractors		
Franchise model					
Fast food	Franchisor (KFC; Pizza Hut)	Franchisee (Morgan's Foods Inc.)	Labor contractor		

	Lead company in variety of sectors	Franchisor (Coverall)	Regional franchisee	Local franchisee	Labor contractor
Janitorial and building services	Lead company in variety of sectors	Franchisor (Coverall)	Regional franchisee	Local franchisee	Labor contractor
Hotels (hybrid model)	Hotel/motel brands (Marriott)	Franchisee/owner (Host Hotels and Resorts)	Brand or independent operating company (Crestline Hotels and Resorts)	Labor staffing company (Hospitality Staffing Solutions)	Subcontracted landscaping or janitorial service
Supply chain model					
Apparel	Manufacturer or retailer (Forever 21)	Contract manufacturer/ subcontractor (CMR Clothing Inc.)	Second-tier contractor (CUI Sewing Inc.)	Third-tier contractor	
Food industry	Food processor	Growers	Farm labor contractors	Farm workers as independent contractors (prior to 1987)	
Computer industry	Computer brand (Apple)	Contract manufacturer (Foxcomm)	Subcontractors	Sub-subcontractor	

composed of multiple employers operating under one roof, new risks arise, and with them health and safety problems, including elevated fatality rates (as we shall see in the case of cell towers).

Part II explores the three major organizational forms that create fissured workplaces and examines their impacts on workers. We start in Chapter 5 with the use of subcontracting. Its use, once a hallmark of a small number of industries, has spread widely. When paired with independent contracting, its consequences can be particularly pernicious.

Chapter 6 looks at a more subtle form of fissuring—franchising. Born out of core strategies focusing on building brands, franchising represents a distinctive form of fissuring that allows the franchisor to focus on core competency while ensuring that the businesses that provide the products and services keep up with standards. Franchising has now spread far beyond the fast-food industry commonly associated with it.

Chapter 7 looks at supply chains in the context of fissuring. Whereas companies like Ford and IBM once built internal empires of suppliers through expansion and vertical integration, modern supply chains achieve even more complicated coordination of hundreds and often thousands of suppliers. But they do so by carefully steering that network from the center, establishing detailed, demanding, and high-stakes requirements and thereby satisfying the core requirements of the lead businesses at their center.

The Subcontracted Workplace

There is nothing new about subcontracting as a form of organizing business, production, and the workplace. It is how the construction industry in the United States has been organized since the 1800s. It has long been a distinctive feature of women's garment manufacturing, for example. And it has been a basic part of the movie industry since the early days of Hollywood.

All of these old-school applications of subcontracting reflect sectors where a substantial part of producing goods requires specialized activities, often combined in different ways to fit highly diverse end uses. Construction is driven by its end use: a commercial building requires one combination of expertise and skills, while a power plant requires something quite different. There is enormous end use variation even within types of construction—a walk along a downtown city street is enough to prove this. Other industries that have drawn on the subcontracting model similarly require specialized activities to create varied products. The women's sector of the clothing industry in the United States, given its far more varied product offerings, has always drawn on more extensive subcontracting than the men's sector.[1] Movies require a wide variety of artistic, cinematic, production, and service tasks, also shifting according to the genre and the specific film being made.

Producing buildings, garments, or movies by hiring specialized companies to do different pieces of the work, particularly where that work requires expertise and investment in skills and equipment that may be used for only a limited period of time, lends itself to subcontracting. A company specializing in electrical work (or embroidery for women's dresses or costume design in film) can invest in its expertise and sell that expertise to multiple parties, each in need of those services for a limited period of time and having no desire to make long-term commitments. The lead company undertaking the work operates through market relationships with a set of subcontractors, drawing on them as the production of the building or the creation of the film warrants.[2]

Subcontracting, however, began to move beyond its traditional sectors as its advantages as a part of fissured strategies became apparent. Its use has spread into new sectors and deepened within those where it was traditionally applied. The use of subcontracting differs both in terms of the types of jobs it targets and its applications in industries where the practice has historically been uncommon. Though the focus of subcontracting and the way it plays out differs across sectors, its effects on the workplace are similar. Employment conditions at the bottom of fissured structures reflect the design of lead company strategies, including the way they choose to parcel out secondary work to other parties. The industries that emerge "underneath" lead players reflect, in part, organizational design decisions aimed at aligning the interests of the parties to the extent possible (particularly to the extent that they support the strategies of the lead players).

As a result, the lower tiers of fissured structures in many industries are very competitive; have low barriers for new entrants; provide services that are relatively easily observed; or draw on contractual provisions, monitoring technologies, and organizational formats that make the consequences of failing to meet standards costly. The upshot is that conditions at the secondary level (and below) are frequently tough: competitive, price sensitive, and subject to fluctuating demand.[3]

A second characteristic of the fissured workplace in subcontracted organizations is coordination problems: the more tasks are divided among different business entities, the harder it becomes to coordinate them. The private incentives pushing toward fissuring the workplace thereby create social problems and costs in the form of increased safety and health risks and, at worst, deaths at the workplace. This chapter illustrates these characteristics with case studies from a number of disparate industries.

We begin by looking at how subcontracting expanded from its traditional focus to a more general employment strategy in a very old industry: underground coal mining. We then turn to a contemporary industry—telecommunications—and examine how the rapid growth of smartphones was accommodated by the application of subcontracting to cell tower maintenance. The impact of subcontracting models on a landmark U.S. business—

Hershey—illuminates how multitiered contracting can make improbable sources of labor (such as university students in a State Department–sponsored visa program) seem plausible and allow egregious violations of safety standards to occur under the nose of historically responsible employers. Finally, we look at how multitiered subcontracting in the cable industry changed what were once employees of cable media companies into independent contractors.

Past as Prologue: Fissured Coal Mines and the "New" Subcontracting

Subcontracting was long used in underground coal mining for reasons similar to those found in construction, the garment industry, and cinema: certain operations require high degrees of skill and expertise but are not part of the day-to-day operation of the mining company. For example, blasting contractors are engaged by mine operators to undertake the dangerous work of opening new seams for subsequent mining. Blasting contractors obtain the work, do their operations, and move on to the next job. Fissured subcontracting in mining was pioneered much more recently, however, and foreshadows various types of subcontracting practices that are now emerging in other industries.[4]

In order to sell coal as an energy source (thermal coal) or as an input for producing steel and other products (metallurgical coal), it must be extracted from the ground, brought to the surface, and taken to processing facilities, where it is sorted, cleaned, and prepared for shipping.[5] Processing plants for coal are capital-intensive, and multiple mines may use a common processing facility. There are therefore economies of scale for a coal operator arising from the processing of coal that—in tandem with the gains from controlling rights to those coal reserves—have led the industry to be concentrated.[6]

At its peak, the United Mine Workers of America (UMWA) represented the majority of coal miners in the eastern United States. Miners covered by the union's collective bargaining agreement earned high wages, were part of the first industry-wide health care system negotiated by a union, received pensions, and were protected by a union-led health and safety system at the mine face that acted as a complement to the Mine Safety and Health Administration (MSHA). The UMWA negotiated with its industry counterpart, the

Bituminous Coal Operators Association (BCOA). But as the union declined in its coverage of mine workers and leverage in the industry, major union and nonunion coal companies began to challenge not only the UMWA at the bargaining table, but also the financial obligations that had been negotiated for current and retired members.

The use of subcontracting to undertake basic mining operations beyond specialty applications is often attributed to the A. T. Massey Coal Company.[7] The so-called Massey Doctrine was based on classifying coal reserves held by the company into three groups:[8] reserves with high-quality coal, in thick seams and good mining conditions; reserves with seams of average height or mining conditions; and reserves with thin seams and difficult mining conditions. The company would own and operate mines of the first type and use subsidiaries or contractors for the second type, while still maintaining some level of control and stake in them. For the third type of reserve, however, the company "desire[d] to have only a brokerage relationship . . . no long-term contractual or financial arrangement. This is the coal that, in a weak market, will be available at the lower price . . . This is the coal that we should buy or market ourselves rather than have it compete with us."[9] The Massey Doctrine does this by having the company or one of its subsidiaries (which controls the rights to the coal reserves, maintains control over access into and out of the mine, and operates the processing facility) hire a small contracting firm to extract coal. The lead mining company specifies the price the contractor will be paid for each ton extracted and provides the contractor with all engineering, mine plans, and other materials needed to undertake the work. It may also lease, sell, and or provide the contractor with financing for the equipment in the mine or for use in mining. The company also specifies to the contractor how, when, and where the coal is delivered, allowing it to adjust both the price paid and the charges for service to the contractor, and to determine quality standards for coal purchased.[10] Of course, the price paid to the contractor is that set by the coal company on the basis of its own internal calculations; the coal operator subsequently sells the coal based on the market price or a price it has negotiated through long-term contracting with utilities (common in the industry). In both cases, the price is well above the price the coal company pays the contractor.

The benefits to a unionized mining company are clear: by subcontracting, it places the union miner outside the boundaries of the firm, placing a contractor between itself and the miner and distancing itself from a set of liabilities associated with being an employer. These include contractual and legislated requirements ranging from accumulated vacation days, health and welfare contributions, and workers' compensation payments to federal and state black lung obligations and other statutory payments.[11] These additional payments for state and federal statutory requirements such as workers' compensation are significant, and for companies with a unionized workforce, the additional costs associated with health and welfare and pension requirements are even more substantial. If the coal company attempts to use subcontracting as a means of union avoidance (as Massey was accused of doing), the potential benefits for the company from contracting are clear.

If the lead company requires contractors to hire former unionized workers (as required by the UMWA/BCOA contract), one would expect no savings arising from shifting employment (since those costs would presumably show up in the costs of the contractor and the price that contractor would be willing to accept for undertaking the mining operations). But if the unequal bargaining power of the coal company in its negotiation with the contractor can achieve a price below that level (perhaps because of the contractor's potential ability to fly under the radar, its inexperience in business, or simply the higher likelihood of insolvency), the lead coal company can reduce its costs through contracting.[12] A lawyer involved in environmental litigation in contracting cases remarked that "depending on specific circumstances, a large company can shift between $3 and $5 (in costs) for each ton of coal mined from its shoulders onto the small mine operator or society at large."[13]

And there was another benefit to lead coal companies like Massey through the arrangement: by using the Massey Doctrine, coal operators were able to shift employment of long-standing employees to the small contractors, who assumed the obligations for future health care obligations. They did so by requiring the contractor to hire from a panel of former employees (often union workers) of the lead company. This was not beneficence, but a means to make the contractor the "last signatory operator" for whom the miner worked, thereby transferring the lifetime health care obligations created under the UMWA/BCOA agreement as well as other health care obligations under the Mine Safety and Health Act to the contractor.[14] In essence, the Massey Doctrine provided a backdoor approach to subvert a variety of long-term commitments to miners and their families negotiated over decades between the UMWA and the BCOA. A spokesman for the BCOA defended the practice, arguing, "Look around in corporate America at what people are doing to avoid health-care and other payments. They're contracting out work. That's the whole point of using contractors."[15]

The arrangement requires a large number of small contractors willing to do the work. This appeared not to be a problem for Massey and other major coal companies. In an investigative report, Paul Nyden reported that Massey used five hundred contractors in Appalachia between the early 1980s and the mid-1990s. An abundance of small operators—sometimes family-owned enterprises with few assets of their own, other times companies that had declared bankruptcy under a different name—bid for the opportunity to work as contractors. Contractors were often undercapitalized and operating under tight margins. Not surprisingly, attrition among this group was exceedingly high.[16] For example, between 1980 and 1993, Island Creek Coal hired sixty different contractors to operate a few small mines in Elk Creek, West Virginia. Of the sixty, fifty-two were out of business by the end of the period, with nine filing for bankruptcy. A similar proportion of Massey's contractors went out of business over the same period.[17]

The doctrine created perverse incentives. Once work had been shifted to contractors, Massey or companies like Island Creek had little incentive to ensure that their contractors contributed required payments to either state funds or, where appropriate, union funds. As a result, Massey and Island Creek owed up to $120 million to the West Virginia Workers' Compensation Fund and over $50 million to UMWA health and retirement funds.[18] Nyden documented at least a dozen contractors that sued Massey or Island Creek Coal (the other focus of his investigative piece) between 1988 and 1993 on the basis of a range of claims including breach of contract, price gouging, mismanagement, misrepresentation, and fraud. For example, a suit by Soho Coal Company against several Massey subsidiaries alleged that the former had lost $650,000 in potential revenues from Massey's practice of rounding its selling price to the lowest dollar figure and on estimated weights of delivery that benefited Massey. The same suit accused Massey of using the contracting arrangement to get out of its liabilities to union miners formerly in its employ.[19] Soho's financial pressures spilled over, in turn, to its subcontractors, including five small mining companies that opened and shut down between 1987 and 1990.

The volatility among contracting firms meant precarious employment for their workforces. As contractors came in and exited, they often left behind a workforce with lost wages, intermittent work, and lost benefits. In many of the cases documented by Nyden, miners in their late forties and early fifties lost long-term jobs with a major coal company, and with them health care coverage for themselves and their families. And with their loss of contract jobs, they faced a labor market with little interest in hiring people in their late forties or older.

Finally, contracting was associated with increased fatality risk during the period. From 1980 to 1993, thirty-eight men were killed in mines affiliated with A. T. Massey Coal and Island Creek Coal. Even though the majority of the coal produces during those years was extracted from mines operated directly by Massey and Island Creek, twenty-seven of the deaths (or 72%) occurred in contract mines operating under those two companies.[20]

In the late 1990s, some states made efforts through legislation and the courts to combat the most harmful effects of subcontracting on the health care, pensions, and wages of miners. In 1993 the West Virginia legislature passed the Wage Payment and Collection Act (WPCA) to clarify contractor versus owner/lessor responsibility for liabilities owed to either miners or the government. Subsequent opinions of the West Virginia Supreme Court of Appeals regarding the act indicated that the court was taking a "broad, reality-based definition of employer under the WPCA which looks beyond contractual relationships to examine the actual relationship between the parties, the employee and the third party."[21] Nonetheless, using corporate restructuring to shift pension and health care liabilities to other parties continues. In May 2013, a court approved a proposal by Patriot Coal Corporation to reduce its pension and health benefit payments to 13,000 unionized miners and retirees as part of its bankruptcy proceedings. Most of the affected miners never worked for Patriot directly, since Patriot acquired pension and health care liabilities when it was created as a spin-off of Peabody Energy in 2007.[22]

The use of subcontracting did not end in the mid-1990s, and actually increased significantly between 1993 and 2011. Figure 5.1 charts the increase in hours and employees among contractors and the decline in both for operators (companies that directly undertake mining). Although contractors still undertake a minority of total production, their share has risen considerably.[23]

Contracting continues to be attractive because of its impact on lowering labor costs for mining companies. It has also proved to be a means of attempting to avoid civil penalties arising from violations of MSHA standards.[24] Take the case of Ember Contracting Corporation, a contract miner.

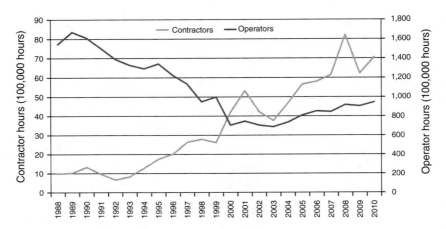

FIGURE 5.1. Trends in contractor and mine operator employment hours in underground coal mining, 1988–2010. *Note:* Data taken from the MSHA self-extracting accident and employment files for underground coal mines. Data available at http://www.msha.gov/stats/part50/p50y2k/p50y2k.htm.

In the early part of 2008, Ember received 247 citations from MSHA for health and safety violations, resulting in total penalties exceeding $225,000. Ember claimed inability to pay because doing so would threaten the company's financial viability, noting that, among other things, the company had lost its line of credit as a result of the penalties. But in subsequent litigation against the company, MSHA found that when Ember stopped its mining activities at sites in the summer of 2009, "its owners sold Ember's assets to a related company, EC Management." It turned out that EC Management was owned by the same two principals that owned Ember. One of the owners "admitted that E. C. Management bought Ember's equipment solely to pay off Ember's debt." Additionally, in January 2010 the two Ember owners formed a separate contract mining company, G. R. Mining, which operates in the same location as Ember and hired many of the employees who previously worked at Ember.[25]

In ruling on the penalty liabilities facing Ember, the administrative law judge ruled that Ember had to pay the entire penalty amount. The judge stated that "Ember has not satisfied its burden of proving that imposition of the total proposed civil penalty would adversely affect its ability to continue in business." Ember should have gone into bankruptcy if it could not continue to operate. However, the company "chose to shift money, business opportunities, and contracts between the other companies owned by its principals like a corporate shell game."

Although coal industry fortunes ebb and flow with the larger energy market (and are certainly at a low ebb at the time of this writing), the burden continues to fall hardest at the lower reaches of the subcontracting chain and on the miners at the mine face. Contract miners in underground operations face significantly higher rates of traumatic injuries than miners working as direct employees of operators in otherwise comparable mines. Even more troubling, miners working for contractors face a 40% higher exposure to fatality risks than those who work as direct employees, even after controlling for a variety of other mine-level characteristics associated with fatalities.[26]

The Massey Doctrine and its influence on subcontracting in the coal industry have broader lessons: subcontracting work is not incompatible with lead companies continuing to maintain substantial influence on the methods and operations of the units working below them—sometimes multiple levels below. By setting out goals regarding output and prices as well as influencing the timing and methods of production, lead companies can draw on multiple tiers of subcontractors while pursuing their core strategies.[27] But by pushing the employment relationship outside of the boundaries of the lead firms, very different pressures arise for the companies and the workforce below them, with smaller and smaller margins at lower and lower levels of subcontracting resulting in increasingly dangerous conditions.

iPhones, Cell Towers, and Telecommunications Fissuring

We all want more reliable cell phone service. Unfortunately, keeping cellular towers upgraded has become a deadly business, in part because of the financially driven strategy through which such jobs are subcontracted. Between 2003 and 2011, almost one hundred workers died building and maintaining towers to support consumers' insatiable demand for smartphone service.

Major carriers like AT&T and Verizon, rather than directly employing workers to build and maintain cell towers, have spun off that work to other parties, who in turn subcontract it to others, who may subcontract out even further. Layers of employment are created, with the lead company setting overall prices for work and often dictating specific conditions regarding quality, scheduling, deadlines, and other requirements that affect how the work is done. In the case of AT&T, this form of subcontracting was developed to rapidly expand and service cellular towers in order to increase coverage and the data capacity demand arising from the introduction of the iPhone. By subcontracting to multiple tiers, carriers are expanding networks to fit a competitive strategy. But such hyper-subcontracting also leads to a loss of control of the workplace, and in particular of safety. The consequence is a fatality rate in cell tower work far in excess of those in industries often regarded as the most dangerous: three times that of coal mining and more than ten times that of construction overall.

Expanding and Maintaining Cell Networks

It is not hyperbole to say that wireless communication usage exploded after 1990. In that year there were an estimated 5 million subscriber connections. By 2011 the number of subscriber connections reached more than 331 million.[28] Texting provides an evocative measure of the exponential growth of wireless communication services in an even shorter period: in the second quarter of 2006, the average number of monthly text messages per mobile subscriber was 79 as compared to 216 phone calls per subscriber. By the second quarter of 2008, the number of monthly texts per subscriber had climbed to 357, leaving in the dust the number of phone calls, which had decreased to 204.[29] The growth in cell phone and smartphone use and wireless communication in general required a similar expansion of the infrastructure to support it. In 1990 there were a total of 5,616 cell tower sites in the United States. By 2011 that number had climbed to 283,385.[30]

Constructing networks that provide the fastest, most extended, and most reliable service has become a major driver of competitive strategy. This means that creating a comprehensive network for mobile users is a core aspect of the business. Developing and coordinating mobile networks is capital-intensive, entailing huge economies of scale (even in the long run, the average costs decline with scale). And given the network economies that are basic to the industry, the bigger the network and the more capable it is of handling the ever-growing demands of digital traffic, the more valuable it becomes to consumers.[31]

Yet developing and coordinating networks does not require that the carrier itself undertake physical construction or maintenance of those networks.

Cell tower construction and ongoing maintenance have been subjected to two levels of fissuring. A major investigative report for ProPublica and PBS Frontline by Liz Day and Ryan Knutson examined this distinctive model of subcontracting that characterizes the industry.[32] The carrier bids out a contract—for millions of dollars of potential work—to a major company, called a turfer.[33] The turfer's contract requires it to provide the carrier with building and maintenance services over a period of time. Other turfers used by the carriers include major construction and engineering firms like General Dynamics and Bechtel as well as firms that specialize in the telecommunications field, like Nsoro.

The Turfer Model of Subcontracting

An agreement between AT&T (then Cingular) and Nsoro LLC Inc. obtained by ProPublica/Frontline illustrates the nature of the subcontracting model.[34] The agreement requires Nsoro to undertake project management for two types of services: those "in support of Cingular's overall new build program" and those to "manage the construction (and related services) of all cell sites at the regional and market levels of the organization. Contractor regional project managers will report to the appropriate Cingular counterparts on the status of the cell site completion and progress toward market goal." The agreement awards Nsoro a base rate of $95,000 (the "Baseline Purchase Order Price") per job under the agreement.

The turfer, however, is a project manager for the carrier and does not directly undertake the cell tower work. Instead, it bids that work out to subcontractors with the crews that actually climb towers, build scaffolds, remove and replace elements on the towers, and do other work on the site. In the case referred to above, Nsoro bid out work to a variety of subcontractors. In one illustrative case documented by Day and Knutson, it subcontracted to a company, WesTower Communications, for a job to "Remove 9 Antennas and Install 9 New Antennas," for which it would be paid $21,000.[35] WesTower Communications, in turn, subcontracted to another company, ALT Inc., which actually undertook the work.[36]

The agreement between WesTower and ALT includes language stating that the subcontractor "shall assume all responsibility and liability with respect to matters regarding the safety and health of its employees and the employees of lower tier subcontractors and suppliers and shall ensure that all such subcontractors or suppliers fully comply with the safety and health provisions contained in this Agreement." It lays these requirements out in detail in an appendix to the agreement and allows WesTower to stop work if it finds evidence of subcontractor failure to follow requirements. But the agreement also makes clear that neither ALT nor any subcontractors working below it "shall be deemed to be WesTower employees or agents, it being understood that Subcontractor and its lower tier subcontractors are independent for all purposes and at all times."

As in other cases giving rise to fissured workplaces, the overall standards for work are set at the top by the carrier. These include performance and technical specifications (the work to be done and the quality standards which must be met), the deadlines for completion of the work, overall caps on pricing over the area serviced by the turfer, and the penalties (liquidated damages) paid by the turfer for failure to meet standards. Carriers like AT&T have an enormous stake in these outcomes beyond the price paid for the work, since they affect the capacity, quality, and speed of their wireless networks. An AT&T contract document obtained by ProPublica/Frontline explicitly lists over one hundred tasks related to cell tower projects and the degree to which the company seeks to have responsibility and to be consulted or informed.[37]

The Cingular/Nsoro agreement includes specific time requirements for responding to "errors or deficiencies in the Site Development Services furnished," including "(i) 4-hour response from receipt of notice for service affecting issues and (ii) 24-hour response from receipt of notice for non-service affecting issues."[38] It also includes language allowing Cingular to conduct an escalating number of quality audits.

Of course, firms at each level of the process incur costs for their services and also seek a return beyond that. At the top of the chain, the turfers claim a large share: the report found that in cases where a pricing record was available, the turfer was paid $187 to install a component on a tower, whereas its subcontractor, which actually performed the work, in turn was paid $93 (about 50% of the revenue from the job).[39] If there are multiple levels of subcontracting (common to the cases studied by Day and Knutson), each level will seek to secure a return before paying the level below it.

The availability of a large number of subcontractors willing to bid for the work drives down the market price, and therefore the amount of money available to pay for labor, equipment, training, and supervision. Not surprisingly, the wage level at the bottom of many of these chains is reportedly $10–$12 per hour (low by construction standards). As in any labor market, such low wages mean that individuals with skills, training, and experience in risky cell tower work may be unwilling to accept them. This raises the need to supervise and train the less-experienced workers doing the work, which often does not happen. Since maintenance work often requires the tower to go offline, carriers usually want this work to be undertaken by the subcontractors between midnight and 6:00 a.m., when cell use is at its lowest and maintenance least likely to be disruptive.[40]

Repercussions of Fissured Subcontracting in Cell Towers

No telecommunications carrier was under greater pressure to expand its network in the past decade than AT&T. Between its merger with Cingular and its original position as the sole carrier supporting the iPhone, the company faced enormous pressures to expand rapidly. It drew extensively on the subcontracting system described earlier to bid work for its rapidly expanding cellular network.

Among the carriers tracked by Day and Knutson, the number of fatalities linked to AT&T far exceeded those linked to other major companies like Verizon, T-Mobile, and Sprint. Between 2003 and 2011, a total of fifty people died while working on cell towers for the carriers. AT&T accounted for fifteen of those deaths (there were five deaths associated with T-Mobile, two with Verizon, and one with Sprint). Fatalities on AT&T sites were concentrated (eleven of the fifteen fatalities) during the period 2006–2008, when iPhone and demands to merge the AT&T and Cingular networks reached a fevered level.[41] In an AT&T document called "Division of Responsibilities Matrix," safety-related tasks are left unchecked, which subcontractors believed "to mean the carrier wanted no involvement with them at all."[42]

A story that played out in the contracting chain described above illustrates the impact of the pressures arising from the system as a whole.[43] William "Bubba" Cotton was working for one of two subcontractors to upgrade a 400-foot AT&T tower in March 2006. One crew was employed by the above-mentioned ALT Inc. and was operating on the tower replacing antennas. Cotton was working for a second contractor, Betacom, on a concrete equipment shelter at the base of the tower. The two subcontractors were operating independently of one another. Figure 5.2 depicts the set of subcontractors on site in 2006 and their relationships.

The ALT crew was lowering an antenna from the tower structure when the rope they were using snapped. The 50-pound antenna fell 200 feet just as Wilson and coworkers were exiting the concrete structure for lunch. Wilson was crushed and died before EMTs arrived on the scene. Occupational Health and Safety Administration (OSHA) investigators later concluded that the rope and equipment used by ALT had not been adequately inspected and that the Betacom crew was not using hard hats on the site. Although OSHA standards did not preclude the practice, the investigators also noted the danger of having two crews, one working below the other, on the site at the same time.

The final point of the OSHA investigation is central: while the WesTower contract included extensive language regarding subcontractor safety, it ceded oversight to its subcontractor, ALT, which used substandard equipment. The consequences of failure to follow safety rules were that ALT lost its contract. Turnover is high among the subcontractors working for turfers—primarily because of the strict quality performance standards imposed by carriers. But there are enough subcontractors to provide sufficient replacements, just as there were enough contract miners to feed the Massey Doctrine system in that industry.[44]

FIGURE 5.2. A fatal example of cell tower subcontracting. *Note:* AT&T was then known as Cingular. (Graphic by Dan Nguyen, ProPublica; cell tower icon by Dima and Christian Hohenfeld, from the Noun Project. Reprinted by permission.)

WesTower also had no control over the presence of a second subcontractor, Betacom, which was contracted separately by Cingular to work at the same time and below the first crew.[45] The Betacom crew failed to use proper protection, although it is unclear whether Bubba Cotton would have survived even if he had been wearing a hard hat. Most importantly, the overall fissuring of work on the tower among multiple players meant that no party coordinated the interactions, with fatal results.[46] This is particularly ironic (but typical) given the stringent audit systems in place in the master agreement between Cingular and Nsoro regarding the quality of work done by subcontractors. Charles Perrow, a renowned analyst of accidents, has shown that serious accidents and fatalities are often the result of the simultaneous failure of multiple systems with complex interactions. The turfer system increases the likelihood of such simultaneous failure across systems given the absence of a party with responsibility for overall coordination of the site.[47]

Sweet Subcontracting: The Hershey Fissured Recipe

In the summer of 2011, Tudor Ureche, a Moldovan college student working at a Palmyra, Pennsylvania, facility that packed chocolates for the Hershey Corporation, sent an email in broken English to the U.S. State Department that read, "Pleas help the miserable situation in which I've found myself cought." Ureche was one of four hundred students, representing a veritable United Nations, hailing from Nigeria, China, Ukraine, Costa Rica, Romania, and twelve other countries, employed at the packing plant and working under the auspices of the J-1 visa program designed decades ago by the State Department to give international students cultural exchange opportunities in the United States. What the students experienced instead were long hours lifting, carrying, and moving 50–60-pound boxes of chocolates in a refrigerated packing facility on shifts that began at 11:00 p.m. and continued through until the morning hours.[48]

Students in the program paid $3,500 to participate. For their work in the plant, they were paid a base rate of $8.35 per hour. Rent, travel expenses, and other charges were deducted from their paychecks, leaving many with limited funds to experience the United States beyond the packing plant environs (with what limited time they were allotted). They were even less likely to earn back the money they paid to participate in the program. Despite e-mails from Ureche and others at the Palmyra plant, it took a walkout by four hundred of the students to induce the State Department to investigate.

The students' trips to the United States were arranged by the Council for Educational Travel, U.S.A. (CETUSA), a nonprofit organization long contracted by the State Department to find jobs, arrange housing, and generally organize trips for the students. Ten years earlier, Hershey would have directly employed unionized workers to pack its products and load them into trucks for customers during the summer peak period. Now, although the chocolates packed in the facility bore the Hershey label, the plant itself was operated by a contractor hired by Hershey to manage operations at the facility that in turn hired a staffing subcontractor, which served as the employer of record for the students. Many of the students discovered that their employer was the subcontractor rather than Hershey only when they received their first paycheck.[49] One might ask how a nonprofit organization created to facilitate international cultural exchanges came to place students in such a bad environment. But even more, one might ask how a global consumer food company came to rely on a third-party staffing subcontractor to employ workers in a packing and shipping facility for its prized products that was just miles away from its headquarters in a town bearing the name of its internationally famous brand.

The answer is that the Hershey story is a poster child of the fissured workplace.

Fissuring Chocolate

Hershey was founded by Milton Hershey in 1894 in his hometown of Derry Church, Pennsylvania. After introducing the famous Hershey's Kiss and later an automated machine to wrap it, the company grew rapidly and introduced other iconic products, including Mr. Goodbar (1925), Hershey's Syrup (1926), and the Krackel Bar (1938). The company cast a long shadow over the town (often called "Chocolatetown, USA") and was known for its paternalistic and sometimes heavy-handed approach toward its employees. Following Hershey's fierce and successful battle to thwart a union affiliated with the Congress of Industrial Organizations in 1938, the Bakery and Confectionery Workers Local 464 (affiliated with the American Federation of Labor) successfully organized the company in 1940. For most of the twentieth century, Hershey directly employed a large, unionized workforce for production, marketing, product development, and distribution of its products.[50]

This business model changed dramatically when Richard Lenny was hired by the Hershey board of directors in 2001 as the first outsider to serve as CEO of the company. From the beginning of his tenure, Lenny pursued a "value-enhancing strategy" focused on shifting production and related activities away from the company via outsourcing.[51] Indicative of this effort, Hershey outsourced elements of production of its chocolate liquor—the chocolate core of products like Kisses—to other companies, leaving only final reassembly steps to its own facilities and workforce.

As a further extension of that strategy, the company announced its "global supply chain transformation" in February 2007. The official objective of the three-year program could not be a clearer statement of fissuring as applied to supply chain strategy. "The transformation program will result in a flexible, global supply chain capable of delivering Hershey's iconic brands, in a wide range of affordable items and assortments across retail channels in the company's priority markets."[52] The plan entailed further reducing the number of Hershey's own production lines, "outsourcing production of low value-added items" to other companies, and building a new production facility in Monterrey, Mexico. Sourcing production to its Monterrey facility and to other international suppliers would give Hershey "increased access to borderless sourcing [and] . . . further leverage the company's manufacturing scale within a lower overall cost structure."[53]

Hershey investors thought well of the strategy, as reflected in the company's stock price, which outperformed the market consistently over the same period.[54] By 2009 Lenny had successfully outsourced most of the production outlined in the strategy, closed six facilities in the United States and Canada, and let go an estimated 3,000 union workers. Hershey further upgraded its supply chain management system, moving cocoa beans, semiprocessed chocolate bars, and other ingredients to be made outside of the United States and Canada and reassembled and packaged by Hershey in a small number of U.S. facilities, where they could then be shipped from subcontracted distribution operations like those in Palmyra.

Subcontracting Production

One contractor for Hershey was Lyons and Sons, based in Camden, New Jersey. Cocoa Services, a subsidiary of another company, and Lyons and Sons were licensed by the city to be a warehousing operation for storage of cocoa beans and semiprocessed chocolate bars from abroad.[55] However, the two companies also had set up an unlicensed operation in the Camden warehouse to take bars of pressed, unsweetened chocolate obtained from Hershey suppliers and melt them in large vats, the contents of which were then transferred into tanks for delivery to other factories contracted by Hershey.[56] At each point, contractors in Mexico, at the Lyons and Sons warehouse, and in other contract factories in the supply chain operated under the exacting product quality standards, delivery requirements, and time and price boundaries established by Hershey.

Melting unsweetened chocolate produced elsewhere was a relatively small operation in terms of manpower requirements. Workers hired as temporary employees stood on a nine-foot-high platform set up above two large vats of molten liquid chocolate, each about seven feet wide and high. According to a report by OSHA:

> They manually drop chocolate liquor slabs into a melting tank. One employee was on each side of a pallet with a one ton box of chocolate liquor slabs, cakes are 1.5-in. by 12-in. by 18-in. One employee would hand the slabs to the other employees standing adjacent to them who then dropped them into the melting tank through the 26-in. square opening. A fifth worker operated a fork lift and would place the boxes of chocolate on an elevated platform.[57]

On July 8, 2009, at 10:30 a.m., a twenty-nine-year-old man named Vincent Smith was one of the workers on the platform. Smith had been employed only for several weeks as a temporary worker at the facility. He was tasked with tossing chocolate blocks into the melting vat for a Hershey order through an unguarded opening in the platform. After the cover to the vat was removed by coworkers below, Smith walked toward the opening in the platform. He was chatting with coworkers on the platform when he took a step forward into the opening and fell into the vat of 120-degree chocolate. Investigators of the fatality later surmised that he was most likely killed by a blow to the head from a large mechanical paddle in the mixing vat. Because of the height of the vat, his coworkers were unable to pull him out until firefighters arrived ten minutes later. OSHA investigators later found that both Lyons and Sons and Cocoa Services had committed numerous serious violations of health and safety standards, including those pertaining to proper floor and wall guarding requirements and confined space requirements.

The Hershey case, like the cell tower case, illustrates the increased likelihood of accidents and risks when responsibility for health and safety is unclear or left in the hands of parties with little incentive to take that responsibility seriously. Back in the days when Hershey produced its own chocolate, it had health and safety departments and joint health and safety committees with the union representing its workers. It directly paid workers' compensation premiums, giving it an incentive to manage risks. And, being a prominent and large employer, it had incentives to follow OSHA standards because of the chance of being inspected—a chance raised by the presence of a unionized and informed workforce.

But Lyons and Sons faced none of those incentives as a small employer flying under the screen of OSHA, workers' compensation insurers, and even local officials, who thought the facility was only a warehouse until after first responders were called. Hershey, now at arm's length from the production of its own chocolates, was not cited by OSHA for the death of Vincent Smith because it could not even remotely be deemed an employer under the structure of current employment laws.

Fissured Distribution

Historically, Hershey considered its shipping functions (managing shipment orders, and packing and loading them onto trucks) to be corporate functions. It negotiated contracts for the workers in its distribution centers, including a large operation in Palmyra that was staffed by unionized Hershey employees.

In 2002, as part of the larger effort to remove itself from the actual production of chocolate, Hershey closed most of its large co-packing operation in Palmyra. Distribution operations were then dispersed to other nonunion locations.[58] To operate a remaining facility in the Palmyra area (still owned by the company), Hershey chose Exel, a major contract logistics provider with over $4 billion in annual revenue managing over three hundred sites in the United States.[59] Exel, in turn, hired SHS OnSite Solutions, a temporary staffing provider (and part of SHS Group LP) to hire the workforce. It was SHS OnSite Solutions that then contracted with CETUSA.

This complicated relationship went largely unnoticed until the four hundred students who spent much of their three-month summer "cultural exchange" in the United States lifting boxes of Hershey's Kisses, stepped forward to protest the conditions under which they worked. After paying to participate in the State Department–sponsored exchange program, students assigned by CETUSA to the Palmyra warehouse were paid $8.35 per hour. Many of the participants in the program had their rent and other expenses directly deducted from their paychecks, leaving them with between $40 and $140 in earnings from their forty-hour workweeks. Students like Yana Bzengey from Ukraine stated that their sponsors threatened deportation in response to complaints: "I pick up boxes that are 40 pounds—I weigh 95 pounds. I complain. I say 'I want another job.' They say if I do not work here they will cancel my visa and I will go home."[60]

With the assistance of the Guest Workers Alliance, the student protest attracted the attention of the State Department, which oversees the J-1 visa program, as well as from OSHA and the Department of Labor's Wage and Hour Division. In subsequent investigations, OSHA cited Exel for violations of health and safety standards (including six willful violations) and assessed penalties of $288,000.[61] After its own investigations, the State Department debarred CETUSA from further participation in its guest worker visa program and also initiated administrative changes to the program to prevent future incidents.[62]

When the Hershey case hit the national news, the company was quick to claim that it knew nothing about the use of J-1 visa workers or of their working conditions in Palmyra. Noting that the company did not directly operate the facility, a spokesperson said, "The Hershey Company expects all of its vendors to treat their employees fairly and equitably." SHS OnSite Solutions similarly distanced itself from the facility, responding, "We don't directly hire these students so we're not really involved in the J-1 Visa Program." Even CETUSA attempted to dodge responsibility. Rick Anaya, its CEO, was quoted as saying he was surprised at the students' negative reaction to their conditions. "We can provide the environment . . . but as far as making contact with Americans, that's up to the kids. We provide the setting, but it's up to them to make the effort."[63]

The Independent Cable Guy

Many of us have waited for a cable installer to arrive. It is such an evocative moment that a movie was even written to enshrine the experience.[64] It turns out that although the installers may wear the insignia of the cable media company or of a major contractor working for it, they may be compensated as if they were working for themselves (that is, as an independent contractor). As a result, the pay they receive would be far less than if they were paid directly by the cable provider.

Time Warner Cable, a major provider of cable services in the United States, at one time would send its own workers to install cable boxes in the homes of customers. Even today, if you search FAQs on the Time Warner Cable website, you may get the impression that scheduling an appointment for installation or service would lead to a Time Warner employee appearing at your doorstep at the designated time. In fact, Time Warner has shifted this work out. In the Dayton, Ohio, area, it hired an intermediary to whom it subcontracted installation services, Cascom Inc., to be the service provider of record.

As we have seen repeatedly, fissuring often leads to more fissuring. In this case, Cascom did not pay its cable installers as employees, but instead set them up as independent contractors. In principle, that meant that each cable installer was a self-standing business that subcontracted the work from Cascom. In reality, however, Cascom determined which homes each so-called independent contractor would visit and how much the contractor could charge (a rate Cascom both set and collected). Cascom precluded installers from taking on new business independently, fined them for work judged (after the fact) to be substandard, and monitored their activities closely.[65]

The one way Cascom treated installers as independent contractors was by compensating them on the basis of jobs completed rather than hours worked. That meant an installer received the same amount of money whether a job took a short or long period of time. This, of course, created high stakes for installers to complete the work quickly (reinforced by the fact that the daily number of service calls was determined by Cascom rather than the installer). Cascom paid installers a rate directly linked to their productivity, rather than on an hourly basis where lower-productivity workers might receive compensation comparable to that of high-productivity workers.

Relying on Cascom to be its general contractor allows the cable giant to pay a far lower cost for installation while maintaining an overall business model built around access to cable content, effective customer service, and price. As the principal contractor, Cascom created its own rigid standards, monitoring, and enforcement systems to see that its subcontractors—in this case individuals employed as independent contractors—met them. By moving installation work outside to the model of contracting created by Cascom, Time Warner ultimately could pay a far lower cost per cable box installed than it would were the installers still within the cable service mother ship. It also gave Time Warner, through the auspices of Cascom, a mechanism allowing it to pay each worker a wage closer to his or her output than if employed inside the media giant.

The case is not unique: many forms of fissured subcontracting end with outer tiers of individuals hired as so-called independent contractors rather than as employees. Independent contracting can be a legitimate form of business organization, but it connotes specific things: that contractors control their own business, maintain multiple clients, are free to bring on and decline clients, and maintain their own equipment, tools, and skills. In reality, the type of independent contracting at the bottom of multilevel subcontracting models often looks like the installers at Cascom: independent in name only.

The Department of Labor's Wage and Hour Division questioned Cascom's form of subcontracting (although it did not raise the role of Time Warner in contracting installation with Cascom). In investigating the relationship between Cascom and its phalanx of individual subcontractors, the agency called into question the idea that the individual installers were truly "independent" from Cascom, given that virtually all aspects of their subcontracted services were determined by it. In an important decision, the district court of the Southern District of Ohio held in favor of the Department of Labor's position that the 250 installers were in fact employees and not independent contractors. As a result, the workers were entitled to overtime pay amounting to over $800,000 and an equal amount of liquidated damages (also paid to the affected workers).[66]

What We Have Here Is a Failure to Coordinate

Subcontracting used to be about the provision and use of specialized services by an employer that could be drawn upon for particular types of work where it would make little sense to have these activities or this expertise in the core of the organization. The external market could provide these services at lower cost and higher quality. Fissured subcontracting differs in that it applies the subcontracting model to core activities of the firm—for example, coal extraction versus blasting; cell tower expansion and maintenance versus one-off service; ongoing manufacturing operations or cable installations versus staffing for peak-demand periods. This type of subcontracting has been adapted in many ways to reflect the balancing required in different industries and to meet the particular needs of lead business organizations.

The contracts that emerge in different cases all specify work at highly detailed levels that maintain the lead firm's leverage regarding price, timing, place of delivery, and so on. And such contracts provide clear standards, guidelines, monitoring, and penalties (sometimes explicit, always implicit) about the consequences to the subcontractor if it fails to meet the guidelines. This is the glue that holds subcontractors to the outcomes that are central to the lead firm's core competency.

Subcontracting often occurs where there is a large pool of potential contractors in the secondary and tertiary markets. In some cases, an intermediary is placed between the principal and the competitive subcontractors, for example, turfers in the case of cellular towers. In other instances, subcontractors bid directly for work from lead businesses. The decision by the lead business to place an intermediary in the mix is based on its need for someone to play a coordinating role, the risk of collusion among those contractors, and the information possessed by various parties in the particular market.[67] But in most of the cases documented here, the lead business calls upon a large group of competitors through an arm's-length relationship, often allowing other subcontracting tiers to emerge under them. This setup requires the presence of a large pool of potential contractors who are willing to take work even under financially questionable terms. In most of the cases—from coal mining to making chocolate—this supply base appears to be more than adequate to fill the needs of lead businesses.

An alternative format places the lower tiers of fissuring in alignment with those of the lead business through a more inclusive business model, but one still requiring explicit detailed standards, monitoring arrangements, and penalties. That format comes from the world of franchising.

Fissuring and Franchising

Lead companies retain activities that are central to their competitive strategy while shedding activities where doing so reduces costs, increases flexibility, and shifts liabilities. But this decision is guided by the constant balancing of the potential impact of shedding an activity that might in the long-term undermine the core competitive strategy. Franchising is an organizational form used to connect the lead company with subsidiary organizations that provides the required glue to keep the pieces of the fissured strategy together. Franchising is an old form of business organization. It historically solved the unique problems faced by manufacturers in finding effective ways to distribute products. In more recent times, it has proved a powerful means to tap the capital and entrepreneurial drive of new business owners who seek opportunities to expand an established product or service. But, less recognized, franchising also provides a way to glue the two pieces of the fissured strategy together.

Franchising potentially provides a lead business with a method of preserving the benefits of a strong brand while controlling labor costs (particularly important for service businesses, where labor represents a significant share of costs). It has become a pervasive form of business organization in a wide variety of industries, spanning fast food, hotels, car rental, home health care, and janitorial services. Since it also allows lead companies to focus on enhancing the gains of branding while using fissured employment to lower labor costs, exploring its use and consequences helps illuminate the broader effects of fissuring.[1] We explore examples of franchising as an organizational form that leads to fissured workplaces in three different settings: fast food, janitorial services, and the hotel/motel industries.

First Principles for Fissured Franchising

Build the Brand

In many of the industries where fissured workplaces have become common, major companies have sought to enhance the value of their products and services to increase revenue streams. Brand-focused competencies enable businesses to create a distinctive bond between customers and the products and services they consume. Successful branding allows a company to differentiate its products in the minds of consumers, who, over time, become willing to pay a higher premium for them. Branding acts on the revenue side of profitability: the more successful the brand, the greater the ability of the business to charge a premium and expand and retain its customer base. Once established, the benefits arising from branding can be expanded by broadening product offerings and managing the expectations of the brand's devoted customer base.[2]

Branding is particularly important in industries where perceptions of the quality, consistency, and variety of the product are critical to competitive performance—that is, in areas where the product or service is not viewed as a commodity.[3] By establishing a brand, a company can differentiate its product and create a large and loyal customer base. Return business for a company and the willingness of customers to pay a higher price are based on a variety of product or service attributes that companies can control through production, by influencing customer perceptions, or both. A branded competency involves major investment in the creation of the brand identity on the production/delivery side and in the realm of marketing. It also requires huge investments in protection of brand image over the long term given that investment. Brand core competencies also require an ongoing ability to manage and expand the brand, in response to competitive brands, threats from new entrants, or the inevitable product fatigue that a consumer group may develop over time.

In the fast-food industry, return business is based partly on the customer's belief that the experience will be the same in any outlet of the company visited.[4] The investment in brand name and protection of its image is therefore a central part of the competitive strategy of national chains and an integral part of the way they make operational decisions.[5] As a result, franchise agreements begin with statements about the importance of adhering to the chain's basic standards. For example, the franchise agreement with Taco Bell states, "You must operate your facilities according to methods, standards, and procedures (the 'System') that Taco Bell provides in minute detail." Not surprisingly, the methods, procedures, and guidelines regarding the creation of a good or the provision of a service are the "crown jewels" of a branded business. The books of standards associated with fast-food or hotel/motel brands are highly confidential documents that are provided only to franchisees who have been approved. Monitoring mechanisms, contract terms, and high-powered incentives (including, in the worst case, loss of the franchise) are associated with adherence to those standards.

One of the key operational decisions made by companies is how to expand. In service industries like eating and drinking establishments, hotels and motels, and rental cars, companies expand by adding outlets. This can be accomplished in a franchised structure in one of two ways. The first way is by opening new outlets that are both owned and operated by the franchisor itself. Expansion through the creation of company-owned outlets is an attractive option because the branded company (or "franchisor") retains control over operational decisions and can therefore be better assured that brand standards are maintained. However, expansion through company ownership entails using the franchisor's capital directly and introduces managerial challenges about ensuring efficient operation of the outlet.

The second way a company can expand is by offering outside investors the opportunity to franchise. Strong brand identity benefits franchisees: by purchasing or operating a franchise of an established brand, a franchisee gains a proven business strategy with a known and trusted name. At the same time, franchising allows for expansion by tapping into the capital of franchisees, potentially expanding the opportunities for growth of the brand. Franchisors receive revenue streams both in the form of upfront fees by franchisees to purchase the franchise and as ongoing payments based on sales. Under a typical franchise agreement, the franchisee purchases the right to own and operate an establishment using the franchisor's brand name and products for a set period of time. In return, the franchisee pays an upfront fee and agrees to provide a portion of revenues (typically around 6%, although it may go as high as 12% in the case of McDonald's) to the franchisor.[6]

Franchising is also an attractive ownership form for geographically dispersed, labor-intensive, and service-based industries. In such an industry, an enterprise's profitability is closely tied to the productivity and service delivery of its workforce. Assuring workforce productivity, in turn, requires effective management, including careful monitoring of the workplace. A large company with geographically dispersed outlets can therefore use franchising—rather than relying on company-owned and -managed outlets—to better align the incentives of the franchisee, whose earnings are linked to the outlet's profitability. For these reasons, restaurants represent the most highly franchised industry in the United States.[7]

Gaining Access to Capital for Second-Tier Firms

Franchising provides a means for the branded company to expand, drawing in large part on the capital provided by individual franchisees. One reason franchising has grown and expanded in scope is the expansion of capital sources for franchisees.

In the developed franchise model found in fast food, part of that start-up capital comes from the franchisor itself. Franchisors provide capital not out of altruism but as an additional source of revenue: by loaning money to franchisees at a higher interest rate than they can access capital for themselves, they earn a nice spread. In many cases, this represents a legitimate way for the franchisor to arbitrage risk itself, benefiting both parties. However, in some cases (such as with janitorial franchising, as we shall see) it represents a pernicious way for franchisors to take advantage of unsophisticated franchisees.

In the hotel/motel industry, with its far higher requirements for capitalization, franchisees draw on more sophisticated sources of capital, including, increasingly in recent years, private equity providers like Nobel Investment Group and Blackstone. A second source of capital is real estate investment trusts (REITs), an investment vehicle expressly developed by Congress for industries like hospitality that allows multiple investors to pool their capital and receive tax benefits from real estate investment.[8]

The other capital market option for franchised industries with lower up-front capitalization requirements such as janitorial services and home health assistance (and, in general, for lower tiers of many fissured structures) is relatively high-interest sources of financing like personal and business credit cards. Small businesses are particularly reliant on credit cards as a source of capital. In 2003 almost 90% used some form of credit. While 60% of small firms used six traditional types of loans, such as credit lines, mortgage loans, and others, about 80% used nontraditional sources such as owners' loans and personal and business credit cards.[9] Nontraditional sources like business credit cards expose small second-, third- and lower-tiered businesses to even more cost pressure and risk, further exacerbating the negative employment consequences of fissured workplaces.[10]

Fissured Fast Food

Although franchising acts as an organizational glue, tensions between franchisors and franchisees still arise in franchise structures. Because franchisees pay royalties that are linked to revenues as opposed to profits, the franchisor benefits financially from increased sales (revenue), while the franchisee seeks to maximize profit (revenue less cost). This can lead to differences in terms of pricing, promotion, and cost control strategy.[11] In addition, although the franchisee has a stake in brand reputation, its stake is not as great as that of the franchisor. A franchisee has incentives to "free ride" on the established brand and may be willing to cut corners to reduce costs or improve its individual bottom line, even if such actions have negative consequences for the branded company.[12] This means that franchisees may be more willing to violate consumer, workplace, or environmental regulations in order to reduce labor costs than would be the case for company-controlled units.

Brand investment by the franchisor also makes investments by potential franchisees attractive. Franchisees, through the agreements signed with the franchisor, must adhere to standards and procedures that maintain the integrity of the brand. But because their profits are determined by the percentage of revenues kept after payment to the franchisor minus their costs, they face incentives to manage costs carefully (if not aggressively).

From one perspective, this puts the franchisor in a position to attempt to "appropriate" (in economics jargon) as much of the profits as possible, leaving franchisees only the bare minimum return to justify their investment. On the other hand, if franchisors are too greedy and take all of the spoils, they will be unable to attract other franchisees and potentially will lose existing ones as well. From a long-term perspective, it makes sense for the franchisor as the lead player to share (although certainly not everything).[13]

As anyone with young children knows, learning how to share is difficult. Not surprisingly, one finds a spectrum of franchisor/franchisee sharing behavior. At one end of the spectrum is the grandfather of fast-food franchising, McDonald's. McDonald's has some of the highest hurdles faced by would-be franchisees in terms of screening, approval, qualifications, and upfront payments. These high performance standards continue after a firm has entered into a franchise relationship, and franchisees pay one of the higher royalty payments (percentage of royalties on revenues) of any fast-food company.

But the company leaves money on the table for its carefully screened franchisees. In a rigorous analysis of the economic profitability of franchising, Kaufmann and Lafontaine show that McDonald's franchisees earned an estimated economic profit of close to 6% on revenues. They conclude that this represented a return above and beyond what a franchisee might receive from a comparably risky investment if they had not become a franchisee.[14] The authors do not provide a comparable estimate of the economic profits of the franchisor side of McDonald's operations, however.

On the other end of the spectrum, many franchisees complain that franchisors do exactly what a self-interested lead firm might be feared to do: take as much profit as possible from franchisees while continuing to reap the economic profits from investment in a national brand reputation. In the early 1990s, this was a common complaint among franchisees of Subway, who complained that the sandwich company was perfectly happy to cycle through failed franchisees as long as it received its upfront payments and at least enough royalty payments to keep the Subway brand on the street. Other examples of franchisors benefiting at the expense of franchisees include a series of suits brought by franchisees of Quiznos.[15]

It's Good to Be the (Burger) King

In a fissured workplace, one would expect the returns to the lead company (here a franchisor) to have higher profitability than a subordinate unit operating at an outer orbit (a franchisee). It is difficult to directly compare the rates of returns of franchisees and franchisors using publicly available information because most franchisees are privately held and because of the difficulty of attributing costs that are often pooled in income statements to either the franchisor or the franchisee.[16] It is still useful to compare profitability to illustrate the differing financial pressures faced by the parties in a franchise agreement. Table 6.1 compares two measures of profitability—return on assets

Table 6.1 Comparative profitability between franchisors and franchisees, Yum! Brands and Burger King Corporation

Company	Brand(s)	Franchisee or franchisor	Return on assets (%)[a]		Return on revenues (%)[b]	
			2007	2008	2007	2008
Yum! Brands (U.S.)	Pizza Hut, KFC, Taco Bell, Long John Silver's, A&W	Franchisor	16.5	19.6	11.4	11.4
NPC International Inc.	Pizza Hut	Franchisee	1.1	1.2	1.3	1.5
Morgan's Foods Inc.	KFC, Taco Bell, combination stores	Franchisee	7.0	1.4	4.0	.8
Burger King Corp.	Burger King	Franchisor	10.6	10.5	11.2	11.4
Carrols Corp.	Burger King	Franchisee	4.8	4.5	2.9	2.5

Sources: United States SEC Form 10-K: Yum! Brands Inc., FY 2007, 2008; NPC International Inc., FY 2007, 2008. Morgan's Foods Inc., FY 2007, 2008; Burger King Holdings Inc., FY 2007, 2008; Carrols Corporation, FY 2007, 2008.
  a. Net income before taxes divided by total assets.
  b. Net income before taxes divided by total reported sales from all sources.

and return on revenues—for two major franchisors with the returns for some of their publicly held franchisees. The table compares both measures of profitability in 2007 and 2008, the years immediately before the Great Recession.

The Yum! company, which owns Pizza Hut, Taco Bell, KFC, and other brands, had return on assets of 16.5% in 2007 and 19.6% in 2008 and return on revenues of around 11% during those years. This compared to return on assets and on revenues of about 1% for NPC International, one of the largest U.S. franchisees (which owned 1,098 Pizza Hut restaurants in 2008). Morgan Foods, another large Yum! franchisee that operates KFC and Taco Bell outlets, had somewhat better performance, with return on assets of 7% in 2007 and 1% in 2008 and return on revenues of 4% in 2007 and a little under 1% in 2008. But these were still far below the level of profitability of its franchisor.

Similar gaps in profitability are apparent for Burger King and one of its franchisees, Carrols Corporation. In 2007 and 2008 the return on assets and return on revenues for the Burger King Corporation ranged around 11%. For Carrols Corporation, the comparable rates of return were around 4.5% (return on assets) and just under 3% (return on revenues). Notably, Carrols Corporation was one of Burger King's largest franchisees.

Since Yum! and Burger King, like most franchisors, encourage growth among their most successful franchisees, it is likely that the rates of return in Table 6.1 among the franchisees represent the higher end of profitability among franchisees of those companies.[17] This would make the franchisee estimates an upper bound, meaning that the gap between the profitability of franchisors relative to franchisees is even larger. To paraphrase that great economist, Mel Brooks, "It is good to be the [Burger] King."

Effects of Fast-Food Franchising on Workplace Labor Standards

The eating and drinking industry employs over 10 million individuals. It is composed of two distinct sectors: full-service restaurants and limited-service (or fast-food) eating places. The limited-service sector accounts for about 37% of employment in the industry, or about 3.3 million workers. The vast majority (88%) of jobs in the industry are low-skilled and relate to food preparation and service. Employment is concentrated in small establishments, which average about seventeen workers per outlet.[18] Average hourly earnings for food preparers and servers in 2006 were $7.23, with a median wage of $7.02 and a tenth percentile wage of $5.79—both well below the current federal minimum wage of $7.25.[19] The large number of low-wage jobs makes the industry particularly prone to minimum wage and hours of work violations.

An estimated 18.2% of workers in the sector experienced minimum wage violations, 69.7% overtime violations, and 74.2% off-the-clock violations.[20] Estimated violation rates were similar for one key occupational group within the sector—cooks, dishwashers, and food preparers: 23.1% experienced minimum wage violations, 67.8% overtime violations, and 72.9% off-the-clock violations. The estimated amount of annual back wages owed by the industry is also sizable: the average amount of back wages recovered during the 2003–2008 period was $12.9 million per year.

Franchisees, who typically own and manage their own outlets, seek to maximize the profit of only their own units whereas the franchisor benefits from increases in sales of all outlets in the chain, whether franchised or company-owned. Franchisors are therefore more concerned about the deterioration of brand reputation, because it potentially affects sales in all units. Given this, a franchisor has a greater incentive to comply with laws that affect consumers' perceptions of the brand. As a result, company-owned units have a greater incentive to comply with workplace regulations relative to franchisee-owned units, which are likely to exert relatively less effort to comply given their incentive to maximize profits only at their own outlets.[21]

A comparison of outlet-level compliance with federal minimum wage and overtime laws between franchised and company-owned enterprises in the top twenty U.S. fast-food companies illuminates the consequences of franchising as a form of the fissured workplace. There are many reasons franchisee-owned outlets might have higher noncompliance than company-owned outlets that have little to do with franchise status itself. In this view, the comparisons are unfair in that they involve outlets that might be very different in other respects, leading one to incorrectly attribute the differences to franchising. For example, franchisees might be more common in areas where there is greater competition among fast-food restaurants. That competition (and franchising only indirectly) might lead them to have higher incentives to not comply. Alternatively, company-owned outlets might be in locations with stronger consumer markets, higher-skilled workers, or lower crime rates, all of which might also be associated with compliance.

To adequately account for these problems, statistical models that consider all of the potentially relevant factors, including franchise status, are generated to predict compliance levels. By doing so, the effect of franchising can be examined, holding other factors constant. This allows measurement of the impact on compliance of an outlet being run by a franchisee with otherwise identical features, as opposed to a company-owned outlet.

Figure 6.1 provides estimates of the impact of franchise ownership on three different measures of compliance for the top twenty branded fast-food companies in the United States.[22] The figure presents the percentage difference in compliance between franchised outlets relative to otherwise comparable company-owned outlets of the same brand.[23]

Compliance differs dramatically between franchisees and company-owned outlets. The probability of noncompliance is about 24% higher among franchisee-owned outlets than among otherwise similar company-owned outlets. Total back wages owed workers who were paid in violation were on average 50% higher for franchisees, and overall back wages found per investigation were close to 60% higher.[24] Not only do these results suggest that franchisees, faced by more competitive conditions and holding less of a stake in the brand than the lead company (the franchisor), are significantly more

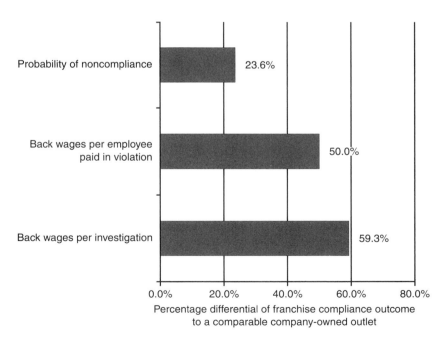

FIGURE 6.1. Effects of franchising on employer back wages and compliance, U.S. fast-food industry, top twenty brands, 2001–2005 (in 2005 dollars). *Source:* Ji and Weil 2012.

likely to fall out of compliance, but they also show that workers directly employed by the lead companies are much more likely to be paid according to the law. Indicative of this is the fact that one-half of the top twenty brands had *no* violations and owed no back wages at *any* of their company-owned outlets even though the franchisees in those same companies often owed substantial back wages to employees.[25]

Franchising and Fissuring in Janitorial Services

For the majority of janitorial service workers, wages are low and benefit coverage minimal. Conditions on the job subject them to workplace injuries and illnesses as well as the ups and downs in employment that are basic to market economies. The janitorial services sector usually ranks high on lists of workplaces with widespread violations of labor standards. In 2009 an estimated 22% of surveyed workers in the security, building, and grounds industries had not received minimum wage payments, and 63% had not received pay for overtime. Based on an occupational rather than industry definition, building services and grounds workers experienced minimum wage violation rates of 26% and overtime violation rates above 71%. Far more than half of workers in this industry and occupation classification failed to receive required meal breaks. An equally high percentage were not compensated for work done at the beginning or end of their shift (that is, off-the-clock violations), such as being asked to clean an area before officially punching in or out for work.[26]

As in other industries, it is not useful to simply attribute high violation rates to the malevolence or venality of specific employers. Instead, they can be traced to the structure of markets and competition arising from the widespread outsourcing of maintenance activities, the consequent creation of a competitive market to provide janitorial services to those organizations, and the emergence of specific types of business models that set market prices and the conditions in which wage policies are set.

Creating the Janitorial Services Market

Like many other business functions, cleaning and maintenance of facilities have been shed by many organizations—public, private, and nonprofit. This outsourcing of maintenance and janitorial services has a logical rationale: a hospital, law practice, software developer, or insurance company does not have comparative advantages in managing cleaning and property maintenance services.[27] The outsourcing of cleaning and maintenance functions to outside companies gave rise to what is now a very large supply base of companies providing janitorial services. In 2007 the sector was comprised of 50,325 firms employing over 940,000 workers and took in $34.7 billion in revenue.[28]

Firms in the industry range in size and organizational structure. At one extreme are large corporations that provide maintenance services for major companies and for venues like convention centers. A small number of very large firms with annual revenues exceeding $100 million (eighty-six companies representing less than 1% of all firms in the industry) account for about 25% of industry employment.[29] These include companies like ABM Industries, a $3.5 billion maintenance, security, and janitorial company with a client list that once included the World Trade Center and now includes major companies like Cisco Systems as well as large organizations like the government of Sonoma County, California, and major school districts in Arizona.

At the other end of the spectrum, thousands of cleaning companies serve small business customers in local markets. Although these very small entities, with annual revenues below $500,000, represent 83% of all firms in the industry, they account for only 19% of industry employment.[30] Small entrepreneurs are drawn to the industry because of the modest capital and formal business requirements, the large potential customer base, and the ample supply of low-skilled labor (often from an immigrant workforce).

In between the large-scale players catering to major clients and the small-scale businesses serving small customers are the bulk of employers, with revenues above $500,000 but below $100 million. This group accounts for 17% of firms but 56% of all employment.

Franchising has become a common form of business organization in this tier of the janitorial services industry, and a growing number of janitorial service companies use franchising as the primary mechanism of business expansion.[31] Franchised operations serve clients through a form of organization that combines common components of franchising with unique features that place particular competitive pressure on their owners as well as the market as a whole.

How Janitorial Franchising Works

There are a number of franchised companies operating across the United States. Examples include Coverall North America, Jan-Pro Franchising

International, CleanNet USA, and Jani-King International.[32] One of the largest franchised firms is Coverall, whose revenues equaled $224 million in 2008. Coverall had over 5,400 franchised outlets at the end of that year, operating in almost half of all U.S. states.[33] Franchisees of the company provide cleaning services to general office facilities; fitness centers and health clubs; child care, health care, and educational institutions; retail, manufacturing, government, and warehouse facilities; auto dealerships; and restaurants. As a franchised company, Coverall advertises a unique system of cleaning to prospective owners.[34] Presumably the distinctive approach gives an interested entrepreneur a leg up in entering the business.

A franchisee in the janitorial service sector pays the franchisor initial fees to acquire a franchise and ongoing fees linked to revenues. The initial franchise fee is related to the size of customer base the franchisee will be provided upon start-up. For example, the initial fee for Coverall franchisees ranges from $10,000 to $32,000 depending on the size of the customer base being "purchased." Janitorial franchisees must also pay the franchisor a fee based on customer revenues, usually broken into a royalty and a management fee; for Coverall, the royalty fee is 5% and the management fee is 10% of gross revenues. The franchisor also earns revenues through the sale of cleaning materials to its franchisees, but revenues from this source are modest. In exchange for the initial and ongoing fee payments, the franchisor provides franchisees with (1) an initial customer list; (2) training in the franchise's method of cleaning; (3) starter supplies and equipment; (4) advice and counseling; and (5) a "brand."

Most janitorial franchisees are organized in geographic tiers. For example, at Coverall, beneath the franchisor are regional or master franchisors who, in turn, sell franchises on a "unit" or territory basis. Unit franchises provide services to a specified list of customers supplied by the company.[35] Most provide the franchisee with a guarantee of this business for a time-delimited period. However, those guarantees are highly contingent on the reasons clients were lost.[36]

The Business Model

Although some of the features described above are standard components of franchising in any industry (for example, fees based on revenues received), others are more distinctive to the janitorial sector. First, the company provides its franchisees with an initial customer base as part of the basic franchise package. This takes the form of a list of customers for the franchisee that together provide revenues equal to the value of the package purchased by the franchisee.[37] In principle, this gives the new business an immediate customer base to serve. However, if the franchisee does not wish to provide services to a customer on the list (due to geographic distance, time required for the work, or other reasons), the franchisor is under no obligation to replace it with another client or clients. That burden falls to the franchisee.

Second, although franchisees work for clients, the primary relationship remains that between the client and the *franchisor*. Most striking, the price for a job is negotiated and set by the franchisor, not the franchisee. The franchisor receives payment for work completed and then forwards the remaining amount (gross revenues less royalty and management fees) to the franchisee. Jan-Pro's franchise agreement, for example, states:

> Each month we will bill your Customers for the services you provide. We will collect the monies we receive on such billings and pay you on a monthly basis on the last day of each month the net amount due to you after deduction of our Royalty Fee, Management Fee, Sales & Marketing Fee, payments due under a Promissory Note, and any other amounts due to us.[38]

Even if a franchisee finds new clients, it must refer them to the franchisor, which then sets terms and conditions for the franchisee.[39] It is not clear how involved the franchisee is in those discussions (which might vary according to the history, size, and relationship among Coverall, the master franchisee, and the unit franchisee). The overall janitorial franchising relationship is depicted in Figure 6.2.

The dominant role of janitorial franchisors in setting the terms and conditions of the relationship in some senses is similar to other franchise settings. Burger King or McDonald's, for example, set most terms regarding how stores function, the menu, and, to a more contested degree, prices for products. But the janitorial model is more intrusive, particularly in that actual revenues flow first to the franchisor and then back to the franchisee.

These relationships potentially set up conflicts of interest between franchisors and franchisees. This can be seen most strikingly in the impact of a franchisee losing a client's business. For the franchisee, customer loss has a detrimental impact on financial operations, for obvious reasons. For the franchisor,

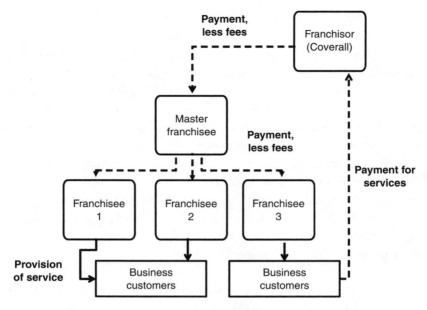

FIGURE 6.2. Janitorial services franchising.

however, if one franchisee loses a client, it becomes available for another franchisee in the system (provided the customer is still willing to work with that franchisor). As noted above, the franchisor has no obligation to find a replacement client under these circumstances. In fact, a client lost by one franchisee provides the franchisor with an opportunity to resell it, along with other clients, to a new franchisee, thus earning additional initial franchisee fees for the franchisor.[40]

Can a Janitorial Franchisee Be Financially Viable?

Can a janitorial franchisee hope to make a reasonable return to compensate himself or herself for the upfront investment in franchise fees[41] and the ongoing payment of royalties? The answer depends in large part on the fees the franchisor negotiates with clients for its franchisee's services. Since the janitorial service market is large, competitive, fractured, and easy to enter and exit, the downward pressure on price—particularly for services to midsized businesses and organizations—is fierce.

Suits and complaints/stories on industry blogs paint a picture of widespread discontent about the revenues franchisees allege they were promised to earn in the business. Although it is difficult to document these promises in writing, they are frequently cited in legal actions brought by discontented franchisees. Similarly, many of the blogs and websites promoting franchising cite figures that average around $25 per hour in terms of what a franchisee can expect to charge a typical client.[42] If franchisees received this level of compensation for their services, our financial models indicate that they could service contracts, pay workers according to legal requirements, and make a reasonable rate of return (see below).

The reality, however, appears very different. A variety of news stories on the sector offer franchisee accounts of earning less—far less—than $25 per hour for services. For example, a 2005 *New York Times* article recounts the case of a Boston-based Coverall franchisee who reported working 280 hours per month and earning $1,262, implying hourly earnings of $4.50. A 2009 report included a similar story of a Coverall franchisee who was assured of receiving between $18 and $20 an hour, but whose actual price turned out to be under $11 per hour.[43]

One reason the hourly figure often quoted to potential and current franchisees is above the actual price paid to franchisees is that clients sign contracts based on a price for service provision, without an explicit statement of hours. As noted, since the terms of contracts are negotiated between the franchisor and the customer (and not the franchisee), the franchisor has less of an incentive to consider the total time required for completion of the service in setting the price.[44]

Hourly prices for basic janitorial services based on prevailing contract rates can be estimated drawing on a variety of sources regarding the terms of contract payment, the number of visits required by a cleaning agreement, the typical service provision (that is, what cleaning services would be provided), and a conservative estimate of the number of hours required to provide services for that type of contract.[45] The resulting estimates are summarized in Table 6.2.

For a small client who requires very basic janitorial services, contracts are often bid on the basis of a price per service visit. A typical price for basic service at a small office (vacuuming, dusting, trash removal, bathroom cleaning) is $25–$30 per visit. The minimum time required for basic services of this

Table 6.2 Hourly pricing for basic janitorial services, market surveys, 2009

	Small office/facility, minimal service	Small office/facility, basic service	Medium office/facility, daily service	Large office/daily service
Contract term	$20–30 per visit	$150–250 per month	$500–$700 per month	$2,000–$4,000 per month
Number of visits	Single visit	8 per month	20 per month	20 per month
Cleaning activities[a]	Vacuuming, dusting, trash pickup and removal, bathroom cleaning	Vacuuming, dusting, trash pickup and removal, bathroom cleaning	Vacuuming, dusting, trash pickup and removal, bathroom cleaning	Vacuuming, dusting, trash pickup and removal, bathroom and kitchen cleaning
Time per visit	1.5 hours	2 hours	2 hours	8 hours
Site characteristics[b]	1–2 offices and restroom	2–3 offices, common space, restroom	2–3 offices, common space, restroom	20,000-square-foot office, restrooms, and kitchenette
Estimated price per hour	$16.67	$12.50	$15.00	$16.67

Sources: Based on pricing, contract term, time, and square-foot estimates from the following sources: Cleaning Management Institute, "2009 Kaviac Inc. Contract Cleaning Benchmarking Survey Report," CMI/NTP Media, 2009 survey; "Office Cleaning Costs: What People Are Paying," Costhelper.com (http://www.costhelper.com/cost/small-business/office-cleaning.html); "Commercial Cleaning Services—Buyer's Guide" (http://smallbusiness.yahoo.com/advisor/commercial-cleaning-services-buyers-guide-144201040.html).

a. Based in part on work hours devoted to particular tasks; CMI/NTP Media, 2009 survey.

b. Based on cost estimates for office tasks and square footage of office area.

kind is around 1.5 hours per visit, leading to an average price for services of $16.67 per hour.

More commonly, customers contract on the basis of monthly rates for the provision of a specific level of janitorial services (for example, $500 per month to clean a branch bank five nights a week). Very basic janitorial service for a medium-size property can run between $100 and $200 a month, assuming eight visits each month, which translates into an hourly rate between $8.33 and $16.67. For a client requiring nightly cleaning services, payment can range between $500 and $700 per month (assuming a conservative two hours for basic cleaning), which implies an average payment of $15 per hour. Basic nightly service for a large office (for example, a 20,000-square-foot property), requiring the use of several cleaners, is priced in the $2,000–$4,000 monthly range. Once again, very conservative assumptions regarding time required for this work implies an hourly rate of around $15.

These estimates therefore suggest hourly payments well below the $20–$25 often quoted to franchisees, and probably closer to a rate of $15 per hour. Although rates vary according to geographic area, quality of service, desire for specialty cleaning requirements (for example, carpet cleaning and special surface cleaning), the figures in Table 6.2 provide conservative estimates for basic service provision.

The Bottom Line: It Pays Not to Comply

As a tool to examine the pressure to not comply with labor standards (and presumably other public policies) given prevailing market prices and the costs facing franchisees, a simplified model of the financials for a franchised janitorial services contractor can be created. The model can be constructed using information from franchise disclosure documents (FDDs)[46] filed by Coverall as inputs for the operational requirements of a typical franchisee in 2009 and, to the extent possible, using estimates and assumptions directly from the company's FDD.[47]

Assume that a franchisee is operating at a scale of more than $500,000 per year in gross revenues. By setting an average price level for services at different hourly rates, and then calculating the franchisee's economic profit, the average rate of pay for employees (given the hours required to complete the work) can be calculated, given the assumption that the franchisee simply seeks to break even on an ongoing basis.[48]

An entrepreneur would find it difficult to break even (pay expenses and a reasonable compensation to him- or herself) and comply with minimum wage laws if the gross hourly price for services falls below $15 (see Table 6.3). If the franchisee seeks to make a positive economic return, the downward pressure on labor costs intensifies further.

These results, coupled with the pricing data reviewed in Table 6.2, imply that the franchised portion of the industry, as currently structured, has a built-in bias toward noncompliance given prevailing conditions for janitorial services in many markets. In essence, a franchisee cannot service the contracts provided by the franchisor at the market prices prevailing in many cases and still comply with labor standards without going into the red. The landscape of compliance becomes tilted toward violations of labor standards (as well as cutting corners in any other way to minimize costs).

But if janitorial franchising is inherently not profitable, why has it persisted—indeed, grown significantly—in recent years? The answer is two-fold. First, the above suggests that franchising cannot be profitable *if* the franchisee adheres to wage and hour laws as well as, presumably, meeting its basic legal obligations (for example, workers' compensation, unemployment, and Social Security payments). Hence the incentive for noncompliance.

Second, the above analysis suggests that a company that does pay workers according to the law—whether because of a desire to obey the law or arising from tight labor market pressures—will have a hard time surviving. This would lead one to predict high rates of turnover among franchisees. In fact, a

Table 6.3   Maximum wage for Coverall franchisee given profit targets

Profit for franchisee (given $500K annual revenues)	If the hourly price for janitorial service is:		
	P = $20	P = $15	P = $12.50
Break even (0)	$11.39	$7.77	$6.02
$25,000	$10.43	$7.07	$5.44
$50,000	$ 9.47	$6.37	$4.86
$75,000	$ 8.51	$5.66	$4.28

Note: Based on model using franchisee royalty and operating fees and information from Coverall franchise disclosure documents; typical amount of debt for upfront franchise payment and baseline assumptions about economic profits based on alternative employment of franchisee at $30,000 annually.

review of data from FDDs reveals such high turnover. The high level of turn-over among some of the leading janitorial franchisees relative to franchisees in the fast-food industry is depicted in Table 6.4. The figures not only indicate high annual turnover—15%—from franchisees exiting the industry (compared with about 3% at KFC, one of the major fast-food franchisors), but also the large number of incoming franchisees (leading to an overall increase in the number of franchisees). The significant supply of prospective franchisees to replace those unable to make the business model work allows franchising to persist (and to benefit the franchisor).

Finally, it should be remembered that while being a law-abiding franchisee in many markets does not offer sustainable profits, this does not imply

Table 6.4   Turnover among janitorial services franchised companies, 2006–2009, and fast-food benchmarks

Franchised janitorial services company	Exits: terminations, nonrenewals, reacquired by franchisor, and ceased operations		Entries: new franchisees (outlets opened)		Net change (average)
	Average no.*	% of franchisees**	Average no.*	% of franchisees**	
Coverall[a]	589	12.4	715	15.1	+126
Jani-King[b]	1,619	16.5	1,255	12.8	−364
CleanNet USA[c]	233	7.3	563.3	17.5	+330.3
KFC[d]	162	3.8	162	3.8	0

Sources:

a. Coverall North America Franchise Disclosure Document, May 2009, p. 39. Accessed through the California Electronic Access to Securities Information and Franchise Information, http://134.186.208.233/caleasi/pub/exsearch.htm.

b. Jani-King of Boston Inc. Franchise Disclosure Document, April 30, 2010.

c. CleanNet of Southern California Franchise Disclosure Document, March 19, 2009, p. 33. Accessed through the California Electronic Access to Securities Information and Franchise Information, http://134.186.208.233/caleasi/pub/exsearch.htm.

d. KFC Franchise Disclosure Documents, September 23, 2010.

* Average annual exits/entries over the period 2006–2008 (Coverall; CleanNet USA; KFC); 2007–2009 (Jani-King).

** Percentage of exits/entries versus the reported number of franchised outlets at the beginning of the relevant calendar year.

that such profits are not attainable for the *franchisor*. Since the franchisor receives payment from royalties linked to revenues but does not face the direct costs of employing workers or the other costs of cleaning, it can still earn reasonable returns even given tough market conditions and downward pricing pressure. In the above models, franchisor profitability (defined as operating income as a percentage of gross revenues) ranged from a low of about 3% for Coverall to 41% for Jan-Pro, with other franchisors in the 8%–10% range.[49]

The large demand for services and the elastic supply of janitorial service providers create market conditions that push prices for services down toward the lowest costs of the existing supply base for a given quality tier. The ready supply of would-be franchisees therefore drives prevailing market prices down toward a level below that necessary to meet basic labor standards required by the law. In effect, by being the lowest-cost suppliers in many commercial markets, franchisees set a baseline price for services, which in turn leads them to be unable to sustain their businesses within state or federal wage and hour requirements (and undoubtedly other requirements such as workers' compensation, unemployment insurance, and even payroll taxes owed to the state and federal government). As a result, the high rates of noncompliance arise from the interaction of the competitive conditions driving the market for janitorial services and the role that a pervasive form of business organization plays in the behavior of individual players and, in turn, the market price on the margin.

Hybrid Fissuring in the Hospitality Industry

Hospitality Staffing Solutions is an Atlanta-based company operating in thirty-six states and more than seventy markets that provides hotel properties with housekeeping, janitorial, stewarding (dishwashing and kitchen support), laundry, food and beverage (waiters and waitresses and banquet help), and grounds maintenance staff. The company summarizes its core strategy succinctly: "Our value proposition is simple: provide the same motivated, reliable workers every day at a lower cost. Hospitality Staffing Solutions© delivers through highly selective grassroots hiring, employee compliance, and inclusive pricing which saves our customers on average 12% on personnel costs." In so doing, Hospitality Staffing Solutions offers to provide hotel clients with "the continuity of full time employees with the scalability to meet their changing needs—from a handful of associates to entire departments." Given the importance of service to both hotel chains and owners of properties, the company assures clients that its staff will meet the particular standards and quality levels of each brand, noting that the hotels it serves "consistently score in the top 20 properties in guest satisfaction for their brands."[50]

In the summer of 2009, Hyatt Hotels Corporation fired ninety-eight housekeepers who worked at its Hyatt Regency Boston, Hyatt Regency Cambridge, and Hyatt Harborside at Logan International Airport properties. The fired employees earned between $14 and $16 per hour with health and other benefits. Most had worked for Hyatt for years—some having more than twenty years of seniority. The employees were replaced by workers from Hospitality Staffing Solutions who were paid $8 per hour and received no benefits. Employees at the Hyatt properties trained the new workers before they were told that they would be replaced by them, on the pretext that the new workers were being brought in to fill in for staff when they were on vacation or out sick (an allegation the company contested). "Everyone was shocked. A lot of people were crying." Lucine Williams, one of the longtime Hyatt employees who lost her job, said to reporters.[51]

In its public statement, Hyatt argued that the "difficult decision to outsource the housekeeping function at our Boston properties was made in response to the unprecedented economic challenges those hotels are facing in the current business environment."[52] Media accounts of the Hyatt decision, however, puzzled over why a company would suddenly treat a trained and devoted workforce so callously. Why change from a beneficent employer to what was portrayed as a heartless penny-pincher? Rather than revealing a sudden change of heart, the Hyatt story illustrates the complex way franchising has combined with third-party management and labor contracting in the hotel and motel industry and its resulting impact on the workforce.

Catering to the Discerning Traveler

Brands have become an increasingly important part of competitive strategy in the hotel industry. Whether for business or vacation travelers, a successful brand creates an image in a customer's mind regarding the quality, standards, amenities, and value of a hotel. Since consumers searching for hotels in most locations have many options, the brand can be extremely valuable if it narrows the consumer's search to a subset of hotels or, even better, to a single brand. As with fast food, travelers typically want to know that they will receive service that is consistent with their past, hopefully positive experience. Once again, a successful brand does this. As a result, at the end of 2007 more than half of U.S. hotel/motel properties were part of a branded company chain, concentrated particularly among twenty-five top brand names (see Table 6.5).[53]

The hospitality market is divided up in terms of customer niches, from economy to high-end users. Major hotel parent companies in the industry own and manage a portfolio of brands representing different customer groupings. Due to industry consolidation, approximately ten parent companies control the vast majority of the major brands in the United States. Table 6.6

Table 6.5   Branded versus independent hotels, United States, 2007

	No. of properties	% of total*	No. of rooms	% of total*
Independent only	22,177	44.8	1,482,421	32.5
Branded only				
Top 5*	6,398	12.9	703,906	15.4
Top 10	11,790	23.8	1,229,363	27.0
Top 25	17,937	36.3	2,020,521	44.3
All major brands	22,142	44.7	2,512,969	55.1
Nonmajor brands	5,167	10.4	563,697	12.4
Total	49,486	100.0	4,559,087	100.0

Source: Analysis by Smith Travel Research (STR), "U.S. Lodging Census Database," based on year-end data, December 31, 2007.

Notes: Top 5, 10, and 25 ranked by number of rooms.

Top 5 STR brands: Best Western, Days Inn, Holiday Inn, Marriott, Holiday Inn Express Hotel.

Top 10 STR brands: Top 5 plus Super 8, Comfort Inn, Hampton Inn, Courtyard, Hilton.

Top 25 STR brands: Top 10 plus Motel 6, Quality Inn, Sheraton Hotel, Residence Inn, Hyatt, Econo Lodge, Hilton Garden Inn, Fairfield Inn, Embassy Suites, Doubletree, Ramada, Extended Stay America, Americas Best Value Inn, Crowne Plaza, Westin.

* Calculated as the percent of hotel type (for example "Top 5") divided by total for the column. Note that the overall total equals the sum of "independent only," "all major brands," and "nonmajor brands" ("Top 5," "10," and "25" are subsets of "all major brands"). Total may not equal 100% due to rounding.

lists the brands held by major brand operating companies. For example, Hilton Worldwide held five major brands ranging from Hampton Inn at the lower end of the business market to premier hotels in its core Hilton brand.

Table 6.6 points to a more fundamental change in the industry. The core product of the parent hotel/motel companies is not the properties they own and manage, but the portfolio of brands, each representing (if executed effectively) a replicable bundle of quality, pricing, amenities, and reputational characteristics, focused on different markets. If you are a business traveler on the road looking for value and Wi-Fi, Marriott can offer you Courtyard.[54] If, instead, you are an upscale consultant looking for style and less concerned about price, try Starwood's W Hotels and Resorts. And the harried parent looking for a clean room at a low price for her family's vacation? Accor's Sofitel is for her. Hilton, Marriott, Starwood, Accor, and other hotel parent companies' share prices reflect their acumen in acquiring, developing, and maintaining a portfolio of brand experiences across markets, not their

Table 6.6 Major brand operating companies and the brands they control (brands held as of March 2011)

Brand operating company	Brand(s)
Wyndham Worldwide Corp.	Baymont Inn & Suites, Days Inn, Hawthorn Suites, Howard Johnson, Knights Inn, Microtel, Ramada, Super 8, Travelodge
Accor North America	Motel 6, Sofitel
Choice Hotels International	Clarion Hotel, Comfort Inn, Econo Lodge, Mainstay Suites, Quality Inn, Rodeway Inn, Sleep Inn
InterContinental Hotels Group	Candlewood Suites, Holiday Inn, InterContinental Hotels & Resorts, Staybridge Suites
Hilton Worldwide	Doubletree, Embassy Suites, Hampton Inn, Hilton, Homewood Suites
La Quinta Management LLC	La Quinta
Marriott International Inc.	Courtyard, Fairfield Inn, Marriott Hotels and Resorts, Renaissance, SpringHill Suites
Carlson Hotels Worldwide	Country Inn & Suites, Radisson Hotel & Resorts
Starwood Hotels & Resorts Worldwide Inc.	Aloft, Four Points, Sheraton, St. Regis, W Hotels & Resorts, Westin
Global Hyatt Corp.	Grand Hyatt, Hyatt Hotels & Resorts, Hyatt Park, Hyatt Regency, Summerfield Suites

skill in providing clean rooms, cheery front desk staff, or prompt curbside service.[55] Scrutiny of those tasks falls to other actors.

Franchising the Brands

Branded parent companies in the hotel/motel industry have largely abandoned the business of owning and managing their properties, turning instead to franchising as the major form of ownership. In 1962 only 2% of U.S. motels were franchised. By 1987 that share had jumped to 64%. Today, more than 80% of hotel properties in the United States are franchised.[56] In 2011 Hilton owned and managed only 22 of its 258 U.S. properties, and Marriott Hotels and Resorts owned and managed only 1 of the 356 properties operating under one of its brands.[57]

Through franchising, major hotel chains are able to expand rapidly, especially in growth markets. Franchising allows the brand to tap capital, expand in multiple markets simultaneously, and draw on geographic expertise of local owners and independent management operators. Brands have expanded their access to capital through franchising in much the same way companies in other industries—notably restaurants—have adopted franchising as the major form of ownership and business expansion.

The attraction of franchising has led entire chains to flip from company ownership to franchising. Choice Hotels, for example, which owns the Clarion, Comfort Inn, Quality Inn, and Rodeway Inn brands, franchised all of its 4,884 hotels in 1999. Also in 1999, Wyndham, which owns the Ramada, Howard Johnson's, Super 8, and Days Inn brands, franchised all of its 6,383 properties.[58]

A distinctive brand image in the hotel/motel industry arises from a combination of architectural and design investments that affect the look of properties; administrative investments that affect the marketing, pricing, and "backroom" practices of properties; and operational investments that directly affect the "customer experience," including how visitors are greeted at the front desk, the range of services available to hotel patrons, and the way rooms are cleaned and facilities maintained. Table 6.7 provides examples of these standards from a variety of hotel brands. Developing and implementing this set of practices is both complicated and costly. But it is the core to assuring that the central branding strategy results in customers' receiving the "experi-

Table 6.7 Franchise agreement statements regarding compliance with brand standards: Hotel and motel industry, selected examples

Hotel/motel brand	Excerpt from franchise agreement
Days Inns	When a licensee buys a franchise from DIA (Days Inns of America), he buys the "Days Inn System," a comprehensive "hotel operating system" that sets hundreds of mandatory "System Standards" that control the manner in which a Days Inn must be operated . . . As the Statement of Undisputed Facts shows in exhaustive detail, the mandatory Days Inn System and DIA System Standards, which DIA can change at any time, address all aspects of the operation of a Days Inn, including: operating policies that "must be strictly observed by each property in the Days Inn System" and requirements for grooming and attire for hotel employees, employee uniforms, hours of operation of the front desk, services that must be provided to guests, the forms of payment the hotel must accept, guest safety and security, swimming pools, restaurants, free continental breakfasts, supplies and furnishings in guest rooms, the responsibilities of the hotel's general manager, employee relations, employee performance, housekeeping, and maintenance.[1]
Microtel Hotels	You operate the Microtel Hotel under the Hotel System. The Hotel System means the concept and system associated with the development and operation of Microtel Hotels. The Hotel System may be periodically modified by us. The Hotel System includes, among other things, (i) the trademarks, service marks, logos, slogans, trade dress, domain names and other source and origin designations that we or USFS periodically designate for use with the Hotel System (collectively, the "Proprietary Marks"); (ii) copyrightable materials that we periodically develop and designate for use with the Hotel System including prototypical architectural plans, designs, layouts, building designs, and a set of confidential constructions/operations manuals (the "Manual"); (iii) a central reservation system (the "CRS"); (iv) a unified platform property management system, management and personnel training, operational procedures and marketing, advertising and promotional programs; (v) all confidential information (see Item 14) and (vi) standards, procedures, policies, specifications and rules associated with the construction, operations, marketing, furnishings and equipment that we introduce and implement for the Hotel System which are described in the Manuals or in other written (electronic or otherwise) directives and which we may periodically modify. We designed the Hotel System for the operation of "super budget" and "hard budget" hotels, and we expect that each Microtel Hotel will comply with Hotel System standards to achieve a relatively uniform and standardized package of services and amenities that are offered to guests consistent with the economy budget sector of the hotel industry.[2]

(continued)

Table 6.7 (continued)

Hotel/motel brand	Excerpt from franchise agreement
Motel 6 Hotels	The terms, conditions, and obligations under which you operate the Motel are described in a franchise agreement that you and we sign before you begin operations (the "Franchise Agreement"). You must also sign a Software Agreement with Motel 6 OLP for the Software used in operating the Motel. Before signing a Franchise Agreement of the Software Agreement, you must sign and submit a franchise application (the "Application") to us. The Application, the Franchise Agreement, and the Software Agreement are referred to in Item 22 below, and copies of the documents are attached as exhibits to this disclosure document.
	To promote uniform Standards of operation under the System, we have prepared a set of confidential operating manuals, which may include more than one volume and periodic supplements (the "Manuals") and which contain mandatory and recommended procedures for operating your Motel.[3]
Omni Hotels	Each OMNI HOTEL operates pursuant to unique methods, systems and programs of operation (the "Method of Operation"). These relate to the establishment, development and operation of OMNI HOTELS that offer distinctive high quality hotel services. The characteristics of the Method of Operation include exceptional décor, design, layout and color scheme; exclusively designed signage, decoration, furnishings and materials; the Omni Hotels Reservation System; hospitality service procedures and techniques; operating procedures for cleanliness and maintenance; other confidential operating procedures; methods and techniques for inventory and cost controls, record keeping and reporting; personnel management and training, purchasing, marketing, sales promotion and advertising.[4]
Red Roof Inns	You will own and operate a Red Roof Inn or Red Roof Inn & Suites lodging facility. A Red Roof Inn lodging facility offers low cost accommodations to all sectors of the traveling public. A Red Roof Inn is generally located at places that attract both business and leisure travelers, such as major highway exit ramps, major intersections, airports, tourist destinations, and business centers. You will operate the business according to our business system and standards, and under the Red Roof Inn trademarks. You will use our prototype architectural plans and drawings in building a Red Roof Inn, or in renovating an existing building to be a Red Roof Inn. A typical Red Roof Inn does not offer full service and management intensive facilities or services, such as in-house restaurants or cocktail lounges, conference rooms,

room service, or banquet centers. However, to meet the needs of guests in certain markets, we offer a Red Roof Inn & Suites lodging facility with enhanced amenities, such as more spacious rooms with refrigerators and coffee makers, exercise facilities, or meeting rooms.[5]

---

1. Plaintiff United States' Memorandum in Support of Its Motion for Summary Judgment, *United States of America v. Days Inns of America, Inc.*, October 27, 1997.

2. Microtel Inns and Suites Franchising Inc.: Microtel Franchise Disclosure Document, March 28, 2008. Filed and accessed through the California franchising database, http://134.186.208.233/caleasi/pub/exsearch.htm.

3. Accor Franchising North America LLC: Motel 6 Franchise Disclosure Document, March 6, 2008. Filed and accessed through the California franchising database, http://134.186.208.233/caleasi/pub/exsearch.htm.

4. Omni Hotels Franchising Company LLC: Omni Hotels Franchise Disclosure Document, April 18, 2005. Filed and accessed through the California franchising database, http://134.186.208.233/caleasi/pub/exsearch.htm.

5. Red Roof Franchising LLC: Red Roof Inns Franchise Disclosure Document, October 1, 2008. Filed and accessed through the California franchising database, http://134.186.208.233/caleasi/pub/exsearch.htm.

ence" that will lead to repeat visits and the ability to maintain price premiums for the franchisor's brands.

Just as with fast foods, the detailed standards for hotel brands are central features of contracts with franchisees, treated with grave secrecy and enforced vigorously. However, because of the complexity of hotel/motel operations, franchising is increasingly accompanied by the hiring of management companies to oversee the operation of properties. In some cases, the brand explicitly requires potential owners to hire other organizations to undertake management activities as a means of ensuring that brand standards are maintained. Parent companies often require management companies to invest in the properties they manage, thereby making them partial "equity partners" and more closely aligning their interests with those of the brand holder.

May I Be of Service?

The competing needs of building brand equity, finding capital for expansion, and maintaining standards require brand operating companies to maintain a complicated balancing act. Creating mechanisms to achieve that balance gives rise to a complicated range of business arrangements that operate "under the hood." As shown in Figure 6.3, when a customer walks into a Courtyard by Marriott, Sofitel, or Doubletree Suites hotel, multiple organizations are responsible for creating the particular customer experience.

A Courtyard hotel could be managed by an independent operating company that is not at all affiliated with the brand. Marriott International could manage but not own the property: the owner may have asked the brand parent company to manage the property or, as a condition of the franchisor or the lender, the owner may have been required to make the brand parent company the manager.

The decision on which organizational form to use is based on balancing the core elements of fissuring: benefits arising from the brand versus benefits from shifting out employment to other entities. The lead enterprises in the hotel industry often choose to manage and sometimes own their premier, full-service hotels. Starwood Hotels and Resorts Worldwide Inc., for example, requires that Starwood manage all W hotels and St. Regis higher-end branded hotels.

Some parent companies have divisions or subsidiaries that act as brand operating companies. For example, Hilton Management Services manages

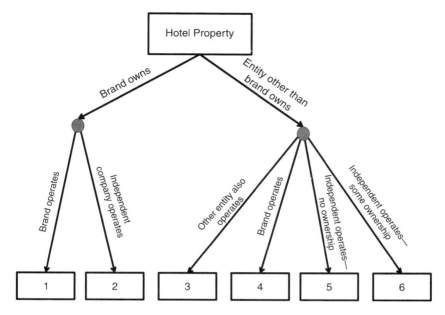

FIGURE 6.3. Branded hotel industry organization.

Hilton brands, and Hotel Management Group manages InterContinental brands. Under such an arrangement, a hotel property carrying one of the Hilton brands might be owned by a private equity firm but choose Hilton Management Services to manage the property. This might be particularly important for a premier Hilton property where concern over adherence to brand standards might be particularly important.

In contrast, an *independent operating company*—sometimes referred to as a management company or third-party management company—provides management and operating expertise to branded properties that are usually owned by an entity other than the brand parent company. The reduction in the number of parent company–owned hotels has shifted many properties into management contracts with independent operating companies. Between 1970 and 2006, the number of management contracts increased dramatically, from 22 to 4,370. A number of major companies have emerged in the national market, with the top ten companies managing 1,192 properties and over 200,000 hotel rooms.[59]

An independent operating company may therefore manage a branded franchised property owned by a real estate investment trust, private equity company, or local group of investors. It is also possible for an independent operating company itself to own or hold an ownership stake in some or all of the properties it manages. In fact, some brands require a partial investment by the operating company in order to increase the latter's commitment to the financial performance of the properties it manages.[60]

More often than not, the independent operating companies are operating hotels with many different brand affiliations and possibly belonging to multiple brand parent companies. This requires them to attend to the provisions of many different management agreements. While those agreements might be similar, it could be the case that the same operating company is more (or less) attentive to certain aspects of hotel management at some properties it manages than at others (as a result of differences in the contracts signed with brand parent companies).

The independent-operator, third-party management scenario (depicted as numbers 5 and 6 in Figure 6.3) is an increasingly common arrangement for several reasons. First, as owners and lending institutions have become more knowledgeable about the hospitality industry, they have become more concerned about the quality of property management where they have a stake. This may lead them to hire a management operating company while still ensuring investment in their ability to implement key brand standards. Second, operators want to expand market share in order to sustain earnings growth in excess of growth in demand, thereby requiring greater management expertise; brands are capturing a large share of contracts for first-class, full-service properties in prime locations, increasing the demand for sophisticated management services. Once again, how much ownership is required of the management company reflects the larger balancing of the fissured recipe.

One Tier More

But the multiple layering of the hospitality industry does not end with the brand or independent hotel management company. In many cases, those operating companies will contract out the staffing of the actual jobs—housekeeping, janitorial, food and beverage—to yet other companies. These may be local staffing businesses offering temporary employees for peak activities or, increasingly, large regional or national companies like Hospitality Staffing Solutions.

Major hotel staffing companies take on the complete set of human resource functions for particular types of jobs: they recruit, screen, and hire workers and then compensate, manage, promote, and terminate them if required. Companies promote their strength in taking on these functions for a workforce (particularly at the low end of pay scales) that might have high levels of turnover and limited experience in the hospitality industry—or in the labor market generally. In so doing, they remove the employment problem from the hands of property owners/franchisees or from the third-party management companies who assume the role of general manager with few employees of their own.

Staffing companies provide workers for multiple brands and properties in an area, usually through a tiered management structure of area managers in charge of building relationships with hotel brands and owners in a geographic area; area supervisors recruit workers and provide day-to-day supervision of workers in different locations.[61] Most employees provided by staffing companies work in the area of housekeeping (cleaning rooms), but these companies also provide janitorial and maintenance workers, waiters and waitresses, kitchen staff (dishwashers and food preparation workers), and laundry staff. Although staffing companies originally focused on providing temporary workers during peak demand periods (for example, at resort properties during holidays), they have gradually grown to provide staffing for entire functions for their clients.

Staffing companies also recognize the importance to their customers—whether property owners or brand or independent operating companies—of providing a workforce that adheres to brand standards. Selection, training, and supervision are guided by the particular standards of the brands and properties to which the staffing company is contracted. For example, Hospitality Staffing Solutions highlights its expertise in regard to its staffing of different functions:[62]

Room Attendants: We're proud to note our room attendants are consistently listed at the top of posted room inspection scores. Your guests will see a difference in sparkling clean rooms that are ready when they check in—a major factor in higher guest satisfaction scores and repeat stays.

Janitorial: Hospitality Staffing Solutions© Janitorial focuses on the typically difficult-to-staff and manage third-shift operation . . . [We] provide turnkey operations including all chemicals, supplies and equipment, as well as professional uniforms for each janitorial team member. Hospitality Staffing Solutions© will create standardized cleaning procedures to fit your property specifications . . . Associates are trained to specialize in the daily detailing of your kitchen operations.

Laundry: Hospitality Staffing Solutions© employees follow your procedures so your linens are handled properly. Area supervisors ensure we consistently meet your expectations.

The use of staffing companies to provide the workforce for different functions results in yet a further tier in employment at hotel properties. And there could be several staffing companies present at one property, operating under a common set of brand standards but each supervised and paid by different business entities (and seeking to meet their own bottom lines). As in other fissured workplaces, the commitment to adhering to quality standards from the lead businesses (the parent hotel brand) is usually accompanied by an effort to devolve responsibility for adherence to the workplace standards required by law to the outermost orbit of business.

Inhospitable Conditions?

Most workers in the hotel industry earn low wages. About 22% of workers in the leisure and hospitality industry earned at or below the minimum wage in 2011.[63] If one uses the common benchmark for low wages as those falling below two-thirds of the median wage (which equaled $11.61 per hour in 2011), about 55% of workers in the hotel/motel industry earned low wages in 2010. The 1.86 million workers employed in the industry comprised about 1.25% of total employment but accounted for 2.4% of all low-wage workers.[64] Almost three-quarters of those surveyed in a three-city survey of workers in 2009 had been paid off the clock at some point (that is, not compensated for some of the hours they worked) in the prior week, and about two-thirds had not received the overtime compensation to which they were entitled.[65]

The operations of hotels are buffeted by multiple incentives arising from the different businesses in orbit around the hotel brand, as depicted in Figure 6.3. This creates conditions where contradictory incentives are present in terms of assuring adherence to quality standards (brands); finding managerial expertise to operate properties (franchisees/investors); and seeking to expand

business operations by ratcheting down costs but not fully facing the consequences of those cost-cutting actions (operators).

The fissured structures that have emerged in hotels lead to significant problems in assuring compliance with basic labor standards such as overtime and
minimum wages. Table 6.8 presents information about Fair Labor Standards
Act (FLSA) violations for major hotel/motel chains during the period 2002–
2008, using four different measures of compliance. Among this group, only
31% of all investigated properties were in compliance with FLSA provisions.
Compliance rates ranged from a low of 18% (Quality) to a high of 58% (Marriott Hotels and Resorts). Average back wages (representing the difference
between wages received by workers and what they were entitled under the
law) owed per employee paid in violation of standards were $435. This also
ranged considerably across the chains, with much higher rates at Marriott
Hotels and Resorts and Holiday Inn branded properties, and relatively
lower back wages owed at Fairfield Inn (another brand owned by Marriott
International).

Compliance is further affected by the combination of parties that together
create fissured hotel workplaces. In particular, properties managed by the top
fifty independent hotel management companies violate the Fair Labor Standards Act at far higher rates than otherwise comparable hotel properties managed by franchise owners or brand operating companies.[66] Back wages were
about $2,500 higher in properties operated by one of the top fifty indepen-
dent companies versus comparable properties not managed by the top fifty.
Properties with a branded operating company serving as the manager tended
to have better relative compliance levels, in part reflecting closer alignment of
the brand with the management of the property.

All of this brings us back to the Hyatt story. Although the workers at all
three Hyatt properties in Boston were nonunion, the union for hotel workers,
UNITE HERE!, brought attention to the situation facing the fired workers
and orchestrated a public campaign against Hyatt. Daily protests in Boston,
coverage in local and national media outlets, and outreach to Massachusetts
political leaders kept the story in the public eye. Hyatt workers in Chicago
and some of the fired employees from Boston protested at the company headquarters. Three weeks after the firing, Governor Deval Patrick of Massachusetts encouraged state employees to boycott Hyatt hotels unless the company
reinstated the workers.

Table 6.8 Compliance among top hotel/motel chains: Investigations 2002–2008 (brand parent companies in parentheses)

U.S. brand	Number of investigations	Total employees paid in violation	Employees paid in violation per investigation	Back wages per employee paid in violation	Percentage in compliance
Holiday Inn Hotels & Resorts (InterContinental Hotels Group)	99	826	8.3	$602	26.2
Best Western (Best Western International)	183	1,009	5.5	$390	31.3
Hampton Inn/Hampton Inn & Suites (Hilton Hotels Corp.)	91	430	4.7	$395	32.9
Holiday Inn Express (InterContinental Hotels Group)	126	854	6.8	$318	20.6
Marriott Hotels & Resorts (Marriott International)	31	121	3.9	$768	58.0
Days Inn (Wyndham Hotel Group)	246	1,386	5.6	$498	22.7
Comfort Inn (Choice Hotels International)	166	1,027	6.2	$415	23.4
Super 8 (Wyndham Hotel Group)	187	795	4.3	$480	24.5
Hilton (Hilton Hotels Corp.)	23	284	12.3	$427	47.8
Motel 6 (Accor)	28	92	3.3	$205	35.7
Quality (Choice Hotels International)	83	692	8.3	$364	18.0
Ramada (Wyndham Hotel Group)	93	800	8.6	$457	23.6
Econo Lodge (Choice Hotels International)	74	352	4.8	$458	29.7
Fairfield Inn (Marriott International)	21	93	4.4	$313	38.0

Source: Violations of the Fair Labor Standards Act for major hotel/motel chains during the period 2002–2008, based on author analysis of closed investigation data from the U.S. Department of Labor, Wage and Hour Division.

In late September 2009, Hyatt offered the ninety-eight fired employees health coverage through the following March and full-time positions with United Service Companies (a Chicago-based staffing organization that the hotel chain used for contract labor) through the end of 2010 at wages comparable to the ones they had lost.[67] Notably, however, Hyatt continued with its agreement to use Hospitality Staffing Solutions for staffing the positions. Despite the unfavorable publicity over its role at Hyatt, the staffing company's Boston area market continued to blossom, and in early 2013, Hospitality Staffing Solutions advertised for a number of entry-level managerial positions for the area.[68]

Franchising and the Workplace: Having It Both Ways, Again

Fast food represents franchising at its most developed: a sophisticated system to align the interests of major brands with individual owners in order to allow both parties to benefit from a branding core competency. Yet tensions in incentives have repercussions on the cost side of the ledger. The result is decidedly different profiles in compliance with workplace laws like minimum wage and overtime between the lead company's own outlets and those run by franchisees.

Franchising in the janitorial services industry is more pernicious. The presence of a tier of franchised janitorial service providers that in many markets cannot be financially viable without cutting corners. Wide-scale noncompliance with labor standards results. Franchising in the hotel/motel industry takes a more complicated form. Because of the significant capital investment in the industry, investors, brands, and managers all have a stake in the management of hotel properties. This has given rise to a complicated mix of organizations with hands-on roles in day-to-day hotel operations. A given property may have four or more businesses with some impact on how work is organized, managed, supervised, and compensated. This complexity leads to downward pressure on wages and benefits (the multiple margins problem found in subcontracting), coordination diseconomies, and contradictory incentives. For the workforce, this can mean at best confusion over who is minding the store and at worst significant violations of workplace labor standards.[69]

Many of the attributes of franchising have beneficial aspects for consumers and investors. A well-structured franchise agreement creates incentives for the owner to provide service and achieve standards that customers expect and from which they benefit. A well-structured franchise agreement solves some of the problems arising from managing large and geographically dispersed operations. And franchising brings to the table new sources of investment capital—such as individual entrepreneurs who wish to start new businesses but may not be ready to create new brands or business models—that may benefit entrepreneurs, franchisors, and their customers.

But franchising also creates social costs, arising from incentives that leave franchisees less committed to compliance than their franchisors; from the pernicious use of the model in the janitorial sector; or from the sheer complexity of the crosswinds of incentives created in its application to the hotel industry. Our workplace laws fail to recognize the complexities created by franchising: as will be seen in Chapter 8, workplace statutes and legal interpretations of them usually hold the franchisor harmless for the actions of franchisees when it comes to employees, even as franchise and commercial law protect the franchisor's right to impose standards on every other aspect of business decision. This creates the fundamental dilemma of the fissured workplace by allowing lead companies (in this case franchisors) to have it both ways: creating, monitoring, and enforcing standards central to business strategy while at the same time ducking responsibility for the social consequences of those policies when it comes to the workplace.

Any effort to improve labor standards compliance in franchised industries must recognize that organizational form's role in creating fissured workplaces. Traditional approaches to enforcement—focusing on the individual enterprise—may bring to light widespread violations of minimum wages, overtime pay, and off-the-clock work. But if not wedded to a larger strategy that attempts to change the forces that drive this behavior, enforcement will be effective only at the margin.

Supply Chains and the
Fissured Workplace

Manufacturing supply chains are composed of the network of businesses companies draw on for the components used in making products. Retail supply chains are composed of the broad network of manufacturers that sell their products through retailers. Strictly speaking, the firms making up a supply chain relate through market transactions: suppliers provide parts, assemblies, and inputs to their customers: retailers or manufacturers. Characterized in this way, supply chains are a very old phenomenon: most producers rely on purchases of inputs from other companies. And, going back to the Phoenicians, these supply relationships often existed internationally as well as within national borders.

What has changed is the degree to which lead companies have shed internal pieces of the production process to other companies and, for reasons described in Chapter 3, the extent to which those companies have increased the degree they specify, monitor, coordinate, and choreograph the activities of suppliers in the network. In manufacturing, the relationship is much closer than arm's-length market transactions because it is often composed of work formerly done within corporate boundaries: this is outsourcing (moving jobs outside the company, but to domestic sources of supply) and offshoring (moving jobs outside the company to firms providing the service in other countries).

Even where work has traditionally been done by other suppliers, the need for greater coordination has increased as products have become more complex, quality standards more demanding, time-to-market demands tighter, and management of inventories more critical. In retailing, information technologies have also transformed arm's-length supplier relationships, allowing retailers to manage an ever-growing scope of products while substantially reducing their exposure to inventory risk.

Consequently, supply chain management results in the pressures that create fissured workplaces and their often deleterious impacts on the people working within them. This chapter focuses on supply chains as a form of fissured employment. The chapter starts by looking at how the core of supply chain operations—logistics—has been changed in distribution centers. Though coordination represents a highly valued core competency for lead businesses in both manufacturing and retail industries, the actual work is done through complex webs of contracted work. The chapter then turns to the intersection of fissured employment and the phenomena of outsourcing and offshoring and examines their close relationship and implications for employment domestically and internationally.

Fissuring Squared in the Logistics Industry

Lean manufacturing is a core production strategy famously developed for the auto industry by Toyota and then widely diffused across the sector.[1] Its objective is to reduce the amount of in-process and final inventory in a production system, carefully matching real-time demand for final products with the quantity of goods moving through the manufacturing and assembly process. In a complex manufacturing system like auto production, this requires high levels of coordination at each step in the process, careful management of capital and labor, attention to quality and factors that affect throughput, and an overhaul of management support systems, from accounting, to inventory management, to compensation.

It also requires a different way of handling logistics—the movement of goods—within a manufacturer, between the manufacturer and its suppliers, and between the manufacturer and the end retailer of goods. As lean manufacturing spread to industries beyond the autos and into the retail sector, the importance of logistics as part of competitive strategy rose as well.

The change is best seen in the evolving activities in a manufacturer's warehouse. If you pay little attention to in-process and final inventory, large stocks of parts accumulate at each stage and in final production. A warehouse is simply the place where you store that inventory—and where that inventory can sit for long periods of time. Warehousing requires tracking and managing where things have been left (perhaps a bit more systematically than in a typical person's basement). It does not require a lot of attention to how quickly those things can be accessed and moved once needed.

In the modern age of lean manufacturing, the warehouse becomes a distribution center—a place where intermediate or final products are efficiently tracked, processed, and moved. In one type of distribution center, a modern cross-docking facility (critical to both manufacturing and retailing), the layout reveals its central role as a means to move, not store, goods. Typically, cross-docking facilities have a rectangular footprint, with one long side devoted to incoming trucks (from suppliers) and the opposite long side to outgoing trucks, destined either for the final assembly facilities or for retail outlets. Between the two walls is a capital-intensive maze of automated conveyance systems, governed by an incoming flow of data regarding incoming shipments (types, quantities, and costs) and outgoing destinations.[2]

For logistics providers—UPS, Federal Express, DHL—and for companies with logistics central to their function—retailers like Walmart, Target, Safeway, and Kroger—operating logistics is the core competency to be nurtured, perfected, and safeguarded. But fissuring has come to logistics. It has popped up in a variety of ways.

Perhaps best known is the case of FedEx. FedEx has long treated drivers servicing its routes as independent contractors.[3] Drivers are paid by the delivery, based on a schedule from the FedEx package terminal where they receive a listing of packages each day. They are given a window of time for drop-offs and can be docked if packages arrive outside of it or if the company receives complaints from customers. As an independent contractor, the driver is required to purchase a truck (as specified by FedEx) that bears the company logo. In addition to financing the vehicle, the driver must pay all expenses (gas, insurance, maintenance). A driver's income is therefore based on the difference between the fees paid per delivery and the costs incurred for servicing the route, rather than on a salary or hourly rate.

As independent contractors, drivers are not covered by overtime or other labor standards or protections against discrimination, health and safety laws, or provisions that would allow them to take leave to care for a sick child or family member. Contributions for Social Security and Medicare taxes fall entirely on the driver, and because drivers are in business for themselves, they are not eligible for unemployment insurance or workers' compensation.

Not surprisingly, FedEx has been the target of state litigation for misclassification of workers by state tax and workplace authorities. Independent contracting status was also the subject of a major IRS audit of FedEx. But in most cases to date, the FedEx position has been upheld: FedEx, as a branded, logistics juggernaut for which time to delivery is central to customer value, need not directly employ the workforce central to that mission.

FedEx is not alone in its use of fissured workplace arrangements for logistics, the centerpiece of modern supply chains. More and more distribution centers are adopting an organizational form where third-party management has been married to subcontracting. Since supply chain management has elements that create many of the preconditions of the fissured workplace, the increasing use of subcontracting and temporary staffing companies within logistics can be considered fissuring on top of fissuring—fissuring squared.

Lean Retailing and the Modern Distribution Center

Like lean manufacturing, lean retailing takes advantage of information technologies, automation, industry standards, and management innovations to align orders from suppliers more closely with what consumers are buying in the store (rather than what purchasing agents, months in advance, think consumers might buy). By using sales information collected through millions of scans of bar-coded labels, retailers reduce their need to stockpile large inventories of products, thereby reducing their risks of stock-outs, markdowns, and inventory carrying costs. The companies that have adopted lean retailing principles now dominate major retail segments, from mass merchants like Walmart and Target to department stores like Macy's.

Core competencies of a modern retailer depend on a combination of traditional practices with the benefits arising from lean retailing. Like traditional retailers, companies using lean retailing must provide their customers with a changing variety of products that lure them into the store. But as lean retailers, they do so while minimizing the inventory they need to hold to service that demand. In contrast to the infrequent, large bulk shipments between suppliers and retailers that characterized traditional retailing, lean retailers require frequent shipments made on the basis of ongoing replenishment orders. These orders are made based on real-time sales information collected at the retailers' registers via bar-code scanning. SKU-level sales data are then aggregated centrally and used to generate orders to suppliers, usually on a weekly basis for each store.

Lean retailing changes the relationship between a retailer and its supply base. Suppliers must replenish orders in three days or sometimes less. Retailers like Saks Fifth Avenue create standards that require frequent replenishment and demand that shipments meet standards concerning delivery times, order completeness, and accuracy.[4] Any disruptions to the weekly replenishment of retail orders by apparel suppliers constitute a major problem for retailers. Not surprisingly, the implementation of standards by suppliers to companies like Saks is carefully monitored (also in real time). And failure to adhere to them can lead to substantial penalties or, even worse, result in canceled orders or cutting off the supplier altogether.

Walmart: Shedding Distribution?

Walmart was a pioneer in lean retailing. More than any retailer of its era, it discovered the importance of managing inventory inside and outside its corporate walls. Its success at using real-time customer information collected at the register, information systems on the status of inventory and orders, automated distribution centers, and sophisticated logistics relations with its customers was (and is) central to its ability to lower the costs of providing products to customers.

But just as hotels gradually turned even core functions over to others, Walmart has begun to do so with logistics. This shift in policy is reflected in the case of distribution centers operating in Mira Loma, California, in the so-called Inland Empire region of Southern California.

Schneider Logistics, headquartered in Green Bay, Wisconsin, provides a wide variety of logistics and transportation services to its customers.[5] Its parent company, Schneider National, was one of the first trucking companies to invest in two-way satellite communications systems for its trucks and to use electronic data interchange (EDI) to handle transactions in the mid-1980s. This coincided with the adoption of similar technologies in retailing (by Walmart and others) to transform how those companies handled information and coordinated logistics.[6]

Schneider Logistics was launched in 1993 to focus on the rapidly growing business of handling the flow of products and materials in the manufacturing and retail sectors, winning a contract to provide General Motors with logistics support for its part suppliers in 1994.[7] It used its access to its own network of trucks, trailers, and drivers, major intermodal facilities and equipment, and sophisticated communication systems. Its core competency, which makes it attractive to customers like Walmart, is its expertise in handling imported goods arriving in shipping containers from ports and processing those goods so that they can be efficiently shipped to retail stores.[8]

With the rapid growth in goods arriving from offshore in the 1990s, retailers like Walmart needed to find efficient means to process, transport from docks, and unload that stock from shipping containers used for ocean transportation, and then sort, record, repack, and load those goods for transportation to regional distribution centers or directly to stores. The work of unloading and processing goods from containers (called "lumping") is more labor-intensive than the typical operations in distribution centers. Schneider Logistics directly employs workers in its distribution centers to do lumping. But it also uses subcontractors—sometimes several layers of them—who often employ temporary workers to undertake these operations. Temp employees working for subcontractors are used to handle increased volumes during peak retailing periods (particularly the run-up to the holiday season). But they have also become a growing share of the main workforce in these operations, representing up to a third of the workforce in nonpeak times and much more in peak periods.

As with cell towers, discussed in Chapter 5, the agreements between Schneider as logistics service provider and subcontractors are very informative about the larger fissured subcontracting structure in play. In the case of the Mira Loma facility servicing Walmart, Schneider contracted with three companies: Premier Warehousing Ventures LLC (PWV), Rogers-Premier Unloading Services, and Impact Logistics Inc. The agreement between Schneider and PWV is typical. In its contract, Schneider explicitly specifies that PWV will provide services for Schneider's Walmart account. The contract states that while Schneider operates warehousing and transloading facilities, the company "desires to concentrate its efforts and expertise on the internal warehouse operations while contracting for trailer loading services."[9] The contract makes clear that PWV will be compensated on the basis of the number of trucks loaded, not on an hourly basis or on the basis of the number of workers used to achieve output targets. It also makes clear that the relationship between the two organizations is a principal/vendor one, where "PWV will, at all times, remain the sole and exclusive . . . employer of any personnel utilized in providing the Services and the Principal of any subcontractor it may elect to utilize."[10] This and other provisions regarding indemnification attempt to establish market-relation distance between the parties.

However, other features of the agreement imply a fuzzier boundary between the responsibilities of the two companies. Section 2 describes in considerable detail the standards to which Schneider holds PWV and the mechanisms it will use to monitor compliance with them. Section 2.06, for example, describes a variety of audit-based performance metrics that PWV will periodically provide to Schneider (at no cost to the latter) regarding average number of cases loaded per hour; number of trailers loaded per week; trailer loading accuracy (a critical dimension for Walmart); and average cubic meters packed in trailers per week. These measures serve as the basis of compensation and for ongoing evaluation of PWV's performance as a contractor. Although PWV is required to provide on-site management of its workers, the agreement also gives Schneider audit rights for performance with the provisions of the contract and requires that PWV rectify any problems within thirty days. It also makes PWV liable for any damages to merchandise in the process of handling it.

The blurred lines of actual employment between Schneider and PWV become evident in section 2.12. The contract notes that Schneider (referred to as SLTD)

> will notify PWV of any problems regarding the Personnel. In the event SLTD is dissatisfied with the performance or conduct of any Personnel, SLTD may request PWV to remove such person from the premises and from their assignment with SLTD immediately. SLTD will not be responsible for the payment of any amounts with respect to such Personnel so removed for that day's assignment or any future assignment of that specific Personnel unless approved in advance by SLTD.[11]

Schneider also reserves the right to audit the immigration status of any of PWV's workforce, in conformance with Walmart's concern that all contractors working for them be in compliance. But the agreement states (in capital letters) that "PWV further acknowledges that SLTD's said audit is in no way intended to waive or release PWV's I-9 compliance obligations . . . or alter the independent contractor relationship between the parties."[12]

Subcontracting and the Workforce: A Refrain

Subcontractors like PWV receive payment on the basis of truckloads completed (or on a similar basis for other output-based metrics). But labor subcontractors must pay their workforce for achieving those output goals. Prior to 2006, subcontractors at the Mira Loma facility paid workers on an hourly basis. Beginning in 2006, however, a new pay system and related policies were created at PWV and Impact that compensated workers on a piece rate, based on the number of trucks loaded or unloaded by the workforce.[13] The formula for loading was a complicated one that allegedly adjusted for both individual and group effort. Like the method Schneider used to compensate its subcontractors, the piece-rate system did not pay for hours worked, but for work completed. A change in scheduling policy coincided with the shift in pay policy, adjusting hours from a standard eight-hour, five-day weekly schedule to four ten-hour-per-day shifts.[14] Separate policies required workers to be present at the distribution center several hours before work commenced (without compensation) in order to reduce potential interruptions from not having enough people ready to load or unload trucks. The new policies also made it difficult for workers to take legally mandated breaks.

In October 2011 the Mira Loma facilities were inspected by the California Labor Department. The company's murky and opaque payroll records and pay stubs associated with the compensation system and the inability of PWV and Impact to produce records verifying hours for workers violated state record-keeping standards. As a consequence, the state levied substantial penalties on Impact ($499,000 for failure to provide itemized wage statements for record-keeping violations) and PWV ($616,250 for similar and related record-keeping violations).[15] At the same time, a group of workers filed a class action suit against Schneider and the three subcontractors for back wages.

However, the worker complaints leading to the October 2011 investigation and penalties did not end the saga. Four days after the investigation, workers who met with investigators and subsequently filed a complaint for lost wages were told not to come to work (despite the fact that the investigation occurred in October, during the peak season for the facility).[16] This led to a series of court rulings that directly addressed the question of the respective roles of Schneider and its subcontractors at the facility. I return to the rulings in this case in Chapter 8.

The number of workers in the logistics industry rose from 474,200 in 1998 to 672,800 in 2008 and is projected to reach 775,700 by 2018, an annual growth rate 2.5 times faster than the overall growth rate in employment for the economy as a whole.[17] The practice of retailers hiring third-party managers to operate distribution facilities who in turn draw on temporary agencies for staffing has spread quickly since 2008 and has been reported across the country.[18]

Implausible Deniability?

Walmart has responded to inquiries about the violations in Mira Loma and other facilities handling the company's local distribution center needs by pointing out that none of the workers involved were employees of the company.[19] With respect to health and safety standards, it cites its codes of conduct for suppliers that, if violated, would lead to repercussions for those contractors.[20] Before the most recent injunctions filed against Schneider Logistics, in 2012, that company similarly cited the fact that labor contractors working within its facilities were "separate corporate entities. The only legal avenue which Schneider has to enforce their compliance would be to terminate the contract with these vendors. We have no plans to terminate the contracts with our vendors; our expectation is that they will comply with all applicable statutes, regulations and orders."[21]

As with the subcontracting cases discussed in Chapter 5, ceding authority to multiple organizations creates complexity, so that enforcement of important workplace policies falls through the cracks—notably safety practices in the case of AT&T and other cell phone carriers, immigration policies for Hershey, and basic labor standards in the Walmart/Schneider case. It also illustrates how these changes alter the wage-setting environment, shifting it ever outward and into increasingly competitive environments, often into labor markets characterized by workers with limited opportunities, fear of job loss, and sometimes precarious immigration status.

Supply Chains, Outsourcing, and Offshoring

Supply chain strategy and management became a major topic in business schools in the 1990s. And for good reason: more and more industries reassessed how products could be made as a result of new information technologies, the falling cost of computers, adoption of common communication standards, improvements in international logistics, and new sources of global manufacturing. Underlying supply chain strategies is the decision whether to build things inside or outside corporate boundaries.

Outsourcing goods—deciding to purchase parts or subassemblies from other companies rather than producing them internally—was the first step in the process. Manufacturing industries core to the U.S. economy—notably automobiles—moved aggressively in this direction, first outsourcing a growing percentage of parts and later entire subassemblies to other companies. The growth of global manufacturing capacity in many industries and the ever-falling cost of transportation transformed outsourcing to offshoring—seeking suppliers for parts and assemblies that had been outsourced to non-U.S. producers. The same technologic and information systems that made outsourcing possible, combined with the reduction of many international trade restrictions, such as quotas and tariffs, enabled offshoring to expand rapidly as a source of intermediate products for manufacturers or as a source for more and more final products for retailers.[22] In more recent years, digital technologies and the growth of higher-level skills in India, China, and elsewhere led to similar offshoring in service industries—in areas ranging from call centers to software engineering.

Outsourcing and offshoring have also been a growing topic of popular debate in the past decade and featured prominently in the presidential campaign of 2012. Offshoring has drawn particular attention because of its perceived impacts on wages and employment of U.S. workers directly affected by it. A *New York Times* report in 2012 found that 86% of those surveyed said buying products in the United States was "very or somewhat important to them," and that 58% believed that "a lot" of unemployment is caused by products sold by U.S. companies being manufactured abroad.[23]

Outsourcing and offshoring share a fundamental characteristic with other organizational forms that create fissured workplaces: they entail a lead company focusing on a core area of competency and shedding activities (manufacturing and assembly) to other businesses, all the while ensuring that technical, quality, and delivery standards are rigorously adhered to by those subordinate suppliers. Successful global manufacturers accomplish this through supply chain management, which comprises the planning, coordination, and control of the activities of that network of suppliers through the creation and implementation of standards.

Offshoring, Trade, and the Impact on Workers

The economic literature on the consequences of trade between nations goes back to David Ricardo's work on comparative advantage in the early 1800s. The focus of discussion has been trade in final goods.[24] But offshoring typically involves the use of outside suppliers to provide intermediate products—

arising from what trade economist Rob Feenstra calls the "disintegration of production." The changing nature of trade—as well as the growing importance of trade in intermediate goods—is illustrated by looking at U.S. imports and exports with respect to their end use over time. Table 7.1 charts the share of U.S. exports and imports by end use from 1925 to 2010.[25]

The destination of U.S. imports and exports in terms of end use has changed dramatically since 1925. Whereas the vast majority of imported goods were in either agriculture or raw materials in the early part of the twentieth century (over 90% in 1925), in the past few decades they have become far more dominated by capital goods (those used in the production of other manufactured products) or consumer goods. The share of imports of consumer goods rose rapidly from the 1960s to the 1980s and doubled from 16% of imports in 1965 to 32% by 2010. But the share of capital goods increased even more rapidly, from 7% to 30% over the same period.[26]

Modern supply chains and the offshoring practices related to them play out on an international stage. The question about who gains and who loses from supply chains therefore begs the more fundamental question of the gains from trade. To the extent that offshoring is simply a specific case of trade between two nations, X and Y, with different comparative advantages, traditional economics argues that both nations benefit from it. If country X can produce a good (or subassembly) at lower cost than country Y, the national economy of Y benefits from letting that work go to country X, thereby freeing country Y's resources for more productive uses.[27]

Many questions arise, however, in the trade literature on the gains from trade where there are other imperfections in product or capital markets. In addition, Ricardo's ideas on gains from trade were built around natural endowments (climate, access to raw materials) conveying comparative advantages to different nations. Two countries producing products where they could translate those endowments into lower costs would benefit from exchanges between them. The situation becomes more complicated if each party can create an advantage through volitional policy (for example, educating its workforce; investing in research and development; devoting significant national resources to developing comparative advantage in an industry), although the overall benefits from trade between those with higher and lower productivity arising from those policies still hold.

Several articles by eminent economists rekindled the debate on the gains from trade. In 2004 the Nobel laureate Paul Samuelson examined in an essay

Table 7.1 Share of U.S. imports and exports by end use categories (percentage)

	1925	1950	1965	1980	1990	2000	2007	2010
Imports								
Foods, feeds, beverages	21.9	30.0	19.1	11.3	5.0	4.4	5.3	6.1
Industrial supplies and materials[a]	68.2	62.4	53.3	31.3	18.2	16.1	17.7	16.6
Capital goods (except autos)	0.4	1.3	7.1	19.0	33.6	33.4	29.0	30.0
Consumer goods (except autos)	9.4	6.1	16.0	21.5	24.3	27.1	31.0	32.3
Automotive vehicles, parts, and engines	0.02	0.3	4.5	16.9	18.8	18.9	16.9	15.0
Exports								
Foods, feeds, beverages	18.7	15.5	19.2	16.9	9.2	6.5	7.8	9.4
Industrial supplies and materials[a]	59.8	45.5	34.8	32.2	25.6	21.8	25.6	27.5
Capital goods (except autos)	8.7	22.4	31.4	35.0	42.4	48.6	41.7	38.9
Consumer goods (except autos)	6.0	8.9	7.0	7.8	11.7	12.3	13.6	14.4
Automotive vehicles, parts, and engines	6.8	7.8	7.5	8.1	11.2	10.9	11.3	9.8

Sources: Estimates for 1925–1990 from Feenstra (1998, table 3, p. 37). Estimates for 2000, 2007, and 2010 based on data from U.S. Census Bureau, *US International Trade in Goods and Services, Annual Revisions*, table 6, "Exports of Goods by End-Use Category and Commodity"; and table 7, "Imports of Goods by End-Use Category and Commodity" (2000, 2007, and 2010).

a. Following Feenstra, the following petroleum categories are excluded from import and export totals for "Industrial supplies and materials": crude oil; petroleum products other; gas—natural; fuel oil; natural gas liquids (export); liquified petroleum gases (import).

late in his life situations where an increase in the productivity of a trading partner reduces its partner's gains from trade relative to the status quo. Samuelson modeled a situation where one country (for example, China) rapidly creates new comparative advantage in a good that its trading partner (for example, the United States) historically had specialized in producing. The ability of the first country to rapidly expand supply of the product results in falling export prices for the second country, thereby worsening the latter's terms of trade. The gains from trade between the two countries are still positive for the second country, but diminished from the period prior to the first country "catching up" to the second.[28]

Studies of the impact of offshoring on manufacturing jobs a decade ago found evidence of positive associations between rising import shares and decreasing employment, but that overall effect was relatively small. Skill-biased technologic change, where new technologies lead to displacement of low-skilled jobs by those demanding higher skills, represented a far larger factor in explaining employment declines.[29] Estimates of service offshoring similarly indicate that the effects have so far been small when compared to the overall size of the labor market. But for those service activities that are vulnerable to outsourcing because they require provision of what the economist Alan Blinder calls "impersonally delivered services," the opportunities for future movement are significant, spanning skill levels from low-skill work like scanning books and newspapers to high-skill work such as architecture and financial analysis, and sectors from parts of health care to financial services.[30]

Even fervent adherents of the classic gains from trade view accept that there may be deleterious distributional impacts from offshoring: the economy can benefit overall, even though certain groups are adversely affected (sometimes severely) by it in the form of lost jobs and earnings. Offshoring also prompts questions about the capacity of the economy to move people from those jobs most affected by it into more productive, higher-skilled jobs so that the gains from trade can hopefully help in part those most likely to be hurt by offshoring.[31]

Apple, Foxconn, and the Global Electronics Supply Chain

Another way to look at the effects of offshoring on the workplace is to focus on the decisions underlying globalization of supply chains. The decisions leading to the offshoring of parts of production arise from balancing the benefits and costs of doing work inside versus outside firm boundaries, similar to other organizational design choices that result in fissuring.[32] Offshored activities are those where the benefits of finding outside suppliers capable of providing subassemblies at lower cost outweigh the benefits of keeping those activities inside the organization in order to preserve competitive advantage or areas of core competency (for example, product design) or the difficulties of coordinating production through arm's-length relationships.

In some instances, this balancing act means that components produced abroad by other companies are brought to the United States to be assembled closer to the final market, a practice that characterizes automobile production.[33] Alternatively, balancing the benefits and costs of offshoring may compel companies to shed virtually the entire production process to other businesses, with the United States serving as the anchor of product development, research, marketing, and retail distribution, as has become the rule in the apparel and electronics industries.

The balancing of inside versus outside work has also moved into nonmanufacturing sectors. This is reflected in the decision by financial services companies, airlines, and other businesses with significant customer service needs to offshore these "impersonally delivered services" to other countries, as has famously happened with call center work.[34] But nothing better portrays the tensions inherent in outsourcing strategies than the global electronics industry and its most famous (and valuable) company.

On February 24, 2012, Apple became the world's largest publicly held company when its stock price hit $526.29, giving it a market capitalization of $487.1 billion.[35] Its role in the U.S. economy was compared to that of General Motors in the mid-1950s when its market share stood at 54% percent and it produced its 50 millionth car. At that time, Charles Erwin Wilson, the former CEO of GM, famously answered a question about personal conflicts of interest during his confirmation hearings to become President Eisenhower's secretary of defense by saying that "for years I thought what was good for the country was good for General Motors and vice versa."[36]

Despite their common achievements, the GM of the 1950s and the Apple of 2012 were fundamentally different kinds of organizations. Design, engineering, marketing, manufacturing, and assembly were intrinsic to what General Motors did throughout its heyday in the post–World War II period. The breadth of its operational scope was reflected in the number of people it directly employed. At its manufacturing peak in 1979, General Motors directly employed 618,365 workers in the United States alone, making it the largest private employer at that time.[37]

Apple's core competency rests on product development and design of an ever-changing array of digital products. It is also a marketing and retail juggernaut. Apple directly employs designers, engineers, and marketing professionals central to its product development strategy. It is not, however, a manufacturer. When Apple achieved its market capitalization peak, it directly employed 43,000 workers in the United States (30,000 of them retail workers employed in Apple Stores) and an additional 20,000 worldwide. This represents a very small number given its market value (by comparison, Walmart employed about 2.2 million people worldwide in the same year). But the scale of direct employment masks how many people are globally engaged in the production of Apple products: in 2012, the company depended on 730,000 workers in global supply chains to manufacture its wide variety of digital gadgets.[38]

In the 1970s and 1980s, U.S. companies in the global electronics sector (IBM, Hewlett Packard) and Japanese producers (Sharp, Hitachi, Sony) were vertically integrated manufacturers, capitalizing on their competencies in research and development, product introduction, and scale economies. But in the 1990s, scale economies became less central as design innovation and technological innovations allowed the modularization of the components making up electronic products like personal computers. A global base of suppliers emerged, facilitated by national development strategies in countries like Singapore, Taiwan, and the People's Republic of China. Falling costs of transportation and coordination further facilitated the disintegration of vertically integrated manufacturers.[39]

Apple's reliance on an international supply chain is therefore not unique to the industry. Hewlett Packard (HP) sold over 64 million personal computers in 2011, all of them produced by an international supply chain of companies. It directly employed a far larger number of people than Apple—some 325,000 worldwide. But it also relied on an international network of 1,000 suppliers located in 1,200 locations. The major subset of suppliers of this group, representing about 90 companies, employed over 260,000 workers.[40] Other major electronics companies, including IBM, Dell, Cisco, and chipmakers like Intel, similarly draw upon a broad and dispersed supply base.[41]

The lead companies in the global electronics business now rely on a small number of major suppliers to act as the spine of their supplier networks. They do so for good reason given the scale of production and assembly that must flow through the system. One of the largest suppliers is Foxconn, a Taiwanese-based electronics manufacturer that employs a staggering 1.2 million Chinese workers in its plants and assembles an estimated 40% of smartphones, computers, and other electronic devices sold in the world.[42] In addition to Foxconn, contract companies like Flextronics, Jabil Circuit, Celestica, and Sanmina-SCI have grown in scale and scope and represent manufacturing powerhouses on their own (albeit unknown to most computer purchasers). Negotiations between these contract manufacturers and leading companies like Apple and HP are not the same as the arm's-length, commoditized relationships that characterize dealings with smaller suppliers.

Even so, profitability remains at the forefront of the supply chain: according to Locke et al., the five most profitable electronics firms (HP, IBM, Apple, Dell, and Cisco) took in cumulative revenues of $350 billion in 2009, earning $122 billion in gross profits from them (or about 35% profits as a percentage of revenue). The top five contract manufacturers in terms of total profitability (listed above) received about $116 billion in revenues and earned gross profits of about $4.4 billion over the same period (or about 3.8%).[43] As happens in multitiered organizational forms documented throughout Part II, as businesses compete in tiers further and further away from the lead companies, margins become thinner as products become more standardized and competition becomes more intense.

Consequences and Having It Both Ways

Despite its size and scope of production, Foxconn has placed unrelenting pressure on lowering its labor costs. The company became notorious for the consequences of its human resource practices, in particular the long work hours it required, the relentless pace of work, serious health and safety problems, and its low wages and lack of overtime pay despite the formal requirements of Chinese labor law. In 2010 stories of numerous worker suicides at Foxconn plants became widely reported. Advocacy organizations undertaking monitoring inside China, such as China Labor Watch and SACOM, documented the pressures and poor conditions facing employees at the company in a series of reports.[44]

In 2012, following a yearlong investigation, *New York Times* reporters David Barboza, Keith Bradsher, and Charles Duhigg published several articles detailing the problems facing workers at Foxconn facilities. The stories, part of a larger series of articles by the three on Apple Computer, documented accidents and serious safety problems. These included two explosions at factories producing iPads that killed four people and injured seventy-seven as well as serious chemical exposures of workers to solvents used to clean iPhone screens. In addition, they documented routine use of excessive overtime and the employment of underage workers, in both cases violating Chinese labor laws and standards (as well as codes of conduct promulgated by Apple for its suppliers).[45]

The mounting public pressure led Apple to join the Fair Labor Association, one of the largest nonprofit labor monitoring groups in the world. The Fair Labor Association conducted audits of Foxconn facilities and issued a report in February 2012. The report confirmed the continuing existence of problems documented by worker advocates and the *New York Times* reporters, including student interns working night shifts and ongoing safety problems that "exposed potentially hundreds of thousands of workers to at least 43 violations of Chinese law and regulation."

In March 2012, Auret van Heerden, the head of the Fair Labor Standards Association, met with Terry Gou, founder and chairman of Foxconn, Jeff Williams, Apple's senior vice president of operations, and other Foxconn senior executives regarding the results of the audit. Gou reportedly turned to his top executives during the meeting and shouted, "This is a disgrace! . . . The world is watching! . . . We are going to fix this, right here!"[46] Subsequently, Foxconn agreed to wide-scale reforms of its policies, including reductions in work hours, major increases in wage rates (amounting to 50% raises for many workers), new policies on health and safety, and reform of practices and conditions on the company's vast assembly lines. Apple also agreed to major changes to its monitoring policies, including tripling the number of people in its social responsibility unit in charge of implementing its monitoring program and recruiting prominent former Apple executives to head up the renewed efforts.

Public scrutiny and the contradiction between Steve Jobs's fabled attention to minute product detail juxtaposed with wide-ranging failure to adhere to labor standards, provoked Apple to recognize that it could no longer "have it both ways" in terms of embracing its attention to design detail while claiming little knowledge of the working conditions surrounding production. Other companies in the sector—notably HP—have similarly accepted greater responsibility to ensure adherence to labor and environmental standards among their principal suppliers, with notable success.[47]

But two tragedies in Bangladesh reemphasized the fragility of such monitoring arrangements in the presence of the competitive pressures placed on extended supply chains. In late 2012, a factory fire at Tazreen Fashions, a large Bangladeshi apparel company, killed 112 workers. Conditions that resulted in the deaths had parallels with the infamous Triangle Shirtwaist fire of 1911 in New York City: locked fire exits, supervisors demanding that workers return to their stations in the face of alarms, and people jumping to their deaths from a burning building. Notably, the facility provided products for a number of major U.S. brands and retailers and had been covered by a workplace monitoring arrangement with Walmart, one of its major customers.[48]

Less than six months later, in April 2013, a multistory building in Savar, Bangladesh, collapsed, killing 1,127 people who worked in the numerous apparel manufacturing companies located in it. The Rana Plaza complex collapse was the deadliest accident in the history of the garment industry. Apparel contractors in the building produced goods destined for such global brands as Walmart, Benetton, the Children's Place, and British retailers Bonmarché and Primark.[49]

• • •

Global supply chains give rise to benefits to the companies that draw upon them, the consumers who purchase goods produced through them, and the workers who are employed as part of them. But supply chain structures also raise the "have your cake and eat it too" conundrum swirling around the fissured workplace. Modern supply chains often represent an intermediate organizational form between arm's-length market transactions and vertical integration. Lead companies at the top of supply chains are deeply integrated with their network of orbiting companies. When Apple specifies the technical standards for Foxconn and hundreds of other core suppliers to exquisite length and operates as a supervisory agent inside the walls of its suppliers, we come back to the same question posed by the practice of franchisors prescribing minute day-to-day activities for franchisees, or AT&T demanding such strict adherence to performance standards by its subcontractors that it virtually drives their business models.

On one hand, companies at the helm of international supply chains— whether in electronics, automobiles, or traditional industries like apparel— create work for people far beyond those directly employed by them, and that is beneficial. But given their deep integration with the supply base and the essential strategic need to carefully prescribe, certify, and conduct ongoing monitoring of adherence to technical, quality, and delivery standards, it seems arbitrary to absolve those lead companies from responsibility for, at the very least, seeing that those suppliers adhere to the labor standards of their home country. The Apple/Foxconn story illustrates that lead firms can take more responsibility. The Tazreen and Rana Plaza tragedies exemplify the failure to do so.

Any effort to address wage levels, health and safety, labor standards compliance, or other aspects of work must recognize that the modern workplace, as redrawn through the organizational forms discussed in Part II, looks less and less like the one enshrined in most public policies. Improving the workplace requires changing the way laws assign responsibility. It requires a reformation in the way government agencies operate. It requires new approaches and roles for worker advocates, employer associations, and other organizations. And ultimately it requires a different relationship between lead organizations and the complicated business networks they rely upon.

How to mend the fissured workplace?

PART III

Mending the Fissured Workplace

The labor economist and policy reformer John R. Commons described an effort to mend a fissured workplace more than a century ago.

> In the year 1902 the City of New York was building its first subway along Fourth Avenue. The contract for construction and operation was made with a syndicate of bankers headed by August Belmont and Company of New York and including the House of Rothschild. About 30,000 Italian subway workers went out on strike, demanding that they should be paid directly "at the office" of the syndicate and not indirectly through the labor contractors. They did not ask for an increase in their wages of $1.35 for ten hours. They asked only for the elimination of the padroni. This demand, if acceded to, would have increased their actual wages considerably by eliminating the extortions of the padroni.[1]

As with many of the cases discussed in Part II, subway construction was being done through a network of subcontractors—in this instance coordinated through small players who acted as agents between the syndicate of investors who financed the subway and the individual workers on the job site. By ceding the authority to hire and pay workers to the "padroni," the syndicate removed itself from the direct employment relationship. The resulting arrangement left the day-to-day problem of recruitment of unskilled laborers to padroni, resulting in a fractured and highly competitive market for those laborers, with ample opportunities for middlemen to use their gatekeeper status to take a slice of the pie and still, presumably, provide the Belmont and

Company syndicate with a lower-wage workforce than if it directly hired the laborers.

Rather than using their collective efforts to improve wages, the subway workers sought to affect the manner in which wage setting occurred in their labor market and, in turn, the trajectory of their wages and working conditions in the longer term. Cutting out the players in the middle would change the basic dynamic of the labor market and potentially give the workers greater ability to set standards and conditions collectively and directly with the party that set the larger conditions in the subway project. Presuming that the subway workers stayed organized (they did not), the effort to shift the focus of discussions to the top of the business structure could have provided the basis for improving conditions for the workforce.

The fissured workplace reflects competitive responses to the realities of modern capital and product markets. The boundaries of firms have been redrawn as a result of new technology and the falling costs of information. As detailed in Part II, the consequences of the fissured workplace are profound. Wage determination changes dramatically, often to the detriment of workers whose work has been shifted outward. Blurring lines of responsibility increase the risks for bad health and safety outcomes. And the pressure to cut corners and not comply with basic labor standards intensifies.

A public policy agenda must look for ways to address these problems. However, crafting responses for the fissured workplace presents its own dilemmas, for a simple reason: federal and state policies are based on a model of employment with a single, well-defined employer with direct responsibility in hiring and firing, managing, training, compensation, and development of its workforce. But that does not conform to the way the workplace is currently organized.

Part III addresses the question of mending the fissured workplace.[2] The emergence of fissuring requires rethinking our basic definitions of employment. It also requires different approaches to how government agencies, labor unions and other worker advocates, and employer associations address its repercussions. An economy dominated by large business organizations with concentrations of employees operating within their boundaries is difficult to police. An economy where much of that employment—particularly of workers with low skills and little market leverage—has been shifted outside of the traditional boundaries of the business organization poses even graver questions about the efficacy of the traditional approach to workplace regulation. Mending the fissured workplace requires mending the way we regulate work.

Chapter 8 focuses on policies that address the overall set of forces arising from fissured employment, particularly the question of responsibility as framed by current and prospective laws and recent court opinions that hint at new approaches to better aligning private and social responsibilities. Chapter 9 explores how new approaches to enforcement of existing workplace laws might better redress the problems of fissuring, drawing on the recent experience of several agencies in strategic enforcement. Chapter 10 looks at other key players that might undertake a different role given the fissured workplace: labor unions, worker advocates, employers and their associations, international monitors, and workers themselves. Once again, it reflects on several contemporary innovative efforts. Chapter 11 examines the impact of further spreading of fissured workplaces on the economy as a whole. It examines their increasing presence in industries and occupations with high skill and education demands, like journalism and law, and then speculates on its implications for income distribution and the macroeconomy. Chapter 12 pulls together the themes of the book to ask the question of where to go from here. ▪

Rethinking Responsibility

The modern employment relationship bears little resemblance to that assumed in our core workplace regulations. Improving conditions where the most vulnerable people in the economy work requires navigating the complicated, fissured environment laid out in this book. Some aspects of the fissured world have desirable aspects—consumers benefit when companies try to market goods and services that conform to their tastes, and there are productivity gains from many aspects of firms focusing on core competencies.[1] Many of the cases in previous chapters illustrate the painstaking systems that lead companies put in place to ensure that suppliers, contractors, and franchisees do not undermine core competencies and the basis of profitability.

While deftly crafting franchise manuals, delivery standards and systems, and monitoring arrangements, these lead companies often profess a lack of knowledge about the work conditions that flow from the very same standards. Or they absent themselves from some coordination functions that might compromise their arm's-length status. And the social consequences of these actions are significant with respect to compliance with labor standards, impacts on worker health and safety, and more generally the distribution of income overall.

This raises a fundamental public policy question: *Should lead companies be allowed to have it both ways?*

This chapter starts with two illustrations of the poor fit between existing laws and the fissured workplace. First, it discusses the difficulty of defining "employer" and "employee" under federal statutes given fissured workplace realities. Second, it explores how liability considerations under the common law exacerbate the problem of coordination arising in the fissured workplace. The chapter then turns to recent court decisions that provide hints of how the law might better align private and social outcomes in the context of the three types of fissured workplace structures discussed in Part II. The chapter concludes with a consideration of broader legislative initiatives and what the passage of other federal workplace statutes in the past quarter-century says about how such an agenda might best be pursued.

Who's in Charge? Defining Employers under Federal Law

Defining who is the employer and who is the employee turns out to be a far less straightforward task than one might imagine.[2] The definitions differ across federal, state, and common law. Federal workplace statutes (the focus of this discussion) do not use a single definition, but rather multiple ones, from fairly expansive definitions that acknowledge the range of relationships that may actually arise in the workplace (as in the Fair Labor Standards Act [FLSA]) to narrow descriptions built around the archetypical large employer (think General Motors) with thousands of employees (as in the National Labor Relations Act [NLRA]).[3]

The FLSA defines an employee as "any individual who is employed by an employer" and that "employer includes to suffer or permit to work." This obscure phrase offers the broadest definition of "employee" of any federal statute. It goes beyond the definition offered by common law focus on the degree of actual control of the employee. Instead, courts have noted that the phrase "to suffer or permit" implies that even broad knowledge of work being done on an employer's behalf is sufficient to establish a relationship. Given the wide latitude implied by this definition, courts have applied an economic realities test to evaluate the particular economic situation surrounding a worker and his or her employer or employers. The broad definition of "employer" under the FLSA (and under most state minimum wage laws) provides the potential for interpretations that capture the complexities of the fissured workplace even though courts have historically tended to hew to relatively narrow definitions of employment.[4] I return to the competing definitions of "employer" offered by different courts below.

The Occupational Safety and Health Act defines "employer" as "a person engaged in a business affecting commerce who has employees." The act requires that an employer "shall furnish to each of his employees employment and a place of employment which are free from recognized hazards that are causing or are likely to cause death or serious physical harm to his employees."[5] The definition of "employer" reflects the act's focus on assuring that such conditions are furnished at the workplace. But this presents obvious problems in the many forms of fissuring described in this book where the party that creates the conditions of work might not actually have "employees." For example, AT&T does not directly employ cell tower maintenance workers, but its use of turfers has clear impacts on hazards (and fatalities) on the tower sites it operates. As we shall see, OSHA has been wrestling with this issue for decades in establishing citation policies for construction and other multiemployer work sites.

At the other end of the spectrum, the NLRA, the federal statute governing union organizing and collective bargaining, uses a restrictive definition and a narrow economic reality test for defining employment, more closely adhering to common law notions. Originally, the Supreme Court in ruling on the NLRA's employer-employee definitions deferred to the National Labor Relations Board (NLRB). In *NLRB v. Hearst Publications Inc.,* the Court explicitly stated that the board's employment definition need not be confined to common law definitions, but could legitimately look, "as a matter of economic fact, to the evils the Act was designed to eradicate." In this particular case, the Court upheld an NLRB ruling that "newsies" (boys who sold newspapers in the street on commission) were in fact employees of the Hearst publishing empire despite Hearst's contention that they were formally independent contractors who purchased papers from Hearst but sold them on their own as "entrepreneurs." The NLRB decision and the Supreme Court's affirmation of it led enraged conservatives in Congress to amend the NLRA in 1947 to specifically exempt independent contractors.[6] This moved the NLRB and the courts to apply the tests for employment created by common law in deciding on issues of coverage under the act.[7]

For many decades following passage of the FLSA and other federal statutes, subtle differences in definitions of employment were less consequential for much of the economy: it was relatively clear who the employer and the employee were, just as were the boundaries of the firm. The more the workplace has fissured, the more the subtleties raised by definitions of employment matter. In effect, what was at one time at the edges of disputes regarding idiosyncratic occupations (newsies) or historically fissured industries (construction and garments) has become a mainstream problem of employment, making the subtleties of these statutes more central to seeing that the objectives of workplace laws are achieved.[8]

The Common Law, Vicarious Liability, and the Nefarious Benefits of Fissuring

The common law bases its views of employment relationships fundamentally on the question of control. It defines control based on the existence of a master-servant relationship between the parties, where the master (as principal) employs the servant (acting as the master's agent) to undertake some action for the former's benefit. The master in the relationship directs and controls the servant in his or her activities.

Under tort law regarding the liability of the principal for the actions of the agent, courts apply a "direct and control" test to ascertain whether those tasks have been sufficiently defined, monitored, and rewarded to establish employment. The question of whether a principal oversees the means (that is, the way work is actually done) versus only the outcomes has important implications as to whether the agent undertaking that activity is an employee or an independent contractor, and therefore whether the principal is liable or not for the actions of the agent. But the important point is that the test itself imposes a high standard in showing that the principal has a significant role in setting out the tasks and activities it expects of its agent.

Troubling Lessons from the Petrochemical Industry

Before the explosion of BP's Deepwater Horizon platform in 2009 that resulted in the death of 11 workers on the company's drilling platform and the largest oil spill in history, a major explosion at BP's Texas City, Texas, refinery in 2005 killed 15 workers and injured more than 170 people. The BP disaster of 2005 was presaged by an even earlier string of petrochemical plant accidents linked to the use of independent contractors.[9] In the late 1980s and early 1990s, a series of petrochemical accidents were traced to the use of contractors. The problem came to public attention when a devastating explosion at a Phillips 66 chemical facility on October 23, 1989, left 23 workers dead and another 314 injured. A report on the explosion requested by President George H. W. Bush focused on the use of contractors as a significant contributing factor.[10]

Petrochemical refineries convert crude oil into multiple products, from high-end ones like jet fuel, gasoline, and other fuels to low-end ones like asphalt. During the course of the year, companies like BP and Mobile rebalance the mix of fuels being produced to adjust to shifts in demand (for example, more home heating oil in the winter, more gasoline in the summer). This requires periodic renovation and "turnaround" operations where major shifts in product mix are undertaken. To do this work, parts of the facility need to be shut down, meaning forgone production. In a capital-intensive business like petrochemicals, it is in the interest of the company to make this downtime as short as possible. However, since operations involve highly combustible materials, the downside of mistakes is considerable. Because refineries differ from one another, as do the operational protocols of different companies, the work also requires knowledge of the specific facility and its operating characteristics. Finally, renovation and turnaround operations involve hiring additional workers beyond the base level required to maintain refineries. Taken together, these requirements create a need for contractors to undertake renovation and turnaround work.

Petrochemical plants face a now-familiar choice between two methods of arranging employment relationships with the contractor. One option would be to treat each contractor (and its workers) exactly as if it directly worked for the major employer: set tasks, jointly determine how the work will be undertaken, monitor progress, interact with the contractor on issues where facility knowledge is important to the turnaround work, evaluate the contractor based on performance, and revise future relationships given performance. In so doing, the petrochemical producer acts essentially as a joint employer with the subcontractor.

Alternatively, the company could create an arm's-length relationship with each contractor, hiring it to do a specified piece of work. The subcontractor in this scenario is left essentially on its own to undertake the turnaround or renovation work.

The common law notions of master-servant relationships play a decisive role in making the choice. If the petrochemical company plays a significant role in oversight of the contractor, it assumes liability if problems arise in the activities of the contractor it has hired. This is because under the common law principles underlying tort law, a master-servant relationship has been created between the parties. If the relationship is successfully structured in a hands-off manner—the market-based relationship of independent contracting

(I will pay you to do a job, and you decide how to do it)—the petrochemical producer shields itself from the liability arising from a close master-servant relationship. More to the point, if the lead company can show it did not have daily operational control of the activities of the contractor, it cannot be held to be "vicariously liable" for problems arising from the contractor's actions.

That is what major petrochemical companies decided to do: limit liability by keeping their contractors at arm's length. On an operational level, this included scheduling the work at times where no plant personnel were present (and therefore potentially in a supervisory role); keeping safety and health oversight functions between the facility and the contractors completely separate from one another; and not providing training on safety procedures to the contractors (assuming that they were skilled and capable of doing so on their own).

Most contractors were left alone to recruit and train their workforce. At the site, supervisory relationships were also kept at an arm's-length distance. Health and safety training and oversight were held to be entirely the concern of the contractor, whose only contact with the petrochemical plants' medical facilities occurred during emergencies. In fact, so distant was the relationship between the entities that less than 60% of the managers of petrochemical facilities even kept records of the accident rates of the contractors they hired.[11]

The decisions on the relationships between the lead petrochemical companies and their subcontractors reflected a calculated risk: the private benefits arising from insulating themselves from liability and the lower costs of not paying workers' compensation and related costs for those workers outweighed the expected costs associated with the relatively low risk of devastating accidents arising from improperly performed work. And devastating those accidents turned out to be.[12]

Vicarious Liability and Fissured Responsibility

The petrochemical cases illustrate how the common law reinforces the incentives to shed work (remember cell towers?). The nature of the relationship between the parties to a subcontracting relationship affects the apportionment of liability. If a "right to control" is established, an organization can be held liable for the actions of its subcontractors. But if a subcontractor undertakes its activities largely under its own direction, the party that hired it is far less likely to be held liable for bad outcomes that may arise.

Vicarious liability refers to liability imposed upon one party because of the actions of another. As in the case of defining who is an employer, vicarious liability requires establishing that a principal party had the capacity to control the activity of its agent if it is to be held liable. As a result, exposure to being held vicariously liable for the actions of a subordinate party affects the degree to which the principal attempts to influence behavior by asserting more direct control over the agents' activities. Imagine a lead organization that decides to contract with small companies to undertake those activities rather than directly employing its own workforce. The question is how to manage those companies in order to meet the lead company's production goals while taking advantage of the competition between them it has created.[13]

Considerations about vicarious liability compound the basic balancing problem underlying fissured employment: on one hand, an employer always has an incentive to have its contractors adhere to a set of standards, practices, and procedures central to its business model (core competency). On the other hand, it will want to have competition among multiple parties who undertake the task while not itself engaging in any supervision that could be construed as "directing and controlling" those parties to the extent it could be held vicariously liable.

This creates very complicated and—as usual—contradictory incentives. Shielding itself from vicarious liability creates incentives for the lead organization to exert as little control over its agents as possible, even in cases where it would be more socially efficient for it to do so. In fact, the incentives become even more problematic: if subcontractors are financially viable (solvent), they will be exposed to the costs imposed by their mistakes or accidents. Although the lead company is not liable in such an instance, contractors will end up forcing it to bear some of these potential costs in the form of higher prices up front. However, if the contractors are financially unstable, they become "judgment-proof"—that is, they will not face the costs of tort actions brought against them, because they will have few or no assets to claim. Such insolvent subcontractors will therefore price their services at a lower level. Hence, lead companies have incentives not only to shift their risk through contracting but also to select agents who are more likely to behave poorly because of their judgment-proof status.[14]

If this seems like so much economic theorizing, think about a characteristic of many of the cases discussed in Part II. Lead organizations draw on contractors that are small, undercapitalized, and financially precarious in the cell tower, coal mining, and logistics industries; franchisors sell franchises to recent immigrants in janitorial and home health care industries whose capitalization and financial resources are thin and volatile; and manufacturers draw on vendors at the bottom of supply chains that are often out of business (and sometimes reborn under new names) in the next season.

The balancing that is a basic part of the fissured recipe therefore creates incentives for the employer to further distance itself from the employment relationship to avoid vicarious liability. It particularly exacerbates the problems of externalities arising from the disincentives it creates for coordination, with disastrous outcomes like those in the petrochemical industry.

The Right to Control under Three Fissured Forms

The "right to control" affects how courts define employees and employers, apply the protections of workplace statutes, and assess liability under tort law. Reconciling existing laws, the often blurred boundaries between organizations, and evolving workplace realities requires returning to a fundamental question posed throughout this book: Should lead companies be able to have it both ways? In recent years, courts have wrestled with aspects of this question under FLSA, OSHA, and other statutes in cases involving the three "fissured forms" discussed in Part II—subcontracting, franchising, and supply chains. Their decisions reveal opportunities and obstacles to rethinking responsibility.

Subcontracting Relationships

Court opinions on joint employment under the FLSA in subcontracting relationships vary widely. Much like vicarious liability, to determine the degree of control exerted on a contractor, courts apply multifactor tests to the specific circumstances under which the relationship operated. For example, in *Rutherford Food v. McComb,* the U.S. Supreme Court held that a joint employment relationship existed between a slaughterhouse and a labor contractor hired to debone meat, on the basis of five factors: (1) the workers did a specialty job on the production line that was an integral part of the production process; (2) the deboning contracts were passed from one supervisor to another without significant alteration; (3) the slaughterhouse's equipment and facilities were used for the work; (4) the workers doing the deboning had no business organization that could be shifted from one slaughterhouse to another; and (5) the manager of the slaughterhouse closely monitored the activities of the workers.[15]

But a multifactor test leaves a great deal of room for interpretation. For example, the Sixth Circuit Court applied such a test to conclude that migrant pickle workers were *excluded* from FLSA coverage because of the temporary nature of their employment relationship, the "lack of control" of farmers over migrant workers given that they were paid on a piece-rate basis, and the skill of those workers. However, in 1987 the court reached an opposite result with similar case facts.[16] Courts also use different factors in addition to those cited in *Rutherford* as well as weighing them in a variety of ways.[17]

Motives also figure into some court readings of whether a subcontracting relationship entails joint employment. The Second Circuit Court in 2003 narrowly interpreted the basis for finding joint employment when it noted that an economic reality test of control "is intended to expose outsourcing relationships that lack a substantial economic purpose, but it is manifestly not intended to bring normal strategically oriented contracting schemes within the ambit of the FLSA." This implies a finding of joint employment only when the intention of subcontracting is avoiding legal responsibility.[18]

In contrast, Judge Easterbrook of the Seventh Circuit Court argued in *Reyes v. Remington Hybrid Seed Co.* that courts must look deeply at the economic reality underlying the relationship between a business and its contractor to establish joint employment. In the *Reyes* case, involving a labor broker hired by a seed corn company to detassel corn plants, the court draws on the same five factors as under the *Rutherford* decision to similarly conclude that the seed company exercised control over the labor broker and was therefore liable for unpaid wages.[19]

Citing similar problems that arise under the doctrine of vicarious liability, Judge Easterbrook argues for the desirability of joint employment in aligning private and public interests given the incentives that arise for firms to draw on insolvent contractors. "If Zarate [the labor broker in *Reyes*] had been solvent, Remington [the seed company] would have to offer him enough that he could pay all of the workers' wages (including the minimum wage and any overtime premium), cover the costs of fringe benefits such as housing, and still be able to make a profit. But when a contractor has no business or personal wealth at risk, he may be tempted to stiff the workers (as Zarate did), and then treating the principal firm as a separate employer is essential to ensure that the workers' rights are honored."

Fissured workplaces arise in some cases solely from a desire to evade responsibility in the manner cited in the *Zheng* decision. But they more generally arise from a fundamental reshaping of the boundaries of business. This requires acknowledgment of the robust economic drivers of joint employment described by Judge Easterbrook in *Reyes*.

Expanding Multiemployer Liability in Subcontracted Industries

Construction continues to be one of the most dangerous industries in the economy, both in terms of the absolute number of injuries and fatalities and in terms of risk exposures. In 2010 there were 774 fatalities in the construction sector out of a total of 4,690 workplace fatalities in the United States as a whole. This was equivalent to a rate of 9.8 fatalities per 100,000 full-time workers versus 3.6 for all workers.[20] Not surprisingly, since OSHA's inception in 1971, construction has been a focal point of its enforcement efforts.

Subcontracting has long been a fixture of the modern era of construction.[21] In large part, this reflects the classic reasons for contracting discussed in Chapter 5: the need for particular skills for a limited time period on any project leads to the efficient organization of production around crafts, with a single entity (the general contractor or construction manager) coordinating overall activity. A construction site will inevitably have more than one subcontractor working at any time; in the case of large commercial or public projects, there could be twenty or more on-site.

OSHA therefore faced the problem of determining responsibility for violations in multiemployer situations.[22] In its early days, if OSHA deemed an employer to have overall responsibility for a work site, it considered the employer liable for hazardous conditions that violated safety and health standards even if its own employees were not directly exposed. The agency narrowed that interpretation in the mid-1970s, however, focusing on whether an employer could have been reasonably expected to either prevent or fix the hazard, given its authority over the site.[23] Procedures for guiding inspectors regarding multiemployer sites were fairly broad and lacked clear criteria. This led the agency to issue more explicit guidance in a 1999 policy statement that remains in effect today.[24]

The policy recognizes that on construction sites, more than one employer may be responsible for a workplace hazard and therefore citable for a violation of health and safety standards. Establishing joint employment responsibility is crucial where coordination of parties can affect exposure to workplace hazards (recall the fatal results arising from failures of coordination in the cell tower and petrochemical industries).

The multiemployer policy creates a two-step process in determining if more than one employer is to be cited. First, inspectors determine "whether an employer is a creating, exposing, correcting, or controlling employer," acknowledging that an employer might have multiple roles. For example, the general contractor on a construction site might have its own workforce (carpenters, laborers) and be a "creating" and/or "exposing" employer for those workers, but in overseeing the site as a whole might also be a "controlling" employer for others on the site.[25]

In the second step, the inspector determines, given the roles established in step one, whether "the employer's actions were sufficient to meet those obligations" that are explicitly outlined in the policy. This requires a review of the actions taken by the employer in addressing safety and health risks given its role on the site. Of particular importance is the definition of the controlling employer in the policy: "An employer who has general supervisory authority over the worksite, including the power to correct safety and health violations itself or require others to correct them. Control can be established by the contract or, in the absence of explicit contractual provisions, by the exercise of control in practice."

In a series of examples contained in the policy itself, OSHA describes how this definition would lead to a citation of the controlling employer where control is established by a contract (with the kinds of explicit provisions about ongoing oversight, monitoring, and evaluation found in the contracts covering cell towers and logistics described in Chapter 5), and the controlling employer failed to exercise that authority as outlined in the contract. Equally, if the contract outlines a policy of supervision by the controlling employer that the employer dutifully undertakes, and a violation of the standard is still found during an inspection of one of its subcontractors, the controlling employer can be found to have exercised reasonable care and would not be citable (although the subcontractor, as the creating and exposing employer, would).[26]

Notably, the policy also describes how a controlling employer might be citable for violations even where a contract formally exempts it from requiring compliance with safety requirements by subcontractors. The policy cites the example of a construction manager that sets schedules and construction sequencing, requires subcontractors to meet specifications, negotiates and resolves disputes between subcontractors on the site, and makes purchasing decisions, all of which have impacts on safety. Even if the contract between the construction manager and the subcontractor states that the manager has no authority over compliance by others on-site (for example, a decision requiring one subcontractor to start work before another subcontractor had constructed guardrails, and the construction manager refused to alter the schedule), the manager could be cited for a violation of fall hazard standards.

Not surprisingly, the multiemployer policy has been extremely controversial, particularly among lead contractors and end users potentially subject to citation as controlling employers, and has been the subject of contested violations as well as reviews by OSHA's Occupational Safety and Health Review Commission (OSHRC) and the courts. Fierce industry opposition and the inevitable ambiguity in applying the criteria in specific situations led OSHA to be reluctant to use its authority to cite controlling employers, particularly after the OSHRC in 2007 (during the Bush administration) overturned an inspector's citation of a general contractor as a controlling employer and explicitly questioned OSHA's authority to issue citations under the multiemployer policy.[27]

But in 2011 the District of Columbia Circuit of Appeals upheld an OSHA inspector's decision to cite Summit Contractors, a general contractor, for its failure to provide ground fault circuit interrupters (which protect workers from shock when using power tools) on one of its job sites. Summit, testing the validity of the multiemployer policy itself, contested the citation, arguing that neither of its two employees at the site was exposed to the hazard.[28] The court upheld the citation, arguing that the company had failed to undertake its role as controlling employer to inspect the electrical boxes used on-site and correct the problem.[29]

The ruling was widely seen as an unambiguous (and, for proponents of the policy, long overdue) affirmation of the authority of OSHA to use the multiemployer policy in construction. But its significance potentially goes beyond construction in helping to rebalance the considerations driving fissured employment. To date, OSHA has not tested the use of the controlling employer concept in its multiemployer citation policy in situations outside construction, like those leading to the fatality at a Hershey contractor/supplier discussed in Chapter 5.[30] Nor did OSHA use the citation policy in any of the cases involving cell tower fatalities, focusing citations only on the immediate subcontractor or in a few cases one contractor above that.[31] The decision in the *Summit* case may create opportunities for OSHA to increase the pressure on lead companies using subcontracted fissured forms through enforcement focused at the top. I return to this issue in Chapter 9.

Franchising Relationships

Franchising raises complicated issues of liability given the intertwined relationships between franchisors and franchisees. On one hand, assuring that franchisees maintain quality and product standards is central to the branding core competency of service industries where franchising is found. Wayward franchisees with poor service or quality quickly undermine the value of the brand, hence the issuing and enforcement of strong standards, as discussed in Chapter 6. However, there is a potential cost for the franchisor: it may become vicariously liable for the actions of wayward franchisees if the degree of control it exercises over them is significant. Vicarious liability means that strategies designed to solve one set of business problems might create other ones in the process. If a plaintiff can establish vicarious liability on the part of the franchisor, what the business might gain from greater scrutiny of quality (and therefore improved revenues from its franchisees) it might ultimately lose from exposure to costly claims.[32]

Courts have indeed held franchisors vicariously liable for actions of franchisees. For example, when Joni Miller bit into a "heart-shaped sapphire stone" while eating at a McDonald's, and sued both the franchisee and the franchisor, the court upheld McDonald's culpability under the vicarious liability doctrine. The court reasoned that the franchise agreement spelled out "equipment layouts, formulas and specifications for certain food products, methods of inventory and operation control . . . and manuals covering business practices and policies." Manuals provided by McDonald's spelled out food handling procedures in even greater detail, and the company sent out field consultants to inspect franchisees; conducted training on procedures related to food preparation; and exercised control over franchisee hours, employees on duty, and uniforms. The court reasoned that the sum of these activities showed that McDonald's, as the franchisor, controlled the procedures used by the franchisee, thereby making the latter vicariously liable.[33]

Courts have followed similar reasoning in holding franchisors liable in other cases where customers have been harmed as a result of franchisee behavior that was potentially under the franchisor's control, particularly where a consumer's expectation was based on the reputation of the product itself (regardless of whether it was being provided by a company-owned or franchised business unit). But in general, most courts have been reluctant to hold franchisors similarly liable for the failure of its franchisees to comply with workplace laws. In part, this stems from explicit language in virtually all franchise agreements stipulating that it is the franchisee's responsibility to comply with all applicable workplace laws. However, as we have seen before, such language alone does not protect a lead company.

In addition, courts hold to a very high standard in concluding that an actual agency relationship exists between a franchisor and a franchisee, requiring evidence of control of day-to-day operations. It is one thing to specify how burgers are to be made (including making sure that employees remove jewelry before working with food). But courts in general have looked at franchise standards as describing *results* of operations, not *means* of achieving them. If franchisees are left to figure out how to manage their franchises to meet standards (and the franchisor is careful not to dabble in activities that might draw it into supervising daily activities), courts have concluded that they alone are responsible.

The incentives created by vicarious liability help explain the different levels of compliance with minimum wage and overtime laws in the fast-food industry discussed in Chapter 6. When running their own facilities, major fast-food companies are quite scrupulous in terms of compliance. Among the largest fast-food companies in the United States operating both franchised and company-owned units, six of thirteen were found to have *no* violations of the FLSA in their company-owned units (at the same time that all fast-food companies had significant numbers of violations among their franchised units).[34] This shows both that franchisors take compliance with the laws seriously and that they have successfully created systems that allow them to do so.

But why tolerate in franchisees what they deplore in their own operations? If they monitor payroll more closely, or included random checks of off-the-clock or other work, franchisors potentially expose themselves to a wider set of liabilities (and potential costs). Imposing closer monitoring scrutiny could be interpreted as evidence of a master-servant relationship and therefore ex-

pose the franchisor to tort liabilities going far beyond the employment relationship itself (e.g., exposing a franchisor to liability from a customer slipping
on a wet floor at a franchised outlet). As a result, franchisors may view franchisee noncompliance with the FLSA (and other workplace regulations)—
including the potentially negative impact noncompliance might have on brand
reputation—as an unfortunate but necessary cost to bear relative to the costs
arising from a wider range of claims under tort law connected to more stringent monitoring.

Yet distinctions between means and results in franchising are much more
blurry in reality. As noted in numerous examples, once a franchisor describes
the results it wants from franchisees in sufficient detail, and essentially sets
the economic returns of its business by specifying royalties, pricing, and factors relating to costs, it is not clear how much wiggle room is left in terms of
the means of action for the franchisee. Recent cases in two areas signal an
awareness of this significant problem.

Franchising as a Form of Misclassification?

In 2005 Pius Awuah, a resident of Lowell, Massachusetts, and an immigrant
from Ghana, purchased a Coverall franchise to provide janitorial services for
$14,500, using $8,500 from credit cards and savings and borrowing the remaining $6,000 from Coverall, to be repaid with interest from revenues from
his new cleaning customers. In exchange, Coverall gave Awuah cleaning contracts potentially amounting to $3,000 in revenues per month, along with
manuals, training, and other materials related to the Coverall brand. As described in Chapter 6 (and Figure 6.2), under the Coverall model, the franchisor directly received revenues from Awuah's clients, deducted royalty fees
and interest and principal payments for the loan, and sent the remainder to
him. Awuah, as an independent contractor, faced all costs for conducting his
business (wages for workers, associated tax, workers' compensation and other
social payments, costs of cleaning materials, insurance, transportation, and
other expenses). Given the prevailing rates for cleaning in Massachusetts (and
at prices set by Coverall), making any kind of margin and complying with
basic labor standards was difficult if not impossible.[35]

Awuah, along with a number of other Coverall franchisees, came to realize
the inherent problems of the franchise model as applied in the janitorial sector
and brought suit against the franchisor under Massachusetts misclassification

law,[36] arguing that he and 115 other franchisees were, in reality, employees of Coverall. The suit, brought by his attorney, Shannon Liss-Riordan, questioned the validity of the independent contractor/franchise status of the Coverall agreements given the top-down nature of the relationship among the franchisor, customers, and individual franchisees. If in fact Coverall was an employer rather than a franchisor in its relationship with franchisees, it would be required to refund franchise fees and royalties; be liable for minimum wage, overtime, and other wage claims; and potentially be liable for misrepresentation, deceptive and unfair business practices, and claims of unjust enrichment.

Drawing on the criteria set out in the state misclassification law, Judge William Young of the U.S. District Court of Massachusetts examined whether the Coverall franchisees were independent contractors given the three conditions required by the law: (1) that the individual independent contractor is free from control and direction in the performance of the service (both under contract and in actual practice); (2) that the service is performed outside of the usual course of business of the employer; and (3) that the individual (in this case the franchisee) is customarily engaged in an independently established trade, occupation, profession, or business. Judge Young ruled that Coverall's franchise model did not satisfy those conditions, particularly the second one.[37]

As a result, the court awarded Awuah and hundreds of other Coverall franchisees in Massachusetts $3 million in damages and required that the franchisor immediately reclassify and treat the franchisees as employees in Massachusetts going forward.[38] In June 2012, in another case brought by Liss-Riordan, U.S. district court judge Mark Wolf ruled that Jani-King Inc., which used a franchising model similar to Coverall's, had similarly misclassified its workers as franchisees.[39]

The rulings in Coverall and Jani-King pose the issue of where employment ends and franchising, as a form of independent contracting, begins. In Massachusetts, they potentially stop the illegitimate use of franchising common in the janitorial sector, where the basic agreement makes it virtually impossible for the franchisee to earn sustainable returns while complying with workplace laws. To the extent that franchised companies operating under this kind of pressure set the prices in markets, removing them from the field (or requiring that former franchisees be treated as employees) will allow prices for services to move upward, hopefully providing a more sustainable basis for wages and working conditions. It is notable that since the Coverall decision, janitorial service companies have stopped establishing franchises in Massachusetts. But it should also be noted that Forbes listed Coverall as one of the "top 10 fast-growing franchise chains that powered through the recession."[40]

Falling Dominos? A New View of Liability under Franchising

The tension created between protecting the brand and shedding employment to others is central to franchising and to fissuring. The careful balance between the two is further amplified by efforts to avoid vicarious liability by franchisors. As noted above, courts have largely been willing to let franchisors have their cake and eat it too when it comes to franchisee liability for compliance with workplace laws.

However, rulings by California and New York courts involving Domino's Pizza potentially open this question to greater scrutiny. In the first case, a Domino's Pizza franchisee was sued by a former employee as a result of sexual harassment and assault by her immediate supervisor (also an employee of the franchisee). The plaintiff named not only the franchisee but also Domino's Pizza LLC as the franchisor in the suit. Domino, citing case law that typically holds franchisees to be independent contractors, thereby removing franchisors from liability, sought a summary judgment by a trial court to remove it from the suit.

Although the trial court granted the motion, the appellate court saw the situation differently, noting that "if the franchisor has substantial control over the local operations of the franchisee, it may potentially face liability for the actions of the franchisee's employees." Although the franchisee agreement explicitly holds the franchisee "solely responsible for recruiting, hiring, training, scheduling for work, supervising and paying the persons who work in the Store and those persons shall be your employees and not [Domino's] agents or employees," the court reviewed provisions of the Domino's manual that provide explicit standards for a wide variety of practices going well beyond food preparation standards. These include setting standards for personal grooming, auditing the franchisee's tax returns and financial statements, setting store hours, advertising plans, customer complaint procedures, signage, equipment and fixtures and décor, and the pricing of items. The court also remarked on the degree of monitoring and control exercised by the franchisor in assuring compliance with standards, including threatening revocation of the franchise itself. In a pithy sentence opening the decision, the court noted, "Here, for purposes of a summary judgment motion, a franchisor's actions speak louder than words in the franchise agreement."[41]

A second case involves current and former Domino's Pizza employees in New York seeking damages and injunctive relief under the FLSA and New York labor law. The employees brought claims against a franchisee, DPNY Inc., alleging that the franchisee owners had paid less than the minimum wage, denied workers overtime pay, required them to work off the clock, and tampered with payroll records (in addition to violating federal and state labor standards in other ways). But the plaintiffs in the case also sought to add Domino's Pizza Inc.—the franchisor—to the claim on the basis that it "promulgated and implemented employment policies including compensation, hiring, training, and management policies for all of their stores, including the defendants' stores."[42]

In a ruling issued in November 2012, the U.S. District Court held in favor of adding the franchisor as a defendant. Citing the broad definition of "employer" under the FLSA and the application of the economic reality tests discussed above, and the mixed record of franchisors being held as liable for actions of franchisees, the court acknowledged that establishing joint employment would be difficult. But the court also indicated that the complaint had sufficient merit to make the case for joint employment plausible, particularly because the franchisee used compensation policies, management systems, and training materials all disseminated by the franchisor. "Most compelling, [the plaintiffs] assert that the Proposed Defendants [Domino's Pizza Inc.] promulgated compensation policies and implemented them through the Domino's PULSE system which was used at the defendants' store and included a system of tracking hours and wages and retaining payroll records which was submitted to the Proposed Defendant for their review."[43]

By looking at the totality of the circumstances surrounding the underlying relationship between Domino's Pizza and its franchisees, both rulings raise the question of whether franchisors can have it both ways given the standards they promulgate and their monitoring and enforcement of those standards on their franchisees. In contrast to the Coverall and Jani-King cases, which question the validity of franchising itself, the Domino's Pizza cases pointedly deal with whether the effort that franchisors undertake to ensure the success of the core business model reasonably raises the bar in their obligations to ensure that other standards—including those related to employment—are also achieved. It is not a question of the capacity of the franchise model to create incentives to achieve consistent standards: the success of business franchising as a form of expanding branded products demonstrates that it does. It ultimately is a question of the franchisor's willingness to do so.

Supply Chain Relationships

Chapter 7 discussed the extensive use of temporary workers in distribution centers, including those providing services for Walmart. The major distribution centers that solely service Walmart's international deliveries are managed by Schneider Logistics, a national logistics company, but many of the distribution center workers are hired as temporary employees through local subcontractors providing temporary workers, in this case Premier Warehousing Ventures (PWV), Rogers-Premier Unloading Services, and Impact Logistics. Workers in those cases won substantial back pay compensation because of the methods used to pay them in the fall of 2011.

More important to the present discussion was how the court treated Schneider Logistics, arguably the lead company in the situation. The U.S. district court ruled that Schneider was covered by the preliminary injunction issued in the case requiring all parties to immediately alter payroll and record-keeping practices at the distribution centers in Mira Loma so that they complied with state and federal labor standards requirements. Schneider argued that because it was not the employer of record, it should not be covered by the preliminary injunction or any subsequent injunctions. Judge Christine Snyder agreed with attorneys representing the plaintiffs, Everardo Carrillo and fellow workers at the distribution centers, and ruled that the preliminary injunction should indeed apply to all parties, since they "bear some responsibility for violations that plaintiffs are likely to succeed in proving and that are causing plaintiffs irreparable harm."[44] The court came to this decision by looking closely at the contracts between Schneider and its subcontractors and noting the substantial authority the company had over the other businesses, including pre-employment screening and training. It also cited Schneider's authority to conduct performance evaluations of the subcontractors and the unilateral right to dismiss individual workers of the subcontractors.[45]

The court's view that obligations to the workers in the distribution centers applied to both the temporary agencies and Schneider was further sharpened by subsequent events. Following the October 12, 2011, inspection of the Mira Loma facility and the announcement of a class action suit by workers at the facilities, PWV and Schneider engaged in a series of what the court concluded were retaliatory actions against workers featuring prominently in the suit and associated press coverage. PWV also notified Schneider on October 21 that it would be "unable to sustain its work under the present terms" of its contract (presumably because of the higher costs it would face given the court rulings, which were not compatible with prices agreed upon in its contract with Schneider). PWV indicated that it would be willing to discuss new terms, but Schneider did not renegotiate with it. On November 18, PWV held a meeting with the employees and distributed termination letters that stated that because Schneider had refused to renegotiate terms, it would be terminating employment as of February 24, 2012. This prompted a new request to the court for a preliminary injunction by affected workers, alleging discrimination for exercising their statutory rights under the California Labor Code and the FLSA.

On February 1, 2012, the court issued a preliminary injunction enjoining Schneider and PWV from terminating the workers. Significantly, it required Schneider to rehire all of the workers let go by PWV, a clear indication of the court's view of the close relationship between the organizations. Yet the saga continued: following the court's order, Schneider elected to offer terminated workers positions as openings occurred based on a randomized list (rather than via seniority), cut workers' starting wage from the average of $12.50 they had earned at PWV to $11.00 as Schneider employees, and denied them benefits, even though other Schneider workers were eligible for such benefits. This led the court on March 21 to hold the company in contempt of court, on the basis that these actions were also retaliatory in nature (under both the California Labor Code and the FLSA). It issued stern and clear guidance to Schneider on how the terminated PWV workers were to be notified of their eligibility for jobs at Schneider, and the terms of those positions.[46]

Notable in this sequence of cases—beginning with the initial court request to review the underlying contracts between Schneider and its subcontractors— was the court's determination to hold Schneider partly responsible for human resource practices at the distribution centers given the company's high degree of involvement in assuring quality standards (leading it to be involved in both the means and ends of service provision).

The fact that PWV could no longer profitably provide its services on the terms set out in its contract with Schneider once it instituted legally required wage rates and payroll policies points to a central problem of fissuring raised by many of the cases in Part II. The economic realities facing businesses at the bottom of fissured structures make sustaining even a normal rate of return incompatible with complying with workplace laws and standards. The court order requiring Schneider itself to assume the role of employer, paying wages and benefits comparable to what it paid its own direct employees— and to do so immediately, through the powerful mechanism of an injunction— represents a particularly powerful response to this fundamental problem arising in many fissured relationships.[47]

Legislation to Achieve Rebalancing in Fissured Decisions

Noah Zatz, a labor law scholar at UCLA, has argued that asking "Who is the employer and who is the employee?" under the NLRA is starting with the wrong question. "The right question to be asking is not 'who is an employee?' but instead 'to what extent should firms be able to choose organizational structures that preclude unionization by avoiding having employer-employee relationships at all?' "[48] This gets at the nub of dealing with the consequences of the fissured workplace more generally.

Successful legislation to address the problems arising from fissured employment would have the same effect as the court decisions reviewed above: they would impact the balancing decision faced by lead businesses by requiring them to include social as well as private benefits and costs in making decisions on employment. In some cases, by changing laws so that the lead business cannot have it both ways, those companies may choose to keep employment inside the organization. But that is not the only outcome legislation should seek. Lead businesses might still choose to move employment outward through contracting, franchising, third-party management, or other organizational forms. However, they might do so with greater scrutiny in the selection, monitoring, and coordination of those subordinate organizations given their heightened responsibility.

Framed in this broader way, public policies amending existing workplace policies, or breaking new ground entirely, can be evaluated in terms of their impact on the decisions made by lead organizations. There are three major objectives for legislative initiatives in this regard. First, legislation can attempt to stop lead organizations from shedding employment simply as a means to avoid workplace obligations created by law. Second, policies placing greater legal responsibility on lead businesses can cause those firms to include the social consequences of the fissured workplace when deciding to shed employment to others. Third, public policies can affect how wages and human resource policies are set in fissured workplace forms.

Thwarting Flagrant Fissuring

Public policies should try to stop egregious forms of fissuring that are solely designed to end-run basic workplace obligations established through existing public policies. The principle is simple: shedding employment simply to avoid workplace obligations established by state and federal laws is not acceptable.

Legislation adopted by the West Virginia legislature in response to rampant subcontracting in the coal industry (the Massey Doctrine discussed in Chapter 5) illustrates such a policy response. In that case, the A. T. Massey Coal Company drew on subcontracting in its mines to get out of its obligations to pay into union health and pension funds (where Massey was covered by them) or to workers' compensation funds maintained by West Virginia.[49] In 1996 the Wage Payment and Collection Act (WPCA) was passed to thwart such bald-faced efforts to subvert contractual obligations for health, pensions, and other benefits by subcontracting.[50] The law adopts a definition of "employee" similar to that used by the FLSA—"any person suffered or permitted to work by a person, firm or corporation"—and defines "employer" as "any person, firm, or corporation employing any employee."

The WPCA importantly requires that anyone who has benefited from a mining operation will be held responsible for paying wages for work that led to that benefit, making them "civilly liable to employees engaged in the performance of work under such contract for the payment of wages and fringe benefits, exclusive of liquidated damages."[51] In a series of cases brought under the WPCA, the state's courts have interpreted this language to include not only the mine operator, but also its "parents": individual owners, joint employers, and property owners.[52]

A related legislative approach would be to focus on the problem created by misclassifying workers as independent contractors. Statutes passed in Massachusetts, New Hampshire, and Indiana, for example, create a presumption of employee status in minimum wage, independent contractor, and/or wage payment laws.[53] The statutes create an "ABC" test that shifts the burden of proof to an employer to show that an individual is *not* an employee. Employers must show that an individual designated as an independent contractor is free from control or direction in the performance of work; that the service provided by the individual is outside the normal activities of the business for which it is performed; and that the activity performed by the individual is usually part of an independently established trade, occupation, or business enterprise. The aforementioned Coverall and janitorial franchising cases were brought under this Massachusetts statute.

Twenty-two states have passed legislation that addresses the classification of workers as independent contractors.[54] While a senator, Barack Obama introduced the Independent Contractor Proper Classification Act of 2007. The legislation addresses misclassification by closing tax incentives that make it more advantageous for businesses to classify workers as independent contractors. Another bill, the Employee Misclassification Prevention Act, reintroduced in 2011, would require strict record-keeping and notice requirements by employers for workers classified as independent contractors and would levy significant penalties for violations of the law.[55]

Rebalancing Fissured Workplace Decisions

Reform of existing workplace legislation and new policy initiatives could broaden the responsibility of lead organizations in the realm of employment so that it is consistent with the roles played in their other relationships with subordinate businesses. The principle here is one of parallelism: if a company exerts minute control over aspects of quality, production, and delivery of services, that control should extend more fully to the domain of employment as well those aspects of business that are directly valuable to the company.

Similarly, if a firm sits at the top of a complicated process of production such that its pricing, technical standards, and quality requirements fundamentally affect the returns available to the network of businesses operating within that system (as in the case of cell towers, for example), public policies should increase incentives for it to oversee coordination—particularly for health and safety—for the system it has, by virtue of its position, created. In effect, such policies say, "We know that you, lead businesses, can create effective systems to achieve quality, price, and scheduling objectives. So you should also play a far greater role in assuring that workplace and public safety are achieved as well."

Several states have enacted legislation that explicitly makes businesses in certain subcontracted industries responsible for activities of subordinate organizations. Both New York and California enacted laws making garment manufacturers or jobbers responsible for subcontractors' compliance with various workplace statutes.[56] California also has a "responsible contractor laws" that imposes some level of accountability on businesses employing construction, janitorial, agricultural, building security, and other workers.[57] In 2005 Illinois enacted a law that requires individuals working for temporary and staffing companies to be provided by those agencies with information about the work they are being offered; establishes record-keeping, meal, transportation, and other requirements for the temporary companies, and, notably, establishes joint employment responsibility for the temporary labor service agency and its clients for violations of the law.[58]

Legal scholars have put forward more ambitious proposals in this realm. One set of proposals focuses on broadening responsibility for violations of workplace standards, placing those companies who benefit from various fissured forms under greater liability. Several build on the model created under a current provision of the FLSA and state legislation that emulates it, referred to as the "hot cargo" provision. The hot cargo provision allows the Department of Labor's Wage and Hour Division to embargo goods in transit if investigations find that the law has been violated at any earlier point of production. This allows, for example, the department to hold the delivery of a manufacturer's clothing shipment if it finds that a subcontractor violated minimum wage standards. Using this provision as part of enforcement strategy is discussed in detail in Chapter 9.

Brishen Rogers proposes a broad expansion of the hot cargo provision to workplace legislation generally, through the creation of a duty-based test that would expand employer responsibility to end-user firms who fail to exercise due care in assuring that suppliers have complied with labor standards. Timothy Glynn goes even a step further, arguing that the nature of "disaggregated" employment requires abandoning fine-grained arguments over immediate or extended employer liability. He argues, instead, that "commercial actors would be held strictly liable for wage and hour violations in the production of any goods and services they purchase, sell, or distribute, whether directly or through intermediaries."[59] Expanding liability to include upstream producers would certainly affect important elements of fissured employment decisions, as the prior discussion of the factors underlying vicarious liability indicates.

Defining more clearly—and broadly—the definition of joint employment would be another approach in this regard. Some of the court decisions reviewed above move in this direction. The *Summit Contractors* decision regarding multiemployer citation policy affirms OSHA's right to cite lead players in construction and potentially other industries under the authority provided by the Occupational Safety and Health Act. Some health and safety advocates have in the past argued for more definitive affirmation of the concept of "controlling employers" through amendments to the act itself. Changes in statutes governing health and safety beyond those covered by OSHA (such as in offshore drilling) have certainly been underscored by the BP Deepwater Horizon disaster.[60]

The idea of joint employment flows more naturally from the broad definition of employment in the FLSA. The Schneider case illustrates how a more expansive application of the definition can be used to challenge fissured structures that seem designed in some sense to subvert it. But courts have not always accepted such a broad view. Legislation that further clarifies joint employment could help what has always been a contentious—and shifting—application of the phrase "suffers from . . ." in practice.

The National Labor Relations Act perhaps stands furthest from the modern realities of the workplace in its narrow and constrained interpretation of "employer" and the very restrictive implications of that definition of coverage. But the chances of changing this through legislation seem least likely to succeed for reasons discussed next.

Altering Wage Determination in Fissured Workplace Forms

Fissuring affects the way wages are determined inside versus outside lead businesses. Over time, shifting work outward has lowered how much people are paid for doing the same type of work in subordinate businesses relative to what they would have been paid when those jobs were done inside lead companies. This distributional impact of fissured employment is the most difficult to affect via legislation. In some senses, the impact of law would be indirect.

If some of the policies described above lead companies to bring work back inside, the fairness norms discussed in Chapter 4 may play a role in future wage setting. The court in the Schneider Logistics case essentially ordered such an upward readjustment for distribution center workers brought "back inside" that company from temporary contractors. But this type of explicit upward adjustment of wages or more subtle, voluntary wage and benefit increases are unlikely to happen in many instances—particularly in the absence of unions or other worker advocates, or significant pressures exercised via tight labor markets.[61]

Alternatively, by placing greater pressure on the continuing responsibility of the lead businesses, legislative reforms described above may prompt changes in how such firms police compliance with workplace standards among subsidiary organizations. This might, in turn, cause them to screen more selectively for better contractors or raise the bar on potential franchisees and, in turn, pay them higher prices so that they are capable of complying. As I discuss in Chapter 9, this kind of change in selection criteria for contractors occurred in the garment industry in response to the aggressive use of the hot cargo provisions of the FLSA in the late 1990s. More wide-scale efforts to challenge the idea that the behavior of businesses at lower levels of fissured workplace structures are "not my problem" could in the longer term lead to salutary adjustments in the private economic relationships at each level of those structures.

Political Realities and Legislative Solutions

In his 2012 book on inequality, the Nobel Prize–winning economist Joseph Stiglitz focuses on the increasingly large role that powerful private interests— particularly what has come to be known as "the 1%"—have on politics. He argues that the economic interests of the few have been increasingly protected and expanded through their greater control of the political process. Thus, tax policy, deregulation, responses to the banking crisis, and macroeconomic policy all have come to favor the very upper reaches of the income distribution while having detrimental impacts on the 99% (particularly those at the bottom and in the middle).[62]

Stiglitz points to the intensifying role played by the very top of economic elites in affecting political outcomes over the past three decades. The point can certainly be made in regard to legislation affecting the workplace. Passage of legislation to improve protections against a variety of workplace problems has been vexing, to put it mildly. One element that has been consistent in efforts to such pass laws has been the adamant and fierce opposition from the business community. Each new workplace proposal is denounced as undermining market functions and ultimately hurting rather than helping working people. Clearly, any of the legislative initiatives mentioned above would quickly face similar opposition.

But the history of workplace legislation also offers insight into how passage of new laws might be accomplished. While the business community has opposed proposed laws, that opposition has not always been unified, and the splits within the coalition are revealing—and politically important—in understanding the prospects of passing legislation related to the fissured workplace. Although outward support for workplace legislation among business groups is rare, segments of the business community have chosen to move from a position of strict opposition to one of negotiation. In these cases, and in the presence of a broad coalition of legislative advocates, Congress has been able to pass legislation such as the Worker Adjustment and Notification (WARN) Act of 1988, cushioning workers during plant closings; the Family and Medical Leave Act of 1993 (FMLA); and most recently the Lilly Ledbetter Fair Pay Act of 2009.[63]

But there have been failures as well. Most strikingly, these have occurred in the area of labor law reform, most recently in the failure to pass the Employee Free Choice Act in 2009 despite an incumbent Democratic president and Democratic control of both houses of Congress. In fact, every legislative effort to reform federal labor laws—including those that would erode management's ability to hire permanent replacement workers during a strike or change the methods used in union recognition elections—has met defeat for more than thirty years.

The key difference between whether these legislative efforts succeed or fail has been the position taken by business interests, which have been unwavering in opposing laws governing union-management relations, but less rigid in other areas. That fracturing in the otherwise "mighty monolith" of business opposition is significant for mapping future legislative strategies regarding policies redressing fissuring. Small business remained for the most part implacably opposed to legislation like WARN and FMLA. However, other segments of the business community began to negotiate about the legislation rather than simply trying to thwart its passage. The divergence arises in part from the underlying motivations driving different segments of the business community. Table 8.1 provides an overview of the political and institutional factors that have affected passage of federal workplace policies.

The strong and consistent opposition to workplace regulation from the small-business community reflects both practical and ideological concerns. From a practical perspective, small businesses tend to have a higher proportion of their costs related to labor, employ a higher proportion of low-wage workers, and generally operate in more competitive product markets. Those factors mean that workplace regulations directly affect their costs and profitability. Ideologically, many of the positions small-business lobbies like the National Federation of Independent Business stake out are based on the premise that attempts to regulate one aspect of the workplace inevitably lead to wider and more onerous regulation. This ideological orientation promoted a highly antagonistic response to virtually all major workplace regulation introduced from the Carter to the Obama administrations.

Larger businesses (the lead employers in fissured workplace structures), on the other hand, sometimes moved away from the reactive to the practical. For example, during the years between the initial proposal of FMLA in 1984 and its passage in 1993, major business representatives seemed to have decided to negotiate for a more limited medical leave policy rather than simply trying to block it—which seemed unlikely to succeed.[64]

Part of that is due to the coalition-driven nature of those laws, which usually expands far beyond unions. With the growing diversity of the labor force, the increase in dual-income and single-parent families, and the resulting impact of household structure on family–work balance, many recent workplace policies have engaged groups beyond the labor movement. Antidiscrimination policies, for example, have engaged political coalition partners from the NAACP, the Urban League, NOW, and groups representing the disabled.

Equally important is the passage of state-level legislation addressing workplace issues. Although business groups might prefer no legislation, in choosing between complying with varied standards and policies across different states and a single policy administered federally, businesses have generally shown a preference for the latter (going beyond just workplace regulatory

Table 8.1 Political and institutional factors regarding passage of selected federal workplace policies

Workplace policy	Small-business opposition?	Large-business opposition?	Broad political coalition partners beyond labor movement?	Related state-level policies prior to federal legislation?	Legislative outcome
Davis-Bacon Prevailing Wage (1931)	Yes, but not well organized	No	Yes	Yes	Passed
Fair Labor Standards Act (1938)	Yes, but not well organized	Mixed[a]	Yes	Yes	Passed
Labor Law Reform (1977)	Strong	Strong	No	No[b]	Failed
Hazard Communication Standard (1983)	Strong	Mixed[c]	Yes	Yes	Passed
Worker Adjustment and Notification Act (1988)	Strong	Moderate	No	Yes	Passed with significant exemptions
Family Medical Leave Act (1993)	Strong	Moderate	Yes	Yes	Passed with significant exemptions
Workplace Fairness Act (1993)	Strong	Strong	No	No[b]	Failed
Employee Free Choice Act (2007, 2009)	Strong	Strong	No	No[b]	Failed
Lilly Ledbetter Fair Pay Act (2009)	Strong	Moderate	Yes	No	Passed[d]

a. Law supported by manufacturers based primarily in northern states; opposed by manufacturers in southern states and those operating in both areas.

b. Federal preemption does not allow state-level policies related to the National Labor Relations Act. Several state-level attempts to restrict the use of permanent striker replacement, for example, were ruled unconstitutional.

c. Standard opposed by business groups that would be required to provide significant levels of disclosure (e.g., Chemical Manufacturers Association); supported by downstream chemical users who saw benefit in disclosure (see Fung, Graham, and Weil 2007).

d. The Lilly Ledbetter Fair Pay Act, an amendment to the Civil Rights Act of 1964 that effectively extends the statute of limitations on equal pay lawsuits, had an unusually short legislative history from its initial introduction in 2007 to being the first law signed by President Obama, on January 29, 2009.

matters). In the cases of WARN, FMLA, and federal minimum wage policy, a variety of states had adopted their own policies on these matters prior to passage of federal legislation. Smaller businesses with a single or a limited number of establishments are more likely to operate in only a single state and therefore oppose federal legislation. But larger businesses with outlets in multiple states face a very different calculus in choosing between state and federal regulation.[65]

This political dynamic could affect passage of federal legislation addressing issues like employee misclassification. Companies operating in multiple states already must comply with state-level legislation regarding independent contracting. Having to comply with different definitions, tests, and enforcement systems in different locations may be less desirable than operating under a single federal standard regarding misclassification. The interests of state and local governments (particularly in seeking lost tax revenue), along with those of community, immigrant, and workers' rights groups, create the basis for a broader coalition to support such initiatives.

One can imagine a similar political pathway developing for new efforts to address the fissured workplace where state governments might experiment with expanding responsibility for particular workplace outcomes. Imagine, for example, a law that made the provision of certain explicit standards in regard to product quality, delivery, and price a basis for greater liability in the safety and health practices of those business entities—whether franchisees, subcontractors, or principal suppliers. Some states whose courts have already signaled a willingness to consider such claims under existing statutes (California, Massachusetts, New York) might be ready to make that approach a part of law. Successful passage of legislation in some states (particularly those with large concentrations of business) might change the political dynamic at the federal level, allowing passage of similar statutes, much as has happened in the area of other workplace laws—and other public policy areas.[66]

While promising, an effort like this would take much time. Almost all of the successful laws mentioned above took years—sometimes more than a decade—to pass.[67] Given the current political climate in Washington, D.C.—to say nothing of the wider political economy realities described by Stiglitz— significant changes in liability or even more modest changes to definitions of joint employment seem unlikely for the foreseeable future.

Focusing on enforcement and implementation of existing minimum wage, overtime, and health and safety policies affords opportunities to address workplace problems now. We turn to the possibilities in this regard next.

Rethinking Enforcement

Responding to the fissured workplace requires rethinking workplace laws, their narrow definitions of "who the employer is," and the structure of liability implied by them and other relevant statutes. But it cannot stop there. The fissured workplace requires new approaches to enforcing existing workplace statutes in order to change employer behavior and begin to tip the careful balancing of core competencies and shedding employment that underlie it in a way that once again protects workers. This requires new approaches very different from those that characterize traditional state and federal workplace policy.

The Resource Challenge

Economics is the study of achieving objectives in the face of limited resources, so to say that limited budgets for workplace agencies represent a major and long-standing problem simply states the basic challenge facing any agency. However, those resources have become more limited over the same period that the number of workplaces covered by laws has grown, creating extremely challenging circumstances. What is more, changes in regulatory oversight over the past decade—ranging from the Government Performance Review Act of 1996 (GPRA) to the expanding role played by the Office of Management and Budget and the Office of Inspector General—have raised performance expectations and the level of scrutiny facing workplace agencies.[1]

The fundamental challenge facing workplace regulatory agencies arises from limitations in the resources available to them relative to the size and scope of U.S. workplaces covered by relevant statutes. As a result of reductions in the size and role of federal and state workplace agencies, employers and industry sectors face trivial likelihood of investigation in a given year. Reduced enforcement, in turn, diminishes the pressure for regulatory compliance in many sectors, thereby contributing to the growth of vulnerable workers in the economy. One can see a demonstration of this long-standing challenge by reviewing trends in enforcement resources relative to the number of workplaces in the U.S. economy.[2]

As the fissured workplace expanded and deepened in many industries, budgets for enforcement for major U.S. Department of Labor regulatory agencies remained remarkably unchanged for more than three decades. Annual enforcement budgets for the four major workplace programs within the Department of Labor—the Wage and Hour Division (WHD), Occupational Safety and Health Administration (OSHA), Mine Safety and Health Administration (MSHA), and Office of Federal Contract Compliance (OFCC)—were virtually flat in constant dollar terms from the Carter administration in the late 1970s through the administration of George W. Bush. Real spending on enforcement, however, rose in the first term of the Obama administration. Overall enforcement spending for the four agencies in current and constant dollars from 1977 to 2012 is shown in Figure 9.1.[3]

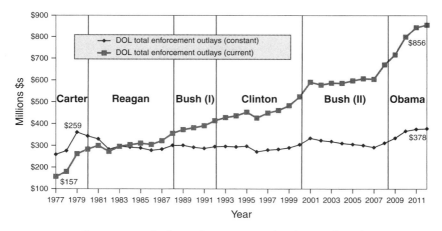

FIGURE 9.1. Department of Labor enforcement spending by presidential administration, 1977–2012 (current/constant 1982–1984 dollars, in millions). Total spending for enforcement for WHD, OFCCP, OSHA, and MSHA combined. *Sources: Budget of the U.S. Government,* various years.

Figure 9.1 masks some differences in trends across the agencies in the four administrations. These are depicted in Figure 9.2, which tracks enforcement spending in constant dollars for each of the four agencies. Expenditures for OSHA enforcement have been virtually unchanged over the entire period, beginning at $101 million (in 1982–1984 dollars) in 1977 and ending at $95 million in the proposed 2012 Obama budget.[4] In contrast, enforcement spending for the WHD has increased significantly over time, from $69 million in 1977 up to a proposed $124 million in 2012. MSHA's budget increased markedly in the late 1970s but then remained flat in real terms until 2006, when a series of major underground coal mining accidents led Congress and the Bush administration to increase enforcement resources for the agency; resources increased further in real terms in the first three years of the Obama administration.

While real expenditures for overall enforcement stagnated for much of the past two decades, the number of workplaces and workers in the U.S. economy grew, increasing from 6.94 million establishments in 1998 to 7.71 million in 2007, representing an 11% increase. Over the same period, the number of paid employees in the United States rose from 108.1 million to 120.6 million, or 11.5%.[5]

The long-term stagnation of enforcement resources and the growth in the number of workplaces and employment over the same period mean that the

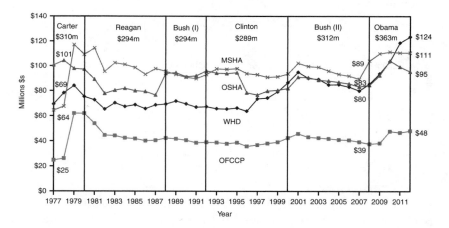

FIGURE 9.2. Department of Labor enforcement spending by program and presidential administration, 1977–2012 (in constant 1982–1984 dollars, in millions). *Sources: Budget of the U.S. Government,* various years.

likelihood of inspections has fallen over time. In fact, workplace investigations are extremely rare events. Examining the probability of receiving an investigation by the Wage and Hour Division is illustrative. Table 9.1 provides estimates for the number of cases, number of establishments, and resulting annual probabilities for eleven industries where the workplace has

Table 9.1   Wage and Hour Division annual investigation probabilities in fissured industries

Industry	(1) Number of establishments (CBP 2008)[a]	(2) Avg. annual WHISARD cases, FYs 2006–2008[b]	(3) Annual probability of WHD investigation (= (2)/(1))
Eating and drinking: limited service (fast food) and full service	431,932	2,164	0.501%
Hotel/motel	48,644	474	0.974%
Residential construction	187,327	259	0.138%
Janitorial services	53,093	174	0.328%
Moving companies/ logistics providers	50,386	54	0.107%
Agricultural products, multiple sectors	22,651	1,212	5.351%
Landscaping/horticultural services	92,167	152	0.165%
Health care services	635,808	1,267	0.199%
Home health care	24,129	73	0.303%
Grocery stores	89,054	519	0.583%
Retail: mass merchants, department stores, specialty stores	707,050	743	0.105%
All fissured industries	2,342,241	7,091	0.303%

Sources: NAICS code hierarchy table, including Census Bureau definitions of codes, http://www.census.gov/cgi-bin/sssd/naics/naicsrch?chart=2007; U.S. Bureau of the Census, County Business Patterns (CBP) data, by NAICS, http://censtats.census.gov/; Bureau of Labor Statistics employment data, State and County Wages: *Quarterly Census of Employment and Wages—QCEW,* http://www.bls.gov/cew/#databases.

a. Based on U.S. Bureau of the Census, CBP data, 2008.

b. WHISARD = Wage and Hour Investigative Support and Reporting Database. Averages based on registered limited and full directed and complaint investigations conducted between 2006 and 2008 and closed by August 2010.

become fissured. In the eating and drinking industry, for example, the annual chance of investigation is about .5%, or 5 in 1,000. Overall, the chance of receiving a WHD investigation is less than 3 in 1,000 (final row).[6]

As low as these annual probabilities of investigation are, they overstate the effective odds of investigation in many fissured industries. This is because the definition of an "establishment" used in calculating the chances of an investigation is "a single physical location where business transactions take place and for which payroll and employment records are kept."[7] In many industries, the definition of "establishment" is a reasonable way to count "workplaces" since the establishment is also the place where employees carry out their work activity. An establishment also is synonymous with a workplace in some industries where fissuring has become common, including hotel and motel, eating and drinking, and parts of retailing.

However, in a number of other industries with fissured workplaces, the definition of "establishment" captures only the location where payroll functions are undertaken and (perhaps) where work is coordinated, not the actual physical location where work is done. An establishment in residential construction, for example, may be a division office or perhaps a trailer where payroll is dispersed, but not the actual building sites where work is undertaken and employees found. In the years immediately preceding the collapse of the home building industry, there was an average of thirteen home building sites to every home building "establishment."[8]

Similarly, agricultural establishments are very different than "farms." The latter are defined by the Census as "any place from which $1,000 or more of agricultural products were produced and sold, or normally would have been sold, during the Census year."[9] This broad definition better captures where farm work itself is carried out. The broadest definition of "agriculture" (the North American Industry Classification System [NAICS], code 11) counted a total of 22,651 establishments in 2008, but this represents only a fraction of the total number of farms, which in 2007 exceeded 2.2 million.[10]

A third example can be found in janitorial services, for which the establishment estimate includes only those locations where janitorial service providers kept payroll records, but not the thousands of locations where their employees provided services. In 2009 the estimated number of customer accounts maintained by a typical commercial janitorial service was sixteen, meaning that a rough estimate of physical locations where janitorial employees undertake their work is closer to 850,000 than the 53,000 reported in Table 9.1.

Table 9.2 provides revised estimates of annual investigation probabilities for a subset of fissured industries where the number of workplaces and the number of establishments diverge significantly. The table underscores the even larger gap between investigation resources and the location of vulnerable workers in residential construction, janitorial services, and agricultural products.[11]

When a more representative measure of the number of workplaces in the three industries in Table 9.2 is used, the annual chance of an investigation becomes vanishingly small: for a residential construction site about 1 in 10,000, and for janitorial services about 1 in 5,000. Of course, these represent simple averages, and the best estimate of the probability of an investigation probably rests somewhere between those in columns 3 and 4 of Table 9.2.[12] But this still implies tiny chances of an investigation in any given year. Even for some

Table 9.2 Revised Wage and Hour Division annual investigation probabilities in selected fissured industries

Industry	(1) No. of establishments (CBP 2008)	(2) Estimated no. of physical workplace locations	(3) Annual probability of WHD investigation (Table 9.1)	(4) Revised probability given workplace estimates
Residential construction[a]	187,327	2,435,251	0.138%	0.01%
Agricultural products, multiple sectors[b]	22,651	350,562	5.351%	0.35%
Janitorial services[c]	53,093	849,488	0.328%	0.020%

Sources: North American Industry Classification System (NAICS) code hierarchy table, including Census Bureau definitions of codes, http://www.census.gov/cgi-bin/sssd/naics/naicsrch?chart=2007; U.S. Bureau of the Census, County Business Patterns (CBP) data, by NAICS, http://censtats.census.gov/; Bureau of Labor Statistics employment data, State and County Wages: Quarterly Census of Employment and Wages (QCEW), http://www.bls.gov/cew/#databases; U.S. Department of Agriculture, National Agricultural Statistics Services, Selected Characteristics of Farms by NAICs in 2007 Census of Agriculture; U.S. Bureau of the Census, housing starts data http://www.census.gov/construction/nrc; number of contracts for janitorial services providers: 2009 Kaviac Inc., *Contract Cleaning Benchmark Survey Report,* reported by NTP Media.

a. Based on the ratio of housing starts to establishments in 2007.

b. Based on the reported number of farms with annual production above $100,000.

c. Based on the reported number of clients per janitorial services per business enterprise.

of the largest companies in fissured industries, the likelihood of receiving a WHD investigation is tiny. For example, the chance that an outlet of one of the top twenty fast-food restaurants (for example, Burger King, Subway) will receive an investigation is about 0.008 in a given year. Many employers operate under an expectation that government investigations are not a matter of first-order concern.[13]

These investigation probabilities underscore why traditional approaches to enforcement are insufficient to address vulnerable workers in fissured industries. Even with the significant increase in resources for enforcement provided by the Obama administration, there are simply too many workplaces given available resources to exercise significant oversight via a workplace-by-workplace model of investigations. Enforcement and other strategies must seek to change compliance at the bottom of fissured industry structures, among lower-tiered employers, by focusing attention at the point where the incentives driving that behavior originate rather than where compliance problems are observed.[14]

This can be illustrated by the evolution of employment structures in the janitorial sector, discussed in Part II. A great deal of janitorial work was done historically by direct employees of larger business enterprises (for example, an auto manufacturer, computer producer, or university directly employed its janitorial workforce). Outsourcing of these activities led them to be purchased as a service. This, in turn, gave rise to a large, self-standing janitorial services industry with its own set of firms and business organizations (including franchises) providing these cleaning services. As a result, rather than having a WHD investigator examine overtime compliance of janitorial workers as part of a review of a larger business organization, fissuring means that those workers no longer work under the auspices of that employer. Instead, janitors must be found at the service provider's clients' sites, which will be widely dispersed.

Investigation protocols need to reflect this changed reality. An investigation at a residential construction site must not only consider where payroll records are kept, but also the set of sites being run from that office. This becomes even more important given the prevalence of off-the-clock practices, under-the-table cash payments, and misclassification, which can be detected only by cross-checking records with interviews of employees. Similarly, investigation of janitorial service providers must identify their customer base and include them as an integral part of the investigation protocol. Only then can patterns of violations detectable at the work-site level be adequately tied to a larger set of practices that often drive noncompliance.

Limits of Traditional Approaches to Enforcement

Traditional enforcement approaches are based on investigations having two types of effects. First, an investigation changes the behavior (compliance) of the individual employer being investigated directly through the finding and correction of past violations. Back wage findings by the WHD are designed to restore wages owed to workers retrospectively. OSHA and MSHA inspections uncover violations of health and safety standards. Civil monetary penalties for repeat or willful violators, as well as injunctive actions or settlement agreements, are intended to ensure that employers comply in the future.

Second, an investigation has deterrent effects on other employers who are making compliance decisions. Raising the probability of investigations—which other employers may become aware of either through the communication efforts of the Department of Labor or through their own communications with other employers in the same industry and/or geographic region—increases the incentives to comply even absent an investigation. The potential of being assessed civil monetary penalties provides further incentives to comply if such penalties impose significant costs on employers. An investigation may also have deterrent effects when, after its completion, the agency issues a press release that includes the violations found and the penalties assessed—a signal to all employers that they could also receive negative publicity for any violations found.

The problem of traditional enforcement in a world of fissured workplaces is illustrated by enforcement of minimum wage and overtime regulations under the Fair Labor Standards Act. The primary recourse under the FLSA is recovery of back wages owed to workers for underpayment of minimum wage, overtime, or other statutory obligations. For many years, the WHD has been evaluated by external constituents—and indeed has measured its own success—primarily through the amount of back wages it recovers (in addition to overall numbers of cases concluded).

Making sure that workers who have been underpaid—or not compensated at all—get fairly paid is of course fundamental, so increasing back wage recovery over time is a laudable objective. But recovery of back wages per se should not be defined as the WHD's principal objective. If the factors that lead employers to decide not to comply with laws do not change, then investigators are forever trying to fix a system that remains broken. An apt analogy would be to occupational health and safety. Although workers' compensation policies provide benefits to workers who have been hurt at the workplace and whose earnings have been impacted, the ultimate objective of health and safety policy (including OSHA) is to reduce or prevent injuries and fatalities in the workplace, not simply to ensure that those injured are compensated (as important as that objective is). Enforcement that cleans up past noncompliance but does not alter behavior puts investigators on a hamster wheel: running very fast and working very hard, but not advancing the larger aim of protecting and enhancing the welfare of the workforce.

Focusing enforcement on back wage recovery alone or on inspections aimed at bringing individual workplaces back into compliance with specific health and safety standards is no longer sufficient if the goal is creating significant and sustainable improvements in working conditions. A strategic focus is required.

Focusing at the Top

Traditional enforcement strategies assume that enforcement efforts should focus at the level where workplace violations are occurring. Yet, as has been argued throughout this book, the forces driving noncompliance in many industries arise from the organizations located at higher levels of industry structures. Strategic enforcement should therefore focus on higher-level, seemingly more removed business entities that affect the compliance behavior "on the ground," where vulnerable workers are actually found.

For enforcement to be effective in a fissured workplace, agencies responsible for enforcing the law need to map the business relationships underlying a sector, carefully tracking all of the different players that impact workplace conditions. The map, in turn, indicates which organizations ultimately must be considered in developing investigation plans. An eating and drinking initiative should, for example, include investigations not only of outlets with violations (for example, those arising from complaints), but also of other units owned by the particular franchisee. It would also include a systematic analysis of all other investigations of the franchisor (brand) in question to detect the presence of multiple instances of violations at other franchisees. Finally, it could entail contacting the brand itself regarding the results of these investigations if it was clear that significant violations extended beyond the boundaries of any one franchisee or owner group.[15]

This approach implies a very different orientation where the government focuses its efforts at the portion of the industry driving conditions that ultimately result in compliance problems. Although this entity may differ from the employer of record, reorienting enforcement attention in this way alters how the various parties up and down industry structures behave in a manner more compatible with better workplace conditions.

A top-focused enforcement strategy would target lead organizations that had a documented history of systemic violations among their subordinate units (for example, franchisees; subcontracted entities; workplaces monitored through third-party arrangements). These lead players could be identified through evaluation of past investigation records (for example, persistent noncompliance across the units in a major hotel brand).[16] Once the lead players are identified, workplace agencies could undertake broad and coordinated investigations in different locations and across multiple franchisees in order to establish the level of system-wide violations and pursue statutory penalties for those violations. As part of the process of resolving the violations, agencies could negotiate a comprehensive agreement covering all outlets/properties, which would entail outreach, education, and monitoring.

Beyond direct enforcement, outreach could also be geared to lead firms in their role as promulgators of standards and practices among subsidiary units, whether as a brand, a major logistic coordinator, or a third-party manager. Specific outreach could be geared to major brands depending on their prior records of compliance. Agencies could reach out to several major brands in those industries with positive employment reputations and a positive record of system-wide compliance and ask them to be leaders in the industry and help ensure compliance with workplace policies across their systems of franchisees. A cooperative agreement could include a commitment by the brand to cascade information through its company-owned properties and outlets and to its franchisees, as well as a commitment to review employment practices with franchisees when other franchise standards are being reviewed—with the intention that such efforts could be a model for other progressive major brands.

In June 2013, the WHD announced an initiative with the fast-food franchisor Subway along these lines. The effort seeks to increase compliance with federal workplace laws through educating franchisees, provision of information to Subway workers, and changes to franchise governing documents.[17] Another example of such a program can be found in Australia. The Fair Work Ombudsman, an Australian agency whose mission includes ensuring compliance with federal workplace laws, launched the National Franchise Program (NFP) for the country's largest franchisors in 2012. The NFP "offers franchisors an opportunity to protect their brand by proactively working with us to support fair and compliant workplaces in their franchise business." The initiative includes education and training programs and materials as well as resources to cooperatively create model franchise agreements promoting workplace compliance among franchise systems.[18]

The Department of Labor has had several relevant experiences with comparable initiatives. One example dates back to the Clinton administration's efforts to improve compliance in the apparel industry. More recently, the Obama administration has undertaken several promising initiatives, which are described below.

Enforcement and Monitoring in Apparel

Garment manufacturing represents one of the oldest examples of a fissured industry, and the government has wrestled with the task of improving working conditions in the industry for more than a century. In 1893 the Committee on Manufacturers of the House of Representatives released a report regarding its investigations of the "sweating system" of production. Among other findings, the committee concluded that 80% of production originated in sweatshops.[19] Several years later, President William McKinley appointed a commission made up of members of Congress and private citizens to study the problem. Arising from its study, running from 1898 to 1901, the commission documented extensive abuses, including long hours, low pay, and unsanitary conditions.[20]

Core characteristics of the product and labor markets in the apparel industry push contractors to cut corners with respect to wages, hours, and conditions. In particular, the women's segment of the industry has always been organized around a splintered production system, where different enterprises carry out the design, cutting, sewing, and pressing/packaging of apparel products.[21] For example, a jobber may sell a design to a retailer, and then contract with a manufacturer for delivery of the product. The manufacturer, in turn, may purchase and cut the product, but then contract out sewing to one or more companies (which may, in turn, further contract out subassembly). Contractors compete to preassemble bundles of cut garment pieces in a market where there is little ability to differentiate services (that is, sewing and associated assembly) except for some operations requiring higher levels of skill. The structure of relations from the retailer down to contractors and subcontractors is depicted in Figure 9.3.

In general, as one goes to lower levels of apparel production (that is, from design and cutting by manufacturers or jobbers at the top of Figure 9.3, to sewing by contractors or subcontractors at the bottom), the level of competition intensifies and the profit margin per garment diminishes. Sewing contractors—often themselves former sewers/cutters and recent immigrants to the United States—compete in a market with large numbers of small companies (employing on average twenty-five to thirty-five workers each in the women's industry), low barriers to entry, and limited opportunities for product differentiation. This creates conditions for intense price-based competition. Because labor costs represent the vast majority of total costs for a sewing contractor, there is great pressure to strike deals with jobbers and manufacturers that are not economically

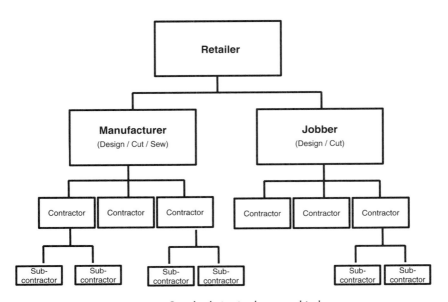

FIGURE 9.3. Supply chains in the apparel industry.

sustainable if the contractor actually complies with wage and hour laws.[22] As a result, noncompliance is predominantly a problem among the large number of contractors and subcontractors that assemble apparel products.

Surveys conducted by the Wage and Hour Division in the late 1990s revealed exactly what one would expect. About one-half of all contractors in Los Angeles in 1998, and one-third of those in New York in 1999, failed to comply with minimum wage laws.[23] The same surveys revealed that a typical garment contractor with thirty-five employees owed approximately $11,850 in back wages annually.[24] Given very low investigation probabilities for any contractor and the modest penalties for violations, a contractor had a very high incentive to underpay workers, even when faced with additional investigations.[25]

Traditional regulatory activity focused on that contractor/subcontractor level of the apparel industry. The primary means of inducing compliance was through direct investigation and the imposition of civil penalties on those repeatedly found in violation. This led to a seemingly endless cat-and-mouse game between the WHD and small-scale contractors, whereby efforts to reduce sweatshop conditions in the garment industry were thwarted by companies constantly going into and out of business, either because of the harsh competitive conditions in the industry or as a means of evading penalties for past violations.

The dynamics of the apparel industry changed dramatically given the emergence of lean retailing. Lean retailing relies on information technology to provide retailers with real-time point-of-sale data for purposes of reordering products and inventory management. These practices reduce the need for retailers to stockpile large inventories, thereby reducing their risks of stockouts, markdowns, and inventory-carrying costs.

Apparel companies supplying to lean retailers must operate far more responsively and accept a great deal more consumer demand risk. Suppliers must replenish products within a selling season, with retailers requiring replenishment of orders in as little as three days. Any disruption in the weekly replenishment of retail orders by apparel suppliers becomes a major problem—one that can lead retailers to assess penalties, cancel orders, and even drop "unreliable" suppliers. The increasing importance of time translates into a potential tool of regulatory enforcement.[26]

Through an initiative begun in 1996, the Wage and Hour Division shifted the focus of enforcement efforts by exerting regulatory pressure on manufacturers in the apparel supply chain rather than on individual small-scale contractors. Section 15(a) of the Fair Labor Standards Act (the "hot goods" provision) allows the Labor Department to enjoin the transportation, shipment, delivery, or sale across state lines of goods that have been produced by any employee who has not been paid the minimum wage or overtime compensation as required by the FLSA.[27] Although the agency's ability to enjoin goods from transportation had limited impact in the traditional retail-apparel supply chain, when long delays in shipments and large retail inventories were expected, invocation of the hot good authority today can raise the costs to retailers and their manufacturers of lost shipments and lost contracts (given the short lead times of retailers). Indeed, invoking this provision potentially creates significant penalties arising from violations that quickly exceed those arising from back wages owed and civil penalties.[28]

The WHD's policy drew on the ability to invoke the hot goods provision to persuade manufacturers to step up regulatory action by making the release of embargoed goods contingent upon *the manufacturer's* agreement to create a compliance program for its subcontractors. The manufacturer must agree to sign two types of agreement: one between the manufacturer and the Department of Labor, and one between the manufacturer and its contractors. The agreements stipulate basic components of a monitoring system to be operated by the manufacturer.[29]

Statistical analyses of these monitoring arrangements demonstrate that they led to very significant improvements in minimum wage compliance among apparel contractors in Southern California and New York City. For example, in Southern California in 2000, stringent contractor monitoring by manufacturers (adopted as a result of agreements with the Wage and Hour Division) was associated with an estimated reduction in the incidence of minimum wage underpayments by covered contractors of 20 violations per 100 workers and a reduction in the level of back wage underpayment by an average of $6.00 per worker per week.[30] These represent very large effects since the overall level of minimum wage violations per 100 workers in a random sample of Southern California apparel contractors was 27, and back wages owed per work per week were $6.50.[31]

By focusing at the top of supply chain, the WHD replaced the cat-and-mouse games that characterized traditional enforcement with a focus on a key party (the manufacturer) that drives subcontracting compliance.[32] As a result, the strategy of using public enforcement power (enjoining transportation of goods) to create private monitoring systems had powerful deterrent effects, which in turn created a platform for sustainable improvements in compliance. The results from Los Angeles for 1998–2000 and particularly those from New York for 1999–2001 indicate system-wide improvement in compliance during that time. What is more, the incentives for manufacturers to find partners who were less likely to cause their goods to be embargoed seemed to raise average levels of compliance among new garment contractors entering the system.[33]

The supply chain approach for garments was put aside during the eight years of the Bush administration. Between 2008 and the 2012, the WHD conducted 1,500 investigations of garment contractors and manufacturers in Southern California and once again found wide-scale violations of the FLSA. A sweep of garment factories in downtown Los Angeles in the summer of 2012 uncovered minimum wage and overtime violations in shops producing products for a number of clothing retailers, including Forever 21, a major apparel retailer.[34]

In a sign of a renewed focus on improving compliance by focusing on supply chain dynamics, in October 2012 the Department of Labor issued a subpoena to Forever 21 to provide documents regarding its manufacturers and contractors operating in Southern California. Ruben Rosalez, the WHD's western regional administrator, noted in a press announcement at the time of the subpoena, "Since 2008, our investigators have identified dozens of manufacturers producing goods for Forever 21 under sweatshop-like conditions," including widespread violations of minimum wage, overtime, and record-keeping requirements among the retailer's domestic suppliers. Noting the retailer's reluctance to provide information to the WHD as part of its ongoing investigation, Rosalez stated, "When companies like Forever 21 refuse to comply with subpoenas, they demonstrate a clear disregard for the law, and the Labor Department will use all enforcement tools available to recover wages and hold employers accountable."[35]

Enterprise-Wide Agreements

Traditional workplace enforcement approaches focus on the workplace where violations are found and seeks remedies only at that level. However, significant violations at one workplace may suggest a wider pattern of violations for the enterprise with which the workplace is associated. A step forward is therefore to assure that the entire enterprise with which the workplace is affiliated also moves toward compliance as a result of the investigation. Many state-level labor enforcement agencies in recent years and the Obama administration have instigated the signing of corporate-wide settlement agreements where there is evidence that widespread problems exist.[36]

One example is an agreement reached between OSHA and Munro Muffler Company, an auto service provider with eight hundred stores across the country. A hydraulic lift at a Munro Muffler shop in Stoughton, Massachusetts, failed, causing a car to fall to the ground. Although no one was injured, the incident led to an OSHA inspection and a fine of $19,000. Munro initially contested the penalty but ultimately came to an agreement with OSHA on a settlement covering not only the garage where the accident occurred, but all of its facilities. Inspections of the Stoughton case revealed that the company lacked a corporate-wide policy dealing with safety risks posed by hydraulic lifts. The agreement requires Munro Muffler to develop and implement an inspection and maintenance program for lifts in all sites covered by OSHA. Program components include training for operators, ongoing inspections of equipment to assure compliance with industry standards, a requirement to remedy problems where they are identified, and provision of written reports to OSHA.[37]

Another illustrative enterprise-wide agreement arose from OSHA inspections of DeMoulas Supermarket (Market Basket) stores that found widespread fall and laceration hazards and resulted in penalties of $589,200. After contesting the initial citations, DeMoulas reached a settlement agreement with the Solicitor's Office of the Department of Labor to both remedy the hazards and initiate a policy to prevent future hazards at the company's sixty stores. Specifically, the agreement requires the company to develop a safety and health program for each store. Each program is required to cover monitoring and evaluation processes to gauge effectiveness, requirements to document and act on identified hazards and violations, and an explicit disciplinary program covering employees (including management) who violate standards. To ensure implementation of the policies, the agreement requires that DeMoulas hire a full-time health and safety director with "authority and responsibility to develop, implement, monitor and enforce the requirements of the company's safety and health program." It also requires extensive training for new and existing employees annually as well as incorporating safety and health performance measures as part of review criteria for store and department managers.[38]

Three elements of the Munro and DeMoulas enterprise-wide agreements are notable and relevant to enforcing workplace laws in response to fissured workplace conditions. First, the enterprise-wide agreements are systemic, creating mechanisms to reduce hazards across the entire organization, not just where hazards are directly observed. Second, the agreements are proactive in nature, not only remedying the immediate problem but creating systems that can detect and act upon new hazards before they result in problems. Third, the agreements create private systems based on public enforcement pressure. They allow businesses to develop internal mechanisms to monitor and supervise ongoing safety and health efforts where they have both the ability and, in conjunction with the requirements of the agreements, the expertise to do so. But the private monitoring is accompanied by public enforcement teeth (the consent agreement itself) that provide greater incentives to adhere to the provisions of the agreements than would arise from voluntary arrangements.

Focusing at the top of the enterprise in coming to these agreements changes conditions at workplaces far beyond what would be achieved through traditional enforcement approaches. Remarking on the Munro Muffler agreement, Marthe Kent, OSHA's regional administrator for Massachusetts, notes, "What's important about this agreement is its multiplier effect. It will enhance safety for Monro employees at service centers in multiple states. That means safer working conditions for thousands of workers at hundreds of workplaces."[39]

Mending Fissured Construction

Two recent efforts by the Department of Labor—one by the Occupational Safety and Health Administration and another at the Wage and Hour Division—apply a top-focused approach to the construction sector. Like lead firms in many industries, general contractors or construction managers set the tone and create overall standards that are followed by the subcontractors on a building site of any scale.[40] The importance of the lead contractor underscores the importance of the multiemployer policy under OSHA, affirmed in the *Summit Contractors* decision discussed in Chapter 8. The controlling employer principle in that policy is a form of focusing enforcement from the top.

The idea of placing greater pressure through the policy is not a matter of going after the deepest pockets. Focusing at the top of the construction site raises the stakes for the general contractor to use its unique and critical role in how it selects its team of contractors (including how it weighs low prices in bids against a contractor's past performance on safety, quality, and related activities); how it undertakes and coordinates health and safety activities on the site in the course of construction; how it monitors the day-to-day running of the construction site; and how it evaluates and rewards or punishes subcontractors based on their performance. The tools of enforcement (including citing and penalizing general contractors and construction managers for failing to fulfill their role in overseeing compliance with specific OSHA standards) therefore create changes in the on-the-ground management of construction as well as what kinds of contractors successfully win work, which could change overall exposure to health and safety risks.

OSHA AND NATIONS ROOF

Residential building tends to be more decentralized than other segments of the construction industry. However, there was considerable industry consolidation among major U.S. home builders before the housing bubble burst in 2007. As a result, at the peak of the building boom, the top ten builders accounted for close to 25% of new single-family homes constructed.[41] Consolidation at the top also led to the growth of some large-scale contractors. An OSHA settlement with one of these national players, Nations Roof LLC, provides one example of an enforcement agreement focused on the top. The case involved a group of roofing contractors, all under the general umbrella of an entity called Nations Roof LLC, but operating as seventeen affiliated companies.

In the past, OSHA enforcement procedures would deal with each company as an independent and separate entity. However, as part of the enterprise-level effort discussed above, OSHA treated violations documented at different affiliated companies as if they were all part of one common enterprise. As part of the complaint associated with the inspection, OSHA cited Nations Roof LLC's own website as evidence of the coordinating role exercised by that entity over its affiliates:

This is a company that owns all its locations, not an affiliation of independents; it is one company that can deliver consistently and on time . . . Nations Roof does not support separate and redundant overhead in multiple locations and business unit presidents are highly motivated owner-partners in the company.

A direct implication of treating the affiliated companies as part of a common business was that violations found in multiple places could be treated as repeat violations and therefore subjected to higher penalties. For example, by considering the various affiliates as part of the national company, citations of serious violations for inadequate protections against roof falls (that is, employees exposed to falls of twenty to twenty-two feet with no fall protection) were reclassified from a "serious" violation to a "repeat" violation, thereby increasing the proposed penalty from $2,100 to $35,000.[42]

A settlement agreement between OSHA and Nations Roof contains a number of novel features that require the parent organization, Nations Roof, to undertake a role as the responsible party for overall safety and health across the sixteen affiliated businesses.[43] First, in exchange for a reduction in penalties, the agreement requires that the management development program for the business managers of all sixteen affiliates be amended to include training on safety and health policies, practices, and standards. Second, it requires that each affiliate appoint a manager to be the health and safety director, with specific responsibilities, including accountability for the creation and administration of a health and safety policy, and engage in specific activities including weekly inspections of construction sites.[44] Third, the settlement requires Nations Roof to review "on a regular basis (e.g. annually, semi-annually, etc.) . . . the performance of each Business Unit Owner/Manager with respect to matters affecting occupational safety and health." Performance criteria include the number and severity of occupational injuries and illnesses at the company's construction sites; the quantity and quality of inspections conducted by the company; and other factors related to the adequacy of its safety and health programs. Fourth, the agreement lays out very specific and stringent requirements for general health and safety procedures, job site inspections, training, daily "toolbox talks" about safety issues, and development of site-specific safety plans on an ongoing basis.

Finally, the settlement agreement requires Nations Roof to "perform random, unannounced inspections of the active jobsites of every Nations Roof

Affiliate . . . Except as otherwise provided in this Section 4(I)(iii), Respondent Nations Roof, LLC shall conduct four Parent Inspections of each Nations Roof Affiliate every calendar year." The latter activities once again make clear the responsibility of the parent organization in overseeing the health and safety activities of affiliates (just as its website describes its role in assuring the delivery of services "consistently and on time").

The WHD and Lettire Construction

Workers on construction sites receiving federal funds must pay wages that comply with local prevailing wages for the different construction trades.[45] Recent efforts by the WHD signal that its enforcement approach will hold general contractors overseeing federally funded construction projects responsible for violations of prevailing wage requirements among their own workforce, but also for violations by subcontractors on those sites. The case involving Lettire Construction, a major affordable housing contractor, is illustrative.

Following an investigation of Lettire Construction and its sixteen subcontractors on two New York–based projects that received funds from the American Recovery and Reinvestment Act of 2009, the WHD cited the company and its subcontractors for numerous prevailing wage violations, including failure to pay required overtime, improper classification of employees, and underpayment of both wages and fringe benefits. In addition to resolving the back wage claims of affected employees of Lettire and its subcontractors, a consent agreement between the company and the Department of Labor requires the company to "ensure its own and its subcontractors' future compliance . . . and to guarantee payment for any future violations committed by its subcontractors on federally funded local, state and federal prevailing projects."

The consent agreement also creates monitoring mechanisms to ensure future compliance of Lettire and its subcontractors by requiring the company to hire an approved third-party monitor to undertake regular compliance reviews of the company and its subcontractors on publicly funded projects. The monitor is also tasked with training both Lettire and subcontractor staff on requirements, and with creating a hotline to allow workers to report noncompliance confidentially. Lettire is also required to screen prospective subcontractors to assess their past compliance history before hiring them (thereby creating positive feedback of pairing compliant contractors and subcontractors, as in the garment effort). Finally, the agreement subjects the company to debarment (that is, inability to bid future federally funded work) for failing to follow the terms of the consent agreement, creating significant incentives to abide by it.[46]

The direct effects of agreements of this type on future compliance with workplace laws on the network of contractors undertaking work are significant in themselves. But the more important impacts may arise from the ripple effects that such settlements may have on how contractors bid, monitor, and screen subcontractors, thereby ensuring that responsible businesses are not undercut by those that gain advantage from violating the law.

Transparency, Reputation, and Striking a New Balance

A strategy complementary to top-focused policies like the examples discussed above is to act on one of the key components underlying fissuring: brand reputation. Reputation-based competitive strategies have become pervasive across industries—even in those producing what were once considered commodity products. They make good business sense: by creating strong consumer allegiances or by assuring tight quality standards (or through a combination of the two), businesses can create margins through higher pricing. This is a legitimate aim that is often beneficial to consumers and the public.

However, these business strategies lead to great sensitivity to any form of threat to image or disruption of carefully crafted standards. Threats to these systems—private, public, or otherwise—lead to businesses putting in place private systems to preempt the loss of reputation among consumers or, more ominously, onerous public interventions. Whether one looks at Nike's response to accusations of its shoes being made in sweatshops, Apple's response to supplier conditions in the factories producing iPhones, or Walmart's responses to any number of labor, environmental, or consumer campaigns, lead businesses are sensitive to reputational attacks.

Targeted transparency—the disclosure of standardized information about organizations regarding their performance to serve a regulatory purpose—has become widespread. Through the power of transparency, disclosing information about workplace practices in fissured industries could create incentives for the development of alternative methods of addressing problems. Although the disclosed information may lead some consumers with a particular interest in working conditions to avoid companies with poor records, this need not be the only channel through which disclosure operates. If violations are perceived as indicators—or reasons—for compromised food or service quality, disclosure creates incentives for lead firms to change practices in order to protect their brand. This includes preemptive responses, which are frequently the result of mandatory disclosure policies.[47]

An interesting example of a public policy revealing variations in the performance of franchisees is the impact of transparency on restaurant hygiene in Los Angeles County. Before the imposition of mandated restaurant disclosure, franchisees within a brand had worse hygiene performance than company-owned outlets of the same brands. In 1998 Los Angeles County required restaurants to publicly post grades, based on restaurant hygiene inspections, in their front windows. This public disclosure led to a narrowing and ultimately elimination of these discrepancies in intra-brand hygiene performance. Eliminating free riding in this way was a consequence of consumer behavior. But it was also a result of the overall threat to reputation leading to greater internal pressure from brands on their franchisees.[48]

These examples imply that reputation can be a source of regulatory jujitsu—even without recourse to legal strategies. Workplace regulatory agencies could map relations—whether subcontracting, third-party management, or franchising—of the entities they inspected routinely to the entities that had an overarching role in their activities and report on violations and investigations to that controlling entity. And these agencies could also provide information on their activities via the Web as a matter of course, irrespective of other enforcement activities.[49]

An effort of the Obama administration picks up on the opportunities to use transparency as a regulatory instrument. As part of its larger effort to promote transparency across executive agencies, the Department of Labor has promoted development of new apps to assist workers in assessing whether they have been paid according to FLSA standards. It has also sponsored development contests to create apps that use WHD and OSHA data to provide end users with information on past compliance behavior. The winner of the first app contest, "eat/shop/sleep," provides this information in a format similar to consumer search apps like Yelp. These have the potential of increasing the salience and impact of enforcement data generally and those connected with fissured enforcement efforts in particular.[50]

Stopping Lowest-Road Employers

Egregious Fissuring

Some forms of fissuring are clearly directed toward end-running basic employment responsibilities, such as deliberately classifying workers as independent contractors who by all recognizable standards are employees. As discussed in Chapter 8, many states became aware of this problem in the past decade, and multiple state-level statutes expressly address misclassification. In 2011 the Department of Labor also announced a major enforcement initiative focused on misclassification, in concert with the Internal Revenue Service and a number of state labor agencies.

These efforts are aimed at stopping forms of fissuring that are not only illegal, but have the secondary effect of creating competitive conditions that undercut legitimate service providers in an industry. The case of the janitorial service industry is indicative. As noted throughout this book, franchising has become a dominant form of fissuring in the janitorial sector in recent years. This particular franchise structure inherently places franchisees in a position that undermines their ability to obey workplace laws and requirements. An analysis of the underlying costs of a typical franchise structure when compared against prevailing prices for janitorial services in those markets implies that a franchisee faces one of two options: either underpay the workforce or fail to receive returns high enough to sustain the franchise.[51]

Any effort to improve compliance in this industry must begin with the market dynamics clearly in mind. Traditional approaches to enforcement—focusing on the individual enterprise—will certainly bring to light case after case of violations of minimum wages, overtime pay, off-the-clock work, and so on. But if not wedded to a larger strategy that attempts to change the market forces that drive this behavior, enforcement will not diminish the prevalence of the problem. Enforcement efforts and other public policies (including those protecting potential investors in franchises) must evaluate whether these forms of business organization not only create conditions inherently disadvantageous to franchisees, but undermine broader public policy objectives by driving down prevailing price levels and, in turn, the ability to meet workplace obligations.[52]

Focusing on the Worst Offenders

A fissured workplace also requires that government agencies use their limited resources strategically even when not part of the type of focused efforts described in the previous section. For example, complaint-driven inspections (which drive a great deal of investigation activity in many workplace agencies, including more than 70% of WHD investigations) need to be integrated into the larger regulatory efforts rather than being undertaken in an entirely reactive fashion.[53]

General enforcement policy should also seek to influence employer behavior through effective use of specific and general deterrence. Ideally, assessed penalties change the subsequent behavior of the inspected firm, leading it to choose to remain in compliance in the future. Affecting the behavior of the parties in this way is termed "specific deterrence." Penalties may also change the behavior of regulated parties prospectively: the prospect of receiving a penalty creates potential costs that regulated parties seek to avoid through voluntary compliance. These *general deterrent effects* of penalties are particularly important when the government is unable to inspect all firms covered by a policy and must instead depend on deterrence to change behavior. The amount of penalties in this case could reflect the benefits of noncompliance or the harm imposed. But it should also reflect the probability of inspection and detection.[54]

One particular aspect of strategic enforcement warrants emphasis: the need to focus on bad actors in an industry—those not only committing significant violations of the law, but doing so on a repeated and willful basis. For reasons discussed below, these organizations can play an outsized role in their sector by sending signals regarding the potential to flout standards to other employers that are similarly situated (or facing similar pressures and vulnerable to tipping toward noncompliance at lower levels of fissured structures). More troubling, their actions may send signals even to compliant employers who may view their persistence as an indication of the lack of fairness of the regulatory system as a whole, leading to an erosion of the overall culture of compliance in an industry. Efforts, therefore, to both identify and deal effectively with the worst actors are a critical complement to an overall approach to fissured industries.

The MSHA POV Program

The Mine Safety and Health Act of 1977 provides the strongest system of inspections, penalties, and enforcement tools of any federal workplace law.[55] It requires a minimum of four inspections of all active underground mining operations per year. It also provides for a high penalty structure (at least relative to OSHA), including a maximum of $7,000 per citation for serious violations and up to $70,000 per violation for willful or repeated violations.[56] Additionally, the law gives the MSHA the authority to close sections or operations of mines in the face of "imminent dangers" and imposes significant consequences on mine operators who fail to abate violations promptly.

As the death of twenty-nine miners in the Massey Upper Big Branch mine disaster of April 2010 attests, however, even with such stronger enforcement devices, mining remains a highly dangerous sector with a continuing presence of recalcitrant operators unwilling to abide by health and safety standards and practices. Noting in its December 2011 accident investigation report that "the root cause of the tragedy" was "unlawful policies and practices" of Massey Energy, MSHA issued 369 citations and assessed $10.8 million in penalties.[57] Massey Energy had been led since 1994 by Don Blankenship, an outspoken critic of MSHA and government regulation in general. The company had been repeatedly cited for significant and substantial violations of MSHA standards throughout his tenure, including in a series of inspections undertaken in 2009 that resulted in 515 citations.[58] Finding ways to pressure such companies beyond penalties became a priority of the agency.

A recent initiative of MSHA provides an important model for targeting the worst violators in the industry and placing significant pressure on them to improve their behavior. Under section 104(e) of the Mine Safety and Health Act, MSHA is granted enforcement tools to deal with operators that have shown consistent disregard for the health and safety of miners. If a mine operator is classified as operating with a "pattern of violations" (POV), each subsequent significant and substantial (S&S) violation found by MSHA investigators results in an order requiring the operator to withdraw miners from the affected area until the cited condition has been corrected.[59] By requiring the withdrawal of miners, the provision essentially gives the agency authority to stop operations until the operator addresses the problem found in the citation. An operator must demonstrate progress in improving the overall conditions that led to the designated POV status.

In practice, the use of these provisions has been limited and has been contested by the industry. Attempts to issue regulations to clarify procedures for implementing these procedures have been controversial and time-consuming.[60] The Obama administration promulgated new regulations to allow the agency to better identify and more consistently assess POVs on recalcitrant operators. First, these new regulations use a broader measure of operator behavior, combining compliance, accident, injury, and illness records to identify problematic mines, and creating thresholds for POV status. The change would both clarify the criteria being used so that they can be more consistently applied and better align those criteria with outcomes to more effectively identify recalcitrant operators who are creating dangerous work environments. Second, information on the POV status of operators would be available via a monthly monitoring tool for patterns of violations available on the Web. The tool allows mine operators to monitor their own compliance record against POV criteria. As noted in the rule:

> Prior to MSHA's creation of the on-line Monthly Monitoring Tool, mine operators had to track each mine's compliance performance and calculate the statistics to determine whether the mine met each of the specific screening criteria. Many mine operators relied on MSHA to issue a POV notice. Now, with MSHA's on-line Monthly Monitoring Tool, they do not have to calculate the statistics. Operators, including those that own multiple mines, can easily monitor their performance.[61]

The online tool therefore enables operators to proactively take steps to improve safety and health and bring mines into compliance.

Third, the regulations allow operators approaching the POV level to work with MSHA to develop an approved health and safety management program where it would lead to appreciable reductions in significant and substantial violations and establish specific benchmarks. Finally, the rule allows MSHA to use all citations and orders (including those being contested by the operator) rather than only final citations and orders for determining POVs. This is important given the high number of contested citations that currently are not taken into account in determining operator status.[62]

Undoubtedly, the POV regulation creates incentives for gaming. In particular, operators face a greater incentive to underreport accident and injury statistics used in assigning POV status. The higher the stakes of crossing the

POV threshold, the greater the incentives to underreport injuries or engage in other record-keeping efforts to reduce POV-related measures. But this is a basic problem in any regulatory system that puts in place significant consequences for noncompliance.

The Lessons of Black Mag

On May 14, 2010, an explosion at Black Mag LLC, a manufacturer of gunpowder, resulted in the death of two employees at its manufacturing facility. An investigation of the explosion at the company's Colebrook, New Hampshire, facilities revealed the presence of fifty willful, egregious, and serious violations. OSHA assessed total penalties of $1.2 million which the employer then vigorously contested. The primary contention of the company was that as a result of the explosion and the size of the penalties, it was unable to continue in business and pay the penalties.

Ultimately, the case was settled between OSHA and the company's president and owner, Craig Sanborn, in an unusual agreement. Black Mag LLC, with Sanborn's concurrence, agreed to withdraw its notice of contest of the penalty and admitted that it had violated the Occupational Safety and Health Act. Sanborn agreed not to "conduct, establish, own or manage by himself, with or through others, any current or future business that is covered anywhere under OSHA's explosives or process safety management standards if that business employs workers or independent contractors." Additionally, he agreed to "have no involvement in any enterprise that has employees if it is located within 1,000 yards of another business that is covered under OSHA's explosives or process management safety standards." The agreement includes a provision that allows OSHA to file in a federal court for contempt if Sanborn violates its terms.[63]

Black Mag represents an extreme case of an employer so dangerous that the public interest is served by barring it from employing workers. But the case also underscores the importance of enforcement policy identifying and fashioning strong responses to deal with the worst violators or those whose activities undermine the competitive position of compliant employers (particularly those operating in highly competitive conditions in fissured structures). Clearly, workers employed where there are egregious, willful, and repeat violations of standards benefit from robust government responses to those situations. These efforts also provide important deterrent effects for other firms, particularly those with a similar inclination to flaut the law. Deterrent effects are further amplified where well publicized, or through a transparency mechanism such as that created under MSHA's current (and prospective) POV system.

Another, more subtle, benefit of instituting tough and well-publicized enforcement measures aimed at the worst offenders is their impact on organizations that are already complying with laws. In their studies of environmental enforcement, political scientists Dorothy Thornton, Neil Gunningham, and Robert Kagan have found that companies that were already largely compliant with standards were aware of enforcement actions taken against the worst offenders in their industry or geographic area. This awareness has beneficial effects on those companies' future compliance decisions because such enforcement actions demonstrate the fairness of the overall system, thereby reinforcing their own behavior.[64]

Rebalancing the Fissured Decision

Given the relatively uncharted waters represented by a strategic enforcement approach to fissured employment, there are many different ways lead organizations might respond with respect to taking greater responsibility for the actions of businesses operating under them. This could include branded companies setting up internal private training systems for affiliated organizations; incorporating more explicit workplace standards in the detailed standards that are central to fissured employment; setting up more formal monitoring systems to ensure adherence across all affiliated organizations; and engaging in more aggressive review and removal of franchisees or subordinate organizations engaged in questionable activities.

In the longer term, when regulatory approaches recognize that fissured employment rests on a desire to balance the benefits of corporate strategies like branding with the benefits of shifting employment responsibility, a whole range of policy options becomes possible. Interventions that can affect the tipping point of lead firm decisions may have the best chance to impact the underlying drivers of compliance behavior and to change them in significant and lasting ways that improve conditions in the workplace.

Public policies that significantly change how firms balance the benefits and costs of fissuring would not lead to the reemergence of large employers organized in traditional ways. But they could result in lead companies assuring that the workplaces operating under their umbrellas do so in a manner consistent with both their rigorous private standards of quality and performance and the public standards of decency and fairness underlying our workplace laws.

Fixing Broken Windows

> If a window in a building is broken and is left unrepaired,
> all the rest of the windows will soon be broken . . . [O]ne
> unrepaired broken window is a signal that no one cares,
> and so breaking more windows costs nothing.
>
> —Kelling and Wilson (1982)

In a famous article on reducing crime, James Q. Wilson and George Kelling argued that the focus of traditional policing was misplaced given its emphasis on responding to serious crimes. "Broken windows," as the notion became popularly known, demanded that policing should deal with reducing disorderly behavior and small crimes that created fear among the public, because fear of crime in turn leads citizens to withdraw from their critical role as the true guardians of civic peace. By using community policing and focused efforts to "fix broken windows" through the reduction of panhandling, graffiti, low-level crimes, and other activities that citizens take as signs of imminent danger, people would reassert themselves in the daily life of their neighborhood and retake their role as the glue that Jane Jacobs called the "small change" of urban life. In short, reducing the major crimes that dominate newspaper headlines requires controlling the disorderly street-level activities that spawn them.

The broken windows analogy is a useful one for the U.S. workplace. In some workplaces—particularly those employing large numbers of low-wage workers—day-to-day experience is replete with violations of basic labor standards. People are asked to set up their workstations before punching into their shift or to clean up their area after punching out; overtime work is required with no additional compensation as required by law; or mandatory break times are routinely ignored. In other workplaces, being paid is an off-the-books, cash-only transaction, where employers flout payroll tax laws and other required social payments. In yet other workplaces, the "word on the street" is to ignore certain safety and health requirements—tying off on roofs for construction; using proper machine guards in manufacturing; adequately ventilating a room when using cleaning solvents—in order to get the job done. Verbal abuse, discriminatory comments, or sexist jokes by supervisors or between coworkers are left unaddressed.

Broken windows on the street send messages about the decline of social order in a neighborhood, leading to retreat from civic life and downward spirals toward more serious problems. Similarly, daily violations of basic workplace standards send powerful messages. If off-the-clock work is routinely tolerated, should one expect safety standards to be seriously respected? If a supervisor can speak disparagingly in public to a coworker with impunity, should one expect fair treatment in resolving a discrepancy in a paycheck or a dispute with a coworker?

Withdrawal from civic life as a result of fear also has its workplace analog. In the presence of persistent violations, keeping one's head down, staying out of other people's business, and turning a blind eye to unfair treatment of others are survival strategies. If my neighbors retreat from the street and lock their doors in the face of widespread disorder, it is perfectly rational for me to do the same. Likewise, if my coworkers don't make waves in the face of small but persistent infractions of the law, why should I be any different?

• • •

Many of the workplaces at lower levels of fissured employment structures suffer from the broken windows problem, for a combination of reasons. On one hand, businesses operating at an "outer orbit" of a fissured structure, far from the lead businesses that drive competitive conditions in a sector, do so with thin profit margins (if they have positive margins at all). This book has documented many, many such examples. Janitorial franchisees and growers of commodity products might or might not be able to make payroll. Third-tier subcontractors lack the money to purchase new safety equipment. Residential housing subcontractors fail to make required workers' compensation payments. And contract operators in mining, janitorial service providers, and small contractors in many other industries cycle in and out of bankruptcy, often reconstituting themselves under different names.

These create baseline conditions that are deleterious to compliance with laws and where day-to-day violations may become common. The feeling that other competitors are similarly cutting corners, making it impossible for my business to act differently, reinforces and spreads these behaviors.[1] Often employees enter into Faustian bargains with employers in such cases, where they decide to neither leave nor raise their voice, in fear that a worse fate—loss of a job with limited prospects for reemployment—is the only other option. This too reinforces the broken windows problem.

Raising One's Voice

> The capacity of our society to mangle people who lack the power to
> stand up for their own rights is virtually limitless.
> —Senator Walter Mondale

The broken windows perspective suggests that workers often do not complain when faced with the equivalent of neighborhood disorder at the workplace. In fact, the more challenging conditions described above may give rise to the counterintuitive result of both worsening workplace conditions and fewer worker complaints. In the face of deteriorating conditions and greater barriers to speaking out (for example, from increased economic vulnerability), people retreat from the "unsafe street," and the likelihood of complaining decreases even further.

Choosing to Speak Out

To see why, think of the choice facing an individual who suffers a perceived violation of a workplace law and is deciding whether or not to file a claim. First, workers must know that laws exist that give them the right to lodge complaints for underpayment of wages under the Fair Labor Standards Act (FSLA), to trigger an OSHA inspection in the face of unsafe practices, or to engage in certain types of concerted activities in the face of bad treatment (whether or not they are represented by a union) under the National Labor Relations Act. A great deal of evidence suggests they do not. More than a decade ago, Richard Freeman and Joel Rogers showed that many workers do not know what workplace rights they have, and that they assume the existence of other rights (particularly regarding protection from dismissal) they do not have. Nonunion workers are largely unaware of the right to engage in concerted activities, even where they are not represented by a labor union, afforded to them under statutes ranging from the Fair Labor Standards Act, the Occupational Safety and Health Act, and the Family Medical Leave Act to the National Labor Relations Act.[2]

Second, even if workers are aware of their rights, they still tend to under-utilize them. The likelihood of exercising rights should be related to the perceived benefits arising from complaining (related to the remedy produced by complaining) versus the potential costs of not doing so.[3] One problem that immediately arises is the "public goods" nature of remedies: if my complaint leads my employer to change behavior, it may benefit not only me, but others in the workplace as well. This is particularly true for complaints related to matters like safety and health, where an intervention (for example, improving ventilation or installing guards) lowers general exposure to a safety or health risk. But as it is the individual complainant who is at risk from possible employer retaliation, that individual will tend to underinvest in complaining.

Third, the potential costs of complaining create another major impediment to speaking out about workplace problems. The largest costs facing workers arise from potential employer reprisals. Reprisals may be subtle, such as losing desired shifts or work assignments; more substantial, such as being passed over for promotion; or very high in the case of losing one's job. In their survey of low-wage workers in three major U.S. cities, Bernhardt and her coauthors found a high prevalence of reported retaliation for exercise of rights among those who spoke out about violations and the strong perception of such retaliation among those who chose not to complain (but perceived that their rights had been violated). Among the workers in the sample who had actually complained about a workplace issue or attempted to form a union in the previous twelve months, 43% reported some form of employer or supervisor retaliation. Reported forms of retaliation varied from reduction in hours or pay or being given a less desirable work assignment (reported by 62% of those who said they had been retaliated against) to threats of being fired or reported to immigration authorities (47% of those reporting retaliation) to actually being fired or suspended (35%). The perception (not the fact) that employers will retaliate also affects whether or not workers will step forward in the face of workplace problems. Bernhardt et al. report that 20% of surveyed workers did not complain during the prior year despite having "experienced a serious problem such as dangerous working conditions, discrimination, or not being paid a minimum wage."[4] The most common reason (cited by 51% of those who chose not to complain) is fear of job loss, followed by the perception that complaining would not make a difference (36%).

Perceptions of the potential benefits and costs of stepping forward are particularly important, since overt discrimination for exercise of rights is illegal under most major employment statutes.[5] One way for people to gauge the cost of complaining is by watching the behavior of others in the workplace: Do they raise their voices when facing problems? If others do not complain in reaction to day-to-day violations of "good" workplace behavior, what does that say about the potential reaction to more egregious violations?

Complaint Behavior: Low and Declining

Given the above benefits and costs, it is perhaps not surprising that filing a formal complaint is a rare event. According to the three-city study by Bernhardt and colleagues, a tiny fraction of workers—a mere 1.2%—who reported taking some action to express dissatisfaction with work in the prior year did so by filing a complaint with a government agency, versus 96% who approached their employer. Since about 20% of workers in their sample reported lodging some type of complaint (through any channel), this implies about 240 formal complaints per 100,000 workers.[6]

Analysis of complaints filed under the Fair Labor Standards Act and the Occupational Safety and Health Act find even lower rates. The overall complaint rates under the two statutes were roughly in the same ballpark: there were about 25 complaints for every 100,000 workers under the Fair Labor Standards Act and about 17 complaints per 100,000 workers under the Occupational Safety and Health Act. These averages mask, however, the fact that complaint rates vary significantly across industries. For example, complaint rates per 100,000 workers ranged from 195 in gas stations, to 54 in eating and drinking establishments, to a mere 3.8 in private households.

One might object that these rates are not self-evidently "low" if the underlying problems giving rise to them are uncommon. A low complaint rate in a high-injury industry should raise more concerns than the same complaint rate with low underlying injury rates. On average, it takes about 130 violations of overtime provisions to elicit a complaint to the Department of Labor's Wage and Hour Division (the federal agency that enforces FLSA) and close to 120 lost workday injuries per complaint to OSHA. Once again, these rates vary by industry. The threshold for complaints is lower in construction for OSHA (51 lost workday injuries per complaint) than for overtime violations (173 violations of overtime per complaint); the opposite is true in eating and drinking establishments, where the rate is about 66 violations per complaint lodged under FLSA, but almost three times that level—188 injuries—per OSHA complaint.[7]

Not only are complaint rates low, but they have declined substantially over the past decade. Using complaints filed with the Wage and Hour Division by workers under the Fair Labor Standards Act, Table 10.1 compares complaint rates in 2001–2002 and 2007–2009.[8] Complaint rates (measured as the number of complaints filed by workers with the Wage and Hour Division per 100,000 workers) declined by 26% over this period, from 21.1 per 100,000 workers in 2001–2002 to 15.6 in 2007–2009. They fell even more pronouncedly in industries like home health care services, retail, grocery, and moving/logistics, where complaint rates declined by more than 30%.[9]

Recent literature on low-wage work makes it difficult to believe that the decline in complaint rates arises from a material improvement in the underlying conditions in the industries shown in Table 10.1. Evidence presented throughout this book and other studies of low-wage work suggests quite the opposite trend over this period.[10]

Any discussion of improving workplace conditions through enhancing voice—whether in the form of choosing to elect unions or simply standing up for one's own rights or those of fellow workers in regard to specific problems—must begin with an acknowledgment that workers became increasingly reluctant to exercise their voice over the most recent decade, even in the face of worsening conditions.

Fixing Broken Windows

A broken windows perspective suggests a different focus for efforts to change the climate in which worker voice is exercised. This includes reducing the prevalence of noncompliance with workplace laws through new forms of enforcement; finding new avenues to inform workers of their rights; and strengthening institutions in and out of the workplace that affect the exercise of voice.

Reducing "Disorder" through Strategic Enforcement

The original "broken windows" essay by Kelling and Wilson calls for shifting police resources from reactive, serious-crime response toward more proactive forms of intervention. The analog to the workplace is reassessing how government inspectors in agencies like OSHA and the Wage and Hour Division undertake enforcement.

Reducing noncompliance in the industries employing large numbers of vulnerable workers given the context described—particularly in regard to fissured employment—requires a different approach to enforcement than the workplace-by-workplace method characterizing traditional inspection strategy. Strategic enforcement as described in Chapter 9 requires inspectors who understand both the forces that drive noncompliance and which players on the workplace street are most likely to cause problems. This implies an enforcement policy that seeks to change underlying employer behavior rather than focusing on goals like the collection of back wages or health and safety citations. Decreasing the prevalence of basic violations sends the same message that reducing small crimes does in the context of broken windows: reducing fear and reestablishing the important role played by workers in assuring fair treatment.

The broken windows framework also argues for a different relationship between the police and the neighborhoods they protect. In particular, it calls for community policing, where the cop on the beat establishes close relationships with people in the neighborhoods. The workplace analog is building better bridges between government agencies and community groups, worker centers, and worker advocates. These efforts can range from long-standing efforts by Department of Labor agencies to reach out to unions, community groups, and religious organizations to more extensive collaborations that would allow problem solving around persistent patterns of noncompliance in specific labor markets or industries.[11]

Finally, addressing broken windows means changing aspects of the market relationship between lead businesses and the firms orbiting around them. In particular, if lead companies are forced to bear more of the costs and responsibilities arising from shedding employment, it implies that different prices need to prevail in their relationships with subordinate businesses. This is not a call for price fixing on the part of subordinate businesses or for government to set prices. Effective efforts to shift responsibility back

Table 10.1 Change in complaint rates, Fair Labor Standards Act, 2007–2009 versus 2001–2002 (ranked by 2007–2009 employment)

Industry[a]	2007–2009 Total employment (average)[b]	2007–2009 Complaint rate: (cases/employee) ×100,000[c]	2001–2002 Complaint rate: (cases/employee) ×100,000[d]	% change, 2001–2002 to 2007–2009
Total/weighted average, whole economy	111,175,322	15.6	21.1	−26.4
Retail—all	15,120,711	13.7	20.5	−33.2
Health care services (does not include state hospitals)	13,196,814	11.6	16.3	−28.9
Retail: mass merchants, department stores, specialty stores	9,315,599	10.2	16.2	−37.1
Restaurants: limited service and full service	7,968,326	30.4	35.2	−13.5
Construction	6,879,048	26.2	30.7	−14.8
Grocery stores	2,484,572	10.2	15.0	−32.2
Gasoline stations/auto repair	1,687,929	42.3	52.5	−19.4
Hotel and motel	1,459,546	37.9	47.0	−19.4
Recreation	1,418,641	14.7	19.8	−26.0

Trucking	1,364,638	48.4	54.4	−11.0
Agriculture	1,159,168	13.7	16.0	−14.4
Moving companies/logistics providers	1,017,273	9.0	14.3	−37.0
Home health care	966,772	14.7	21.3	−31.0
Janitorial services	934,009	39.6	42.7	−7.2
Residential construction	796,325	47.6	24.3	95.5
Landscaping services	647,415	20.7	27.3	−23.9
Nail, barber, and beauty shops	490,139	16.7	13.9	20.2
Apparel manufacturing	193,367	44.1	35.7	23.5
Car washes	140,657	44.3	45.3	−2.1

a. Industry based on 3-, 4-, and/or 6-digit North American Industry Classification System (NAICS) (available from the author).

b. Total employment: Extract from Bureau of Labor Statistics, Quarterly Census of Employment and Wages (QCEW), Private Employment Only, 3-digit industries with more than 100,000 employees, 2007–2009.

c. Complaint rate based on average annual number of complaints lodged with WHD classified as pertaining to Fair Labor Standards Act. Includes all full and partial investigations, conciliations, and audits registered in 2007–2009 and closed by third quarter 2010 (June 10, 2010).

d. Complaints registered in 2001–2002 and closed by third quarter 2010.

on lead companies can result in an upward movement in the market prices received by contractors, suppliers, and franchisees if their expenses begin to include the full costs (private and social) of providing services or making products. I return to this aspect of fixing broken windows at the end of the chapter.

You Have the Right . . .

Overcoming the broken windows problem at the workplace requires improving knowledge about workplace rights.[12] The basic idea is to make sure that workers are well informed of their rights under statutes, particularly those related to filing complaints for alleged violations and protections against retaliation.

Notification about employee rights is required by the Fair Labor Standards Act, the Occupational Safety and Health Act, the Migrant and Seasonal Worker Protection Act (MSPA), Title VII of the Civil Rights Act of 1964, the Americans with Disabilities Act, and the Family Medical Leave Act as well as other federal workplace laws.[13] In addition to similar requirements under state labor standards statutes, a number of states in recent years have passed laws that require posting information for employees in areas of emerging public policy concern, such as for temporary workers at agencies.[14]

The legal requirement to post rights is not synonymous with an understanding of them. The Department of Labor has sought to better inform workers of their rights with respect to laws, even where posting is required. These initiatives span Republican and Democratic administrations, going back in some cases to the passage of laws such as the Occupational Safety and Health Act. The Department of Labor during the Obama administration has renewed outreach efforts in its We Can Help campaign through social media and by translating materials into Spanish and other languages. The We Can Help campaign therefore seeks to supplement required posting with information about basic rights provided via the Web, targeted advertising campaigns, and the creation of more engaging materials. The effort, however, has provoked responses from congressional Republicans, the business community, and the conservative media. Criticisms focus particularly on those parts of the effort directed to Hispanic workers, under the premise that this results in informing undocumented workers of their rights under workplace laws. The highly politicized reaction to a straightforward educational effort (and one pursued by prior administrations) well illustrates the charged nature of workplace policy at this time.[15]

Informing workers of their rights under the National Labor Relations Act offers its own unique challenges. The act is the only major federal workplace statute that does not currently require that employers post notices informing workers of their rights under the law. In 2010 the National Labor Relations Board announced a proposed rule to redress this long-standing situation. The proposed rule would require covered employers to post workplace notices informing employees of their rights. Not surprisingly given the highly contested environment of labor law reform, the proposed NLRB rule elicited heated reactions, including 7,000 comments during the public response period. The rule was challenged in a number of suits, most recently leading the District of Columbia Court of Appeals to temporarily enjoin it from taking effect on April 30, 2012.[16]

Addressing the Collective Action Problem

As noted above, one reason people are reluctant to exercise their rights is that they often receive only part of the benefit of complaining, but fully bear the potential costs. They therefore complain too little from the perspective of fellow workers. The solution to a classic public goods problem where others gain from the creation of an individual action is through some form of collective action. Addressing the collective action problem is therefore critical to fixing broken windows in the workplace.[17]

LABOR UNIONS AS COLLECTIVE AGENTS

While a number of different organizations can potentially address the collective workplace action problem, labor unions are obviously the most logical given their basic roles in the workplace. As the elected representative of workers, a union has incentives to act on behalf of the collective interests of members in the bargaining unit.[18] Unions are able to gather and disseminate information on workplace laws and rights at low cost, and provide this information through educational programs and apprenticeship training or by alerting members of their rights where a problem or issue arises.

Unions also offer individual workers assistance in the exercise of their rights. This may result from the operation of committees established under collective bargaining, as is common in safety and health, or via the help of union staff who can trigger inspections, oversee pension fund investments, or help members file unemployment claims. Most importantly, unions can substantially reduce the costs associated with potential employer discrimination by helping affected employees use antidiscrimination provisions of the labor policies and providing this protection via collective bargaining agreements regulating dismissals.

There is now over two decades of evidence demonstrating that workers are more likely to exercise rights given the presence of a labor union. Workers in unionized workplaces are more likely to exercise rights under the Occupational Safety and Health Act, the Mine Safety and Health Act, the Family Medical Leave Act, and a variety of other federal statutes. In addition, unionized workers are more likely to receive unemployment insurance and workers' compensation benefits than comparably qualified nonunion workers.[19]

Though unions are cogent collective agents, the reality is that they are found in an ever-decreasing number of workplaces. Continuing a three-decade erosion, overall union membership fell further in 2012, to 11.3% of the workforce and to 6.6% of the private sector workforce, the lowest level of union density since 1916. Union density in industries where the workplace is fissured was also for the most part in single digits: 1.2% in food services and drinking places; 6.5% in accommodation (hotel and motel); and 4.6% for retail trades. Union density among fissured occupational groups in 2012 was 0.5% for building and grounds cleaning and maintenance occupations; 8.3% for health care support; and 6.6% for personal care and service occupations.[20] Since labor unions are largely absent from the private sector workplace, the practical question is, How does one overcome collective action problems in largely nonunion workplaces, where individual complainants have lots to lose by stepping forward?

SEARCHING FOR OTHER WORKPLACE AGENTS

Many workplace policies allow individual and class action claims arising from statutory violations. The plaintiff bar can therefore act on behalf of workers in the absence of unions. Lawyers acting on behalf of workers can press claims against employers for back wages, restitution for discrimination, and other civil remedies. This particular avenue has grown significantly over the past two decades. The number of civil cases filed in U.S. district courts for all workplace laws went from 13,841 in 1990 to 14,142 in 2000 and rose to 18,824 by 2010.[21]

Pursuing complaints in this way creates incentives for employer compliance because of the threat of lawsuits. It is unclear, however, how much it changes the propensity for workers to exercise rights at the workplaces where suits are filed. It seems unlikely (although largely unexplored) that lawsuits or even class actions have spillover effects on worker voice or employer compliance in other workplaces. What is more, the right of workers to pursue individual claims or class actions in employment litigation is in significant flux. In particular, recent Supreme Court rulings have upheld prehire agreements where workers waive their right to pursue grievances or actions on statutory claims as a condition of employment.[22]

Worker centers, community organizations, immigrant rights groups, and other advocacy groups play a variety of informational and educational roles for workers both inside and outside the workplace. Some also function as labor market intermediaries, particularly in day labor markets.[23] However, both legal restrictions and the practical fact that worker centers and related organizations operate outside the walls of the workplace complicate their role in this regard.

Undertaking the role of collective agent requires worker centers and related groups to operate through labor markets and the social networks embedded in them. The supply side of a labor market is affected by where people live, learn, socialize, and search for work. Wage expectations are affected by one's peers at work and by reference groups within geographic, ethnic, and immigrant communities. Recent labor market studies find that social networks of low-wage workers with geographic proximity have important effects on how people find work and who is hired, particularly in some ethnic communities. The social networks embedded in a labor market also shape norms that are acted on by people once employed. Attitudes about when to speak out in the workplace constitute one of type of message passed on through these networks.[24]

The social network for an immigrant worker group, for example, may foster attitudes that encourage or discourage the exercise of rights and voice at the workplace. Attitudes will be shaped by factors like immigrant workers' experiences with unions and government institutions in their home country and the United States; the role of religious organizations in the community;

and the strength of ties within the community and with family and friends in countries of origin.[25] The challenge facing organizations like worker centers is to influence these social networks in order to encourage greater exercise of rights and use of voice at the workplace over time.

Several recent cases suggest it is possible to do so. Nail salons are notorious for high rates of labor standards violations, exposure to chemical health risks, and generally poor working conditions. Ethnic dynamics between owners and workers have often diminished the likelihood that workers will step forward and complain about these conditions. Nonetheless, in December 2009, a small group of nail salon workers in New York City (all Chinese immigrants) brought suit against their employers for violations of minimum wage laws and abusive behavior. After a protracted legal battle, a jury in March 2012 awarded the workers $250,000 in back wage compensation. The ongoing legal effort and related efforts by activists have had ripple effects in the tight-knit communities surrounding the industry. As Sarah Ahn, an organizer in a coalition of advocacy groups working with the salon workers, noted, "Organizing within the nail salon industry has been difficult . . . Victories show there is a way that if you come forward, you can fight and win."[26]

The Taxi Workers Alliance in New York City also suggests the possibilities of new organizations and collective actors in the workplace. Because of their designation as independent contractors, taxi drivers are not covered by the National Labor Relations Act. Nonetheless, since 1993 the Taxi Workers Alliance, led by Bhairavi Desai, has brought together drivers from diverse immigrant communities by focusing their efforts on issues of common interest. This has led the organization to take on a range of issues of growing scope and scale, from safety and disciplinary matters, to responding to the economic downturn following 9/11, to involvement in rate-setting proceedings that fundamentally affect drivers' earnings. In 2011 the Taxi Workers Alliance became the first worker organization not directly engaged in collective bargaining to become a full affiliate of the AFL-CIO in nearly fifty years.[27]

Workplace organizations outside of traditional unions are also emerging among fast-food workers, car wash employees, day laborers, and domestic workers. The trajectory of these efforts illustrates the importance of building individual and collective resolve to exercise voice as an essential foundation for improving the climate for exercising voice and longer-term efforts to represent workers.

The Role of Employers and Their Associations

Many of the case studies in this book provide evidence that lower-tier employers are placed in a highly competitive environment by lead companies, or via the actions of intermediaries like turfers in the cell tower industry, jobbers in the garment industry, general contractors in construction, or third-party management companies in a wide variety of other industries. The pressure to lower costs given prevailing market prices, and the fact that labor is often one of the major costs facing them, leads to pressures to reduce wages and eliminate benefits, and often to skirt compliance.

Part of the challenge faced by public policy makers, worker advocates, and others concerned about workforce vulnerability is affecting the prices faced by businesses operating at lower tiers of fissured industry structures. Chapters 8 and 9 described how this might be done through new policies or more strategic enforcement of existing ones. Efforts to encourage use of rights by workers could also address aspects of the broken windows problem and affect the tacit acceptance of noncompliance that permeates many workplaces. But something must also be done to change the business dynamic.

Franchisee Associations: Meet the AAHOA

One set of organizations to look to in this regard are associations of employers at lower levels of fissured structures. Employer associations often form to attend to issues of common concern in the political realm. Some of the most influential organizations in Washington focusing on regulatory, tax, and fiscal issues of concern to small businesses, they include the National Federation of Independent Business, the Chamber of Commerce, and the National Restaurant Association. As discussed in Chapter 8, these small-business political advocates have opposed many of the workplace laws introduced in the past half century.

But there are other employer associations that play a different role in particular industries. In the hospitality industry, for example, the Asian American Hotel Operators Association (AAHOA) was formed to provide common educational, training, and advocacy assistance to independent hotel owners, particularly those who immigrated to the United States from India. An interesting role played by the AAHOA is dealing with the inherent tension between the objectives of franchisors and franchisees regarding pricing, service standards, capital improvement requirements, supplier requirements, and other matters related to compliance with brand standards. Inevitably, this entails brands wanting greater investment in standards (including upgrading them) with the franchisee footing the bill, and franchisees seeking to pay only for those that directly benefit them.

Given the relative power of franchisors over franchisees, the AAHOA and other franchisee associations in hotels, fast food, and other industries play a role in providing a collective voice to address areas of tension with franchisors.[28] For example, in 2008, at the deepest trough of the Great Recession, AAHOA reached out to the major hotel parent organizations seeking relief from requirements to upgrade properties and amenities, decreasing royalty fees for "franchisees who are encountering severe financial hardships," and limiting expansion of hotels to new properties.[29] AAHOA provides its members with an annual rating of different brands, based on its "12 Points of Fair Franchising" regarding matters such as early termination and liquidation; brand expansion; minimum performance and quality guarantees; and franchisee relationships.[30] Associations of franchisees play similar roles elsewhere. The Federal Trade Commission acknowledged the importance of this advocacy role played by franchisee associations with respect to franchisors when it added requirements to existing disclosure requirements that franchisors make prospective franchisees aware of these associations as part of providing basic disclosure.[31]

One can imagine that these associations could play a productive role if lead organizations in fissured structures assumed greater responsibility in assuring that standards and workplace conditions were being met. Monitoring systems to ensure compliance could in part involve such associations. Equally, independent franchisee associations could also play a role in working out financial recognition of the costs of improved workplace conditions throughout all levels of fissured structures.[32]

More generally, lead businesses in fissured structures facing greater responsibility for workplace outcomes could spawn innovations in how they are discharged. As has been repeatedly pointed out throughout this book, lead companies are remarkably adept in creating systems to ensure that subordinate businesses comply with technical, product, delivery, and scheduling outcomes central to their core competencies. Similar creativity could be brought to addressing problems arising from fissuring and improving workplace conditions.

Lessons from the Food Sector

It would be hard to identify a case of employers and workers facing more competitive pressure than those operating at the bottom of the food supply chain. At the top are branded food processors like Campbell Soup and Vlasic Pickle, or retailers like Sam's, Costco, and Safeway, which are increasingly selling packaged food under private labels (brands created by the retailer). Other growers sell to major fast-food providers like Wendy's, Taco Bell, and McDonald's. While there are certainly very large and powerful food providers in some supply chains, in others the growers at the bottom are small price takers, often operating at very thin margins.

Consider the case of cucumbers grown to be used for pickles. Large numbers of farmers grow cucumbers. Although there are different varieties (sizes, shapes) and quality levels, in the end, a cucumber is still a cucumber. That means farmers have little to compete on in terms of product characteristics, requiring them, in true Economics 101 fashion, to compete on price. Falling transportation costs and trade barriers, improved technologies for transit and preservatives, and a large number of nations anxious to sell in the U.S. market mean that the barriers to entry have fallen (as the geographic boundaries of the potential suppliers have expanded). Add these factors together and you have the basis for high levels of competition among cucumber growers.

If you are furiously competing on the basis of price, how do you cut costs? In agriculture, the major input costs are seed, fertilizer, pesticides, water, capital costs associated with equipment, and labor. Recall that seed, fertilizer, pesticides, and farm equipment are provided by multinational companies like Archer Daniels Midland (seed), Dow (pesticides and fertilizer), Deere, and International Harvester (tractors). Since the farmers purchasing products are small potatoes in those markets, the prices paid for those inputs are largely beyond their control. That leaves labor (which constitutes about 40% of direct costs) as one of the only factors in control of growers.

But the picture is not yet complete: farmers must sell cucumbers to someone. In many major agricultural markets, the end user is not the consumer, but a food processor (Vlasic or Mt. Olive pickles for cucumbers, Campbell Soup for tomatoes); a major user (for example, McDonald's or Taco Bell for lettuce producers); or a major food retailer. Once again, the relative market power is clearly skewed toward the buyer. What is more, not only are major buyers in a position to set prices (particularly where they have offshore sourcing options), but they usually have stringent standards in terms of product quality, delivery, time requirements, and even, in the case of cucumbers, requirements that growers do some of the preparatory work that transforms the produce into a final product. The upshot is that price is largely determined by powerful buyers.

It is no wonder that agricultural work is so often rife with violations of the most basic labor standards, or that efforts to improve conditions, whether through enforcement of labor standards regulations or organizing labor unions, are resisted with a fervor commensurate with the growers' desire to stay in business. It is also easy to see that efforts to enforce the Migrant Seasonal Protection Act (the federal legislation setting labor standards for agricultural workers) or successful efforts to organize farm workers (remember Steinbeck's *In Dubious Battle?*) are at best Sisyphean feats: what is gained in one season is quickly lost in the next. Simply put, individual growers paying higher wages, providing better housing, or complying with pesticide or health and safety provisions set themselves up to be at a competitive disadvantage regarding the only part of their income statement over which they have a measure of control. Sending more investigators to check on individual farms or attempting to "take wages out of competition" through farm-by-farm labor organizing is swimming against very strong currents.

Yet in this environment there are two models that seek to address the problems of the fissured workplace in a comprehensive manner. One model has at its center the Farm Labor Organizing Committee (FLOC), an AFL-CIO–affiliated union that represents farm workers in Michigan, Ohio, and North Carolina; the North Carolina Growers Association (NCGA) and its member growers; and food processors like Vlasic, Campbell, and Mt. Olive Pickles. After several years of unsuccessful efforts organizing migrant farm workers who picked tomatoes in Ohio on a farm-by-farm basis, FLOC turned its attention to the major buyer of those crops, Campbell Soup. The union began what turned out to be an eight-year campaign to bring pressure on Campbell (through its very popular and established brand) to improve conditions for farm workers. The company's first reaction was something seen elsewhere in this book: it argued that farm workers were not its employees, so that conditions in the fields were not its responsibility. This remained the company's position for many years, as the union expanded its coalition partners to include other unions, church groups, immigrant rights organizations, and others concerned with conditions in the fields.

In 1985 Campbell Soup approached John Dunlop of Harvard University with a request that he intervene and help to fashion an agreement that could resolve the situation. The resulting agreement was unique in several respects. First, it created a private means to allow workers on farms supplying Campbell Soup to vote on being represented by unions.[33] Second, once FLOC had been certified as a bargaining representative, the agreement created the basis for a tripartite collective bargaining mechanism that included growers, food processors, and the union. The agreement included provisions regarding wages, benefits, and housing for workers as well as a dispute resolution procedure for worker griev- ances. Growers who signed the agreement received assurances that they would receive prices for their products high enough to allow them to remain finan- cially viable. The fact that food processors were "at the table" (although they are no longer formal signatories to the agreement) created a sustainable basis for improving working conditions on the ground. The collective agreements ex- panded to include growers working for other food processors (Vlasic; Dean Foods) and have continued to be renewed since that time to the present.

In 2004 the relationship among the union, growers, and food processors took another unique turn when FLOC signed a collective agreement with NCGA providing the first and only collective bargaining coverage of guest workers (H2-A) in the United States. The agreements provide a system of grievance administration, procedures for seniority, and other protections that include the regulations for the guest program established by the Departments of Labor and State. The FLOC/NCGA agreement has been renewed by the parties multiple times and now covers some 120 growers and 6,500 workers at the height of the growing season.[34]

The second example, also from the food sector, is a set of agreements be- tween Yum! Brands (which owns Taco Bell and other fast-food brands), Mc- Donald's, and Burger King and the Coalition of Immokalee Workers (CIW), which represents workers on farms providing produce to those companies. The agreements, much like those involving FLOC, arose from sustained cor- porate campaigns focused on the lead companies, connecting the brand with the poor conditions facing workers on farms supplying produce to those com- panies. The agreements generally require the lead company to pay a specified amount of money connected to production volumes (currently a penny per pound) for specific produce purchased by the companies. The payments go into an industry fund administered by CIW that provides wage supplements for the workers covered by the agreements.[35]

These arrangements in the food sector are particularly noteworthy in that they address all three consequences of the fissured workplace: the FLOC agreements with growers are designed to ensure that growers comply with labor standards of MSPA and the H2-A program; those agreements also provide methods for addressing externalities associated with health and safety in the fields, safe transportation of workers between growers, and adequate housing in seasonal labor camps. More fundamentally, both the FLOC and CIW agreements address the distributional tension underlying fissured decisions by making the lead food organization (Campbell, Vlasic, and Mt. Olive in FLOC; Yum!, McDonald's, and Burger King in CIW) adjust the price it pays (and therefore the return it receives) to accommodate better conditions for workers at the base of the supply chain.

Global Supply Chains and International Monitoring

In the past two decades, public pressure on companies like Nike, Walmart, HP, and Apple has led them to adopt codes of conduct, agree to higher levels of transparency in their supply chains, and create monitoring mechanisms regarding their labor and environmental practices. Since these cases often involve pressure brought to bear by consumer, worker, and environmental activists on companies that draw on suppliers in other countries, these agreements arise outside of the purview of national laws and regulations. In fact, many of the early proponents of international monitoring argued that voluntary codes of conduct and monitoring offered a substitute for the often weak labor laws and inspectorates in many of the developing companies where production of apparel, electronic products, and food was increasingly based.[36]

The responses by advocacy groups and labor unions, companies, suppliers, and national governments have evolved considerably over this time period. As noted at the end of Chapter 7, recent developments within the supply chains of Apple and HP provide hopeful signs of lead companies modifying policies and taking greater responsibility for the workplace consequences of their activities. The policy changes at Foxconn, in particular, including substantial pay increases and reduction in work hour policies as well as efforts to improve health and safety outcomes, are notable, as are the resources and attention Apple and HP have devoted to developing better capacities to monitor and improve labor and environmental practices in their supply bases.[37] At the same time, the death of more than five hundred Bangladeshi workers in factory fires between 2006 and 2012 and the collapse of the Rana Plaza factory complex leading to more than 1,100 fatalities in 2013, all in facilities primarily serving apparel export markets points to the continuing huge challenges faced in this arena. This point is underscored by the fact that most of those who died worked in factories that were technically covered by codes of conduct or some type of international monitoring arrangement.[38]

A complete discussion of the impact of codes of conduct, transparency, and voluntary monitoring occurring across the boundaries of national workplace policies raises issues beyond the scope of this book and requires separate assessment.[39] But several general points about recent efforts to address this particular driver of fissured workplaces can be made here.

First, many of these agreements occur outside of the realm of national laws. International Labor Office conventions have limited methods of persuasion, and there is great variation in the scope, depth, and mechanisms of emerging agreements. Many of the early codes of conduct from the 1990s are now widely viewed as fig leaves, focused more on quelling public relations problems than on addressing underlying problems. More recent efforts have involved greater sophistication, exploration of alternative models, and invention. Some involve direct monitoring of code compliance by the lead companies themselves. More problematically, others rely on certification by third parties paid for by suppliers. In other models, companies hire independent third-party organizations such as the Fair Labor Association or the Workers Rights Consortium. Many of the certification systems have proven weak reeds, given the conflicting incentives of certifiers and suppliers on one hand and the limited capacity (or resources provided) of the companies drawing on certification on the other. However, stronger monitoring arrangements such as those favored by organizations like the Workers Rights Consortium—which incorporate independent labor unions and forceful monitoring standards— have been able to push companies to higher levels of compliance, but have thus far proven hard to scale. Given the multiple forms of monitoring, there is a great need for evaluation of their comparative impact on achieving sustainable change in supply chain conditions.[40]

Second, monitoring arrangements that are not closely linked into the manufacturing, sourcing, and central supply chain decisions of the companies that sponsor them have limited impact on workplace outcomes. Monitoring efforts focus on checklists and surface measures of compliance with codes of conduct in supplier plants but have limited impact on either the sourcing decisions of companies or the workplace policies of suppliers. Multiyear evaluations by Richard Locke and colleagues have shown that Nike's efforts at supply chain monitoring had their largest impacts when wedded to that company's more central business functions.[41]

Third, transparency plays an important role in such systems, going beyond the initial exposure of the problems by providing ongoing information to all parties about conditions on the ground. One of the ongoing sticking points between labor and environmental activists and companies who are the focus of monitoring efforts has been the degree of disclosure those companies are willing to make about their supply base. The most sophisticated systems are usually found where companies have agreed to provide extensive information on their supply base. Resistance to disclosure arises where monitored companies are asked to provide public disclosure about suppliers with specialized, proprietary, or innovative capabilities, or other key strategic capacities.

Finally, experience to date suggests the fundamental flaw of the early view that voluntary codes, standards, and monitoring could substitute for weak labor protections and scarce resources for enforcement of labor inspectorates in the nations where suppliers are based. At best, voluntary monitoring systems can act as complements to national labor inspectorates, leveraging and helping to increase their effectiveness at providing direct and deterrent effects on suppliers. But the vastness and dispersion of international supply chains inevitably limit how far even well-resourced international monitoring arrangements can go. National labor policies and the capacity of labor inspectorates to implement them remain fundamental.[42]

The long-term question of monitoring arrangements will rest on their impact not only on the behavior of those plants directly monitored by them, but on how those efforts ripple outward to other manufacturers and ultimately back to consumers of those products. As David Autor, an MIT economist, commented in regard to Foxconn, "When people read about bad Chinese factories in the paper, they might have a moment of outrage. But then they go to Amazon and are as ruthless as ever about paying the lowest prices."[43] Critics of international monitoring efforts often point out that the bad conditions found in the supply base of prominent international companies may still be far better than those in factories and workplaces providing products to less prominent customers. To the extent that other companies continue to skirt national laws and undercut the standards of more responsible suppliers, the efforts of better players will be undermined and monitoring efforts will have limited and unsustainable impacts. However, if international monitoring systems, in conjunction with national labor inspectorates, change the way lead companies review, source, and relate to suppliers, they are more likely to change the behavior of the larger sector of suppliers in those countries and their resulting compliance with workplace standards and laws.[44]

Safe Streets, Fair Workplaces

In 1961 Jane Jacobs described what defined "public peace" in a city:

> The first thing to understand is that the public peace—the sidewalk and street peace—of cities is not kept primarily by the police, necessary as police are. It is kept primarily by an intricate, almost unconscious, network of voluntary controls and standards among the people themselves, and enforced by people themselves. In some city areas—older public housing projects and streets with very high population turnover are often conspicuous examples—the keeping of public sidewalk law and order is left almost entirely to the police and special guards. Such places are jungles. No amount of police can enforce civilization where the normal, casual enforcement of it has broken down.[45]

If we reframe the question of workplace governance and regulation in light of Jacobs's idea, it creates a very different lens through which to view the problem of workplace governance. Rather than focusing on outcomes like compliance with laws, wage levels, or specific working conditions, Jacobs focuses on the conditions that lead to the public peace—in particular those that can be influenced through some type of intervention.

In the workplace, the "network of voluntary controls and standards" is the culture and standards created by the employer and influenced by workers and (if present) their union representatives. Clearly, in the workplace the employer has by legal right a far greater ability to set these conditions. The history of workplace regulation is one in which public interest in employment conditions placed boundaries around the ability of employers to unilaterally set controls and standards. But legislation provides only the right to set terms—it does not necessarily lead to the attainment of those rights in practice. Declining enforcement, erosion of unionization, a growing skepticism toward government, and a shift (legal and cultural) to more individually focused views of the workplace in many sectors have undermined the ability to attain public objectives in setting conditions in the U.S. workplace.

The troubling working conditions and sometimes egregious behavior of employers found in low-wage settings echoes Jane Jacobs's accounts of deterioration of civil society in neighborhoods and streets in Chicago. A tipping point arguably exists in many sectors affected by fissuring where the day-to-day experience of working people represents Jacobs's urban jungle, where even the most fundamental rules of workplace fairness (for example, being paid for work completed; being allowed breaks; receiving benefits promised at the outset) have broken down.

Seen in this light, the question of workplace governance can be reframed in light of the impacts of the fissured workplace. It starts with the idea that workplace conditions arise from a combination of economic and social forces akin to Jacobs's account of the city. If one recasts the Jacobs quotation for the workplace, it might go like this:

> The first thing to understand is that *workplace fairness—the day-to-day fair and equitable treatment of working people, abiding by the laws of the land*—is not kept primarily by *government inspectors,* necessary as *those inspectors* are. It is kept primarily by an intricate, almost unconscious, network of voluntary control and standards among *workers and employers* themselves, and enforced by *both parties* themselves. In some *workplaces—nonunion, gloves-off workplaces* with very high *employee* turnover are often conspicuous examples—the keeping of *workplace fairness* is left almost entirely to the *government.* Such places are jungles. No amount of *inspectors* can enforce civilization where the normal, casual enforcement of it has broken down.

Rewritten in this way, the quotation emphasizes the importance of the unwritten signaling of day-to-day activities that defines for individuals in a workplace what is and is not permissible. This is best illustrated by workplaces that have become "jungles": where the daily experience displays unfair treatment, flouting of basic standards of behavior, failure to abide by even rudimentary legal requirements, and so on. It is not any one activity—or any one penalty—that leads employees to feel they cannot complain, exercise voice, or respond to risky situations. It is the totality of conditions in the workplace—and, in some cases, the entire sectors—that leads workers to the conclusion that nothing can be done.

The broken windows analogy—and Jacobs's related peaceful street imagery—suggests that community safety improves over time through an evolution of civic conditions. As disorder declines, people come back and begin to participate in public life on the street. Economic activity fills in, neighborhood groups form, civic pride rises. As vibrancy returns to the street, individuals and institutions change their roles in ways that reinforce civic engagement and safety. Jacobs's "peaceful streets" that emerge over time would be unrecognizable from where they began.

What is the end point of fixing broken windows and creating peaceful streets in workplace settings? It is not seeking to increase complaint rates as an end in itself. Instead, its aim is altering perceptions about the common willingness to take affirmative steps to address workplace problems large and small. Just as in Jacobs's safe street, neighbors less encumbered by fear begin to look after other neighbors, allowing civic life to deepen. Changing the climate for exercising voice in the workplace can alter assumptions about what is acceptable behavior in domains regulated by law (for example, labor standard requirements) and those that are not (basic treatment at work).

Fixing broken windows now could eventually lead to an expansion of the opportunities for all parties, including employers, to assure more fair and productive workplaces going forward.

The Fissured Economy

Look around in corporate America at what people are doing to avoid
health-care and other payments. They're contracting out work.
That's the whole point of using contractors.
—Spokesman for the Bituminous Coal Operators Association, 1993

You just described my life!
—Young attorney to the author, 2012

Like cracks in rocks, once fissuring starts it deepens and spreads. It deepens
in the sense that fissuring of one activity—such as janitorial services, security, or staffing operations—leads to further fissuring of that activity. Janitorial services are split out from the regular activities of lead companies. Once
outside the boundaries of the firm, they become part of a self-standing market which splits further apart. Contractors use subcontractors, who in turn
farm out work to individuals who operate as so-called independent contractors. Or, transferred to a franchising model, lead franchisors create regional
franchisors, who then sell to local franchisors.

Fissuring also spreads. Successful fissuring in one area begets fissuring in
other functions. The benefits found in fissuring what are seen as peripheral
activities become experience to be applied to moving out other activities once
considered central to the enterprise. Manufacturing companies shed corporate functions like IT and human resources, then outsource activities like
maintenance and security, and finally turn to components of production itself. Hotels start with landscaping, move on to janitorial services, and soon,
often through the agency of a management operating company, shed beverage and food services, room cleaning, and even front desk service.

Finally, fissuring spreads outward from sector to sector. The fissured workplace started in industries where the characteristics of production require contracting (for example, construction, garments, movie production). But it has moved outward into manufacturing, retail, services, health care, and even the nonprofit and government sectors.

An economy increasingly characterized by fissured employment will operate differently than one characterized by large companies who directly employ their workforces. The research underlying this book has focused at the industry level downward. But an understanding of how the pieces of the fissured employment model fit together provides a basis for speculating on its larger impacts on the way our economy operates. This chapter presents some thoughts on the future path of the fissured workplace and its implications for the broader economy.

I begin with the difficulty of gauging the extent of fissuring and the need for better measures of its prevalence in the future. I then look at its spread into new spheres and discuss the likelihood that it will continue to do so. Finally, the chapter turns to the broader economic impacts of fissured employment, exploring how the evolution described in this book helps explain changing income distribution and the business cycle. In so doing, it suggests the outlines for future research on these linkages.

How Pervasive Is the Fissured Workplace?

Measuring the extent of the fissured workplace is not easy. As previous chapters have shown, fissured employment structures are not always bounded by one industry. Employment in some industries may be highly fragmented but still have pockets where traditional employment structures remain. Other industries may have fissured workplaces affecting only some occupational groups, or be in the midst of organizational changes that will gradually result in more fissuring.

Many of the fissured workplaces discussed in this book are characterized by low wages, limited benefits, and job insecurity. A number of those industries account for a disproportionate share of low-wage workers. For example, while food services and drinking places employed about 6.4% of the workforce, it comprised about 12.4% of all low-wage workers in 2010; retail workers comprised 10.2% of the workforce but 18.9% of low-wage workers; and the roughly 1.8 million workers in the hotel and motel industry accounted for 1.2% of employment but twice that percentage of low-wage workers.[1] Although fissured employment certainly gives rise to low-wage work, it is not synonymous with industries having large concentrations of low-wage workers. How else might one gauge its prevalence?

Fissured employment represents both a *form* of employment (for example, temporary agency employment; independent contracting) and a *relationship* between different business enterprises (subcontracting, franchising). It reflects not only who does the work, but also the structure of contracts and the relative power between those enterprises that contract for and those enterprises that are contracted to do the work. Estimating the number of workers or businesses with fissured employment is therefore difficult since there is currently no government data series that captures both aspects of the fissured workplace. Several approaches must be used to estimate its prevalence.

One approach is to look at business practices that lead to fissured workplaces, such as subcontracting or outsourcing. Several studies use national surveys of businesses to measure the prevalence of subcontracting. On the basis of a representative sample of 500 private sector businesses, Houseman finds that 44% of those surveyed used contract workers to accomplish specific business tasks. Rates of use of contracting varied across sectors: 25% in agriculture; 33% in trade; 48% in service; 52% in manufacturing; and 61% in mining and construction. The survey also reveals that a larger percentage of businesses contracted out work that had previously been done inside the company (17%) than reported bringing back in work that had been contracted out (9.5%).[2] Using a different representative sample of national businesses, Kalleberg and Marsden estimate that over 50% of establishments used either temporary help or contract companies in one or more specified activities. The most common activities were security (57% of establishments reported contracting out); janitorial (42%); and repair/maintenance (57%).[3] These surveys underscore the widespread use of subcontracting as a business practice.

One of the most comprehensive recent estimates of domestic outsourcing by Dey, Houseman, and Polivka draws together several different sources of government data to measure its occurrence.[4] Overall, the researchers find evidence of increased outsourcing across industries and within selected occupations. The number of workers employed in industries that provide contract/temporary services directly increased from 1.98 million in 1992 to 4.17 million by 2002. Manufacturing accounted for the largest share of outsourced workers (39% in 2005), followed by professional and business services (18%), trade, transportation, and utilities (14%), and finally health care and social assistance (12%). Outsourcing of work also increased over time for occupations discussed throughout this book, including security guards, janitors, truck drivers, and a variety of computer occupations.[5] This evidence is suggestive of the increasing prevalence of the fissured workplace.

An alternative method to measure the prevalence of workers associated with fissured workplaces is to use nationally representative worker surveys. One approach is estimating the number of workers classified in the different forms of "contingent" employment. The Census Bureau defines contingent workers as "those who do not have an implicit or explicit contract for ongoing employment."[6] The Contingent Work Supplement to the Current Population Survey classifies a number of different kinds of workers under that category.[7]

- *Agency temporary workers (temps):* Individuals who work for temporary employment agencies and are assigned by the agencies to work for other companies ("client firms");
- *Contract company workers:* Individuals who work for companies that provide services to other firms under contract (for example, security, landscaping, computer programming services);
- *Day laborers:* Individuals who get work by waiting at a place where employers pick up people to work for the day;
- *Independent contractors:* Individuals who obtain customers on their own to provide a product or service (and may or may not have other employees working for them). These can range from day care providers, construction companies, and housecleaners to realtors, graphic artists, and management consultants;
- *Direct-hire temps:* Temporary workers hired directly by companies to work for a specified period of time, such as seasonal workers in the retail sector;
- *Self-employed workers:* Workers not classified as independent contractors (who therefore do not pay payroll taxes, workers' compensation, and other standard employment costs).[8]

Using data from the Contingent Worker Survey, the U.S. General Accountability Office (GAO) calculated the prevalence of these different types of contingent workers, which are presented in Table 11.1. About 31% of workers worked in contingent employment situations in 2005, if one characterizes contingent workers as those not employed in standard, full-time settings. The absolute number of workers employed in all forms of contingent work increased between 1995 and 2005, although as a percentage of the workforce it fell slightly over the same period, from 32.1% in 1995 to 30.1% in 2005.

But there are important differences between contingent work as measured in Table 11.1 and the concept of the fissured workplace. Many categories of contingent work that are closely related to fissured employment grew substantially between 1995 and 2005. In particular, the number of workers classified

Table 11.1 Fissured workplace practices: The use of contingent workers in the United States, 1995 and 2005

Category of worker	Employment, 1995[a]		Employment, 2005[b]	
	Total employed (000s)	Percentage of total employment	Total employed (000s)	Percentage of total employment
Contract company workers	652	.5	813	.6
Agency temporary workers	1,181	1.0	1,217	.9
On-call/day laborers	2,014	1.6	2,736	2.0
Independent contractors	8,309	6.7	10,342	7.4
Direct-hire temps	3,393	2.8	2,972	2.1
Self-employed workers	7,526	5.9	6,125	4.4
Standard part-time workers	16,813	13.6	18,360	13.2
Standard full-time workers	83,589	67.9	96,385	69.4
Total workforce	123,477	100.0	138,950	100.0

Source: U.S. General Accountability Office (2006).

a. Based on GAO analysis of data from February 1995 Contingent Work Supplement to the Current Population Survey.

b. Based on GAO analysis of data from February 2005 Contingent Work Supplement to the Current Population Survey.

as independent contractors grew from 8.3 million to 10.3 million, and also increased as a percentage of total employment, from 6.7% to 7.4%. Workers categorized as day laborers grew by 36% and contract company workers by 26%, while over the same period the overall workforce grew by 13% and standard full-time workers by 15%.

Similar increases in the use of contingent work, measured in terms of part-time and temporary workers, occurred in a number of countries affiliated with the Organization for Economic Cooperation and Development (OECD) between 1995 and 2011. Among OECD nations, the weighted average of part-time employment rose from 11.6% in 1995 to 16.5% in 2011. The incidence of temporary employment among OECD nations also grew, from 10.6% in 1995 to 12.0% in 2011. The growth in contingent practices was particularly dramatic in Germany, France, Italy, and Canada.[9] Also striking was that the rate of growth in part-time and temporary employment was faster over this period among men than among women, even though those practices were historically concentrated among women.[10]

However, other categories of contingent work in Table 11.1 are less closely aligned with the concept of fissured workplaces. This includes self-employed workers (not categorized as independent contractors) and standard part-time workers. Including those categories when estimating the extent of fissured employment would tend to overstate its extent. For example, many self-employed workers are not linked in the close supplier, franchised, vendor, or subcontracting relationships central to fissured employment. And part-time employment can be a feature of virtually any type of work arrangement.

But restricting estimates to conventional definitions of contingent workers may also substantially undercount the prevalence of fissured workplaces in other respects. Many forms of fissuring still result in what is characterized as standard full-time work. Franchising is a business form that allows lead companies to implement the key features of the fissured employment strategy, but would be measured as creating standard work arrangements. Similarly, many people are employed in subordinate businesses that at one point would have been within the boundaries of lead business enterprises but now exist as part of one of the orbiting moons doing work for them as subcontractors or suppliers. Though workers in those subordinate businesses may be classified as employed on a standard, full-time basis, the relationship between the lead firms and those where these workers are employed may be fissured and therefore likely to have the characteristics of precarious employment.

As a result, it is difficult to get a comprehensive estimate of the extent of fissured employment by relying on industry data regarding wage levels or working conditions, firm surveys relating to business practices, or worker surveys regarding type of employment relationship. The complexity of employment arising under fissured workplaces inevitably creates problems for its measurement.[11] But its impacts on the workforce, on compliance with workplace laws, and on the wider economy make measuring its prevalence of growing importance.

New Frontiers of the Fissured Workplace

The majority of cases analyzed in this book involve the impact of fissured workplaces on workers in low-wage occupations and industries. But emerging trends in law, journalism, and finance suggest that fissuring is also affecting jobs and restructuring companies for highly skilled and educated workers. The fissured workplace is appearing at the very top of the professional ladder. As the young lawyer quoted at the opening of this chapter said to the author, "You just described my life!"[12]

Fissured Law

It is an old saw that Americans cannot do anything without a lawyer present. Those who have refinanced a home in certain states can attest to this. The final stage of refinancing requires the borrower to sign a mountain of paperwork in the presence of a notary—and in many states, like Massachusetts, that notary must be a lawyer. In many cases, the bank refinancing the loan hires a company to do title work and handle the legal aspects of closing. The company doing title work hires a local attorney to preside at the closing. This entails assigning this work—which ebbs and flows, often with limited lead time—to attorneys who typically must travel to the home of the borrower. A common practice now is to subcontract this work to lawyers working as independent contractors, compensating them on a per closing basis, rather than assigning lawyers from the firm itself. The assigned attorney is expressly forbidden to offer any legal advice during the closing, and is there simply to oversee the signing process as required by the law.[13]

Outsourcing has arrived in the legal profession. Many of the economic forces acting on companies discussed in Chapter 3 have also put pressure on them to reduce the costs of outside legal counsel. This has, in turn, placed increasing pressure on law firms of all sizes to reduce their billings to clients and, respectively, the costs of providing legal services. A sequence of cost-saving changes, similar to those in other private sector organizations, has rippled through law firms: it starts with outsourcing information technology, human resources, and, increasingly, legal research / library functions from the law firm to other organizations. It continues with using lower-cost paralegals (who still work in-house) to do work formerly done by lawyers.[14] But now it has moved into the shedding of legal work itself.

Outsourcing legal work itself is relatively new, beginning around 2004 with the emergence of legal process outsourcing (LPO) firms that provide different types of legal services to other law firms as well as end users. Controversial initially, it has become a large and growing market increasingly drawn upon by law firms and other organizations.[15]

The types of legal work done by law firms can be usefully broken into three main segments.[16] At the top is high-end legal work requiring the specialized knowledge of experienced lawyers. This can be thought of as the core competency of many law firms, residing in the expertise and reputation of senior partners. It represents the most remunerative but also the smallest proportion of work. In the middle segment is business law, requiring the supervision of experienced lawyers but also involving more mundane legal work that can be delegated to junior lawyers and paralegals. This type of work is fairly common in law practices, implying that many firms are capable of providing it. A significant share of legal work falls in this second segment. The highest-volume work falls into the "commodity" category, where little specialized client knowledge is required and much of the work does not require legal training per se. This means that this type of work can be supplied by many providers.[17] While at an earlier point a law firm would undertake all three tiers of work, pressures to reduce legal fees have meant that firms draw on higher-priced internal staff to handle the top tier and parts of the middle tier, while contracting out work in the commodity category.

There are now hundreds of firms offering legal research, analysis, and brief writing. For example, LRSolutions, a New York–based provider, notes on its website: "LRSolutions will handle your most challenging legal issues, while providing you with the highest quality legal research analysis and brief writing. All for a reasonable, fixed price determined and approved in advance." The company offers a range of possibilities for its clients:

Our legal products and services range from proactive multi-state surveys and summations of law in particular areas, formulated as objective memoranda[,] to advocacy papers such as motions/responses for summary judgment, motions/responses to dismiss, trial briefs and appellate briefs. We can produce a summary and evaluation of opposing arguments, handbooks on the law, and instructive manuals.[18]

As in other areas, the outsourcing of legal work started with legal research, standardized searches, document processing, and other commodity work. But the supply of firms providing LPO services is growing and broadening in scope and experience, changing the type of work done inside versus outside law firms. This has created a large competitive market of LPOs undertaking commodity-type legal work for other law firms and corporate clients; a market of large firms using a combination of inside and outside resources to efficiently provide the middle tier of legal services; and a small (but well-compensated) set of boutique firms specializing in high-end work (and drawing once again on LPOs for support services).[19]

This transformation of how law is done affects the future demand for lawyers and their expected earnings upon leaving law school. The changes in the legal market have already resulted in a dramatic decrease in applications for law school admission, which fell by an amazing 38% between 2010 and 2013.[20] It has also resulted in declining median starting salaries for new law school graduates, which were 17% lower for the graduating class of 2011 than for the class of 2009, and in a growing bifurcation of the earnings distribution of lawyers, between an upper tier with very high salaries (averaging $160,000 at large, top-tier firms) and a growing lower tier with more modest salaries (averaging between $40,000 and $65,000 for all other jobs).[21]

Fissured Reporting

It is well known that the newspaper business is facing what some have called an existential crisis. The Internet has brought the print newspaper business model to the brink, given the latter's inherently higher-costs of production. Newspapers rely on circulation (subscriptions plus sales by vendors) and advertising as sources of revenue. While circulation revenue for the industry was $10 billion in 2011, virtually at the same level it had been for more than a decade, total advertising revenue was $23.9 billion, less than half of its peak of $48.7 billion in 2000.[22]

Efforts to replace falling revenue from print circulation and advertising with business models related to "new media" have so far restored only a small portion of the lost revenue. The good news in 2011 was that online advertising had increased by $207 million compared to 2010. The bad news was that print advertising had fallen by $2.1 billion over the same period.[23] Equally significant, the use of new models for paid content for Internet stories developed, most notably at the *New York Times*. But once again, these have proven modest sources of revenue, although the model of a partial pay wall (free access for a limited number of page views with an option to pay for unlimited content) has expanded.[24]

Plummeting revenues led newspapers to dramatically cut costs to remain solvent. Early conflicts focused on the back room—the print rooms where some of the strongest unions of the first part of the twentieth century resided. Reductions in printing staff, renegotiation of collective bargaining agreements with unions, and early pension buyouts were common. Other newspapers outsourced printing to contract printers.[25] More recently, some newspapers, among them the *Christian Science Monitor,* have abandoned print versions entirely to become solely digital publications. In some major metropolitan markets, rival newspapers either went out of business or in some cases produced joint editions of certain editions to save money.

But in more recent years, the newsroom has been a focal point of cost cutting. Collective agreements have been reopened (particularly in regard to pensions). Chains have consolidated copyediting and layout in centralized facilities rather than having the work done by individual papers. And newsrooms have had their staff slashed: in 2011 there were 40,600 professionals at newspapers, compared with 56,400 in 2000.[26] Cutting has been focused on coverage of government in suburbs, small towns, and cities, as well as feature stories and specialty beats.

Newspapers have also turned to a variety of forms of subcontracting to replace in-house reporting, particularly in areas like local reporting.[27] One model, using what are sometimes called "content farms," draws on freelance reporters who use information aggregated from the Web or by other contractors to write stories. The Journatic case is indicative of such outsourcing.

Rather than relying on local reporters to gather news, the Journatic model scours the Web to piece together stories with what Brian Timpone, cofounder and CEO of the company, calls "hyper-local content": police reports, high school sports scores and accounts, building permit announcements, court actions, and other disputes that have a Web-facing presence. Journatic de-scribes its core strategy as follows: "Founded in 2006, Journatic is a leading provider of content production services to media companies and marketers. Using a transformative, data-driven approach, Journatic delivers rich, origi-nal community news to some of the largest media companies in the U.S."[28]

Information for these articles is assembled in the Philippines and then shipped back to Journatic to be turned into stories, edited, and then provided to major newspapers, including the *Houston Chronicle, Chicago Tribune, Chicago Sun-Times, San Francisco Chronicle,* and other news organizations (whose iden-tities are not circulated for reasons discussed below).[29] It provides these sto-ries in a format that the purchasing news organization can use as its own (including, most notoriously, by employing fictitious by-lines). Importantly, part of what the company sells is a behind-the-scenes role in providing the content for news organizations whose core competency is about reporting. For example, those writing stories for Journatic are told to use the name of the newspaper Journatic is working for in following up a story, rather than that of Journatic. As Anna Tarkov writes, "If you've never heard of Journatic, that's kind of the idea."[30]

It is difficult to get information on the financial model employed by the company, as it is privately held.[31] Journatic earns its revenues by contracting with newspapers to provide local news content that is gathered and reported in the way described above. It has fifty full-time employees (who reportedly recently began to receive benefits) but relies on thousands of freelancers who are paid low wages and often recruited from places like Craig's List. Report-edly, wages can be as low as $10 per hour with no benefits.

Wage levels for print journalists (except those at the top-tier newspapers) have fallen in recent years. Expansion of Journatic and similar content farm subcontracting models would increase the low end of the pay distribution for professional journalists (compounded by the large and growing supply of free-lancers, given ongoing downsizing).

Many of the concerns about the Journatic model go beyond the workplace to its impact on the quality of reporting, given that the stories arise from data pieced together from the Web rather than from the work of reporters nested in and knowledgeable about those communities. It also places greater pressure on the news organizations relying on that work to check content and verify its veracity, this at a time when copyeditors and editorial staff are also being re-duced. Journatic came under fire when a public radio program broadcast the story of one of its freelance reporters, Ryan Tyler, who discussed his experiences, including the fact that the company often used fake by-lines for its pieces.[32] In July 2012 several news organizations announced that they would end their relationship with the company, while several others, including the *Chicago Tribune* (both a customer of and an investor in Journatic) announced a suspension of its use pending investigation into the use of fabricated by-lines and quotes.[33]

The competitive pressures facing news organizations will continue to push out conventional models of reporting (and the kinds of jobs associated with it).[34] It is not yet clear whether Journatic or companies employing similar business models will expand to realms beyond the "hyper-local" news and routine business reporting where it is currently been used.[35] But it would not be the first time that fissured subcontracting started in one corner of an industry and worked its way outward.

Full-Circle Fissuring

Demands from the financial markets drove the move to the fissured workplace. It seems only fitting, then, that the model would come full circle and alight on that sector. In July 2012 the *New York Times* reported on a trend among the main Wall Street investment firms of "shifting jobs out of the area and expanding in cheaper locales in the United States, threatening the vast middle tier of positions that form the backbone of employment on Wall Street."[36] In this regard, Gary Cohn, president of Goldman Sachs, noted in a presentation on the company's "high-value location strategy" that by locating mid-level work outside of New York, London, and other financial hubs, Goldman could save between 40% and 75% on job-related expenses.

Although companies like Deutsche Bank, Goldman Sachs, and JPMorgan Chase described in the story remained the employer of those mid-level workers shifted from New York City to states like Utah, North Carolina, and Florida, it is not hard to see this as only the first step. First, separate out the core work and jobs that need to be done on Wall Street. Second, move those jobs to other, lower-cost locales, thereby separating the wage linkages between the two. Third, once that work is relocated, explore the possibilities of having other companies provide those services. Finally, reevaluate the remaining jobs in the company and repeat the process, reducing the core group of workers directly employed by the lead financial firm. Given that there are far more people paid to do mid-level jobs than those at the top of Wall Street firms, the potential to ratchet down costs is significant.[37]

Fissured Workplaces and Income Inequality

For almost fifty years between the beginning of the Great Depression and the early 1970s, the trend in income distribution in the United States was toward greater equality. In 1928, as the Gilded Age reached its apex, the top 1% of families in the U.S. income distribution held 23.9% of national income. The Great Depression brought the share of income held by the top 1% down to 15.6% four years later. By the end of World War II that share had fallen to 12.5%. It continued to fall until leveling off around 10% by the mid-1950s, where it remained for nearly twenty-five years.[38]

During roughly the same postwar period, from 1947 to 1979, productivity increased by 119% while average hourly wages increased by 72% and average hourly compensation rose by 100%.[39] The gains accruing to the U.S. economy during its most sustained period of economic expansion went to its growing middle class in the form of rising real compensation.

Many factors account for the fact that the typical American worker shared in the post–World War II economic boom. Growing demand for U.S. products around the world fueled expansion of core manufacturing, construction, and mining sectors of the economy, and with it the demand for workers. Collective bargaining between management and labor (at a time when unions reached their highest density) created a mechanism to share those gains. Progressive taxation policies, coupled with social expenditures for Social Security, the GI Bill, and major investments in infrastructure such as the national highway system, further reinforced the trend.

The way lead businesses in the economy were structured, discussed in detail in Chapter 2, contributed to this era of shared growth. The organizational structure of private sector businesses that drove the postwar economy lent itself to sustained sharing of gains. Wages and benefits of the diverse workforce employed inside the walls of large corporations like General Motors, Hilton, General Electric, and Westinghouse moved together. Workers on auto assembly lines received salary increases, but so did the janitors, maintenance personnel, clerical workers, and many others employed in those enterprises. While wage and benefit gains were often driven by collective agreements in unionized sectors like steel and autos, workers in large nonunion firms also shared in the growing postwar economy. Business models and principles of fairness necessary for the operation of large enterprises reinforced one another.

All of that began to change dramatically by the late 1970s. The percentage of income going to the top 1% of the population began to climb once again, from 10% in 1980 to 14.5% at the end of that decade, to 20% by 1999, and to 23.5% in 2007—virtually the same level as before the Great Depression in 1928.[40] The shift in income back to the top has intensified in particular during the past two decades. In the period from 1993 to 2010, real income grew by 13.8%. For the bottom 99% of the income distribution, the real growth rate was 6.4%, while for the top 1% the real growth rate was 58%. That meant that almost 52% of all real income growth in the economy went to families at the very top of the income distribution. Even more remarkably, income for the pinnacle of the distribution—the top .01%—almost doubled, from 3.4% in 1993 to 6.2% in 2007.[41]

That the economy has ceased to broadly share its benefits over the past thirty years is further illustrated by the reversal of the postwar pattern of wage and productivity growth tracking one another. Between 1979 and 2009, productivity rose by 80%. Over the same period, however, average hourly wages increased by only 7%, and average hourly compensation (wages plus benefits) increased by 8%.[42]

Once again, many factors account for what Paul Krugman calls the "Great Divergence," marked by stagnating wages and earnings for much of the workforce.[43] The growth of international competitors in many manufacturing industries led to declining employment in the core industries of the postwar era and the growth of the nonmanufacturing sectors. Unions began their long, multidecade decline. Tax policies dramatically reduced marginal tax rates on top salaries and wages (just as they began a long climb upward) as well as lowering capital gains and taxes on other sources of income for those at the top of the income distribution. At the same time, social welfare policies that benefited those at the bottom of the income distribution were being reduced.

Stagnating wages for many workers also stemmed from changes in technology and skill demand in this period. Skill-biased technologic change led to increased demand for workers in jobs requiring higher skills and more extensive educational background. As the demand for jobs requiring college-level skills outpaced the supply of workers with them, wages for this group increased. At the same time, the supply of workers with a high school education or less grew faster than the demand for those lower-skilled workers, leading to declining or stagnant wage growth.[44]

The emergence of the fissured workplace, however, must be added to the above list of factors that led productivity and wage growth to be detached from one another over the past thirty years. The process of shedding activities and shifting wage setting from inside lead companies to businesses operating in more competitive markets also meant that the beneficiaries of economic expansion changed. With more of the workers responsible for creating economic value operating outside the walls of the lead companies—whether through sub-contracting, outsourcing, franchising, or other organizational forms—more of the gains flowed to executives in lead companies and their investors.[45] And as the economy slowly recovers from the effects of the Great Recession, the trends toward increasing inequality persist. The latest estimates indicate overall real income growth of 1.7% between 2009 and 2011. But that anemic growth masks two very different trends: real income *grew* by 11.2% for families at the top 1% level but *declined* by 0.4% for the other 99% of families.[46]

Employment and Wages over the Business Cycle

The dot-com recession of the early years of the twenty-first century and the Great Recession of 2007–2009 have been followed by very different recoveries than accompanied business cycles of the past. Two characteristics are particularly troubling. First, in both cases, employment recovered much more slowly than in the past, leaving large numbers of workers unemployed, underemployed, or out of the labor market entirely for longer periods of time. Second, the wage profile of job growth in recent recoveries has proved quite different than in the past.

The Great Recession has been devastating in many respects, but nowhere so much as in the depth of job loss and the slow pace of recovery. This is shown in Figure 11.1, which compares the Great Recession with prior recessions in 2000, 1990, and 1981 in terms of the relative loss of jobs and the time required to bring them back. The vertical axis of the graph charts the percentage of jobs in the economy in each month relative to total jobs immediately preceding the beginning of the recession. Not only did the financial crisis and the accompanying contraction in the economy lead to a far worse

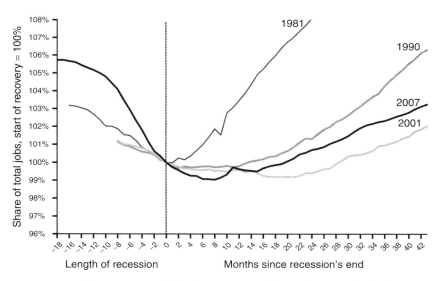

FIGURE 11.1. Job recovery in the last four recessions. *Source:* Economic Policy Institute 2012, based on Bureau of Labor Statistics data, Current Employment Statistics public data series, available at http://stateofworkingamerica.org/files//Jobs_recession-job-loss -comparison-SWA-live11.png.

loss in jobs than during any recession of the past thirty years (or more), but job recovery is taking far longer—much longer even than during what was called the jobless recovery of the 2000 recession.

Once again, it would be a significant overstatement to attribute the extended time required for recovery entirely to the effects of fissured workplaces. Financial downturns like the Great Recession are always deeper, more tumultuous, and more difficult to recover from than more typical business cycle downturns.[47] Equally, the political paralysis in fiscal policy that has hamstrung macroeconomic responses also contributes to the slow rate of economic growth and, correspondingly, to job creation.

However, there is reason to believe that the restructuring of industries discussed in this book has a role in the lengthening of recoveries, decade by decade, depicted in Figure 11.1. As discussed in Chapter 3, capital markets increasingly place pressure on companies to use downturns as opportunities to restructure employment. That means greater incentives for lead businesses to cut their own workforce and diminished incentives to rehire workers coming out of a recession. This contrasts to hiring decisions in the 1960s, 1970s, and early 1980s, where lead businesses often "hoarded" labor—that is, they kept on more workers than they needed, despite economic downturns.[48]

When lead companies do bring back workers, those new employees are likely to be from a more narrow swatch of jobs and occupations than prior to the beginning of recession. What is more, hiring in an industry characterized by fissured workplaces occurs through multiple, lagged steps, since many jobs have been shifted to subordinate tiers of employers. Only when the lead businesses are sufficiently convinced of the wisdom of expanding production will they draw upon the services of those "orbiting" businesses that in turn do much of the hiring (or turn to their subordinates to hire). This implies a longer response time between increases in demand and expansion of employment.

The above account also implies that the jobs coming out of a recession will look different than those going into it: in particular, that the jobs coming out of a recession will be skewed more toward low-wage jobs than those that were lost at its inception. That turns out to be precisely the pattern in the current recovery. Employment losses during the recession were widely spread, but concentrated in mid-wage occupations. However, during the current recovery period, lower-wage occupations grew 2.7 times as fast as mid-wage or higher-wage occupations. Based on an analysis of Bureau of Labor Statistics data, the National Employment Law Project finds that lower-wage occupations (median hourly wage ranging from $7.69 to $13.83) constituted 21% of employment losses but 58% of employment growth coming out of the recession; mid-wage occupations (median hourly wages between $13.84 and $21.13) accounted for 60% of losses but only 22% of employment growth; and higher-wage occupations ($21.14–$54.55) constituted 19% of losses and about 20% of growth. Over the past decade, lower-wage occupations grew by 8.7% and high-wage occupations by 6.6%, but mid-wage occupations actually declined by 7.3%.[49]

David Autor calls the longer-term trend in occupational employment growth at the top and bottom of the wage distribution and the accompanying decline of the middle "job polarization." Job polarization arises from the impact of automation (and to a lesser extent outsourcing) of routine jobs in the economy that tend to be in the mid-wage range. What remains are two types of jobs, both requiring nonroutine tasks. The first type of nonroutine job draws on manual tasks and is found in areas like personal services, cleaning, food service, and retail, which tend to be low-wage. The second type of nonroutine job requires undertaking more abstract tasks (managerial, professional, technical) and therefore greater educational background. These tend to be high-wage. Both types of jobs continue to grow in the economy, explaining their positive growth in contrast to the decline of routine jobs in the middle.[50]

The larger change in the distribution of occupations in the economy is certainly an important part of the explanation of these trends (and their impact on income distribution more generally). But focusing solely on occupations and the median wages associated with them misses the effects of the fissured workplace on shifting the location of where a given job is undertaken and its impact on wages. Chapter 4 presented evidence that janitorial or security work done inside a larger organization pays more than the same job done when performed by a contractor. Chapter 5 provided evidence that work done in logistics and mining or on cell towers paid less (and exposed workers to increased hazards) the further out one went from the lead company. And Chapter 6 showed that an employee is more likely to be underpaid in a fast-food operation if he or she works for a franchisee than directly for the franchisor.

Equally, the fissured story in journalism and law implies that even non-routine abstract jobs will pay differently given where that job is located. A world of lawyers working for LPOs or journalists working for companies like Journatic looks different than one where those professions sit inside traditional law firms or media companies. The job polarization story, therefore, explains part of the changing job profile of economic recovery, but neglects the intersection of the organizational location where nonroutine jobs are undertaken and its resulting influence on earnings.[51]

Economists and policy makers are painfully aware that the way our macroeconomy operates has changed significantly in the past few decades. Understanding the impact of the fissured workplace on how industries and the economy as a whole operate may help in fashioning new approaches and responses to the challenges posed by trends in income distribution and economic recovery.

A Path Forward

If I hire another organization to go run a part of my operation,
I'm not directing their day-to-day activities, and I'm not responsible.
A lot of organizations have cafeterias in their facilities, a third
party coming in and running the cafeteria. I'm not responsible
for those employees. That's not part of my operation.

—David Sarvadi, attorney for major logistics providers, 2012

You can take the captain of the ship approach. You can say that
Randall Stephenson is responsible because Randall Stephenson's the
CEO of AT&T. But what impact . . . would [that] have on the
eventual safety of future crews? I think that's too far to connect.

—Ed Reynolds, former president of AT&T network services, 2012

When the largest company raises wages and cuts hours, it forces every
other factory to do the same thing whether they want to or not.
A firestorm has started and these companies are in the
glare now. They have to improve to compete. It's a huge
change from just 18 months ago.

—Tony Prophet, senior vice president at Hewlett Packard
in regard to Foxconn's decision to dramatically
improve its workplace policies

Economic history runs in one direction. As much as we might like aspects of the past, the age of the large corporation directly employing a very wide cross section of American workers has passed. Absent public policies that rebalance the benefits and costs facing businesses, fissuring will continue to deepen in those industries where it has already taken root and will expand to new industries like finance and law. The fissured workplace is here to stay.

The ethos of fissuring has become embedded in how companies think and how markets operate. Share prices of companies respond positively to news of employment reductions. Companies used to "hoard" labor during recessions to retain workplace talent they did not want to lose. Now they use downturns as times to revise their corporate boundaries, actively shedding parts of production or service delivery that will not be reattached during the recovery. And while politicians may make patriotic stands against offshoring, they take domestic outsourcing as an inevitable part of business practice.

As the Great Recession fades in memory—at least for those comfortably employed—the economic, technologic, and organizational drivers leading to the fissured workplace are likely to be stronger than ever. Public discussions may become temporarily focused on striking stories of its impacts in one place or another: a scandal arising from outsourced legal work; a popular consumer brand relying on a network of contractors using misclassified workers or drawing on vendors who flagrantly violate health and safety standards; or a major accident with multiple fatalities resulting from coordination failures of complex systems with no one overseeing the big picture. And Labor Day will bring the usual round of stories about the decline of unions, the loss of opportunities for those lacking college credentials, and continuing wage stagnation for many workers in the "99%."

But if public attention continues to focus on the symptoms of fissured employment, without adequate understanding of how these stories are part of the new way our economy is and will remain wired, there is little reason to believe that these trends will change. Staying on the current pathway will lead to increased fissuring in more sectors of the economy and the problems that come with it.

A second, alternative, pathway forward is possible. It depends on crafting public and private policies that reflect an understanding of the boundaries of the lead businesses in the economy and of the way modern employment has changed. The drivers behind fissured workplaces are decisions balancing the need to protect and expand core competencies weighed against the benefits of shifting out the employment problem to others. This book has provided many examples of lead businesses balancing those factors carefully and fashioning sophisticated systems to establish standards, monitor performance, and reward or punish compliance or noncompliance. It is clear that lead organizations do not lack the capacity to monitor and oversee behavior or the creativity to find different organizational forms to implement improved standards, nor do they lack the technologies and systems to make monitoring of the tiers of businesses surrounding them cost-effective. They simply lack the legal requirement that they consider important social consequences of the fissured workplace when they are making those decisions.

Lead businesses operate in complicated, multiparty structures and have been successful in making them work. Not only do their investors benefit from many of the organizational forms that lead to the fissured workplace, but consumers and the public do as well. The point is not that producing goods and services using more flexible organizational relationships is inherently wrong. But if those decisions skirt the social costs resulting from that flexibility, we will continue to experience the problems described in this book.

Many of the cases examined here suggest that innovative solutions could be created by reestablishing that lead companies have some shared responsibility for the conditions arising in the network of workplaces they influence through their other activities. In fact, successful public policies should harness the creativity and drive of private organizations to fashion policies and create systems that promote the private aims of lead companies (in product or service quality, value, and delivery) as well as the public aims of the laws protecting the workforce (providing safe and fair workplaces).

- Many petrochemical plants, construction projects, and manufacturing facilities carefully supervise their subcontractors, drawing on needs for particular skills, peak demand, or unusual circumstances in order to achieve production targets, quality standards, and difficult scheduling deadlines. Why can't these goals also incorporate achievement of significant health and safety risk reduction?
- Many franchised systems operate with very high quality standards achieved by their franchisees. Why not just transfer this excellence to the domain of consistent compliance with workplace standards and an environment where workers feel safe in voicing concerns when there are problems?
- Companies producing digital products demonstrate their ability to rely on highly complex networks of suppliers to deliver products that meet demanding specifications and create products that end users adore. If they can specify standards for technical performance, why not assure the same for their workplaces?

A positive path forward requires revisions of existing workplace laws so that they adequately recognize the far more complex nature of the modern workplace and the growing presence of multiple organizations with roles in employment decisions. It requires public agencies to change the way workplace policies are implemented and enforced so that they create incentives for industry and business structures that can lead all parties—not just those most proximate to the workplace, who might lack the ability to change conditions—to play a role in reducing risks and complying with established laws. And it requires private actors in the workplace—unions, worker advocates, and employer associations—to fashion creative, flexible, and effective systems to see that workplaces live up to standards adopted in our laws while continuing to meet the product and service objectives they are designed to produce.

Some companies already follow this alternative pathway, because the private benefits and costs of overseeing subordinate businesses lead them to do so; because collective agreements with unions require it; or because of commitments that business leaders have to socially responsible behavior. But many companies do not and will not until public policies change in ways that alter the private calculus underlying fissured employment decisions.

Requiring lead businesses to incorporate the social costs of shedding employment into the standards and systems they use to monitor the network of businesses they rely upon or the prices they pay to subsidiary organizations working on their behalf would create ripple effects on that wider web of workplaces. This book has argued that fairness plays a vital role in the functioning of the workplace. We are coming out of a long period where wages, working conditions, and standards of fairness at the workplace have been diminished. Realigning the incentives driving businesses at the lead of industries in our economy could move the standards upward once again, making the network of workplaces that underlie many industries better places for workers at all levels of skill and education even while enjoying the advantages that arise from harnessing new ways of organizing production.

This is the path toward mending the fissured workplace.

Notes

1. The Fissured Workplace and Its Consequences

1. For example, retailers have always relied on temporary workers (and agencies) to supply additional employment during the holiday season. Erickcek, Houseman, and Kalleberg (2003) describe the use of temporary workers in the automobile supply and hospital sectors as originally motivated by the need to find workers in tight labor markets. The authors explain that company managers came to use temporary agencies for more and more of their employment needs as other benefits of the arrangement became evident.

2. I review examples of misclassification in Part II. For other examples, see Carré and Wilson (2004); National Employment Law Project (2004); U.S. General Accountability Office (2009).

3. The Federal Trade Commission requires that all franchisors disclose franchise agreements for prospective franchisees. This example is taken from the Dunkin' Donuts Franchise Disclosure Document (FDD), April 17, 2009. The FDD is filed and accessible through the California Franchising database (http://134.186.208.228/ca leasi/Pub/Exsearch.htm).

4. Microtel Inns and Suites Franchising Inc., Microtel Franchise Disclosure Document, March 28, 2008. Filed and accessible through the California Franchising database (http://134.186.208.228/caleasi/Pub/Exsearch.htm).

5. See Saks Fifth Avenue, *Vendor Standards Manual,* June 20, 2013 (https://www .saksincorporated.com/vendorrelations/documents/SFAVendorStandardsManual06 -20-13.pdf).

6. These findings are reviewed in detail in subsequent chapters. The data cited here is from the following sources (also discussed more extensively in the book): (1) wages, pension coverage, and CEO / production worker pay gap: Economic Policy Institute, State of Working America website, http://stateofworkingamerica.org/ (accessed September 2, 2012); (2) labor standards violations: Bernhardt, Milkman, et al.

(2009); (3) back wage findings: U.S. Department of Labor, FY 2012 Annual Performance Report (http://www.dol.gov/dol/budget/2014/PDF/CBJ-2014-V1-01.pdf).

7. See Boushey et al. 2007; Ghilarducci 2008. Osterman and Shulman (2011) find significant differences in the level of pension coverage: 77.3% in the low-wage group are not included in a pension plan versus 25.7% in the group with 1.6 times the median wage or more. One must be cautious in interpreting these figures, since they reflect the answers for a household member in the Current Population Survey (CPS), and may reflect a decision to opt out of pension coverage for both rational and sometimes irrational reasons (see Osterman and Shulman 2011, 21–22). For example, people may turn down pension contributions by employers in a matching program even though this is essentially leaving money on the table (see Thaler and Sunstein 2008 for a summary of this evidence).

8. See Boushey et al. (2007). Osterman and Shulman (2011) show that the percentage of workers without employer-paid health care is inversely related to wage/ salary level. Using the CPS, they find that 67.5% of those earning below the poverty level for a family of four do not have health care paid at least in part by their employer. This compares with 21.9% of those who are 1.6 times or more above the median wage. The authors point out that one must use this figure cautiously, since some people choose not to have coverage because someone else in their household is covered. Still, if the proportions of those groups are roughly similar, the fact that the two groups differ by a factor of three indicates significant gaps in health care coverage for low-wage workers.

9. And, of course, some large companies continue to the present to resist regulations and compliance with standards for their own workforce. Recent major discrimination suits and wage and hour settlements by Walmart best illustrate this point.

10. See Bernhardt, Milkman, et al. (2009).

11. See U.S. Chemical Safety Board website for reports provided in the July 2012 hearing: http://www.csb.gov/investigations/detail.aspx?SID=96&Type=1&pg=1&F _All=y (accessed September 1, 2012). This issue is discussed in greater detail in Chapters 5, 9, and 10.

12. Direct and control test has become central in the area of misclassification laws regarding whether workers have been incorrectly classified as independent contractors rather than employees. I discuss this in Part III.

13. 29 U.S.C. §§ 201–219 (1994). Not surprisingly, the application of this broad doctrine is very case-specific and often controversial. I discuss this in Chapter 8.

14. Even the right of the agency created to implement the legislation to exercise judgment on the interpretation of definitions of "employer" has been contested, particularly in the case of the National Labor Relations Board, which administers the National Labor Relations Act.

15. See Stone (2006), Rogers (2010), and Jost (2011) for a discussion. This is discussed in detail in Part III.

16. In fact, in the case of real estate investment trusts (REITs), one of the most common forms of ownership in the hotel industry, ownership precludes any formal role in the management of hotel properties. I discuss this further in Chapter 5.

17. Federal estimates in Weil (2010); state-level estimates taken from Schiller and DeCarlo (2010). In highly fissured industries like residential home building and janitorial services, the annual probability of an investigation can be below 1 in 5,000. I discuss this challenge in Part III.

18. See Economic Policy Institute, State of Working America website, http://stateof workingamerica.org/ (accessed September 2, 2012).

19. See Picketty and Saez (2003) and updated estimates by the authors, available for download on the Web at http://elsa.berkeley.edu/~saez/ (accessed September 2, 2012). The highest level of concentration prior to 2007 was in 1928, when the top 1% held 23.9% of national income.

20. Employment growth by wage group based on National Employment Law Project (2012). Real income growth for the top 1% based on estimates by Picketty and Saez, table 1, "Real Income Growth by Groups, 1993–2010," available from downloaded data (http://elsa.berkeley.edu/~saez/, accessed September 2, 2012). Both trends are discussed in Chapter 11.

21. Popular accounts include Bobo (2011), Greenhouse (2008), and Ehrenreich (2008). Academic studies in this area (many funded by the Russell Sage Foundation over the past decade) include Appelbaum, Bernhardt, and Murnane (2003); Bernhardt, Milkman, et al. (2009); Kalleberg (2011); Kochan (2005); Osterman and Shulman (2011); and Weil (2009, 2010).

22. Peter Cappelli (1999) argues in "Career Jobs Are Dead" that the stability of this postwar period has been overplayed and that it in fact represented a fairly atypical moment in employment history. Instead, he argues that contracted employment characterized the workplace for a much longer period of time prior to this period. I take this view up further in Chapter 3.

23. For example, in a recent article on working conditions in the poultry industry by Charlotte Alexander (which she describes as a leading example of "peripheral labor"), cost reduction is cited as the obvious and sole reason for the poor conditions prevailing in that industry: "If the answer to the question of *why* firms rely on peripheral labor is that it is cheap and it is effective, I explore *how* conditions on the periphery came to be" (Alexander 2012, 6). Although reducing labor costs represents a major part of the story, this oversimplifies the underlying model pursued by major chicken processors as it does in other industries discussed in this book.

2. Employment in a Pre-fissured World

1. The ten largest U.S.-based corporate employers in 1960 were GM, AT&T, Ford, GE, U.S. Steel, Sears, A&P, Exxon, Bethlehem Steel, and ITT. By 2000 only GM, Ford, and Sears remained on that list (see G. Davis 2009, table 3.1).

2. This account is taken from Marc Levinson's detailed study of the rise and fall of "the Great A&P." See Levinson (2011).

3. Ibid., 81–84. Levinson quotes a Federal Trade Commission report of 1919 that noted, "The cost of these individual delivery systems . . . is a large item to be figured into the wholesale prices" (83).

4. The advantages of internalizing inventory management were huge, as shown by "inventory turns," which is the amount of time required to turn over the inventory held by a retailer. At a time when its principal competitors' inventory turns were four months (requiring paying interest, committing storage space, and bearing the risk of unsold goods for that amount of time), A&P had reduced its turns to a mere five weeks (ibid., 89).

5. A&P's size in fact led fretful congressional leaders to pass the Robinson-Patman Act of 1936, which prohibited chain stores from receiving better pricing than smaller retailers.

6. See Coase (1937).

7. Williamson notes, "I submit that the modern corporation is mainly to be understood as the product of a series of organizational innovations that have had the purpose and effect of economizing on transaction costs" (1985, 273).

8. One problem with the transaction cost approach is that such costs are not directly observed and are difficult to define, making it challenging to test the theory in practice. The property rights framework provides a more formal way of modeling the consequence of incomplete contracts on how markets and organizations solve coordination problems. See, for example, Grossman and Hart (1986) and O. Hart and Moore (1990).

9. For Chandler (1977), the managerial revolution of the late nineteenth century and the first half of the twentieth century can be thought of as the mechanism by which corporations implemented the advantages theoretically described by Coase and Williamson. The increasing absorption of transactions and tasks usually allocated by markets into the operation of the business organization is the story of the evolution of the modern corporation and the management systems used to guide it.

10. See ibid., 249–258.

11. Livesay (1975, 102–106).

12. See Chandler (1980, 26). Williamson (1985, 274–279, provides a nuanced discussion of the particular type of transaction costs that lent themselves to new solutions in the railroad industry.

13. See Chandler (1977), chapters 3–6, in regard to railroad and telegraphy, and chapter 7 in regard to retailing. The sea change that retailers like Sears represented was as transformative as Walmart would be more than a century later. Chandler notes that by 1905, Sears filled 100,000 mail orders each day—more than a typical merchant might have handled in a lifetime of work. Chandler (1990) examines the creation of managerial hierarchies required to manage production and distribution systems built on economies of scale and scope.

14. The property rights framework discussed above (e.g., O. Hart and Moore 1990) explains the emergence of a single firm providing multiple products in this way arising from the "complementarity" of assets and tasks—that is, by using one asset or doing one task, it raises the payoff from other related assets or tasks. If such complementarities exist, a single firm will better capture the cumulative gains from doing them under one roof relative to the case of undertaking them by contracting across several independent firms. The larger the number of firms that must be contracted to produce a common good with complementarity at its core, the greater the incentive for integration.

15. Williamson (1985) notes, "The M-[multidivisional] form furthermore effected a split between operating and strategic decision-making and reserved the latter for the general office. Providing the general office with an internal incentive and control capability was required lest the potential benefits of the division of effort be dissipated" (296). Once again, more recent theorists operating from property rights frameworks focus on the incentive problems that arise from trying to organize such complicated processes through arm's-length contracting. Because of the difficulty of observing the actions of contracted partners and the consequent need for high-powered incentives to induce desired behaviors, organizational structures create an alternative arrangement that moves parties in desired directions with lower-powered (less costly) incentives. Grossman and Hart (1986) provide a foundational discussion of this perspective; Rebitzer and Taylor (2011) provide a helpful overview of the literature and its implications, particularly in regard to labor market incentive structures.

16. See Ferguson (2008) for a sweeping discussion of the history of money and finance.

17. Although not yet the modern form of the corporation, the Boston Manufacturing Company was established by Lowell in 1813 as a joint-stock enterprise allowing multiple investors to pool their capital in a form quite distinct from partnerships. Lowell needed and used the capital he raised to build his first textile factory in Waltham, Massachusetts, which integrated ginning, baling, spinning, and weaving in one factory. See Abernathy, Dunlop, et al. (1999), chapter 11, for a short history of Lowell and his efforts; see Dalzell (1987) for a more detailed discussion.

18. Berle and Means (1932, 9).

19. Ibid., 313.

20. Sloan quoted in Williamson (1985, 287). The Ethyl Corporation therefore was made a self-standing enterprise (with investment by GM) rather than an operational division.

21. Chandler and Tedlow (1985, 737–738). See Seligman (1995, 418–437) for a discussion of the conglomerate merger wave.

22. This justification can be found in a popular analysis of the day by Neil Jacoby (1969): "By definition, the conglomerate firm combines operations unrelated in respect to raw materials, technologies, or markets. The annual sales or profits of its different operations will be negatively correlated. In the aggregate they will produce a more stable return through time. For any given rate of return on investment, risk will be less; for any given risk, expected reward will be higher."

23. Galbraith (1971, 89).

24. See Doeringer and Piore (1971). In describing the employer considerations driving the adoption of internal labor markets, Doeringer and Piore describe factors that are still weighed by lead businesses in now deciding whether or not to shed them (1971, 28): "Three kinds of cost considerations appear to militate in favor of internal labor markets: (1) the value of such markets to the labor force, (2) the cost of labor turnover to the employer and the role of such markets in the reduction of turnover, (3) the technical efficiencies of an internal labor market in the recruitment, screening, and training of labor."

25. In fact, some labor economists and industrial relations scholars of the time worried about the negative consequences of the low levels of mobility occasioned by internal labor markets, in what Clark Kerr (1977) famously described as the "balkanization of the labor market," which created limited desire—or ability—to move out of one organization and into another. More formally, by reducing mobility, internal labor market conditions gave employers some level of monopsony, allowing them to pay wages below what they might otherwise have been required to pay workers of comparable skills and abilities in a more open labor market setting. I discuss monopsony and its consequences for employment in Chapter 4.

26. Many in recent years have harkened back to this "golden age" of employment that was accompanied by both growing productivity and wage growth (and a sustained period of overall wage compression and an increase in income equality) as a period of greater corporate responsibility and management accord with labor. While some part of this period of greater labor/management accord may have arisen from the common, searing experience of the Great Depression and World War II, the arrangement also proved profitable. See Cappelli (1999) for a presentation of the latter view.

27. See, among other accounts of this, Dunlop (1993).

28. For example, Foulkes (1980), in a comprehensive review of nonunion personnel policies at the peak of the postwar period, notes that "promotion from within is an important cornerstone of the personnel policies and practices of all the companies

studied, although the methods and the selection criteria by which the companies implement promotion from within vary" (143).

29. The estimates are based on Dobbin and Sutton (1998), using a stratified random sample of 279 public, for-profit, and nonprofit organizations in thirteen sectors with offices in California, New Jersey, or Virginia. The growth was particularly dramatic in personnel / human resource functions dealing with discrimination and affirmative action, with no company respondents reporting an office (or officer) with such responsibility in 1967, up to 25% so reporting in 1977, and over 40% so reporting by 1987.

30. C. Brown and Medoff (1989) provide the most comprehensive evidence that workers in large firms and large establishments earn significantly higher wages even after controlling for the above factors as well as occupation and industry. They also show that the large-firm wage premium cannot be explained by hidden worker quality (as evidenced by the fact that employer size wage effects do not shrink much for workers who switch jobs); by differences in working conditions (that is, that higher wages in large workplaces are not compensating for worse conditions in them); by union threat effects (large-firm wage premiums persist even in industries with very low union density); or by differences arising from the relative market power of large firms located in industries with higher economic profits. Finally, Brown and Medoff show that the large-firm effect even impacts piece rates, which are higher for comparable levels of output relative to piece rates offered in smaller firms. See also Brown, Hamilton, and Medoff (1990) for an extensive discussion of the differences in human resource policies between large and small business enterprises.

31. Gibson and Stillman (2009) show persistent large-firm wage effects using more detailed control for skill than the original Brown and Medoff findings. Hollister (2004) presents evidence on the decreasing size of the large-firm wage effects in the 1990s. Researchers differ in their explanations for the persistence of higher wages in larger firms and internal labor markets with regard to the degree that the supply and demand for labor underlie the wage effect, and the extent to which large-firm wage premia reflect individual versus group choice. Researchers also differ with respect to the extent that wage premia and internal labor markets generally respond to changing conditions surrounding firms—their "rigidity," to use Doeringer and Piore's (1971) term.

32. Oi (1983, table 2.6, p. 89). Oi's estimates of wages as a percentage of total compensation are based on a survey of large firms by the Chamber of Commerce. Bob Hart (1984) uses the Chamber of Commerce survey data but a somewhat different methodology than Oi for estimating total compensation and finds a sixfold increase in benefits as a percentage of salary and wages between 1929 and 1951, from 1.9% in 1929 to 11.5% in 1951.

33. See Oi (1983, table 2.7, p. 90). Firm pension and health care coverage estimates for 1979 are based on the Current Population Survey.

34. A large literature, following the groundbreaking work of Michael Piore and Peter Doeringer in the late 1960s, documented the existence of "segmented labor markets" divided between primary labor markets with higher wages, greater job security, union representation, and benefits and a secondary labor market with few of these features. See for example Bowles (1973); Reich, Gordon, and Edwards (1973); and Gordon, Edwards, and Reich (1982).

35. It should also be noted that the arbiters of the "bottom line" were also less demanding in the postwar period: simpler capital market structures were far less dominated by the factors that have come to push corporations to focus on quarterly returns (for better and worse). With fewer institutional investors and the revolution in financial arbitrage decades in the future, public markets for capital had less sway on the day-to-day operations of firms. In fact, a literature dating back to the late 1930s (Berle and Means) was more concerned about the complete separation of ownership and management, a concern that in the late 1960s would lead financial and organizational economists to think about ways to create greater incentives for risk taking by managers. Chapter 3 discusses this issue in detail.

36. Union membership data for 1930–1972 are from U.S. Department of Labor, Bureau of Labor Statistics (1975, 389). Estimates of the number of persons employed for 1930–1993 are from U.S. Department of Labor, Bureau of Labor Statistics (2003, 158; 1994, 182). For a comprehensive set of union membership and density estimates, see http://www.unionstats.com, a site maintained by Barry Hirsch (Georgia State University) and David Macpherson (Trinity University) that provides alternative measures of density.

37. One measure of this is that the size of the large-firm wage gap found by C. Brown and Medoff (1989) and others began to decline. Hollister (2004) estimates that the large-firm effect declined by about one-third between 1988 and 2003. The strongest factors associated with these changes in her study are "shifts in organizational structures, particularly a decline of internal labor markets" (673–674).

38. Peter Cappelli argues that the rise of internal labor markets was in itself a singular and relatively brief phenomenon between the 1940s and the early 1980s, reflecting a stabilizing macroeconomic climate and the dominant position in global trade held by the United States as well as the relatively high density of the labor movement. Economic and market stability led employers to accept the "bargain" of having relatively high commitments to job security and paying decent wages, not because employers were more decent or committed to such outcomes, but because it made good business sense at that moment in time. As international competition intensified and capital market pressures became more demanding, employers looked for methods to unwind these practices and move toward other arrangements. It was not that employers lost their commitment to good practice, but simply that they concluded that the postwar model no longer fit with the prevailing environmental conditions. See Cappelli (1999) as well as critiques of his view in S. Jacoby (1999).

3. Why Fissure?

1. In a famous essay at the time, Milton Friedman (1970) raised a very different concern related to the same detachment between ownership and management. He argued that the growing discussion among business executives about social responsibility was naïve at best and counterproductive at worst, since the prime responsibility for management was to maximize shareholder value. "In a free-enterprise, private-property system, a corporate executive is an employee of the owners of the business. He has direct responsibility to his employers. That responsibility is to conduct the business in accordance with their desires, which generally will be to make as much money as possible while conforming to the basic rules of the society, both those embodied in law and those embodied in ethical custom." Given this responsibility, "businessmen who talk this way [about social responsibility] are unwitting puppets of the intellectual forces that have been undermining the basis of a free society these past decades." It is interesting that in the essay, Friedman implicitly assumed wide latitude on the part of management in focusing a little or a lot on social responsibility, with little discussion of the disciplining role of capital markets, which would soon become central to this discussion in economics and corporate finance.

2. For the classic statement of this view, see Jensen and Meckling (1976).

3. Ferguson (2008) gives a history of the long-term evolution of money and financial markets, and Johnson and Kwak (2011) provide an account focused on more recent evolution in the United States. Recent popular accounts of the emergence of major institutional players and their impacts on business, financial markets, and the economy can be found in Cohan (2009) and M. Lewis (2009, 2010). G. Davis (2009) places these developments in relation to the changing nature of companies, following the work of Hacker (2006), although with a greater emphasis on its impact on the ideology underlying political and economic decision making.

4. Less than half of the workforce receives any form of pension, but overall participation rates show the same shift from defined benefit to defined contribution plans: in 1980 an estimated 28% of all wage and salary workers were in defined benefit plans, 8% were in defined contribution plans, and 11% had both a defined benefit and a defined contribution plan. By 2010 only 8% of wage and salary workers had defined benefit plans, while 31% were in defined contribution plans (and 6% held both). Estimates from the Center for Retirement Research, based on data from the Federal Reserve Board's Survey of Consumer Finances.

5. Estimates are based on the annual fact book of the Investment Company Institute (2012), which tracks industry-level trends among investment companies. For 2011, 9% of household financial assets were invested in 401(k) and other defined contribution plans, and 10% of household financial assets were in individual retirement accounts (IRAs). The rest were in a mix of investment vehicles. A total of 52.3 million households (or 90.4 million individuals) owned a mutual fund (ibid.). In

2010 about 50% of families had stock holdings either directly or indirectly. The median level of holdings for families with stocks was $29,000 (in 2010 dollars), down from $42,000 in 2001. Stocks represent 47% of family financial assets (vs. 56% in 2010) (Bricker et al., 2012, table 7). Mutual funds managed 55% of the assets in defined contribution plans in 2011 (versus 13% in 1991) and managed 45% of IRA assets.

6. That number fell from a prerecession peak of $12 trillion in 2007 (Investment Company Institute 2012, figure 1.1).

7. Ibid., figure 1.5. Equity funds made up 45% of mutual fund assets in 2011 (ibid., 24). The percentage of 401(k) funds invested in equities declined after the recession. For example, in 2000, 51% of participants in their fifties had more than 80% of their 401(k) account balances in equities; by 2010 only 26% of participants in their fifties had that percentage in equities. Similarly, in 2000, 40% of participants in their sixties had 80% of their account balances in equities versus only 21% in 2010 (see ibid., figure 2.6).

8. Ibid., figure 2.2.

9. Based on estimates by G. Davis (2013). See also Susanne Craig, "The Giant of Shareholders, Quietly Stirring," *New York Times,* May 19, 2013.

10. Bernstein (1992) provides a very readable account of the interplay of academic ideas and capital market developments.

11. Turnover is measured as the percentage of a fund's holdings that changed over a year (weighted by overall assets). See Investment Company Institute (2011, figure 2.7).

12. In recent years even more high-powered funds, with shorter time horizons, have emerged. Exchange traded funds (ETFs) are investment companies (e.g., Black-Rock, Charles Schwab, Vanguard) that hold assets including stocks, bonds, and commodities whose shares are traded on stock exchanges. Investors can buy or sell ETF shares through a broker or brokerage account. Unlike mutual funds, ETFs can be bought and sold on a stock exchange like other stocks. However, only authorized participants such as institutional investors buy or sell shares directly from the fund manager, in large blocks (25,000–200,000 shares, or "creation units"). The price of ETFs is therefore continuously changing on stock exchanges. Arbitrage on valuation drives price. ETFs have grown rapidly in the past decade: in 2001 there were 102 at year end; by 2007 there were 629; and by 2011, 1,134. Total net assets of ETFs went from $83 billion in 2001 to $608 billion in 2007 to $1.05 trillion in 2011. ETFs held $229 billion in large-cap domestic stocks and $89 billion in mid-cap and small-cap domestic stocks. See ibid., figures 3.7, 3.1, and 3.6, respectively.

13. This influence goes beyond buying and selling of shares, but also directly from the role that institutional investors play in corporate governance via the exercise of voting rights, influence on who holds seats on boards of directors, as well as activities in other governance forums.

14. Although the terms are often used in popular discussions interchangeably, private equity funds and hedge funds differ in a number of important respects. Both financial organizations historically primarily served very large institutional investors and operate in a relatively unregulated environment compared to banks, mutual funds, or investment banks. Private equity funds, on one hand, are typically focused on a small number of very large deals where investors expect their money to be locked in place for many years. Hedge funds, on the other hand, make a much larger number of short-term investments, focused on finding arbitrage opportunities (instances where a price differs in two markets) or using other methods to provide high returns to investors. As a result, while investors in private equity funds may be locked in for three to five years, hedge fund investments are liquid. See Ferguson (2008) for an interesting discussion of the origins of modern hedge funds.

15. These figures are presented in Appelbaum and Batt (2012, figure 1, p. 11).

16. See ibid. for an excellent description of the private equity model.

17. These lenders, in turn, often securitize the loans made to the company in acquisitions, which are then sold to secondary markets, often including other hedge funds. As a result, the acquired company faces the most concentrated risk arising from the transaction, since the private equity funds, limited partners, and lenders can all diversify their own exposure to the risk of default by the acquired company.

18. Bain Capital was formed out of the consulting firm Bain and Company, in part because of the belief of Mitt Romney and other Bain executives that many companies were unwilling to implement the consulting advice they provided. By using private equity to actually acquire the company, the new owners would be able to implement policies and realize gains from the share price appreciation of the company over time. See Lemann (2012) for a history of Mitt Romney and the evolution of the Bain Capital model.

19. Increasing returns also requires solving other problems arising from incomplete contracting—including the difficulty of observing the actions taken by executives in pursuit of improved performance—discussed in Chapter 2. See Jensen and Murphy (1990) for the classic argument in favor of providing high-powered incentives for executive compensation.

20. Estimates are based on Frydman and Jenter (2010), using constant 2000 dollars for the top fifty firms in the United States. The rate of growth of compensation for a wider group of all firms in the S&P 500 reveals a similar trend in growth, rising an annual average rate of 10% in the 1990s, from a median (average) level of $2.3 (3.0) million in 1992 to $6.1 (8.2) million by 2008 (see ibid., table 1, panels A and B, p. 41).

21. Historic trends in the components of executive compensation are estimated in ibid. The percentage of compensation from salaries, bonuses, options, and stocks is estimated and reported in figure 2, panels A and B, pp. 38–39.

22. In principle, the boards of directors of corporations select a subset of directors to act as a compensation committee charged with setting pay and establishing performance objectives for executives. Members of compensation committees are supposed to be independent in the sense that they are not former members of the corporation and are unaffiliated with the business except for their role on the board. See Bebchuk and Fried (2004), particularly parts I and II.

23. Mishel et al. (2013). The data presented here is drawn from the Economic Policy Institute website associated with *The State of Working America*, accessed September 2, 2012, http://stateofworkingamerica.org.

24. In this view, famously articulated in an article by Robert Hayes and William Abernathy (1980), businesses in the late 1970s and early 1980s became overly fixated on immediate returns, which led managers to make investments and acquisitions, and adopt strategies, that looked good to investors in the short term but often led to underinvestment in the kinds of activities needed to make businesses sustainable and competitive over the long haul. Hayes and Abernathy argued that the ascendency of Japan was a result of the long-term focus of investors (and the government) in that country versus the short-term preoccupation of U.S. businesses, in large part because of the financial system. See Lazonick (2010) for a related discussion.

25. Early examples of this literature include Quinn, Doorley, and Paquette (1990); Prahalad and Hamel (1990); and Quinn and Hilmer (1994).

26. In what is often considered a seminal article in the early business school literature on the topic, Prahalad and Hamel (1990) examine the idea by contrasting the performance of the then-rising upstart information technology company NEC with the declining fortunes of GTE in the high-tech sector. They attribute NEC's success to its focus on building a set of competencies involving the intersection of computing and telecommunication. By making decisions focused on strengthening its unique expertise in integrating computing, communications, and components, they argue, NEC secured an advantage in developing new products and entering new markets that kept it ahead of GTE and other competitors. Products, activities, and existing business units that did not support further development of that unique competency were put aside or shifted to other entities to allow NEC to further pursue its core competency. In contrast, "no such clarity of strategic intent and strategic architecture appeared to exist at GTE. Although senior executives discussed the implications of the evolving information technology industry, no commonly accepted view of which competencies would be required to compete in that industry [was] communicated widely." Ibid., 80–81.

27. Apple outsourced design activities to Frogdesign, printers to Tokyo Electric, and marketing to a small company called Regis McKenna. See Quinn and Hilmer (1994, 43–44). For an early history of Apple, including the development of the Apple II series, see Moritz (1984).

28. Employment numbers and the exchange between Jobs and President Obama reported in Charles Duhigg and Keith Bradsher, "How the U.S. Lost Out on iPhone Work," *New York Times,* January 23, 2012. The story was part of a larger investigative report on Apple published as "The iEconomy." See http://www.nytimes.com/interactive/business/ieconomy.html (accessed December 21, 2012).

29. In its staff report, the FTC recommended that the "Securities and Exchange Commission immediately require pooling of interests to be eliminated as the normal mode of accounting for acquisitions involving the exchange of stock." Federal Trade Commission (1969, 119–134). Seligman (1985) provides a detailed account of government accounting scrutiny of conglomerates in this period.

30. See Seligman (1995, 418–437). Williamson (1985) notes: "Indeed, one would expect, and events have borne the expectation out, that the 'go-go' conglomerates would become unglued when adversity set in—as it did in the late 1960s. Those firms found it necessary to reorganize along M-form lines (divisional structures), to simplify their product lines, or to do both" (289).

31. The merger wave had been enhanced by creative accounting techniques that allowed companies to hide some of the costs associated with mergers and acquisitions activity, making the acquisitions look more attractive than they often were. This led to investigations by the Federal Trade Commission and the Securities and Exchange Commission (SEC). As a result of growing public and investor concern with the issue, Congress passed the Williams Act in 1968, requiring disclosure of cash tender offers resulting in changes of ownership of more than 10% (later lowered to greater than 5%). The SEC also required greater disclosure of product-level data in acquisitions. See Fung, Graham, and Weil (2007, 107–109) for a discussion of financial disclosure policies arising from the conglomerate period.

32. This account is based on Gazel (1990), who provides a history of the rise and demise of Beatrice.

33. A well-known ad indicative of the company's reach far beyond core food brands in the 1980s proclaimed, "We're Beatrice. You've known us all along." A notable commercial from the 1970s with the "We're Beatrice" tag line can be seen at https://www.youtube.com/watch?v=1SRT1y6xmng (accessed June 22, 2013).

34. The institutionalization of human resource and personnel functions is examined in Dobbin and Sutton (1998) and Dobbin and Kelly (2007). Pfeffer (1998) reviews the large literature on strategic human resource policy.

35. Adler (2003) points out that some of these payroll providers further subcontract out more specialized activities, such as processing workers' compensation, to other firms. The creation of multiple tiers of subcontractors is a phenomenon common to fissuring, as we shall see in later chapters.

36. See Adler (2003) generally regarding human resource outsourcing. He provides a detailed case study of the BP outsourcing effort (see pp. 57–59). See also Gilley, Greer,

and Rasheed (2004), who report positive financial performance effects of human resource outsourcing.

37. Firms in the emerging industries of outsourced payroll activities and human resource functions grew and consolidated rapidly. For example, shortly after BP and other major companies hired Exult, the human resources consultant was purchased by Hewitt in 2003; Hewitt later became part of Aon, a very large integrated human resources company. This type of reconsolidation of activities that have been shed is not uncommon and is often pushed forward by private equity companies. I take up this aspect of fissuring and its implications in Part II.

38. Results of annual surveys conducted by Computer Economics (2000).

39. Barthélemy (2001), in a survey of fifty IT outsourcing cases, reports that 78% of respondents outsourced some data center activity; 56%, network management; 56%, user support; and 52%, application maintenance (p. 62).

40. Computer Economics (2012). The survey estimated that outsourcing among its panel of respondents had grown 43% by 2011, after experiencing some decline during the recession.

41. Private businesses were not alone in this regard. Many nonprofit entities—hospitals, public agencies, charitable institutions, and universities—found the logic of shifting work outward equally compelling.

42. Milkman (2006) describes this evolution in Los Angeles. See also Mines and Avina (1992) for an earlier discussion.

43. See Dey, Houseman, and Polivka (2010, figure 7); they use the Occupational Employment Statistics for a set of identified occupational groups (including janitors and guards). Estimating contracting-out is difficult for a variety of reasons explored by the authors. Dube and Kaplan (2010) also estimate the percentage of outsourcing among these groups, but derive somewhat lower figures (22% of janitors and 50% of guards for the period 1998–2000) using estimates from the Current Population Survey. Both studies show a rise in the use of contracting for these positions. Abraham and Taylor (1996, table 6), using a different estimation method, also find evidence for significant growth in business service contracting during the 1980s beyond what would be expected because of overall growth in employment. Cleaning, security, and building maintenance work has also been increasingly contracted out in other countries. Blanchflower and Bryson (2010) report that in the United Kingdom, the share of workplaces with twenty-five or more employees that subcontracted janitorial services increased from 55% in 1990 to 72% by 2004; contracted security increased from 33% to 45% over the same period.

44. Reengineering efforts often resulted in layoffs, and a common critique of the approach was that it was used to provide cover for large-scale downsizing (for example, see Bluestone and Harrison 1990). A more amusing critique of the nefarious side of reengineering can be found in the 1999 film *Office Space* (http://www.imdb.com/title/tt0151804/).

45. Hsiao et al. (2010) break this evolution into four levels of logistic outsourcing: (1) transportation, (2) packaging, (3) transportation management, and (4) distribution network management.

46. Hsiao et al., in ibid., provide a review of the performance literature on logistic outsourcing.

47. See Erickcek, Houseman, and Kalleberg (2003). The only case where there were no temporary workers was a unionized plant with very strong collective bargaining language prohibiting the practice.

48. Ibid., 381.

49. Note that this is a key feature of franchising: the franchisor holds many rights over the franchisee in terms of length of contracts, options to renegotiate and sell the agreement, etc. The stronger the franchisor (because, for example, of the strength of the underlying brand), the less successfully the franchisee will be able to use its hold-up power.

50. See Brynjolfson and McAfee (2011) on new capacities created by IT technologies and the rapidly expanding range of activities created by them.

51. Traditional franchising goes back to the mid-1800s and is attributed to major manufacturers like McCormick Harvesting Machine Company and Singer Sewing Machines Company. Traditional franchising allowed sales representatives, who were given exclusive geographic territories, the right to sell the manufacturer's products. Some companies, like McCormick, created company-owned branches to oversee the sales agents in a region. Others, like Singer, created a mix of company-owned and independent sales agents, with the latter given explicit guidance on how operations were to be run. Business format franchising emerged in the 1920s and 1930s in companies like Hertz Car Rentals, A&W Restaurants, Howard Johnson's, and Arthur Murray Schools of Dance. But it did not become a ubiquitous form until the 1950s and its use in fast food (discussed in Chapter 6). See Blair and Lafontaine (2005, 5–8) for further discussion of this history.

52. This improves the capacity of the principal (company) to monitor its agent (trucker) and, with attendant incentives, to increase the payoff for the firm to continue to directly hire its workforce. OBC from this perspective decreases subcontracting by addressing the incomplete contracting problem. See Baker and Hubbard (2003).

53. Baker and Hubbard say that the dual effects help explain how a fall in communication costs in the nineteenth century as studied by Chandler led to *increased* concentration, while a similar fall in communication costs arising from OBC led to smaller, less integrated firms. They conclude: "We find that the answer to the question: 'Has IT adoption led to larger or smaller firms in trucking?' is 'Yes,' and show how the organizational implications of IT's incentive- and coordination-improving capabilities systematically differ" (ibid., 1351).

54. In the auto supplier case described above, they attempted to do so by offering the most highly ranked temporary workers permanent positions. However, the

resentment of these workers at being paid at a lower level meant that many of the best workers left the company and sought better positions elsewhere (possible given the tight labor market conditions at the time of the study). This meant that the hiring practice was increasingly at odds with the quality standards desired by the company—although not enough so to tilt the balance back toward its higher-paid permanent workforce.

55. Formally, this requires that the costs of locating the activity inside the firm must be greater than or equal to the cost of activity from outside divided by the relative productivity of outside option relative to inside option.

56. This is famously characterized as the "lemons problem" by George Akerlof, a Nobel Prize–winning economist. In the used car market, the underlying quality of cars is hard for buyers to observe. Because many people sell cars because of problems they have with them, buyers in the market assume the worst (in part because they cannot easily see the quality of any given car). Because of this expectation, the price for used cars is pushed down, so that even the seller of a good car will be forced to receive a lower price than the true value of the vehicle warrants.

57. A well-known problem arising from this is moral hazard, where a principal ends up creating precisely the wrong incentives for agents. For example, when selling fire insurance to customers, the insurer hopes that they will be careful in regard to fire safety. But since the customers now know that damages will be covered, they become more, rather than less, careless.

58. Some literature asserts by assumption that contracting is impossible with little acknowledgment of the often heroic efforts made by businesses to map out many aspects of the relationships between business organizations. The effort to keep such documents private evinces their importance to core firm strategy. I discuss this, for example in relation to franchise disclosure documents and handbooks, later in this chapter and in Chapter 6.

59. Saks Fifth Avenue, "Technology Requirements," in *Vendor Standards Manual,* June 20, 2013, p. 9 (see https://www.saksincorporated.com/vendorrelations/docu ments/SFAVendorStandardsManual06-20-13.pdf, accessed June 22, 2013).

60. Dunkin' Donuts Franchising LLC: Dunkin' Donuts Franchise Disclosure Document," retrieved via BlueMauMau.org., http://www.bluemaumau.org/ufocs_free _and_without_a_salesman_attached (accessed March 28, 2008).

61. Taco Bell Franchise Agreement, Franchise Disclosure Document, 2009, section 3.

62. The general terms and some of the operating requirements and standards are offered to prospective franchisees as part of franchise disclosure documents (FDDs), which are required by the Federal Trade Commission and many state business agencies. I discuss (and draw on) these documents in Chapter 6. The operating manuals provided to franchisees, however, are proprietary and confidential, and therefore dif-

ficult to gain access to. Most franchise agreements regard the operations manual as on loan to the franchisee. Often prospective franchisees are only allowed to review the table of contents of the manuals in advance of being approved by the franchisor. The FDD for Chipotle, for example, says, "The Operations Manual contains our trade secrets and you may not copy, duplicate, record, or otherwise reproduce any part of the Operations Manual." See "Chipotle Mexican Grill, Inc., Information for Prospective Franchisees," May 20, 2004, item 11, pp. 20–21.

63. And that is not all: "Cingular may continue to add audits in a market in 5% increments until Vendor's Major Defect rate is less than the 1% baseline provided herein." See https://www.documentcloud.org/documents/365742-cingular-contract -with-nsoro.html#document/p30/a58894, at pp. 79–80.

64. Taco Bell Franchise Agreement, Franchise Disclosure Document, 2009, section 9.

65. Saks also asserts that "all risks, claims, storage or handling charges on refused, rejected, returned, postponed or cancelled goods are Your [the vendor's] full responsibility, regardless of other terms of sale or passage of title." See Saks Fifth Avenue, *Vendor Standards Manual,* June 20, 2013, p. 15 (https://www.saksincorporated .com/vendorrelations/documents/SFAVendorStandardsManual06-20-13.pdf, accessed June 22, 2013).

66. See Master Supplier Agreement between Betacom Incorporated and Cingular Wireless LLC, effective date November 29, 2001 (https://www.documentcloud.org /documents/365750-cingular-contract-with-betacom.html#document/p1, accessed July 15, 2012).

67. The Pizza Hut Franchise Agreement states: "If any inspection indicates any deficiency, Franchisee will correct or repair the deficiency within 48 hours after Franchisee receives a written report of the deficiency from PHI [Pizza Hut Incorporated]. If (a) the deficiency is one that Franchisee has a right to cure under Section 18.2 and (b) the deficiency cannot be cured within 48 hours, Franchisee will not be in default if Franchisee begins the necessary corrections or repairs within the 48-hour period, and diligently pursues the work to completion. If the deficiency is one that imminently threatens the health or safety of Franchisee's employees or the consuming public, PHI may (instead of terminating this Agreement . . .) require Franchisee to cease operating the effected [*sic*] System Restaurant until the deficiency is corrected. If Franchisee does not cure the deficiency within the permitted time, PHI may make, or hire someone else to make, the corrections or repairs. Franchisee will reimburse PHI, upon demand, for all of PHI's repair expenses." See Pizza Hut Incorporated Franchise Agreement, State Amendments and State Addenda to Disclosure Document, 2009, section 6.4.

68. For example, the Taco Bell FDD states, "If the Franchisee defaults in the performance or observance of any of its other obligations hereunder or under any other

franchise agreement with the Company, and such default continues for a period thirty (30) days after written notice to the Franchisee, the Company may at any time thereafter terminate this Agreement as well as any other such franchise agreement upon written notice to the Franchisee" (article 15.0, p. 14).

69. S. Davis et al. (2011, 30–32).

70. See ibid., table 7. In contrast, where independent firms are acquired by private equity firms, net employment grows by 10.5% two years after the transaction year. Divisional buyouts and other forms of buyouts yield net employment losses two years after the transaction of 1.5% and 6.5%, respectively. Post-transaction behavior also varies significantly across broad industry groupings. See pp. 28–31. An earlier version of the paper using a larger sample of target firms and establishments found larger negative impacts on employment growth in the target establishments relative to controls, and no difference in gross job creation. See Appelbaum and Batt (2012) for a critique of the Davis et al. results, particularly their inclusion of acquisitions and divestitures by targeted firms in estimating overall net employment effects.

71. See S. Davis et al. (2009), which employs a similar methodology of matching manufacturing firms acquired by private equity with a constructed control group of firms that were not acquired, and comparing the pre- and post-acquisition labor productivity trajectories of the acquired firms and their establishments against the controls.

72. The fact that employment reductions were largest in public-to-private buyouts in service and retail (S. Davis et al. 2011, figure 8), sectors where fissuring is a more recent occurrence than in manufacturing, is consistent with this interpretation.

73. See "GM Looks to Cuts to Boost Stock Price," *Detroit Free Press,* June 13, 2012.

74. See Farber and Hallock (2009) and Hallock (2009).

75. Hallock and Farber measure pricing impact by using cumulative excess returns based on the Center for Research in Security Prices data on stock price movements. Excess return of a stock measures the part of a stock return that is not correlated with overall market fluctuations in returns, and therefore reflects unanticipated, company-specific changes in valuation. The authors use an "event window" framework (measuring changes prior to and after the job loss announcement) as their key variable, controlling for other characteristics of the firm. Different lengths of the event window do not affect the overall results reported above. See Hallock (2009) and Farber and Hallock (2009).

4. Wage Determination in a Fissured Workplace

1. Even here, labor law scholars would be quick to qualify this statement, as suggested by voluminous court rulings on when plant closings or statements about the

effects of a union winning an election do or do not transgress what is a remarkably fuzzy line.

2. These estimates by Hallock (2012, 40–43) are based on data from the National Compensation Survey for 2011. The averages mask differences in the components of employer hourly costs across workers, occupations, and industries. For example, wages and salaries for service workers account for 71% and legally required benefits account for 9.3% of employer hourly costs because employees in service industries typically receive far lower insurance and retirement benefits than workers in other industries.

3. In making more employers responsible for providing health care coverage to their workforce, the Affordable Care Act of 2010 changes these dynamics both for lead and subordinate businesses in complicated ways. For example, the costs of providing health care benefits may be lower per worker for a larger versus a smaller business. If subordinate businesses are now required to provide coverage, their costs of providing services to lead businesses will increase, thereby changing the private calculus of hiring additional workers versus using a subcontractor or temporary agency to provide them. I discuss the "rebalancing" of the fissured workplace decision in Part III.

4. This assumes that the supply of labor is upward sloping—that is, in order to induce additional people into a labor market, employers must pay an increasingly higher wage rate as they increase employment. How quickly the wage needs to increase to entice additional people into the market (measured as the elasticity of labor supply) affects the degree that a labor market is affected by a monopsonistic employer. See Manning (2003, chapter 4) for a complete discussion.

5. The economist Joan Robinson coined the term *monopsony* (as a general term applied to any case where a single buyer had market power) and developed how it affected labor markets in particular in 1937. For a recent discussion of monopsony, see Ashenfelter, Farber, and Ransom (2010) and Manning (2003, chapter 2).

6. Even coal towns are rarely controlled by a single employer. But major coal companies do loom large over local labor markets. And, as we shall see in Chapter 5, they too fissure employment.

7. In a competitive labor market, the supply of labor facing a firm is totally elastic, meaning it can purchase as much labor at a certain skill level as it wants at the market price. But search frictions reduce the willingness of workers to move, which means the supply of labor slopes upward and firms have an ability to set wages (Boal and Ransom 1997; Manning 2003). Ransom and Oaxaca (2010) estimate elasticity of labor supply for men and women in the grocery store industry and show that the supply of labor for women is less elastic than for men, and as a result their wages are more affected by the monopsony position of employers in that industry—specifically that the relative pay of women is lower. Staiger, Spetz, and Phibbs (2010) find evidence of

very low supply elasticity in the labor market for nurses working in the Department of Veterans Affairs.

8. The observation by the Webbs at the outset of this section (1897, 281) has been substantiated in more contemporary times. See, for example, Slichter, Healy, and Livernash (1960); Foulkes (1980); Brown and Medoff (1989); and Bewley (1999), who all document the presence of "standard rates" for workers of varying productivity. Brown and Medoff, for example, conclude, "Large employers are more likely to have single-rate wage policies within job categories for their blue-collar workers, and they are less likely to opt for a separately determined wage for each worker" (1056).

9. See Oi (1983) and Becker (1964). Both models help explain why, as John Dunlop often commented, "labor markets are not a bourse" and instantaneous wage rates do not allocate labor efficiently on their own. The presence of either quasi-fixed costs of labor or the need to provide specific training (i.e., training that benefits a worker at a specific employer) creates a compensation problem that firms must find a way to solve by acting as if, in the Oi model, only a portion of compensation costs are variable or, in the case of Becker, thinking about compensation policy as part of a human capital investment that the firm must recover over time.

10. This view is developed in Milgrom (1988). For an overview of implicit contract theory in employment, see Rosen (1988).

11. The ultimatum game and a wide variety of variants of it (e.g., the "dictator game," where the proposer's split is imposed without the consent of the second player) have been used both as experiments, where people play the game with real money but in a decision laboratory, and in the field, where experimenters try to create similar conditions but with more realistic setups. They have also been replicated at different levels of payoffs—that is, with much larger pots of money at stake. In general, the same results hold up. Fehr and Schmidt (1999, 2002, 2007) and Camerer (2003) provide detailed discussions and extensive references about these results.

12. Early work on the fairness of wage cuts was done by Kahneman, Knetsch, and Thaler (1986). Bewley (1999), whose work I discuss below, provides rich qualitative evidence on how anticipation of fairness affects personnel and human resource managers. See also Kahn (1997) for empirical evidence of nominal wage stickiness.

13. The incomplete nature of information gives rise to "search frictions," discussed above—that is, imperfections that limit my ability to do a full-scale search for a job that best matches my qualifications. The more limited a job searcher's information is in relation to an employer's, the more such search frictions convey power to the employer.

14. The vast majority of managers (87%) in Bewley's study of compensation policies agreed with the statement "Most or all employees know one another's pay." See Bewley (1999, table 6.6, p. 80).

15. Seniority-based pay for workers in a given pay grade or job classification is one imperfect way to vary wages based on differences in average productivity that strikes

most as fair. See Medoff and Abraham (1980) for empirical evidence on the use of seniority as a fundamental device for setting compensation over the course of a worker's career at a firm.

16. Using data from the 1890 Census, Claudia Goldin finds that piece rates were used more extensively in firms where both men and women were employed in comparable occupations (although women were rarely employed at the same occupations and the same firms as men at that time). In those firms, men tended to earn more than women from the piece rate (set at a similar level for both). Goldin writes: "Why were females and males both employed at piece rates when they were given the same occupational title? One reason may be that males were more productive than were females because the existing technology rewarded their greater strength, or because males had a greater incentive to work more intensively than females. Data from the 1895–96 Report of the Commissioner of Labor indicate that the average ratio of earnings for females to males, when both worked at piece rates at the same firm and at the same occupation, was about 0.8. If these same workers were employed on time, their earnings would have differed (for a given occupation, at the same experience level, and so on). Even in the late nineteenth century unequal payment by gender for identical work would have damaged labor relations within the firm" (1986, 13).

17. Foulkes (1980, 185).

18. In economic terms, employment relationships are "incomplete contracts" where much of what the employer is contracting for cannot be directly observed or measured.

19. This problem was pointed out in a 1942 Bureau of Labor Statistics assessment of piece rates: "In computing workers' pay for their output, the more complex incentive systems make use of formulas that are confusing to most of the workers. The pay is not calculated according to the mere number of pieces produced or the number of hours of work but by means of some special unit [measure]. Workers claim that the use of a complex formula for wage payment facilitates rate cutting, because actual changes in production standards which affect the unit of measurement must be concealed from them. Whether rate cutting occurs or not, the worker finds it difficult to check the relationship between his pay and his output or effort." Joiner (1942, 6–7).

20. One problem with piece rates, for example, is that they can reward quantity at the expense of quality. Tailoring them to do both is difficult, although not impossible, as pointed out by Koller (2010) in his interesting account of the use of piece rates at Lincoln Electric, a Cleveland-based arc welding manufacturing company. Rebitzer and Taylor (2011) show why crafting the correct incentives in a case where there are multiple performance outcomes is difficult and can often have undesirable consequences.

21. While one might expect that selfish players would push out the fairness-focused players, a large number of experiments show that the opposite turns out to be the case. In one typical setup, participants are paid a certain wage but can choose how much

effort to exert in doing a task. A purely selfish individual would simply exert the minimum effort necessary to obtain the wage, and if everyone behaved this way, the level of effort would quickly descend to the minimum. However, if there are even a small number of fairness-focused players who feel they should reciprocate the higher wage by expending higher effort, the selfish players have an incentive to mimic the behavior of the fairness-minded players (and therefore exert more effort) out of fear of being revealed as selfish shirkers. As a result, effort of the group migrates to the higher level (see M. Brown, Falk, and Fehr 2004).

22. Just under 50% cited "job performance" and only 7% cited "avoidance of discrimination suits" as the major reason for internal pay equity. Bewley quotes a human resources manager in a unionized manufacturing company with 27,000 employees remarking: "Unfairness can cause upheaval within an organization and lead to dysfunctional activities. People want to be treated fairly and to see that their contributions are recognized and that this is done on a consistent basis from one location to another and from one profession to another." See Bewley (1999, 79, 81). For a related formal model of how fairness concerns play out in workplaces, see Stark and Hyll (2011).

23. See Manning (2003, chapter 5) for a summary of this literature. See also Card and Krueger (1995) and Erickson and Mitchell (2007).

24. The horizontal equity imperative is exemplified in management scholarship of the period. For example, Herbert Meyer, on the basis of his research on personnel policies, recommended that firms give "all employees judged to be performing at a satisfactory level the same percentage increase whenever salaries are adjusted upward." In so doing, "a predictable salary progress schedule not only should help to reduce uncertainty about future pay but also should prevent the development of false expectations. In addition it should minimize dysfunctional competition between individuals for favored treatment." Quoted in Foulkes (1980, 186).

25. Fehr, Goette, and Zehnder (2009, 378). The literature on loss aversion and "framing" in psychology is extensive. The seminal papers are Tversky and Kahneman (1974) and Kahneman and Tversky (1984). Kahneman (2011) provides an overview of the extensive research in the field in the decades following those landmark works.

26. Slichter, Healy, and Livernash (1960) explained the common practice of uniform pay increases with job grades with minimal performance evaluation in union and nonunion facilities as an outgrowth of union avoidance and the constant problems of defending merit-based evaluations in the minds of workers. "The path of least resistance has been to develop automatic, or nearly automatic increases" (606).

27. Foulkes (1980, 153) similarly notes, "The pay policies of the companies [large nonunion employers] are designed to provide and demonstrate equity."

28. In regard to the need to have a fairly fixed relationship among the different wage levels within a wage system, a human resources officer at a four-hundred-person

division of a nonunion manufacturing company commented: "The jobs are in a fixed relationship with each other. The relationships have a history. The important thing is to pay consistently by some sort of yardstick. As soon as you change the system, you have a problem." See Bewley (1999, table 6.4 and discussion on pp. 75–79).

29. See Card and Krueger (1995) and Manning (2003) as well as a recent set of empirical papers estimating the degree of monopsony power, summarized in an opening essay by Ashenfelter, Farber, and Ransom (2010).

30. Bewley (1999) finds evidence of this in his study comparing wage setting for what he calls "primary sector workers" (those hired on a permanent basis) and "secondary sector" workers (those hired on contract, temporarily, or on some contingent basis). "The greater flexibility of hiring pay (for secondary workers) derived from the lesser importance of internal pay equity. In both sectors, the pay of existing workers was rigid downward, but in the secondary sector the pay of new hires was less tied to that of existing workers. In contract labor, there are no comparable existing employees, for temporary workers usually do not relate their pay to that of permanent employees" (18–19).

31. Rebitzer and Taylor (2011) summarize literature on problems arising from more complex monitoring/agency where workers have multiple aspects of effort to monitor. If there are two aspects of effort, for example, and they are complementary, but one aspect is not observable, the employer faces a difficult problem in creating a compensation model. Shifting this work to an independent contractor is desirable in such cases in that the payment becomes one more directly related to output of the provider than to the input of the worker.

32. The complementary nature of switching from employment to contracting in order to deal with the variation (economists call it heterogeneity) of workforce productivity and "focusing on core competencies" can be seen most clearly here.

33. Ironically, it would also remove the resource distortion introduced by monopsony, since under these circumstances the employer would end up hiring additional workers to the point that would be found in a competitive market. However, unlike the situation in a competitive market, the monopsonist would capture the "bonus" received by workers whose wage rate exceeded their marginal contribution to production (i.e., the rents of inframarginal workers).

34. More technically, successful core competency in branding or product development means less elastic demand for those companies (and therefore a greater ability to price at higher levels for a given level of costs). In those cases, the reduction of labor costs arising from fissuring can go primarily to investors. In core competency areas of coordination (think retailing) or with economies of scale, lead companies may still face more competition in their product markets. Labor cost savings are more likely to flow into reduced prices for consumers (as well as to higher returns for investors).

35. See Dey, Houseman, and Polivka (2010, figure 7).

36. Abraham and Taylor create a careful measure of wages to capture whether the establishment is a high-wage or low-wage organization (see 401–403), which allows them to measure the relation of a firm's overall wage structure to its decision to contract out specific types of work. See Abraham and Taylor (1996, tables 4 and 5 and pp. 407–410).

37. See Berlinski (2008) and Dube and Kaplan (2010). The cited differences control for a variety of factors that might be associated with differences in the workforce as well as the places where the work is done. The Dube and Kaplan study provides a particularly rich set of estimates that allow the authors to rule out a number of potentially "unmeasured" characteristics of contract vs. in-house workers. This includes estimating the impact of contracting for workers who switched from in-house to contract work (and therefore presumably had similar skill sets). In addition, the fact that health benefits and wages were worse for contractors (and that hours of work were similar) contradicts a "compensating wage differential" story where lower wages reflect better coverage or other more desirable aspects of work.

38. The negative effects of contracting on health coverage remain even when other characteristics of workers and work are controlled (Dube and Kaplan 2010, 297–299).

39. In this kind of empirical work, the question of omitted variables that might be driving observed associations between dependent and independent variables looms large—in this case, unmeasured characteristics of the workers that are associated both with their status as contractors and with their pay. There is always the chance that some unmeasured characteristic of janitors who continue to work inside companies makes them more productive than contractors, hence explaining the pay gap for reasons other than their contract status per se. That three careful studies, drawing on different methods (and data sets), derive similar results makes this seem less likely here.

40. In their very careful study of the determinants of wages and benefits for janitors and security guards, Dube and Kaplan (2010) reach a similar conclusion, noting, "Overall the recent increase in the use of service contractors seems to be associated with some shifting of rents away from workers" (305).

41. Cleeland, quoted in Milkman (2008, 80).

II. The Forms and Consequences of the Fissured Workplace

1. Greenhouse (2008, 4).

2. Studies on the growth and impacts of low-wage work include Appelbaum, Bernhardt, and Murnane (2003); Bernhardt, Boushey, et al. (2009); Kalleberg (2011); Osterman and Shulman (2011); and Weil (2009, 2010).

3. There is overlap between these organizational forms: supply chain structures in some sense can be characterized as more elaborate forms of subcontracting. Franchisees often decide to subcontract out particular activities (an increasingly common

practice in many industries). I discuss some of these hybrid cases, such as those found in the hotel and motel industries where franchising is often combined with different types of subcontracting.

5. The Subcontracted Workplace

1. This was particularly true in the clothing industry's formative era, when diversity within and across product types was far greater on the women's side. See Carpenter (1972) for a wonderfully detailed account of the evolution of the women's industry in New York City.

2. The boundaries are interesting too. In construction, historically, general contractors were the lead firm, working directly for the end user and in charge of hiring, managing, and coordinating subcontractors for a project. However, since some trades could be expected to be on-site virtually for the duration of the project (in particular what are called the "basic trades" of carpenters, laborers, and in some cases operating engineers), they were often directly employed by the general contractor. This relationship changed beginning in the 1960s, partially as a means to weaken the power of building trade unions, with the emergence of "construction managers" who coordinate work but do not directly employ any trades. See Weil (2005a).

3. Mookherjee and Tsumagari (2004) show how different forms of subcontracted relationships dominate other forms from the perspective of different parties. In particular, they show the importance of (1) information, (2) collusion among suppliers/contractors, and (3) substitutability/complementarity between the inputs of suppliers or subcontractors.

4. This section draws from a series of articles by the investigative reporter Paul Nyden published in the *Charleston Gazette* between 1993 and 1995 that document in detail the increasing use of subcontracting in underground coal mining. It also draws from Crandall, Starrett, and Parker (1998), which provides a detailed discussion of subcontracting in mining in the context of legal issues raised by the practice. I am grateful to Doug Parker for conversations sharing material on subcontracting from this period as well as to Marric Buessing for discussions of the incentives for vertical integration between different stages of mining production.

5. Although I focus here on underground coal mining, which is concentrated primarily in the eastern half of the United States, a large percentage of coal is mined through open mining operations (strip mining) in parts of the East Coast as well as predominantly in the western half of the country.

6. See Buessing (2013) for a detailed empirical analysis of the recent trend to vertical integration.

7. This is the same company that in a later incarnation as Massey Energy Company was responsible for the death of twenty-nine miners in April 2010. A. T. Massey Coal Company was founded in 1920, originally as a coal broker. It expanded into the

coal mining and processing business in 1945. Following investments by a number of energy companies including Royal Dutch Shell in the 1970s, it became a wholly owned mining subsidiary of the Fluor Corporation (an international engineering and construction firm) in 1981. It was spun off from Fluor in 2000 and renamed Massey Energy Company. Following the Upper Big Branch disaster, the company was acquired by Alpha Natural Resources in January 2011.

8. The name refers to a confidential document, "The Massey Coal Company Doctrine," circulated by then-president E. Morgan Massey to his top executives in 1982.

9. Massey Doctrine, quoted in Paul Nyden, "Massey Contracting Made Controversy," *Charlestown Gazette,* November 30, 1993, 1–5.

10. All coal is not the same, but varies in terms of its heat, sulfur, ash, and other contaminant content. Reject rates are based on whether the coal meets standards for these attributes. For example, given environmental restrictions on the amount of sulfur dioxide that can be emitted by electricity companies, utilities purchase coal with specified levels of sulfur content as well as heat content. Metallurgic coal requires lower sulfur and ash content and therefore higher costs for cleaning and processing. Coal companies retain the right to set and change the standard and therefore potentially reject coal that has already been mined by the contractor.

11. Subcontracting also insulates the mining company from any concerted worker activity focused at the lead company, since it no longer is the direct employer, making such actions a violation of the National Labor Relations Act prohibition of secondary boycotts.

12. For example, Nyden documents the case of Nobel Coal, a tiny subcontractor for Soho Coal Company which subcontracted for a Massey subsidiary. Nobel mined $50,000 worth of coal but reneged on paying its men for the four weeks of work it required, promptly shutting down thereafter. Several days later a new subcontractor (owned by the same couple as Nobel) reopened the mine under the name R&B Mining Inc., rehiring the men, but this time failing to pay state taxes or royalties to the UMWA health and pension funds. See Nyden, "Massey Contracting Made Controversy," 5.

13. Thomas Galloway, quoted in Paul Nyden, "Coal Contracts: Shifting Mining Danger, Responsibility," *Sunday Gazette-Mail,* November 7, 1993, 5.

14. The use of subcontracting also created opportunities to avoid cleanup responsibilities under the Resource Conservation and Recovery Act (RCRA) and other environmental laws. This became and remains a very active area of environmental litigation for the Environmental Protection Agency and the U.S. Department of Justice.

15. Nyden, "Coal Contracts," 1.

16. See ibid., 3. Nyden also reported that 80% of the 250 contractors used by Island Creek Coal Company, another major coal producer in the 1990s, were out of business by 1993.

17. See ibid., 3. See also Nyden, "Mining Contractors Owe Millions in Fees, Fines, Wages," *Sunday Gazette-Mail,* December 26, 1993, 1.

18. Nyden, "Mining Contractors Owe Millions," 1.

19. Nyden notes, "When Soho lost its contracts [to Massey subsidiaries] it laid off 80 union employees who once worked directly for Massey. Soho, not Massey, owed the men and the UMW benefits funds more than $1.2 million." See Nyden, "Coal Contracts," 5.

20. Paul Nyden, "Small Mines Shunt Safety Concerns for Large Profits," *Sunday Gazette-Mail,* December 19, 1993, 1. See also Buessing and Weil (2013) regarding the relationship between contracting practices and fatalities and injuries in the underground coal industry.

21. See Crandall, Starrett, and Parker (1998, 566). The changes to liability in the act will be discussed at greater length in Chapter 10.

22. According to briefs filed by the UMWA during the bankruptcy proceedings, at the time it was created, Patriot received 16% of Peabody Energy's assets and 40% of its liabilities. Patriot took on additional retiree liabilities in 2008 when it acquired Magnum Coal, which had been spun off by Arch Coal in 2005. When Magnum was created, Arch provided it with 12% of its assets and 97% of its retiree healthcare liabilities. U.S. senator Joe Manchin commented, "This ruling is a travesty. It is wrong that Peabody can set up a company such as Patriot, fill that company with its liabilities and then spin that company off for the sole purpose of avoiding its contractual and moral obligations to its workers." The bankruptcy decision was being appealed to federal court at the time of this writing. See Tiffany Kay, "Patriot Coal Wins Leave to Cut Retiree Pensions, Benefits," Bloomberg.com, May 29, 2013 (http://www.bloom berg.com/news/2013-05-29/patriot-coal-wins-approval-to-cut-retiree-pensions-ben efits-1-.html, accessed June 24, 2013).

23. Coal mining industrial structure is divided between controllers (who own and sometimes operate processing and mining facilities); operators who are directly involved in coal mining (and may be the controller or a subsidiary of the controller); and contractors. There is some difficulty in separating out what I call "traditional" subcontracting at the opening of the chapter (e.g., blasting and specialty contracting) from fissured contracting. In 2010 there were about 150,000 employees of mine operators and 20,000 employees of contractors in the underground coal mining industry (Buessing and Weil 2013).

24. The incentives to avoid penalties increased in 2006 because of amendments made to the Mine Safety and Health Act in that year. The loss of nineteen miners in three successive accidents during the first five months of 2006 led Congress to introduce a wide-ranging set of changes, the Mine Improvement and New Emergency Response Act (MINER Act), which was signed into law by President George W. Bush. The law increases penalties for violations of health and safety standards

and also requires mine operators to adopt more extensive emergency response planning to allow evaluation of miners who may be trapped, or, if they cannot evacuate, to provide places for them to retreat underground.

25. Ember claimed that G. R. Mining was a separate company with no relation to Ember's operations. This argument hinged on the point that G. R. Mining used a continuous miner (a type of mining where the mining operation cuts or rips coal and other material from the mine face and then directly loads it onto a moving belt, providing continuous extraction) whereas Ember always used a conventional "room and pillar" mining method. In addition, G. R. Mining entered into contract agreements at mine sites that Ember had never worked. This narrative is based on Federal Mine Safety and Health Review Commission, *Secretary of Labor MSHA v. Ember Contracting Corporation,* Office of Administrative Law Judges, November 4, 2011. I am grateful to Greg Wagner for flagging this case and to Andrew Razov for additional research on it.

26. These estimates are based on quarterly mining data from 2000–2010. Using statistical modeling techniques, two different measures of traumatic injuries and a direct measure of fatality rates are associated with contracting status of the mine operator as well as other explanatory factors, including mining method, physical attributes of the mine, union status, size of operations, year, and location. The contracting measure includes all forms of contracting. See Buessing and Weil (2013).

27. Joseph Yablonski Jr., a lawyer for the widows of seven men killed in a contract mine owned by Island Creek Coal, commented: "Island Creek very carefully monitored everything that occurred on their coal lands and simultaneously disclaimed any responsibility for safety." Paul Nyden, "Small Mines Shunt Safety Concerns."

28. International Association for the Wireless Telecommunications Industry (hereafter CTIA), "Semi-annual Wireless Industry Survey: 2011" (http://files.ctia.org/pdf /CTIA_Survey_Year_End_2011_Graphics.pdf, accessed July 14, 2012). The estimates are based on a semiannual voluntary survey conducted by the CTIA. The organization notes, "For December 31, 2011 . . . CTIA received responses from companies serving 95% of wireless subscriber connections."

29. Nielsen Company, "In U.S., SMS Text Messaging Tops Mobile Phone Calling," *Nielsen Wire,* September 22, 2008 (http://www.nielsen.com/us/en/newswire/2008 /in-us-text-messaging-tops-mobile-phone-calling.html, accessed June 24, 2013).

30. CTIA, "Semi-annual Wireless Industry Survey: 2011."

31. See Shapiro and Varian (1999) for an overview of the economics of industries like telecommunications and related sectors where the growth of the customer base increases the value of services for all users.

32. The account of cell towers is primarily based on a major investigation by Day and Knutson. The PBS Frontline episode "Anatomy of a Cell Tower Death" (originally aired on June 6, 2012) and three associated articles by ProPublica can be found at http://www.pbs.org/wgbh/pages/frontline/social-issues/cell-tower-deaths/anatomy

-of-a-cell-tower-death/. I am grateful to Liz Day and Ryan Knutson for extensive discussions of their research and findings.

33. Carriers, however, use multiple turfers. In the example described below, Nsoro competed against nine other vendors to win the contract with AT&T.

34. The complete contract between Cingular (AT&T) and Nsoro can be found at https://www.documentcloud.org/documents/365742-cingular-contract-with-nsoro .html#document/p30/a58894. The scope of work is contained in appendix B of the document; the standards, pricing, audit, liquidated damage, and other provisions are contained in appendix A.

35. A purchase order from Nsoro to WesTower Communications can be found at https://www.documentcloud.org/documents/365730-nsoro-to-westower-purchase -order.html.

36. The agreement between WesTower and ALT can be found at https://www .documentcloud.org/documents/365731-westower-to-alt.html#document/p2. It is not clear from the master agreement how much WesTower paid ALT for the work.

37. The document explicitly lists a set of activities where AT&T asserts primary responsibility, including "establish overall program level schedule for each market"; "Maintain the development of National site development standards"; and "Provide Network Architecture and Network Engineering disciplines." The matrix is available at http://www.propublica.org/documents/item/358228-turf-scope-of-work-con tract#document/p6/a57721 (accessed July 15, 2012).

38. It also includes a lengthy section regarding liquidated damages related to delay in construction completion, deficiencies detected by Cingular in quality audits, and a cap on the "average base line ground lease" costs achieved by the turfer, which cannot exceed 105% of the average for Cingular. See Nsoro/Cingular agreement, pp. 77–80.

39. The base rate for services specified in the Cingular/Nsoro agreement is $95,000. The amount paid by Nsoro to WesTower for this work in the case tracked in the report is $21,000 (22% of the base price). It is not clear if WesTower received the full $95,000 in its base agreement for this particular job, nor is there an invoice reflecting the amount paid to ALT for its work on the project.

40. The contract between Cingular and Betacom, one of its many subcontractors, states, "SUPPLIER shall insure that its representatives, including employees and subcontractors will while on or off CINGULAR's premises, perform Services which (i) conform to the Specifications, (ii) protect CINGULAR's Material, buildings, and structures, (iii) do not interfere with CINGULAR's business operations" (https://www .documentcloud.org/documents/365750-cingular-contract-with-betacom.html #document/p1, accessed July 15, 2012).

41. See Ryan Knutson and Liz Day, "Methodology: How We Calculated the Tower Industry Death Rate," May 22, 2012 (http://www.pbs.org/wgbh/pages/frontline/social -issues/cell-tower-deaths/methodology-how-we-calculated-the-tower-industry-death -rate/, accessed June 10, 2012).

42. See Ryan Knutson and Liz Day, "In Race for Better Cell Service, Men Who Climb Pay with Their Lives," May 22, 2012 (http://www.pbs.org/wgbh/pages/frontline /social-issues/cell-tower-deaths/in-race-for-better-cell-service-men-who-climb-towers -pay-with-their-lives/, accessed July 15, 2012). The AT&T Division of Responsibilities Matrix can be viewed at http://www.pbs.org/wgbh/pages/frontline/social-issues/cell -tower-deaths/in-race-for-better-cell-service-men-who-climb-towers-pay-with-their -lives/ (accessed June 24, 2013).

43. See Ryan Knutson and Liz Day, "Anatomy of a Cell Tower Death," June 6, 2012 (http://www.pbs.org/wgbh/pages/frontline/social-issues/cell-tower-deaths/anatomy-of -a-cell-tower-death/, accessed July 13, 2012).

44. Also similar to the coal industry, the Frontline/ProPublica investigation found examples of subcontractors going out of business under one name and reforming and reopening under a new name.

45. Also noteworthy in this regard is the clause in the master supplier agreement between Cingular Wireless and Betacom Incorporated. Article IV, "Special Clauses" section 4.1(c)(iv), states that the subcontractor shall "(iv) perform such Services with care and due regard for the safety, convenience, and protection of CINGULAR, its employees, and property in full conformance with the policies specified in the CIN-GULAR Code of Conduct." The list does not reference the presence of other subcontractors on site. See "Master Supplier Agreement between Betacom Incorporated and Cingular Wireless LLC," November 29, 2001 (https://www.documentcloud.org/docu ments/365750-cingular-contract-with-betacom.html#document/p1 at p. 33, accessed July 15, 2012).

46. In a letter from the OSHA area director Roberto Sanchez to Betacom regarding the accident, Sanchez notes: "In the interest of workplace safety and health . . . I recommend that you take the following steps voluntarily to eliminate or reduce your employees [sic] exposure to the hazards described above: 1. Barricade the immediate area where the lifting/lowering of materials is being preformed [sic] to prevent employees from entering the hazard zone and being struck by falling loads. Inform all employees working on site when overhead work being preformed [sic] and its location so they remove themselves from the hazard." (Document available at https://www.docu mentcloud.org/documents/363148-betacom-inspection-foia.html.) This presumes that Betacom would be aware of when other subcontractors would be working overhead.

47. Perrow (1984) discusses the role played by unseen interactions among the elements of a complex system. Many of his examples occur within the boundaries of one large organization operating a sophisticated technology such as a nuclear power plant. But unseen interactions may also occur where multiple contractors operate in the same locale without information about the activities of the different parties. For a related argument, see Johnstone, Mayhew, and Quinlan (2001), who examine the impact of subcontracting on health and safety risk in Australia.

48. This account is based on two articles by *New York Times* reporter Julia Preston: "U.S. Checks Conditions for Workers in Walkout," *New York Times,* August 24, 2011; and a full exposé in "Pleas Went Unheeded as Students' U.S. Jobs Soured," *New York Times,* October 17, 2011, A1, A16.

49. A photograph in Julia Preston's article shows a paycheck with "SHS Staffing Solutions" in an upper corner of the pay stub and the name "Exel" next to each itemized payment in the pay stub.

50. For a history of Hershey, see Brenner (2000); for a history of union organizing efforts at the company and in the chocolate industry generally, see Kaufman (1986).

51. This included a more aggressive stance toward the Bakery, Confectionary, Tobacco, and Grainmillers Union, which represents Hershey's workers. In 2002 the breakdown in negotiations over wages and benefits led to a forty-four-day strike. Although the parties settled the strike, the longer-term effort to reduce jobs continued.

52. See "Hershey Announces Global Supply Chain Transformation," PR Newswire, February 15, 2007 (http://www.prnewswire.com/news-releases/hershey-announces -global-supply-chain-transformation-57933727.html, accessed July 21, 2012).

53. In addition to corporate documents and contemporaneous accounts, this section is based on Cleeland (2009).

54. Weekly stock price increases outpaced the Dow Jones Industrial Average consistently from 2002 through the first half of 2007. Both Hershey and the Dow Jones tracked downward throughout the depth of the recession from the latter part of 2007 through the beginning of 2010. At that point to March 31, 2013, however, Hershey stock once again outperformed the DJIA. Comparison assembled by the author via data in MarketWatch.com.

55. Both companies listed the same man as president. Cocoa Services rented the facility from Lyons and Sons. This brings us almost full circle to the kind of subcontracting arrangements that arose under the Massey Doctrine in coal mining.

56. The facility had been undertaking the unlicensed processing operation for "six or seven years" prior to 2009, according to a spokesman for Lyons and Sons.

57. The description is based on the official OSHA inspection report regarding the July 8, 2009, event. See OSHA Accident Investigation Summary, 201773405 (http:// www.osha.gov/pls/imis/establishment.inspection_detail?id=313074213, accessed June 24, 2013).

58. See Bill Sulon, "Palmyra, Pa., Hershey's Workers Fear Packaging Plant May Close." Knight Ridder/ Tribune Business News, August 29, 2001.

59. Exel began in 1985 in the United Kingdom as part of the privatized National Freight Consortium. An Ohio office was opened in 1992, and the company quickly expanded its warehouse and distribution center management in the United States

as well as Canada and Latin America. Exel was acquired by Deutsche Post DHL (an international express mail, transport, and logistics firm and the self-described sister company to DHL Express) in 2005 and now operates as a wholly owned subsidiary of it. See http://www.exel.com/exel/exel_about_exel.jsp (accessed July 10, 2012).

60. Bzengey, quoted in Nick Malawskey, "Foreign Students Who Work at Hershey Warehouse Say 'We Have Our Rights,'" *Patriot News,* August 17, 2011 (http://www.pennlive.com/midstate/index.ssf/2011/08/foreign_students_who_work_at_w.html, accessed July 1, 2012).

61. See U.S. Department of Labor, Office of Public Affairs, "US Labor Department's OSHA Cites Two Companies, Proposes $288,000 in Fines for Workplace Safety and Health Violations Involving Foreign Students," OSHA Regional News Release, February 21, 2012.

62. In its five-month investigation, the State Department found that the students at the Palmyra facility had no cultural activities connected with their program and cited the "laxness" in the health and safety environment at the workplace. The State Department also announced that it was tightening its rules regarding sponsor commitment to health and safety and was considering banning factory and industrial jobs from the program. See Julia Preston, "Company Banned in Effort to Protect Foreign Students from Exploitation," *New York Times,* February 1, 2012 (http://www.nytimes.com/2012/02/02/us/company-firm-banned-in-effort-to-protect-foreign-students.html, accessed July 1, 2012).

63. Hershey official quoted in Leo Sun, "Hershey's Chocolate Sweatshop Sullies Its Image," *Investorguide.com,* August 24, 2011. SHS OnSite and CETUSA officials quoted in Malawskey, "Foreign Students."

64. See, of course, the 1996 film *The Cable Guy* (http://www.imdb.com/title/tt0115798/). Fissured or not, it was a terrible movie.

65. Cascom also required installers to purchase their own tools (or purchase them from the company via "convenient" payroll deductions) and provide their own vehicle or lease one once again from the company. On the other hand, it would not allow installers to independently advertise their contractor services.

66. See *Solis v. Cascom Inc. et al.,* Civil Action No. 3:09-cv-00257, U.S. District Court, Southern District of Ohio, Western Division at Dayton.

67. There is a theoretical literature on the optimal structure for subcontracting, where different organizational forms are employed by a principal in order to maximize profits while dealing with the problems of adverse selection and collusion among the potential agents. Mookherjee and Tsumagari (2004) show that the organizational form that best serves the principal's interests is affected by the degree of collusion among the agents, the information possessed by the middleman, and the type of service provided by the agents (in particular, whether they are substitutes or complements).

NOTES TO PAGES 122–123

6. Fissuring and Franchising

1. Franchising originated in the late 1800s for very different purposes: distribution of products by the emerging group of mass-market manufacturers, such as sewing machines for household use by the Singer Company as well as typewriters, cash registers, and other new creations. Since the need for service and maintenance was significant for these inventions, the companies required specialized marketing services for purposes of presale demonstration as well as postsale service. Rather than depend on the retail sector, which had more limited incentives to invest in detailed product-specific information, manufacturers drew upon franchised dealers. These franchisees were required to sell only the products of the manufacturer and provided assistance and coordination from the manufacturer, but operated with their own revenues and costs. Franchising also was used for distribution purposes in the petroleum industries (gasoline retailing). See Chandler (1977, 402–411).

2. Research on branding is summarized in Keller (2008). There are myriad business books on the topic of brand development. In one, two marketing consultants discuss why companies should focus on the luxury end of whatever product line they have branded and on the part of the customer base able (or at least willing) to spend more than most consumers on "new luxury goods": "The New Luxury 'sweet spot' is where companies are able to move off the traditional demand curve and achieve high margins and high volumes at the same time. Our research show[s] the New Luxury goods typically account for up to 20 percent of a categories [*sic*] unit volume, but 40 percent of its dollar volume and a remarkable 60 percent of its profits." See Silverstein and Fiske (2005, 20).

3. But even here, companies have created brands where products were once thought to be commodities. The processed chicken industry is a great example, where companies like Perdue have created a brand perception among consumers that their products are superior and therefore warrant pricing premiums over commodity (retail store) chicken.

4. This strategy was most famously pioneered by Ray Croc, the founder of McDonald's, who originally built the national chain around a narrow selection of products. The strategy was followed by others who sought to emulate McDonald's consistent customer experience but also to differentiate products (e.g., Burger King's emphasis on "flame-broiled" hamburgers) and speed and convenience of service, including ubiquitous locations. Jeffrey Bradach quotes the vice president for public affairs of KFC as saying, "KFC chicken should taste the same and be served with the same friendly service regardless of whether it is purchased in Tiananmen Square in Beijing, China or in Louisville, Kentucky" (1998, 16–17). See also Kaufmann and Lafontaine (1994) for a discussion of this fundamental aspect of franchised brands.

5. Williamson (1985) states this challenge in terms of finding ways to overcome an externality problem faced by the brand holder generally, who must distribute goods

through a second party. "Externality concerns arise in conjunction with a branded good or service that is subject to quality debasement. Whereas a manufacturer can inspect, thereby better to control, the quality of components and materials it purchases . . . it is less easy to exercise continuing quality controls over items sold to distributors . . . If the quality debasement efforts of distributors give rise to negative interaction effects, the costs of which can be incompletely assigned to the originators, failure to extend quality controls over distribution will result in sub-optimization" (112).

6. The upfront fee is usually between $10,000 and $50,000 and is often, but not always, required for each store a franchisee wishes to open. Most royalty fees are set as a constant percentage at all levels of sales, with some contracts specifying a minimum monthly royalty payment. See Blair and Lafontaine (2005). Most agreements also have a separate advertising fee, typically less than 3% of sales and paid with the royalty fee, to fund any national or regional advertising conducted by the franchisor.

7. It is difficult to compare the extent of franchising across industries for a number of reasons, but most measures (value of shipments, number of establishments, employment) place restaurants at the top of the list. See Blair and Lafontaine (2005) for a discussion of different measures of the prevalence of franchising by sector.

8. By law, REITs do not allow the owners to manage operations, thereby requiring that management and related functions are shifted to other businesses as a basic feature of ownership. Major REITs in the hotel industry, each with values of about $1 billion, include Host Hotels, LaSalle Hotel Properties, RLJ Lodging Trust, and Strategic Hotels and Resorts. See Liu (2010). Fueled by the significant tax savings for REITs under federal law, their use has expanded dramatically in recent years and goes far beyond hotel/motel companies. Companies operating privately run prison and detention centers (Corrections Corporation of America), data and document storage operations (Iron Mountain), and casinos (Penn National Gaming) have been approved by the Internal Revenue Service for REIT status. See Nathaniel Popper, "Restyled as Real Estate Trusts, Varied Businesses Avoid Taxes," *New York Times,* April 22, 2013, A1, B5.

9. A study of financing for small businesses by the Small Business Administration found that 41% of small-business owners indicated that they used business credit cards, supplied largely by banks. See Ou and Williams (2009, tables 2 and 3).

10. A few large lenders are active in the business credit card markets for small credit (below $100,000). Ou and Williams (2009) estimate that the twenty largest business credit card lenders accounted for 75% of the total small loans made in 2007. This represented a growing share of the overall credit market to small businesses (see table 12). The authors note: "It is fair to conclude that a nationwide market for small business credit cards has emerged, with a dozen national lenders promoting business credit cards to small firms through extensive mail solicitation. To what extent the promotion of business credit cards has complemented or replaced the availability of

working capital in the form of credit lines to very small firms in local markets requires further study" (18).

11. One reason franchisors use revenues rather than profits for this purpose is that revenues are more transparent for monitoring purposes. Since in many franchised relationships the franchisee purchases its products from the franchisor, the larger company has an accurate means of monitoring franchisees' revenue. If the fee were related to profits, franchisors would require far more information about cost factors (particularly those related to labor) and other inputs that are harder to monitor or are more easily manipulated by the franchisee.

12. To illustrate, imagine an individual fast-food outlet along a major interstate highway. The franchisee may be willing to cut corners in terms of service quality by hiring lower-quality employees if it believes that the majority of its customers represent nonrepeat business (e.g., because most are simply driving by on the highway and will not return). Although the franchisee might benefit from increased profits due to lower labor costs, the poor service experience at that outlet may lead customers to avoid the restaurant elsewhere. For a discussion of this issue, see Blair and Lafontaine (2005); Lafontaine and Kaufmann (1994); and Lafontaine and Shaw (1999, 2005).

13. Another advantage that franchisors have is their control of information relative to franchisees. But if there is greater information sharing as well as opportunities for collusion among the franchisees, the value of the organizational form diminishes from the perspective of the franchisor. Franchisors will therefore be resistant to sharing information that may improve the bargaining position of franchisees. For a related theoretical argument, see Mookherjee and Tsumagari (2004).

14. See Kaufmann and Lafontaine (1994). The authors did this analysis for two periods—1982 and 1989—and found evidence of economic profits (profits above and beyond a normal rate of return) of 5.8% and 5.7%, respectively, for a midsize McDonald's franchisee. In addition to calculating the operating profit to the franchisee, economic profit calculations also include the opportunity costs to the franchisee of his/her time (e.g., the salary one might earn from employment elsewhere) and the forgone returns on capital invested in the franchise that might have been used for a comparably risky investment.

15. A lawsuit by a group of Quiznos franchisees in 2008 alleged that the company engaged in "a 'pattern of racketeering' and generates 'grossly inflated profits' at the expense of franchises that usually fail." See Richard Gazarik, "Quiznos Franchise Owners Sue Company," *Pittsburgh Tribune-Review,* July 10, 2008. An interesting calculation by a Quiznos franchisee in 2005 indicated that for an outlet with $480,000 in annual sales, the franchisee could expect to earn annual operating profits of $34,220. However, this calculation does not include opportunity costs to the franchisee (see note 14 above). If these were included, the franchisee would clearly be operating at a

negative rate of economic profits. Quiznos sued the franchisee over the site but ultimately lost the suit. The estimates were widely cited among franchise blogs. See Ryan Knoll, "What a Quiznos Franchisee Makes," franchise pundit.com, April 10, 2005 (http://franchisepundit.com/gossip/what-a-quiznos-franchisee-makes/, accessed June 25, 2013).

16. The analysis is based on financial information from the 2007 and 2008 10-K reports of Yum!, Burger King Corporation (both franchisors) and NPC International Inc., Morgan's Foods Inc., and Carrols Corporation (all publicly traded franchisees). Most franchisees are privately held companies, and their financial information is therefore not available to allow this type of comparison. Profitability measures for all companies are based on reported net income before income taxes divided by reported total assets (return on assets) or by total sales (return on revenues). Several caveats about this analysis should be noted. Estimates for Yum! and Burger King include revenues from company-owned operations and royalty payments from franchisees. Expenses for the franchisors include costs of operation for company-owned facilities as well as selling, general, and administrative expenses, including those related to advertising for the franchise system. The NPC International Inc., Morgan's Foods Inc., and Carrols Corporation analyses include all revenues from their outlets and operating expenses as well as advertising expenses specifically related to franchisees (beyond those paid as royalties to the franchisor).

17. Note also that the incentives to "share" are highest for a large, successful, multiunit franchisee. See Ji (2010).

18. U.S. Bureau of the Census, *County Business Patterns: The United States* (Washington, DC: GPO, 2004). (http://censtats.census.gov/cgi-bin/cbpnaic/cbpcomp.pl, accessed June 25, 2013).

19. U.S. Bureau of Labor Statistics, *Occupational Employment and Wage Estimates, NAICS 722211, Limited Service Restaurants,* May 2006. The minimum wage increased to $7.25 on July 24, 2009. The minimum wage for tipped workers is considerably lower ($2.13 per hour, although employers are required to see that the total of tipped earnings and direct wages meets the minimum wage standard of $7.25). However, work at most fast-food restaurants is paid on an hourly basis since there is seldom table service.

20. See Bernhardt, Milkman, et al. (2009). The estimates represent violation rates for low-wage workers in the three major metropolitan areas (Los Angeles, Chicago, and New York City), based on a sampling methodology that sought to survey "low-wage workers who may be hard to identify from official databases, who may be vulnerable because of their immigration status, or who are reluctant to take part in a survey because they fear retaliation from their employers."

21. Cappelli and Hamori (2008) show that franchised restaurants have better basic human resource practices, such as training, than nonfranchised outlets. Their

comparison, however, is between branded and nonbranded restaurants rather than a comparison of human resource policies *within* franchised restaurants (that is, between franchisees and company-owned units). As a result, the effects they document are related to the impact of branding itself on human resource policies rather than the impact of franchising, the concern here.

22. Data collection and matching for the eating and drinking analysis focused on the period 2001–2005; all tables and figures, unless otherwise noted, refer to that period. There were a total of 1,768 physical investigations of the top twenty branded fast-food outlets in the United States during the study period.

23. Back wages are the difference between the wages paid to workers by their employers and the amount they were entitled to earn given the standards established by the Fair Labor Standards Act.

24. It should also be pointed out that these represent the most conservative estimates in the study. Using other statistical methodologies to control for potential differences between franchisee- and company-owned outlets leads to even larger estimated differences, as does examination of a subsample of the data that better reflects a random sample of the eating and drinking population (Ji and Weil 2012).

25. In a separate paper, Ji (2010) shows that very large franchisees that own large numbers of outlets start behaving like major companies, given their far higher investment in maintaining reputation. These major franchisees, who own an average of 345 outlets, have about the same levels of compliance with laws as do the franchisors.

26. See Bernhardt, Milkman, et al. (2009, chapter 4, 29–39).

27. This fissured story is one where a function has been separated off by companies in order to find lower cost sources of the service. The decision by multiple companies—in different industries—creates a different source of fissuring with similar dynamics at the bottom of the chain. But here it is not clear whether any level of the fissured industry earns high rates of return, although janitorial franchisors have higher returns than their franchisees.

28. U.S. Bureau of the Census, County Business Patterns and 2007 Economic Census for NAICS 56172, Janitorial Services (http://censtats.census.gov/cgi-bin/cbp naic/cbpdetl.pl, accessed June 25, 2013).

29. The number of major companies earning about $100 million is imputed from the table because the Census does not provide breakdowns above $99.99 million of annual revenue to protect confidentiality of respondents. See County Business Patterns, NAICs 56172.

30. U.S. Bureau of the Census, County Business Patterns and 2007 Economic Census for NAICs 56172, Janitorial Services.

31. Although this chapter focuses on the use of franchising, it is not the only problematic workplace practice in the janitorial sector. Another common practice is subcontracting janitorial services and classifying workers as independent contractors,

similar to the cable installers discussed in Chapter 5. This practice—common in office cleaning in many metropolitan services—can lead to multiple tiers of janitors. The Justice for Janitors campaign created by the Service Employees International Union in the 1990s was in direct response to this practice and provided a mechanism to place pressure on end users (Lerner, Hurst, and Adler 2008). The Wage and Hour Division has also investigated the use of misclassification of employees as independent contractors in janitorial services, including recent investigations in Chicago. See "US Department of Labor Sues Two Chicago-Area Cleaning Companies, Owners to Recover Unpaid Wages and Damages for 135 Employees," Wage and Hour Division press release No. 11-1710-CHI, December 8, 2011.

32. There are also franchised companies that serve residential customers, such as Merry Maids (a division of Service Master). The residential janitorial market relies predominantly on very local cleaning service providers that operate in a different market environment than described here. Although the two are undoubtedly linked (e.g., individuals enter the business cleaning individual homes and decide to move up to commercial customers and franchising opportunities on the basis of that experience), I do not consider the residential market here because of its very different product market structure.

33. See Franchise Disclosure Document, Coverall North America, chart no. 3 (Coverall FDD, April 27, 2009).

34. The Coverall franchise disclosure document states: "We distinguish ourselves from our competitors with our Health-Based Cleaning System program. Our innovative cleaning program consists of: initial and on-going Franchise Owner training to ensure a consistent, quality clean for each and every customer; EPA-registered, hospital-grade disinfectant chemistry proven to eradicate disease-causing germs and reduce the spread of infection; innovative cleaning equipment and methods to remove illness-causing germs and reduce cross-contamination and spread of infection; research & development on cutting-edge, state-of-the-art online training." Coverall North America, Franchise Disclosure Document, May 2009. Accessed through the California Electronic Access to Securities Information and Franchise Information, pp. 2, 4, 13.

35. Coverall works entirely through a system of franchisees. Other franchised janitorial service providers—Jan-Pro and Jani-King, for example—use a mix of company-owned and franchised units.

36. For example, the Coverall franchise agreement states: "We guarantee your Initial Business. You may qualify for either a 12 month guarantee or a 6 month guarantee, which begins on the date that you begin servicing the customer. We only guarantee customers lost through no fault of your own [underline in original]. If you qualify for either guarantee, we will replace the dollar volume of the lost customer with one or more customers of equal dollar volume. If the replacement customer(s) has a dollar volume in excess of that lost by you, you may have to pay us for the excess

dollar volume." Establishing who is responsible for the loss of a customer becomes highly contested, as noted below (Coverall FDD, "The Initial Business Guarantee," p. 26).

37. The franchisee receives its customer list in a geographic area close to its base of operations (and within a region of a master or regional franchisee). However, this is not the same as being an exclusive geographic territory, but simply an area of clients in proximity to the franchisee. For example, the Coverall agreement states: "Due to the nature of the franchise business, you will not receive [underline in original] an exclusive territory or exclusive territory rights. You may face competition from other Coverall franchisees . . . You may offer and render janitorial services to commercial customers only within the area(s) in which the Coverall office, through which you have purchased your franchise conducts business; and only in the form and manner approved by us. We have established and will continue to establish other franchises, each licensed to use our service mark that may compete with you. In addition, we may sell supplies directly to customers" (Coverall FDD, 12, "Territory").

38. Jan-Pro Unit Franchise Disclosure Document, May 2010.

39. For example, the Jani-King of Boston agreement notes: "Franchisee may solicit potential clients to provide cleaning and maintenance services through their franchise, but (i) all contracts under which terms services are provided by any Jani-King franchisee are the sole property of Jani-King; (ii) all contracts for the provision of services by Franchisee must be drafted by Jani-King; and (iii) all contracts for the provision of services by Franchisee must name Jani-King as the sole party to the contract." Jani-King FDD, section 4.20.2. Coverall's franchise agreement is even more blunt: "The customers that you service through your franchise are Coverall customers. This is true even if you obtain those customers yourself" ("Restrictions on What the Franchisee May Sell").

40. For example, Coverall's franchise agreement states: "We retain the right to maintain the viability of the accounts you are servicing through periodic inspections, phone contacts, and the provision of comprehensive services . . . If we determine through inspection or complaint that an account is receiving poor service, we have the right to terminate your service to that account." This kind of provision has led to a number of suits brought by franchisees against Coverall, Jani-King, and other franchised janitorial companies that claim that the company deliberately sought out negative customer complaints in order to remove the existing franchisee and resell the client to others. The argument against this critique is that Coverall would risk its reputation if it continually engaged in this activity. However, the turnover among franchised janitorial service providers is high, and it is not clear how much brand equity the company risks losing.

The Federal Trade Commission in its disclosure document for potential janitorial service franchisees warns about this particular aspect of janitorial service franchising: "To meet its obligations, the franchisor may offer you more than one cleaning account. But given time conflicts, distance issues or other problems, you may not be able to accept all the accounts the franchisor offers. What's more, the franchisor may offer the same accounts to several franchisees on a first-come, first-served basis. If you can't accept an account because you can't get to the location, or if another franchisee accepts the account first, the franchisor may have satisfied its obligation to offer you accounts. Because the franchisor may not tell you about this policy before you buy the 'package' of accounts, you should not count on receiving all the revenue that the franchisor promised at first" (Federal Trade Commission 2001).

41. The initial franchisee fee is another aspect of the business where, at least judging by litigation, the interests of the franchisor and franchisee are in conflict. The franchise agreement makes recovery of the entirety of the initial fee extremely difficult, thus making it a sort of unrecoverable bond from the perspective of the franchisee. Although the majority of janitorial franchisors' revenues come from ongoing royalty and management fees, the initial fees still provide a significant stream. For Coverall, the company reported annual sales revenues ranging from $14 million to $17 million for franchise sales between 2006 and 2008 (representing about 6%–8% of total revenues).

42. Indicative of the range of prices found on many blogs and e-magazines promoting franchised businesses are the following examples: "Base your time at $20 to $50 per hour" (http://ezinearticles.com/?Janitorial-Cleaning-Service—Getting-Started &id=49257); "For special large-scale cleaning jobs, the average one-time cost is around $20 to $50 per hour" (http://www.ehow.com/how_5052280_estimate-cost-office -cleaning.html); "Generally, small cleaning operations earn the equivalent of between $15 to $40 per hour and more" (http://www.homebiztools.com/questions/cleaning-bid -estimates.htm); "Hourly rates are anywhere from $15 to $40 per hour depending on the type of services that you provide" (http://ezinearticles.com/?How-Much-Should -I-Charge-For-My-Commercial-Cleaning-Services?&id=385906).

43. See Steven Greenhouse, "Lawsuits Charge Fraud in Cleaning Business," *New York Times,* July 13, 2005, and David Segal, "In Search of Work, but at What Cost?" *New York Times,* December 26, 2009. The blog *Unhappy Franchisee* (unhappyfranchisee.com) includes similar accounts of actual rates being far below those cited by Coverall, Jan-Pro, and other franchised janitorial companies.

44. In fact, the situation represents a classic case of divergent interests, where the franchisor, whose profits depend on revenues collected across all franchised units, has an incentive to set a lower price, while the franchisee, who must bear the costs of providing the service, would favor a higher price.

45. Because of the localized nature of pricing and the variety of formats in which that pricing is presented, it is difficult to find a single source for market rates. The analysis draws on pricing information from a variety of geographic locations to make these estimates. The rates are from several sources: Cleaning Management Institute, "2009 Kaviac Inc. Contract Cleaning Benchmarking Survey Report," CMI/NTP

Media, 2009; "Office Cleaning Costs: What People Are Paying," Costhelper.com (www.costhelper.com/cost/small-business/office-cleaning.html); "Commercial Cleaning Services—Buyer's Guide" (http://smallbusiness.yahoo.com/advisor/commercial -cleaning-services-buyers-guide-144201040.html, accessed June 25, 2013).

46. The Federal Trade Commission requires franchised companies to provide potential franchisees with representative financials and operational requirements. These financial disclosure documents are available through a variety of organizations, including a public disclosure library made available by the state of California.

47. I also compared the cost breakdown for my model with the cost breakdowns available from the 2008 Service Annual Survey conducted by the U.S. Bureau of the Census for NAICS 561. The percentage of costs for employees is similar to that in the Census data; expenses for materials, parts, and supplies represent a higher percentage of costs in our models, although the Census data is based on a broader NAICS code that includes but is not limited to janitorial services.

48. The assumptions for the analysis can be found in the footnotes to Table 6.3. The basic idea is calculating both the franchisee's operating profit (revenues after franchisee fees have been paid, less all relevant expenses) and economic profit (operating profits minus the forgone income and return available to the franchisee had it not become a franchisee). I use the latter financial measure to set the "break-even" target level since this represents the amount of true economic return earned by the franchisee. See Weil (2012b) for further details of these calculations.

49. It is difficult to construct comparable estimates of profitability for the franchised firms because of limited information in their FDDs. However, using data available from the company's financial disclosure documents, I estimate the following income as a percentage of revenues for these franchisors: CleanNet USA earned 8.7%; Jani-King, 9.5%; Coverall, 9.3%; and Jan-Pro, 41% (in 2007).

50. See Hospitality Staffing Solutions (www.hssstaffing.com/, accessed February 7, 2013).

51. The accounts of the Hyatt story are based on Steven Greenhouse, "Hyatts Face Protests after Layoffs in Boston Area," *New York Times,* September 24, 2009; Katie Johnston Chase and Megan Woolhouse, "Hyatt Offers Ninety-Eight Cleaners New Jobs," *Boston Globe,* September 26, 2009, A1, A9; and Steven Greenhouse, "Massachusetts: New Jobs Offered," *New York Times,* September 26, 2009.

52. Hyatt statement quoted in Greenhouse, "Hyatts Face Protests after Layoffs in Boston Area," *New York Times,* September 24, 2009.

53. See O'Neill and Mattila (2010) for a discussion of hotel branding strategy.

54. Indicative of the portfolio strategy, in 2013 Marriott International (the brand operating company) initiated a campaign for its Marriott Hotels and Resorts brand to attract younger business travelers who, the company believes, care about technology access, sleek design, and stylish experiences (and are willing to pay a premium for them). The new campaign, named "Travel Brilliantly," will cost an estimated $30

million to develop and involves changes to advertisement, hotel technology, and facilities as well as more mundane things like hotel key cards, guest room directories, and even "do not disturb" signs. One critic of the campaign sniffed that the Marriott Hotels brand was "everything but brilliant. It's safe, reliable, consistent. Things work the way they should. But it's not a boutique chain, a cutting-edge chain or terribly innovative." See Jane Levere, "A Campaign from Marriott Aims Younger," *New York Times,* June 17, 2013, B4.

55. A number of studies have measured the impact of brands on market valuation as well as revenues and profits. O'Neill and Xiao (2006) found that hotel brand influences market value significantly after accounting for profitability, occupancy rates, average daily rates (ADRs), and scale measured in terms of room size, as well as location and chain scale. O'Neill and Mattila (2006) also found that brand affiliation, name recognition, and reputation for service quality contributed up to 20%–25% of the "going-concern" value of a hotel.

56. Eyster and deRoos (2009, 10–12).

57. At the very top of the industry, the percentage of company-owned properties is even smaller: in 2011 only 3% of the properties among the top twenty-five branded hotels were company-owned. Figures based on "Top Brands," *Lodging Hospitality,* June 1, 2011, data as of March 31, 2011.

58. As with the case of the eating and drinking industry, a franchise is a written agreement between the franchisor (the grantor of the franchise) and its franchisees (those who acquire a franchise), granting the franchisee the right to operate under the name of the franchise (brand) and use/market its products and services for a specified period of time in a particular territory.

59. Leading companies include Interstate Hotels and Resorts; White Lodging Services; John Q. Hammons Hotels; and Tharaldson Lodging. See "Top of the Top Ranking," *Lodging Hospitality,* June 1, 2010.

60. The amount of ownership among independent operators varies. Tharaldson Lodging, for example, manages 23 properties for other owners as well as 200 properties in which it has an ownership stake. Crestline Hotels and Resorts Inc. (CHRI), on the other hand, manages almost all properties for others (64 in total), while it owns and manages only 6 hotel properties. The contract between an owner and a brand operating company is for between ten and twenty years, reflecting the power of brands, which benefit from a long commitment by the owner in such negotiations. In contrast, the typical length of contracts between owners and independent operating companies is between one and ten years, exhibiting the more equal power of the two entities. See Eyster and deRoos (2009) for a comprehensive discussion of these arrangements.

61. Hospitality Staffing Solutions is one of the larger players in this market. In 2012, it had 2 senior vice presidents, 6 vice presidents, 25 area managers, and 150 area supervisors to service the 70 markets in which it provided hotel staff.

62. See Hospitality Staffing Solutions (www.hssstaffing.com/, accessed February 7, 2013).

63. Estimate by the U.S. Department of Labor, Bureau of Labor Statistics based on the Current Population Survey. Detailed estimates of the number and percentage of workers earning at or below the minimum wage are available at http://www.bls.gov /cps/minwage2011tbls.htm#5 (accessed June 25, 2013).

64. The figures are based on research by Paul Osterman and Beth Shulman, who estimate low-wage work for major industries in the United States in 2010 using the Current Population Survey. See Osterman and Shulman (2011) for a detailed discussion of different definitions of low-wage work, including the above benchmark.

65. See Bernhardt, Milkman, et al. (2009).

66. Compliance is also affected by other factors, such as the location of hotels geographically (those in urban areas tend to have the highest rates of compliance, those near airports the lowest); and chain scale (luxury hotels have the highest rates of compliance, economy hotels the lowest). The above estimates hold constant those factors and still find significantly higher rates of noncompliance associated with third-party management.

67. Rick Simon, president of United Service Companies, was quoted as saying that the housekeepers could end up getting hired permanently: "I'm positive by 2010 and probably long before 2010, all will be placed in permanent jobs at a similar wage scale" to what they were earning at the Hyatt. See Johnston Chase and Woolhouse, "Hyatt Offers Ninety-Eight Cleaners New Jobs," *Boston Globe*, September 26, 2009, A1, A9.

68. The job announcement is for an area supervisor and is described on the website as an entry-level management position "that will serve as a liaison between team members and client hotels. He or she must display a warm and friendly demeanor, professional appearance and have the ability to recruit, screen, manage and assist in training of team members, establishing and developing strong relationships with our current and new customers" (http://www.hssstaffing.com/, accessed February 7, 2013).

69. Indicative is the tale of one of the research assistants working on my project who had been employed as a lifeguard at a resort hotel. When I asked him who his supervisor was employed by—the hotel brand, management company, property owner, or labor contractor—he started to laugh and said with some amusement, "I actually don't even know who was my supervisor!"

7. Supply Chains and the Fissured Workplace

1. See Womack, Jones, and Roos (1991).

2. For a discussion of the technology, information systems, business strategies, and public policies that enable modern lean retailing, see Abernathy and Volpe (2012).

3. The company advertises "independent contractor opportunities" on its website: "If you're an independent contractor, select from the following links for information

about opportunities with the FedEx family of companies." The choices include FedEx Custom Critical Owner/Operator; FedEx Ground Independent Contractor; and FedEx Home Delivery Independent Contractor (http://www.fedex.com/us/indp/inde pendentcontractors.html, accessed February 8, 2013).

4. This model of retailing has also become common in many other segments, most strikingly in food retailing, where strategies such as "efficient consumer response" seek to similarly reduce inventory exposure through use of point-of-sale information, efficient logistics, and replenishment programs for perishable and nonperishable products.

5. The company developed Schneider National Inc., which began as a trucking company in the 1930s and grew into a major "double-breasted" (union and non-union) carrier in the 1970s and 1980s. It created Schneider Logistics Inc. as a wholly owned subsidiary in 1993.

6. See Abernathy, Dunlop, et al. (1999), chapter 14, regarding adoption of EDI and related technologies by retailers and the manufacturers that supply them.

7. See Schneider Logistics, "History: Driving the Wheels of Commerce for Seven Decades" (http://www.schneider.com/About_Schneider/History/index.htm, accessed July 18, 2012).

8. The logistics demands of importing are different than in the movement of goods for domestic distribution via cross-docking facilities. In the latter case, retailers need to move goods from trucks arriving from domestic suppliers. In many cases, retailers impose detailed standards regarding the methods of shipment, including how goods are packed and marked with bar-coded shipping containers, and sometimes even required to be floor-ready upon arrival at stores. As a result, a cross-dock facility is simply moving goods from one side of the facility to another (still requiring manual loading and unloading of trucks). Imported goods require more handling since they must be removed from containers, sorted, and then reaggregated for delivery to specific stores (or distribution centers). This tends to require more manual work and therefore higher labor costs.

9. See "2011–2013 Mira Loma, CA Loading Services Contract between Premier Warehousing Ventures, LLC and Schneider Logistics Transloading and Distribution Inc.," article I, section 1.01. The contract was made public through discovery as part of the litigation filed by workers at the facility, discussed in this section. I will refer to this as the Schneider/PWV Service Contract. A similar agreement between Schneider and Rogers-Premier sets out the tasks more broadly as providing "excellent customer services, products, and service in connection with temporary staffing services described herein."

10. Schneider/PWV Service Contract, article II, sections 2.01 and 2.03. The contract also enumerates the roles PWV will play as the "sole employer of the Personnel" in section 2.05.

11. The agreement also allows PWV to use its own subcontractor(s) to perform work, but requires that the company give Schneider notice and information about

the subcontractors and gives the latter the right to approve their use. "Only subcontractor(s) approved by SDLT shall be used by PWV." See section 2.13.

12. See section 2.15. Walmart's extensive use of janitorial subcontractors employing undocumented workers in 2003 led to significant fines and adverse publicity. The requirement that Schneider audit its subcontractors with respect to immigration status reflects this concern.

13. Other subcontractors to Schneider working in Joliet, Illinois, reportedly instituted similar practices in 2006 at processing facilities also servicing Walmart. See Jamieson (2011) and Kari Lydersen, "Wal-Mart Warehouse Workers File Class Action Wage Theft Lawsuit," *In These Times*, February 28, 2011 (http://www.inthesetimes.com /working/entry/7009/wal-mart_warehouse_workers_file_class_action_lawsuit/, accessed July 18, 2012).

14. California law requires the workforce (union or nonunion) to be given a chance to vote on such a change. The Mira Loma workers did so in 2008, but subsequent investigation brought into question the validity of the vote. Workers were found to have been denied overtime wages because of the ten-hour workday, paid at straight-time wages.

15. See California Department of Labor, "California Labor Commissioner Issues Citations for Numerous Labor Law Violations at a Riverside County Warehouse," DIR press release #2011–19, October 12, 2011; California Department of Labor, "California Labor Commissioner Issues Additional $616,240 Citation in Riverside County Case," DIR press release #2011–24, November 17, 2011. See also Jack Katzanek, "Warehouse Operators Face Labor Law Heat," *The Press Enterprise*, October 13, 2011 (http ://www.pe.com/business/business-headlines/20111013-workplace-warehouse-opera tors-face-labor-law-heat.ece, accessed July 18, 2012).

16. One case is found in the deposition of Jose Martinez Arceo: "Last Wednesday, October 12, 2011, the California Department of Labor conducted an on-site inspection at the warehouses. During that inspection, I was one of the workers interviewed by the Department inspectors in full view of the supervisors and managerial personnel of Schneider and Premier. On Monday, October 17, 2011, a lawsuit was filed in federal court protesting violations of California law at my workplace . . . A press conference was held at noon the next day, October 18, 2011. The next day, Wednesday October 19, 2011, a leaflet . . . was distributed throughout the warehouse. The leaflet bore my picture and I saw the leaflet distributed to my fellow employees and supervisors. The same evening . . . I received a call at 5:30pm from my supervisor, Jose Rosas, telling me that I should not show up for work today. On Sunday night my supervisor called me to tell me that I should not come to work on Monday. I felt that these days off were punishment for my cooperation with the Department of Labor and participation in the lawsuit . . . There is no shortage of work at the warehouse right now." See Declaration of Jose Martinez Arceo, Case No. CV11–8557 CAS (DTBx), U.S. District Court, Central District of California, Eastern Division, declaration dated October 20, 2012.

17. Figures are for the NAICS category warehousing and storage (493). See Woods (2009, 76).

18. Multiple stories have documented the practice in areas with concentrations of distribution hubs, such as Chicago, one of the six largest transportation hubs in the United States. See Kari Lydersen, "A Thriving Industry Built on Low-Compensated Temp Workers," *New York Times/Chicago News Cooperative,* August 26, 2010 (http:// www.nytimes.com/2010/08/27/us/27cncdryport.html, accessed January 15, 2013); Spencer Soper, "Amazon Warehouse Workers Fight for Unemployment Benefits," *Morning Call* (Lehigh Valley, PA), December 17, 2012 (http://www.mcall.com/business /mc-amazon-temporary-workers-unemployment-20121215,0,7418365,full.story, accessed January 15, 2013).

19. For example, Jamieson quotes a Walmart spokesman who was asked about the problems at Mira Loma as replying that the company "is not involved in this matter" and responded similarly in regard to problems found among subcontractors at distribution centers providing services for Walmart in Illinois. See Jamieson (2011).

20. A company statement of standards from 2011, quoted by the Bureau of National Affairs, says that "all suppliers must provide workers with a safe and healthy work environment" and "must take proactive measures to prevent workplace hazards." See Bloomberg BNA, "California Warehouse Workers Allege Unsafe Working Conditions at Wal-Mart Warehouse," *Occupational Safety and Health Reporter* 42, no. 28, July 12, 2012, 627–628.

21. See Jamieson (2011). However, later court rulings, discussed in Chapter 10, forced Schneider to take a more active role in rectifying problems that surfaced in the investigations at the Mira Loma facilities.

22. Grossman and Helpman (2005) distinguish outsourcing from offshoring mostly in terms of the proximity of the lead company (principal) to its suppliers (agents). The main cost of distance is that it reduces the ability of the principal to monitor its agents, thereby increasing the risk that the latter will do things not in keeping with the interests of the principal.

23. The survey also found that 67% of respondents said that U.S. companies bore "a lot" of responsibility to keep manufacturing jobs in the United States (versus 9% who said they had not much or no responsibility). For complete survey results, see "Poll: Apple Products," January 25, 2012 (http://www.nytimes.com/interactive/2012 /01/26/business/apple-poll-document.html?ref=business, accessed July 25, 2012).

24. Ricardo famously illustrated comparative advantage when describing trade in cloth and wine between England and Portugal in his book *On the Principles of Political Economy and Taxation* (1817).

25. This table builds on the analysis by Feenstra (1998). It uses the same framework of examining the percentage of imports or exports for a given year that go to the five major categories of end users. Following Feenstra, petroleum products are excluded, as are the "other" category, which is composed of low-valued items, re-exports,

military items, and miscellaneous product categories. The estimates for 1925–1990 are taken from ibid., table 3. Estimates for 2000 and 2007 are by the author from sources listed in the table.

26. The changing impacts of organization of production can also be seen in shifts in imports/exports for particular categories. In 1995 the United States imported $5.5 billion worth of computers and exported $10.2 billion. By 2010 the U.S. imports of computers increased tenfold to $55.3 billion, while exports had only increased to $14.7 billion. Based on analysis of export/import by end use for goods classified as computers (capital equipment), 1995 and 2010. See Table 9.1 for sources of this data.

27. Even if country Y is more productive in both traded goods (i.e., it has an absolute advantage in them), country X will still benefit from trade. By purchasing from country Y the good that country X is less productive in creating, country X frees resources so that it can produce more of the good where it is more productive (which it will, in turn, use in trade with country Y).

28. See Samuleson (2004). Ralph Gomory and William Baumol (2000) examine a related situation where new technologies create economies of scale for the producing nation and also "agglomeration" economies of scale at a global level, where individual firm scale economies improve even further as the global industry expands. The resulting shift in global production could lead to rapid redistribution of the gains from trade and could diminish one nation's welfare relative to the period before the introduction of the new technology. Another preeminent economist, Alan Blinder (2006), notes that a country increasingly dependent on personal services for a substantial part of its GDP (as a result of offshoring of goods that can be shipped and impersonal services that can be performed at lower cost abroad) faces economic challenges in that those services typically are less amenable to productivity improvement, even if they cannot be offshored.

29. There was a large literature in the late 1990s on the impact of trade on wages and employment versus other explanations of growing income inequality (in particular skill-biased technological change). For widely cited studies from this scholarship, see Berman, Bound, and Griliches (1994); Berman, Bound, and Machin (1998); Bernard and Jensen (1997); Cline (1997); Feenstra and Hanson (1999); and Kletzer (2001).

30. See Blinder (2006) and Gereffi, Humphrey and Sturgeon (2005).

31. Kletzer (2002) describes the difficulty of providing opportunities for workers in industries and jobs highly impacted by trade including outsourcing. This arises in part in the varied profile of displaced workers and their capacity to find jobs given characteristics (including location and age) in their prior employment.

32. Grossman and Helpman (2005) offer a theoretical model that shows that the choice of offshoring versus internal production (via multinational structures) depends on the incentives different models provide to either internal parties or external parties, particularly as driven by the ability to monitor parties (arising, in part, from

their distance, but arguably related to other characteristics of the production process itself). Grossman and Helpman show that firms are more likely to choose to outsource if they are highly productive internally but can exert greater pressure on external parties because they have more at stake than an internal player (they say by fronting the cost of the inputs needed to manufacture components). The benefits of keeping activities within the boundaries of the multinational firm arise from the opportunities to monitor (which decline with distance). For reasons discussed in Chapter 3, the ability to monitor external parties has fallen appreciably in recent years, increasing the attractiveness of outsourcing (in their model) or fissuring.

33. See Baldwin and Clark (1997); MacDuffie and Helper (2007); MacDuffie and Fujimoto (2010); and Sturgeon and Florida (2004) for discussions of the evolving global production of automobiles.

34. For an overview of service center outsourcing, see Batt, Holman, and Holtgrewe (2009) and Batt and Nohara (2009).

35. Although its stock price receded considerably after reaching this high-water mark, it remains a noteworthy moment in business history. Some comparisons provide a sense of the scale of Apple's market value: in 2012 dollars, prior record holders for becoming the largest public company in terms of market capitalization were IBM at $192 billion in 1967; Walmart at $119.5 billion in 1992; General Electric at 128.4 billion in 1993; Microsoft at $380.8 billion in 1998; and Cisco at 707.9 billion in 2000. See James Stewart, "Confronting a Law of Limits: Apple Surges to No. 1 in Size." *New York Times,* February 25, 2012, B1, B6.

36. The statement came in response to a question during the hearing whether Wilson, a major stockholder of GM, would be able to make a decision that would be against the company's interest. He answered yes but added that he could not envision such a situation and then made his famous quote. It has often been misquoted as "What's good for General Motors is good for the country." Wilson was confirmed for the post by a vote of 77 to 6.

37. General Motors global employment was 853,000 at that time.

38. See Stewart, "Confronting a Law of Limits," B1, B6, and David Segal, "Apple's Retail Army, Long on Loyalty but Short on Pay," *New York Times,* July 23, 2012 (http://www.nytimes.com/2012/06/24/business/apple-store-workers-loyal-but-short -on-pay.html?pagewanted=all, accessed July 23, 2012).

39. A research volume edited by Kenney and Florida (2004) contains a number of industry studies that examine the shift toward international supply chains in different segments of the electronic industries (see in particular Curry and Kenney in that volume). Cowie (1999) stresses, however, that moving work in search of lower labor costs began well before the 1990s in the electronics industry. In his history of RCA Corporation, Cowie charts how the company moved production through the twen-

tieth century within the United States in order to lower labor costs and avoid unions. However, in this period, companies like RCA continued to hire those workers as their own employees rather than rely on outside suppliers.

40. These estimates are based on Locke et al. (2012), which provides an in-depth study of the impact of labor and environmental monitoring in the HP supply chain. It will be discussed further in Chapter 11.

41. The exception to this model is Samsung, which continues to undertake a larger share (although by no means all) of the manufacturing of its own products— and those of other electronics companies, including Apple. Samsung directly owns and operates twelve very large factories in China as well as drawing on many suppliers in that country. In 2012 it employed 220,000 people worldwide. See Brian Chen, "Challenging Apple's Cool: As a Phone Rival, Samsung Takes a Different Tack," *New York Times,* 2/11/13, B1, B6.

42. David Barboza and Charles Duhigg, "Pressure, Chinese and Foreign, Drives Changes at Foxconn," *New York Times,* 2/20/12, B1, B2.

43. See Locke et al. (2012, 7–9) for a discussion.

44. See, for example, Students and Scholars against Corporate Misbehaviour (SA-COM), "Foxconn and Apple Fail to Fulfill Promises: Predicaments of Workers after the Suicides," May 6, 2011 (http://sacom.hk/wp-content/uploads/2011/05/2011-05 -06_foxconn-and-apple-fail-to-fulfill-promises.pdf, accessed February 13, 2013); China Labor Watch, "Tragedies of Globalization: The Truth behind Electronics Sweatshops," July 12, 2011 (http://www.chinalaborwatch.org/pro/proshow-164.html, accessed February 13, 2013).

45. See Charles Duhigg and David Barboza, "In China, Human Costs Are Built into an iPad," *New York Times,* January 25, 2012 (available at http://www.nytimes .com/2012/01/26/business/ieconomy-apples-ipad-and-the-human-costs-for-workers -in-china.html, accessed February 10, 2013). The series, called The iEconomy, appeared in January and February 2012 can be found at http://www.nytimes.com/interactive /business/ieconomy.html.

46. See Keith Bradsher and Charles Duhigg, "Signs of Changes Taking Hold in Electronics Factories in China," *New York Times,* December 26, 2012 (http://www .nytimes.com/2012/12/27/business/signs-of-changes-taking-hold-in-electronics-fac tories-in-china.html, accessed January 15, 2013).

47. See Locke and Romis (2007) and Locke et al. (2012) for evaluations of HP's ongoing efforts in monitoring labor and environmental practices.

48. See Vikas Bajaj. "Fatal Fire in Bangladesh Highlights Dangers Facing Garment Workers," *New York Times,* November 25, 2012.

49. See Liz Alderman, "Public Outrage Over Factory Conditions Spurs Labor Deal," *New York Times,* May 19, 2013; Jim Yardley, "Report on Deadly Factory Collapse in Bangladesh Finds Widespread Blame," *New York Times,* May 22, 2013.

III. Mending the Fissured Workplace

1. Commons (1935, ix).

2. There are many other policies regarding the labor market that are separate from the phenomenon of fissuring (although affected by it) that I do not consider here. This is not because I judge them as unimportant or inconsequential. Part III focuses on those aspects of fissuring that might be addressed by public policies and private actors. For very useful discussions of other public policies that also address issues of low-wage work, workforce vulnerability, and stagnating wages in many parts of the labor market, see Freeman (2007); Kalleberg (2011); Kochan (2005); Levy and Murnane (2005); and Osterman and Shulman (2011).

8. Rethinking Responsibility

1. The tension between fair pay and conditions for workers and low prices for consumers is certainly not a new issue. In 1926 Hutchins and Harrison described the tension as it played out in passage of early factory legislation in England: "Unfortunately, in the absence of regulation, the evil tends to increase and the sweated trades to spread. In the all-pervading competition of the modern world market, each industry is perpetually struggling against every other industry to maintain and to improve its position . . . tempting the consumer by cheapness continually to increase his demand for its commodities, inducing the investor by swollen profits to divert more and more of the nation's capital in its direction, and attracting, by large salaries, more and more the nation's brains to its service" (Hutchins and Harrison 1926, xii).

2. This section does not attempt to provide a detailed analysis of the statutory, judicial, or academic writing in this area, or even provide a basic overview. Instead, it simply seeks to paint the overall picture in which the definitions of employment relationships were grounded in a time when most employer/employee relationships were fairly obvious and not highly contested, but that now are more problematic. An early but very insightful discussion of the definition of "employee" can be found in Perritt (1988). Davidov (2006) and other essays in Davidov and Langille (2004) also provide a useful survey of legal issues surrounding employment definitions, as do other legal writings cited in this section.

3. In *Nationwide Mutual Insurance Co. v. Darden,* 503 U.S. 318 (1992), the U.S. Supreme Court held that when a statute does not explicitly define "employer" or "employee," courts should apply common law principles of master-servant relationships to determine responsibility.

4. 29 U.S.C. §§ 201–219 (1994). Senator Hugo Black, the sponsor of the FLSA, noted in 1937 that the definition of "employer" is "the broadest definition ever included in any one act" (Black quoted in *United States v. Rosenwasser,* 323 U.S. 360, 363n.3 (1945)). The U.S. Supreme Court in *Rutherford Food Corp. v. McComb,* 331

U.S. 722 (1947) affirmed the idea that the FLSA provided a broad definition of employment given that the statute "contains its own definitions comprehensive enough to require its application to many persons and working relationships which, prior to this Act, were not deemed to fall within an employer-employee category" (728–729).

5. Employers are defined in the Occupational Safety and Health Act at 29 U.S.C. 652; employer and employee duties are specified at 29 U.S.C. 654.

6. *NLRB v. Hearst Publications, Inc.,* 322 U.S. 111 (1944). The case was the basis of *Newsies,* a Disney movie, a play, and most recently a Broadway musical (http://www .imdb.com/title/tt0104990/). Undoubtedly, more high school students have been exposed to a memorable moment from U.S. labor history due to local performances of *Newsies* than from the scant coverage of the topic in most history curricula. See Zatz (2010) for a discussion of this case and an overview of the debate on employer/employee definitions under the NLRA.

7. For example, in *NLRB v. United Insurance* (390 U.S. 254 (1968)) the Court held that "there is no doubt we should apply the common-law agency test here in distinguishing an employee from an independent contractor" (at 256). A recent opinion of the District of Columbia Circuit Court in *FedEx Home Delivery Inc. v. NLRB* (563 F.3d 492 (D.C. Cir. 2009), however, seems to apply a new test for independent contracting, quite different from that used under the common law, regarding whether the contractor has significant "entrepreneurial opportunity for gain or loss." For a discussion of this new stream of reasoning and its potential impact on further expanding the legal underpinning for use of independent contractors, see Jost (2011).

8. See Stone (2006) Rogers (2010), and Jost (2011) for related discussions.

9. See Rebitzer (1995) and Wells, Kochan, and Smith (1991).

10. For a detailed report on the Phillips 66 explosion, see U.S. Department of Labor, Occupational Safety and Health Administration (1990). The string of accidents also led Congress to have OSHA conduct a study on the role of contract workers in those incidents (undertaken in Wells, Kochan, and Smith 1991).

11. See ibid., 95–96.

12. The 2009 BP accident also reveals problems in the risk perception and resulting management decisions by companies like BP that dramatically underestimated the consequences of their reduced control over contractors. That they committed such errors in repeated situations suggests larger managerial problems. One example was BP's reliance (in both 2005 and 2009) on personal injury rate levels as early warning signals of problems rather than measures relevant to management processes related to potential accidents. In this regard, the Chemical Safety Board's chairperson, Dr. Rafael Moure-Eraso, remarked: "A number of past CSB investigations have found companies focusing on personal injury rates while virtually overlooking looming process safety issues—like the effectiveness of barriers against hazardous releases, automatic shutoff system failures, activation of pressure relief devices, and loss of containment of liquids and gases. Furthermore, we have found failures by companies

to implement their own recommendations from previous accidents involving, for example, leaks of flammable materials." See U.S. Chemical Safety Board site for reports provided in the July hearing (http://www.csb.gov/investigations/detail.aspx?SID=96& Type=1&pg=1&F_All=y, accessed September 1, 2012).

13. See Arlen and MacLeod (2005) for a relevant discussion of the problematic effects of the doctrine of vicarious liability on the incentives of parties in principal/ agent relationships.

14. Arlen and MacLeod note, "Thus vicarious liability creates perverse incentives for principals to prefer independent contractors over employees when the risks fall primarily on third parties in the very situation in which control may be most socially beneficial, when agents are judgment-proof" (2005, 132).

15. See *Rutherford Food Corp. v. McComb,* 331 U.S. 722 (1947).

16. See *Donovan v. Brandel,* 736 F.2d 1114 (6th Cir. 1984) and the different conclusion given similar facts in *Secretary of Labor v. Lauritzen,* 835 F.2d 1529 (7th Cir. 1987). More generally, see Goldstein et al. (1999) and Ruckelshaus (2008) for detailed discussions of the employer/employee definition under the FLSA.

17. For example, in *Wirtz v. Lone Star Steel Co.,* 405 F.2d 668 (5th Cir. 1968), the circuit court drew on a different five-factor test than in *Rutherford* that included the company's power to fire, to hire, or to modify the terms and conditions of employment and whether the employees of the contractor could refuse to work for the company. The Ninth Circuit Court in *Torres-Lopez v. May,* 11 F.3d 633 (9th Cir. 1997) drew on an eight-factor test to determine if a joint employment relationship existed. Along with factors included in other cited decisions, the court looked at the degree of initiative, judgment, and foresight required for the work, whether the employee had an opportunity for profit or loss, and the permanence of the employment relationship.

18. *Zheng v. Liberty Apparel Co. Inc.,* 355 F.3d 61 (2d Cir. 2003).

19. *Reyes v. Remington Hybrid Seed Co.,* 495 F.3d 403 (7th Cir. 2007).

20. The lost workday injury rate (the number of cases with an injury leading to a loss of one or more days from work per 100 full-time workers) for the industry was 2.1, versus 1.8 for all private sector industries. For injuries, see U.S. Department of Labor, Bureau of Labor Statistics (2011). For fatality data, see U.S. Department of Labor, Bureau of Labor Statistics, "Fatal Occupational Injuries by Industry and Event or Exposure, All United States, 2010," http://www.bls.gov/iif/oshwc/cfoi/cftb0250 .pdf (accessed September 2, 2012).

21. In 1904 the father of industrial relations research, John R. Commons, wrote: "The building industry in New York, as well as elsewhere in the United States, is conducted, unlike in England and Europe, on a system of sub-contracting. The mason builder, or general contractors, secures the contract from the owner, or 'client,' and generally puts up the brick-work; but he sublets, by competitive bidding, all of the other work to as many contractors as there are kinds of work. This system enables the contractor to enter the field with little or no capital, since it is usually

arranged that partial payments shall be made by the owner to the general contractor, and by him to the sub-contractors, as the work progresses" (Commons 1904, 410).

22. The Occupational Safety and Health Act requires employers to provide for all of its employees a workplace free from recognized hazards and to comply with all health and safety standards promulgated by OSHA (section 5). This creates both a "general duty" obligation related to an employer's own employees and an obligation to furnish a workplace that complies with all OSHA standards, regardless of employer status. The latter issue raises the question of multiemployer workplaces.

23. This more narrow interpretation arose from the introductory language in the section of the Code of Federal Regulations dealing with construction (20 C.F.R. 1910.12(a)), which states: "The standards prescribed in part 1926 of this chapter are adopted as occupational safety and health standards under section 6 of the Act and shall apply, according to the provisions thereof, to every employment and place of employment of every employee engaged in construction work. *Each employer shall protect the employment and places of employment of each of his employees engaged in construction work by complying with the appropriate standards prescribed in this paragraph*" (italics added).

24. See OSHA, Multi-Employer Citation Policy, Directive No. CPL 2-0.124, issued December 10, 1999. The directive became incorporated in the OSHA *Field Inspection Reference Manual* used by inspectors. It can be found at http://www.osha.gov /pls/oshaweb/owadisp.show_document?p_table=DIRECTIVES&p_id=2024 (accessed August 29, 2012).

25. The definitions of each type of employer are as follows: A creating employer is "the employer that caused a hazardous condition that violates an OSHA standard"; an exposing employer is "an employer whose own employees are exposed to the hazard"; a correcting employer is "an employer who is engaged in a common undertaking, on the same worksite, as the exposing employer and is responsible for correcting a hazard" (e.g., an employer given the responsibility to install or maintain safety equipment at a factory); a controlling employer is "an employer who has general supervisory authority over the worksite, including the power to correct safety and health violations itself or require others to correct them. Control can be established by the contract or, in the absence of explicit contractual provisions, by the exercise of control in practice." See OSHA Multi-employer Citation Policy, CPL 2-0.124, sections X.B–X.E, for definitions and examples.

26. See ibid., section X.E.5, for a series of very detailed examples with analysis contained in the policy.

27. The case involved Summit Contractors, a general contractor that was building a dormitory in Little Rock, Arkansas. Summit had subcontracted brickwork to another company. OSHA inspectors found that workers for the subcontractor were laying brick more than ten feet above the ground without any type of guardrails or

protections. OSHA cited both the subcontractor (as the creating and exposing employer) and Summit (as the controlling employer) for violations of fall protection standards. Summit appealed the citation, which was upheld by an administrative law judge but then overturned by the OSHRC. However, when the Obama administration took office, the OSHRC's decision in the case was appealed by the solicitor of labor. In 2009 a U.S. court of appeals overturned the OSHRC's decision and affirmed the original citation. The U.S. Court of Appeals for the Eighth Circuit in a 2–1 decision held that OSHA had an unambiguous right to issue citations to employers for violations even where the latter's own employees are not exposed to hazards related to that violation. The court in its opinion noted that "the controlling employer citation policy places an enormous responsibility on general contractor to monitor all employees and all aspects of a worksite." However, the decision was narrowly drawn and explicitly did not weigh in on the overall multiemployer policy. See *Solis v. Summit Contractors Inc.,* 2009 U.S. App. LEXIS. 3755 (8th Cir. 2009).

28. Summit was cited as both the controlling employer (because of its overall site authority) and the creating employer (since it obtained the power generator that was not equipped with the grounding protection). The citation against Summit had been affirmed by both the administrative law judge and OSHRC when Summit appealed it to the court as a challenge to the broader multiemployer policy, which, as mentioned in the previous note, Summit had already made a legal run against during the Bush administration. See *Summit Contractors Inc. v. Secretary of Labor and Occupational Safety and Health Review Commission,* No. 10-1329, 2011 U.S. App. LEXIS. 25011 (D.C., Dec. 14, 2011).

29. The court also provided strong legal support of the multiemployer policy itself, rejecting Summit's contention that the policy should originally have gone through formal rule-making procedures, thereby affirming its use by inspectors.

30. In the Hershey case, OSHA focused only on the two contractors—Lyons and Sons and Cocoa Services—responsible for the chocolate mixing operations. The penalties assessed were modest ($21,750 for Lyons and Sons, brought down to $16,312; $17,450 for Cocoa Services, reduced to $13,087).

31. Jordan Barab, the deputy assistant secretary of labor for occupational safety and health, commented to the Frontline/ProPublica investigative reporters covering that story: "Generally, we can only cite employers when their employees are at the work site. As you go up the line, it becomes much more difficult to actually hold the companies at the top responsible." See Ryan Knutson and Liz Day, "Built for a Simpler Era, OSHA Struggles When Tower Climbers Die," May 24, 2012 (http://www.pbs.org/wgbh/pages/frontline/social-issues/cell-tower-deaths/built-for-a-simpler-era-osha-struggles-when-tower-climbers-die/, accessed September 2, 2012).

32. Findings by Jin and Leslie (2009) concerning the gap between franchisee and company-owned restaurant hygiene prior to the imposition of mandatory grade cards

can be similarly understood through the lens of vicarious liability. The imposition by franchisors of stringent monitoring of outlet hygiene practices could support a claim that they exert a direct role in operational decisions and therefore expose them to liability claims. Franchisee free-riding behaviors (lax hygiene practices) were reduced only by allowing consumers to directly see outlet hygiene status in the form of posted restaurant grades.

33. *Miller v. McDonald's Corp.*, 150 Ore. App. 274, 945 P. 2d 1107 (Or. Ct. App. 1997). In the decision, the court notes that Miller went to the franchisee "under the assumption that [McDonald's] owned, controlled, and managed it." As far as she could tell, this was the case. It had the same look and offered the same products as any other McDonald's, and the McDonald's name was the only one she could see. "To the best of [Miller]'s knowledge, only McDonald's sells Big Mac hamburgers." Particularly important to the decision was the franchisor's control over the creation of hamburgers to make it liable, and the customer's belief that the burger being purchased was a McDonald's product (irrespective of whether it was provided by a franchisee or franchisor), a concept in tort law called "apparent agency."

34. These results are from Ji and Weil (2012) based on analysis of complete investigation records of twenty top fast-food companies in the United States. The study is discussed in detail in Chapter 6.

35. See Katie Johnston, "Cleaning Company Took Franchise Fees Illegally, SJC Rules," *Boston Globe,* September 1, 2011 (http://www.llrlaw.com/pdfs/coverall_Globe _09_01_2011.pdf, accessed July 14, 2012).

36. Massachusetts General Laws, chapter 149, section 148B.

37. *Awuah v. Coverall N. Am., Inc.,* 2010 U.S. Dist., LEXIS 29088 (D. Mass., March 23, 2010). The court focused particularly on the second condition: that franchisees were engaged in a demonstratively different activity than Coverall itself. Coverall claimed that it, like most franchisors, was primarily engaged in the business of franchising, not in commercial cleaning per se. In essence, the court argued that Coverall itself was a cleaning service relying entirely upon its franchisees to undertake its work and in that way using franchising as an illegitimate way to avoid employment obligations.

38. Since the case was brought under Massachusetts's misclassification law, it did not apply to Coverall franchisees located elsewhere. However, given similar misclassification laws in many other states with Coverall franchisees, and the larger issues of the franchising model used by Coverall (and other janitorial franchisees), the case sent ripples throughout the franchise sector. See Carol Tice, "Franchisor Nightmare: The Scandal at Coverall," *Forbes,* May 11, 2012 (http://www.forbes.com/sites/caroltice/2012 /05/11/are-some-franchisees-really-employees/, accessed July 2, 2013); Julie Bennett, "'The Sky Is Not Falling' although Ruling in Coverall Case Could Cause Sweeping Changes," *Franchise Times,* May 2012 (http://www.franchisetimes.com/May-2012 /The-Sky-is-Not-Falling/, accessed July 1, 2013).

39. The Federal Trade Commission had been warning potential franchisees about the dangers of purchasing janitorial cleaning services like those offered by Coverall and Jani-King, given their structure and economic terms, for almost twenty years, as had state franchising business offices in Maryland and elsewhere. Despite this, janitorial franchise sales had increased over that period, particularly targeted to immigrant communities.

40. According to Forbes, the company added 2,315 units between 2008 and 2010. See Carol Tice, "Top 10 Fast-Growing Franchise Chains That Powered through Recession," *Forbes,* May 9, 2012 (http://www.forbes.com/pictures/feji45fh/coverall-2/#gallerycontent, accessed August 31, 2012).

41. See *Taylor Patterson v. Domino's Pizza, LLC, et al.,* California Court of Appeal, Second Appellate District (June 27, 2012). Of particular importance to the court in regard to the control Domino's exercised in enforcing provisions of the franchise agreement and manual was the testimony of Daniel Poff, the owner of the franchise. Poff testified that he complied with the wishes of Domino's area leaders because otherwise he would be out of business "very quickly."

42. See *Gil Santiago Cano et al. vs. DPNY Inc. d/b/a Domino's Pizza et al.,* U.S. District Court, Southern District of New York, Memorandum and Order (Case No. CV 07-100-(ALC) (JCF)), filed November 8, 2012, p. 4.

43. See ibid., 15.

44. See *Everardo Carrillo et al. vs. Schneider Logistics Inc. et al.,* U.S. District Court, Central District of California, Western Division, Order Granting Preliminary Injunction (Case No. CV 11-8557 CAS (DTBx)), pp. 2–3.

45. As a result, Judge Snyder required all parties—including Schneider—to immediately account for how all workers were paid; document the piece-rate formula used by some of the subcontractors; institute electronic or mechanical pay systems that would account for hours and wages; and make a number of other record-keeping changes.

46. The court, in short, was not amused by Schneider. In its preliminary injunction and contempt ruling of March 2, 2012, the court ordered that Schneider immediately (1) pay workers a wage equivalent to what they were earning as Premier employees; (2) publish a seniority list of workers and provide employment opportunities to all employees in the suit based on their seniority; (3) provide the court with a contact list for all employees affected by the termination; (4) provide a written notice (to be approved by the court) stating that all affected workers would have jobs available to them, giving their position on the seniority list and information on how to contact them, and asking the workers to contact Schneider about their interest in the jobs; (5) provide the court with a list of all class members who did not contact Schneider within four weeks of the mailing; and (6) inform all class members of the jobs and procedures via telephone outreach. See *Everardo Carrillo et al. vs. Schneider Logistics Inc. et al.,* U.S. District Court, Central District of California, Western Divi-

sion, Plaintiff's Motion for Further Preliminary Injunction and Contempt (Case No. CV 11-8557 CAS (DTBx)), March 21, 2012, pp. 11–12.

47. On January 7, 2013, the district court granted the plaintiffs' request to amend the complaint against Schneider Logistics, PWV, and the other temporary agencies to include Walmart as a defendant. This ruling grants the plaintiffs' request to make Walmart a party to the complaint but does not yet indicate the court's view of the retailer's responsibility in setting and enforcing standards. Stay tuned. See *Everardo Carrillo et al. vs. Schneider Logistics Inc. et al.,* U.S. District Court, Central District of California, Western Division, Plaintiff's Motion for Leave to File Third Amended Complaint (Case No. CV 11-8557 CAS (DTBx)), January 7, 2013.

48. See Zatz (2010, 11).

49. This discussion draws from Crandall, Starrett, and Parker (1998).

50. Interestingly, in 1914 Judge Learned Hand of the Second U.S. Court of Appeals had rejected a much earlier attempt by a coal company to use independent contractors to avoid responsibility for injuries. In that case, Lehigh Valley, a coal company, had kept miners working in its mines at arm's length by paying them as individual contractors or through other miners working as subcontractors. As a result, miners would be unable to sue Lehigh Valley if injured (that being the only recourse for those hurt on the job at the time). This, Judge Hand ruled, was unacceptable in that injured miners could only seek relief from "one of their own, without financial responsibility or control of any capital" (*Lehigh Valley Coal Co. v. Yensavage,* 218 F.546 (2d Cir. 1914)). The case is discussed in the context of the more recent decisions regarding the independent contractor status of FedEx drivers in Jost (2011).

51. Definition of "employee" in West Virginia Code, section 21-5-1(b)(1996); definition of "employer" in West Virginia Code, section 21-5-1(m) (1996); "Prime Contractor Statute" in West Virginia Code, section 21-5-7 (1996).

52. In coal mining, a company can own coal reserves and then hire a coal operator to undertake mining of them. The operator in turn can (and does) subcontract that work to others. It is not uncommon for a parent company to own reserves and operate processing plants (used to prepare coal for shipping to various markets depending on the coal's energy, sulfur, and ash content) but mix its use of operators for actually mining the coal. See Buessing (2013) for a discussion of the incentives for vertical integration in the industry given this structure. A series of cases by West Virginia courts applies this obligation to landowners who are joint employers in the case of farmwork; to "passive investors" in the case of defunct employers; and for corporate officers. See Crandall, Starrett, and Parker (1998, 568–571).

53. See Massachusetts (M.G.L.A. 149 § 148B); New Hampshire (N.H. Rev. Stat. §§ 275:42(II) and 279:1(X)); Indiana (IC § 22-2-2-3)(limited version).

54. The list includes California, Colorado, Connecticut, Delaware, Hawaii, Illinois, Louisiana, Maryland, Massachusetts, Michigan, Minnesota, Missouri, Montana, New Jersey, New York, Pennsylvania, Utah, and Washington. See also http://www.dol

.gov/whd/workers/misclassification/ for a discussion of joint initiatives between state agencies and the Wage and Hour Division regarding misclassification.

55. The Independent Contractor Proper Classification Act addresses the section 530 safe harbor provision of federal tax law, which is a loophole that allows employers to classify workers as independent contractors. In addition to thereby allowing those businesses to avoid paying taxes, workers' compensation, and unemployment insurance, it imposes those costs on the individual worker (and also creates tax compliance problems in many instances). See "S. 2044—110th Congress: Independent Contractor Proper Classification Act of 2007," GovTrack.us (database of federal legislation), 2007 (see http://www.govtrack.us/congress/bills/110/s2044/text, accessed September 2, 2012). The Employee Misclassification Prevention Act, H.R. 3178—112th Congress, was introduced by Representative Lynn Woolsey (see http://www.govtrack.us/congress/bills/112/hr3178, accessed July 1, 2013).

56. See New York: McKinney's Labor Law § 345-a.; California: Cal. Labor Code § 2677.

57. See California: Cal. Labor Code § 2810.

58. See Illinois Day and Temporary Labor Services Act (820 ILCS 175/). There were over 300,000 temporary employees and 150 day and temporary labor service agencies with 600 branch offices in Illinois at the time the law was passed in 2000.

59. See Rogers (2010) and Glynn (2011, quote at 109). Other workplace legal scholars have also called for significant legislative change to redress aspects of the problems arising from fissured employment. Katherine Stone (2004), Guy Davidov (2004), and Cynthia Estlund (2010) have also addressed how the devolution of employment decisions has led the law to diverge increasingly from the reality in the workplace.

60. The U.S. Chemical Safety Board, in a 2012 hearing on the accident, noted, "On the Deepwater Horizon, a little over a month before the Macondo blowout, there was a delay by operators in responding to a 'well kick'—an unanticipated, hazardous influx of hydrocarbons into the wellbore that can precede a blowout. BP investigated the incident but after informal verbal discussions with Transocean, evidence indicates that Transocean did not implement changes based on the findings." The investigation is ongoing as of this writing. See U.S. Chemical Safety Board site for reports provided in the July hearing: http://www.csb.gov/investigations/detail.aspx?SID=96&Type=1&pg=1&F_All=y (accessed September 1, 2012).

61. Many of the ideas of horizontal and vertical equity (fairness) discussed in Chapter 4 emerged in an era when these jobs were already inside the boundaries of the organization. The norms and benchmarks relevant in that earlier period have changed significantly and are unlikely to be as strong even in instances where a job was brought back inside. Research on the pattern of wages in such instances would be informative.

62. Stiglitz argues that the economic rules of the game—both regulatory and macroeconomic—are "slanted in favor of the 1 percent. At least part of the reason is that the rules of the political game, too, are shaped by the 1 percent" (Stiglitz 2012, 119). This results both from successful efforts to shape the opinions of the public so that they are aligned with the opinions of those at the top (but not necessarily with their own interests) and from efforts to affect the political process itself—particularly in terms of who participates in it. See ibid., chapters 5 and 6.

63. This section draws from a larger study on the political economy of workplace legislation (Weil 2008a) as well as a study of the factors affecting passage and subsequent improvement of laws that use transparency as a form of regulation (see Fung, Graham, and Weil 2007, chapter 5).

64. These dynamics within the business community were important to passage of earlier rounds of state legislation as well. See Fishback and Kantor (2000) and Fishback (2007) for a discussion of these earlier episodes.

65. One example is the passage of an increase in the federal minimum wage in 2007 after a battle of almost a decade. Along with the change in political control of Congress, passage was spurred by the adoption of higher state-level minimum wage policies in more than thirty states by July 2007.

66. Notable in this regard is the passage of laws regarding transparency. Fung, Graham, and Weil (2007) show that the passage of many types of transparency laws in the area of consumer products, health, and the workplace began as state legislation, splitting unified opposition at the federal level.

67. For example, both the WARN and FMLA took over a decade to pass from the first time legislation was introduced until they became law. The one exception is the Lilly Ledbetter Fair Pay Act of 2009, which was first introduced in the House of Representatives in June 2007 and in the Senate in July 2007 and ultimately passed by Congress in January 2009, becoming the first law signed by President Barack Obama, on January 29, 2009.

9. Rethinking Enforcement

1. GPRA, a legislative initiative championed by former vice president Al Gore, requires agencies of the government to provide Congress with ongoing measures of their performance to expand the type of information used in appropriation, budgeting, and oversight. Many federal agencies have adopted internal strategic planning and budgeting processes that link to GPRA reporting requirements.

2. Unless otherwise noted, all figures reported in this section are based on analysis of data from the WHD's Wage and Hour Investigative Support and Reporting Database (WHISARD). To the extent possible, I use data from 1998 to 2008 in order to show trends over as long a period of time as possible. When there were questions

about the reliability of WHISARD data in earlier years, I restricted my analysis to the time period 2003–2008. Included for analysis are all cases with FLSA findings (including findings of no violations) and closed by the end of fiscal year 2009. I do not include investigations for which FLSA findings were not recorded, e.g., those cases with only child labor findings.

3. Figures from the *Budget of the U.S. Government,* various years, for reported spending for enforcement by the Occupational Safety and Health Administration, the Mine Safety and Health Administration, the Wage and Hour Division of the Employment Standards Administration (ESA), and the Equal Employment Opportunity enforcement effort of the ESA. All numbers are in constant 1982–1984 dollars. The figures are based on actual expenditures for enforcement, as defined in the president's budget for the four agencies for 1977–2010. The figures for 2011 represent expenditures based on the Continuing Resolution budget by the Congress, and 2012 figures reflect the estimated expenditures for the 2012 budget proposed by the Obama administration.

4. The reported expenditures are for federal OSHA enforcement programs only and do not include expenditures of those states with a state-administered OSHA program or the expenditures that OSHA provides to those states.

5. Estimates for the number of establishments and employees based on the U.S. Department of Commerce's County Business Patterns series.

6. The number of cases represents the average number of physical investigations (directed and complaint) conducted by the WHD. The footnotes to Table 9.1 provide the data and methodology used to derive them.

7. This is the definition by the U.S. Bureau of the Census, which tracks the number of establishments and firms in the economy over time.

8. This estimate is based on a comparison of the number of reported residential construction sites and the number of housing starts. Since a housing start represents a physical location where the Census has verified that a home is being built, it is a better representation of a work site. Estimates are based on total housing starts data collected by the Bureau of the Census, 2005 and 2006 (available at http://www.census.gov/construction/nrc/) and establishment data for the same period (available at http://www.census.gov/econ/susb/data/susb2007.html). I use 2005–2006 data to capture activity before the collapse of the housing market. Following the housing bust, the ratio fell to twelve starts per establishment, demonstrating that the number of active residential construction sites remains multiple times the size of the reported number of establishments.

9. Based on definitions in the Census of Agriculture and found at http://www.agcensus.usda.gov/Publications/2007/Full_Report/usv1.pdf, accessed July 2, 2013).

10. There is one additional issue in regard to my estimates for agricultural products. Over 94% of the Department of Agriculture investigations in my universe were registered under some act other than the FLSA. (For all other industries, 12.7% of

investigations with FLSA findings were registered under some act other than the FLSA.) When we look just at agriculture investigations with FLSA findings that were *also registered under the FLSA,* the probability of investigation drops from 5.351% (shown in Table 9.1) to 0.35%. The probabilities in the final column of Table 9.1 would shrink even further.

11. There is no readily available or reliable data on the number of physical work sites in landscaping and home health care, although it is very likely that there would be a large disparity between the Census definition of workplaces and the number of physical workplace locations in those cases.

12. Column 3 in Table 9.2 overestimates the likelihood that workplace investigators will actually visit the physical locations where violations might be observed. On the other hand, column 4 probabilities understate the role of a central location in coordinating the activities on dispersed work sites and its resulting deterrent effect. In the case of agriculture, the large number of farm sites also reflects the myriad locations where small farm operations may not even employ workers. However, even if one restricts the number of farms to those producing more than $100,000 each year, there are about 350,000 farms, relative to the 22,651 establishments in that industry.

13. Estimates based on Ji and Weil (2012). Other industrial nations face the same enforcement challenge due to the declining presence of government regulators and the growing number of workplaces. For example, in the United Kingdom, "each year since 1999–2000, HM Revenue and Customs [the government agency in charge of minimum wage enforcement] has made around 5000 visits to an employer . . . There are around 1.6m employers in the UK. Therefore a typical employer can expect a visit from HMRC once a millennium." See Metcalf (2008, 499).

14. Table 9.2 also illustrates that the actual location of work in many of the identified fissured industries is not reflected in the way government data track workplaces or the assumptions on which traditional enforcement practices are often based. Although in many of the industries of greatest regulatory concern in the past—in particular manufacturing—establishments and workplaces were synonymous, this is clearly no longer the case. Fissuring means that the location of workers has been splintered from the business organizations that may coordinate, manage, and keep payroll for that work.

15. Alternatively, in an industry like residential construction, greater attention should be paid to systemic violations among contractors working under the umbrella of a national home builder, who typically employs a minimal number of construction workers directly, but contracts and subcontracts work. A WHD strategy would then consider focused investigations of contractors for patterns of violations and, if violations are present, outreach to the home builder's division or, if there are patterns of more wide-scale violations, across multiple divisions of projects undertaken by the home builder's national office.

16. For example, in the fast-food sector, Ji and Weil (2012) found significantly higher back wage violations among particular brands even after statistically holding

constant other factors that might also explain noncompliance. In particular, compared to typical McDonald's outlets (which had the best overall compliance record among the top twenty branded companies studied), Subway, Domino's Pizza, and Popeye's Chicken all had back wages per investigation that were substantially higher.

17. See U.S. Department of Labor, "U.S. Labor Department's Wage and Hour Division and SUBWAY Franchisor Collaborate to Boost Restaurants' Compliance with Federal Labor Laws," WHD news release 13-0687-NAT, May 8, 2013.

18. The Fair Work Ombudsman is a statutory office created by the Fair Work Act 2009. The program was announced in early February 2012. For details on the National Franchise Program, see http://www.fairwork.gov.au/about-us/franchise-assistance /Pages/national-franchise-program.aspx.

19. See U.S. Congress, House of Representatives, Committee on Manufacturers, "The Sweating System," House Reports, 52nd Cong., 2nd sess., vol. 1, no. 2309, 1893, iv–viii.

20. Reports of the Industrial Commission on Immigration and on Education (Washington, DC: Government Printing Office, 1901), vol. 15. A discussion of the history of regulating labor standards in the apparel industry can be found in Abernathy, Dunlop, et al. (1999, chapters 2, 10, and 15).

21. In the United States, men's clothing—from the 1920s onward—has primarily been produced in factory-type settings, with manufacturers designing, cutting, sewing, pressing, and packaging products.

22. Labor market conditions also tend to push wages toward the legal minimum or below. In the women's segment, many entry-level sewers can reach the standard rate for sewing in a matter of months, making it relatively easy to substitute workers in the event of turnover. Given its low skill barriers, the apparel industry has always been attractive to immigrants (for example, Slovaks, Germans, and Eastern Europeans at turn of the twentieth century; Hispanic, Chinese, and Asian workers today). The ample supply of workers and the relatively low skill level required of sewers keep wage levels low and the incentive to work long hours—even in inhospitable work environments—high. The illegal status of many workers, language barriers, and cultural norms further undercut the bargaining power of these workers. See Gordon (2005).

23. As part of the innovative efforts in focusing at the top of the garment industry during the Clinton administration, the Wage and Hour Division began to use "random investigation-based surveys" as a way to gauge program impacts in industries where the WHD had major initiatives. A random sample of workplaces in the targeted industry is selected prior to the beginning of the initiative. Those workplaces receive full investigations that assess their compliance with the law (similar to a directed or complaint-driven investigation). At a later point, after the enforcement program has been in place for a period of time, another random sample is investigated and compliance once again measured. The change in compliance provides a measure

of program impact. The results described in this section are based on random investigation-based surveys undertaken in Los Angeles and New York. See Weil (2005b) and Weil and Mallo (2007) for details.

24. This estimate is based on data collected from investigation-based compliance surveys of randomly selected contractors conducted by the WHD. The estimate is based on taking the average back wage owed per worker per week for the subsample of contractors who had not been inspected prior to the time of the randomized survey by the WHD. This estimate is then annualized and applied for a shop employing thirty-five workers.

25. In fact, the incentives for noncompliance are large enough that an employer may choose not to comply with the law even if it is investigated, found in violation of minimum wage requirements at one point in time, and faces a much higher probability of investigation and penalty subsequently. The detailed calculations behind these estimates are discussed in Weil (2005b).

26. As in other fissured industries, apparel suppliers require subsidiary organizations— apparel manufacturers and their contractors—to follow specific and stringent standards and guidelines. Indicative are Saks Fifth Avenue's supplier guidelines: "Now that supply chain efficiencies are the key to remaining competitive and satisfying our customers, it has become critical that we develop collaborative partnerships with vendors who have a similar commitment to these technologies. We expect our vendors to support us by shipping their merchandise 'floor ready,' trading with our required EDI transactions, and following our Transportation, Packing, and Invoicing guidelines." Saks Fifth Avenue, *Vendor Standards Manual,* June 20, 2013 (https://www.saksincor porated.com/vendorrelations/documents/SFAVendorStandardsManual06-20-13.pdf, accessed July 2, 2013).

27. See Fair Labor Standards Act, section 15(a)(1), 29 U.S.C. § 215(a)(1). The provisions specifically allow the Department of Labor to seek temporary restraining orders and preliminary and permanent injunctions forbidding the transportation of goods produced in violation of the provisions of the FLSA.

28. Leonard (2000) provides a detailed discussion of the hot cargo provisions of the FLSA and their application to employers and industries beyond apparel.

29. These agreements, however, are entered into voluntarily by the manufacturer, and their terms are therefore negotiated between the government and the manufacturer/jobber. The terms described here are taken from the Department of Labor's model agreement language specified in formal policy documents (U.S. Department of Labor 1998a. 1998b).

30. These estimates are based on random enforcement-based investigations of contractors. The estimates compare rates of violations and back wages owed per worker by contractors that had one or more manufacturing customers with stringent monitoring (defined as monitoring requiring payroll review and surprise inspections) with comparable contractors having no such monitoring by manufacturers. Weil and

Mallo (2007) provide similar estimates for Southern California in 1998 and for New York City in 1999 and 2001. Both articles argue that the estimated impacts arise primarily from the effects of the monitoring arrangements rather than the self-selection of contractors.

31. Detailed results are reported in Weil (2005b) and Weil and Mallo (2007).

32. A policy focused at the top, of course, would place regulatory pressure on the ultimate driver of the dynamics of the supply chain, the retailer, rather than on the manufacturer. However, legal and regulatory opinions and agency procedures have generally held that retailers are not covered by hot goods provisions since they are not considered directly involved in the production of the good. In particular, a purchaser such as a retailer cannot be held in violation of the hot goods provision if acting "in good faith in reliance on written assurance from the producer that the goods were produced in compliance with [labor standards]." See Leonard (2000, 17) and generally for a detailed discussion of hot goods policy.

33. Weil and Mallo (2007) provide evidence that sorting effects led to better compliance among new contractors (those in business for less than two years) than overall average compliance. Given the high rate of business turnover, this effect leads to systemic compliance improvement over time.

34. See "Federal Court Orders Forever 21 to Surrender Supply Chain Information Subpoenaed by U.S. Department of Labor," WHD news release 13-0447-SAN, March 14, 2013 (available at http://www.dol.gov/opa/media/press/whd/whd20130447.htm, accessed July 2, 2013).

35. See "US Labor Department Seeks Enforcement of Subpoena Issued to Forever 21," WHD news release 12-1989-SAN, October 25, 2012 (available at http://www.dol.gov/opa/media/press/whd/WHD20121989.htm, accessed February 15, 2013). In March 2013, U.S. District Court judge Margaret Morrow ordered Forever 21 to produce documents demanded by the administrative subpoena but that had not yet been provided to the Labor Department. See *Hilda L. Solis, Secretary of Labor, United States Department of Labor vs. Forever 21, Inc.,* U.S. District Court, Central District of California, Order Granting Petition to Compel Respondent to Comply with Administrative Subpoena (Case No. CV 12-09188 MMM (MRWx)), March 7, 2013.

36. OSHA, in conjunction with the Solicitor's Office of the Department of Labor, has signed a series of corporate-wide agreements since 2010. A compendium of them can be found at http://www.osha.gov/pls/oshaweb/owasrch.search_form?p_doc_type=CWSA&p_toc_level=0&p_keyvalue=&p_status=CURRENT (accessed February 16, 2013).

37. The agreement covers facilities in states with federally administered OSHA programs. Because the agreement was between federal OSHA (which covers the Massachusetts site where the incident occurred) and Munro, the twenty-five states with state-administered OSHA programs are not covered by it. However, the corporate-wide agreement states: "The parties to this Agreement recognize that some of Respon-

dent's worksites are located in states that have assumed authority for the enforcement of OSHA standards pursuant to Section 18 of the Act ('State Plan Worksites'). These state plan states are encouraged to honor or agree to the terms of this Agreement." See Agreement between OSHA and Munro Muffler Brake Inc., September 12, 2011 (available at http://www.osha.gov/pls/oshaweb/owadisp.show_document?p_table=CWSA &p_id=2194, accessed February 16, 2013).

38. See "DeMoulas Super Markets Agrees to Correct Hazards, Enhance Employee Safety at All Market Basket Stores in Massachusetts and New Hampshire," OSHA regional news release, Region 1 news release 12-841-BOS, May 7, 2012 (available at http://www.osha.gov/pls/oshaweb/owadisp.show_document?p_table=NEWS _RELEASES&p_id=22350, accessed on February 16, 2013). The agreement can be found at http://www.osha.gov/pls/oshaweb/owadisp.show_document?p_table=CWSA &p_id=2185 (accessed February 16, 2013).

39. Kent quoted in "Monro Muffler Brake Reaches Agreement with US Labor Department to Protect Workers against Hydraulic Lift Hazards at Multiple Company Locations," OSHA regional news release, Region 1 news release 12-1570-BOS/ BOS 2012-159, August 24, 2012 (available at http://www.osha.gov/pls/oshaweb/owadisp .show_document?p_table=NEWS_RELEASES&p_id=22884, accessed February 16, 2013).

40. In sectors like major commercial and public construction, a lead contractor takes on the responsibility of coordinating construction activities and is typically responsible for ensuring that a project is completed on time and within budget. In prior decades, the lead "general" contractor played this role and also directly employed the workers who would be present throughout the project, while subcontracting specialty trades to others. In more recent times the lead player has a strictly coordinating role ("project manager"), meaning that even the basic trades functions are undertaken by subcontractors. The move from general contractor to construction manager reflected in part an effort to reduce the leverage of unions in the construction industry. In the traditional construction collective bargaining model, general contractors signed agreements with the "basic trades" (carpenters, laborers, and often operating engineer unions) that included a requirement that all work on the project would be done with unionized subcontractors. By removing direct employment from the key contractor's role, the construction manager could sign individual agreements with all contractors and subcontractors, thereby opening the door for a mix of union and nonunion contractors on a building site. This change occurred at the same time that the percentage of union members in most of the trades in the construction industry declined, sometimes precipitously. These changes in the industry structure are discussed in Weil (2005a). A benchmark description of the historic structure of construction can be found in Dunlop (1961).

41. Even more, the top five home builders accounted for much more than one-third of single-family homes built in major metropolitan markets like Las Vegas, Houston,

and Dallas at the peak of the building boom in 2005 and 2006. An important factor driving consolidation was the access of national home builders to lower-cost capital for acquiring or optioning land as well as lower costs for the crucial (and complicated) land development phase of construction. See Abernathy, Baker, et al. (2012) for a discussion of the emergence of national home builders in the years leading up to the housing bust.

42. See *Secretary of Labor v. Nation's Roof of New England, LLC and Nations Roof LLC,* Occupational Safety and Health Review Commission, Docket 10-1674, Region 1, Inspection no. 311593180, December 3, 2010.

43. The following terms are taken from the settlement agreement reached between representatives of Nations Roof of New England LLC and Nations Roof LLC and the U.S. solicitor of labor. See *Secretary of Labor v. Nation's Roof of New England, LLC and Nations Roof LLC,* Docket 10-1674, Region 1, Inspection no. 311593180, Settlement Agreement, July 28, 2011.

44. The agreement also stipulates that the designated safety and health director at each affiliate spend at minimum one-third of his or her time on safety and health activities.

45. The Davis-Bacon Act requires that all contractors and subcontractors performing work on federal and certain federally funded projects pay workers prevailing wages and fringe benefits as set by the Department of Labor. The Contract Work and Hours and Safety Standards Act creates similar requirements for businesses receiving federal service contracts.

46. See "US Department of Labor Resolves Action Holding Lettire Construction Corp. Responsible for Labor Violations," WHD news release 12-1532-NAT, July 26, 2012 (available at http://www.dol.gov/opa/media/press/whd/WHD20121532.htm, accessed February 15, 2013).

47. The increasing use of transparency directed toward regulatory purposes is discussed in Fung, Graham, and Weil (2007).

48. See Jin and Leslie (2009) for a study of the effectiveness of the Los Angeles County restaurant grading system.

49. One recent example is the California Transparency in Supply Chains Act of 2010. The law requires major retailers and manufacturers doing business in California to disclose their efforts to stop slavery and human trafficking from their direct supply chains. See http://www.state.gov/documents/organization/164934.pdf. The Clinton administration used a pre-Internet version of transparency in its garment enforcement effort, discussed above. The WHD issued a quarterly "garment enforcement report" listing all apparel suppliers (manufacturers, jobbers, and contractors) found out of compliance in the prior quarter. These written (and later PDF-based) reports provided manufacturers and retailers concerned with potential embargoes under the hot goods program with information on suppliers who might pose problems in this regard. Given the significant costs of dealing with a contractor potentially subject to

embargoes, such information could have powerful impacts on sourcing and therefore on compliance decisions.

50. For the DOL-Timesheet app, available via Apple iTunes, see http://itunes .apple.com/us/app/dol-timesheet/id433638193?mt=8. For the eat/shop/sleep app, see http://informaction.challenge.gov/submissions/4585-eat-shop-sleep.

51. This section is based on Weil (2012b).

52. There are numerous cases currently pending against a number of nationally franchised janitorial service providers (e.g., several cases against the Coverall and Jani-King franchises). These cases challenge whether the franchise contracts are in fact either efforts to subvert a basic employment relationship between the franchisor and franchisees or pernicious and unsustainable business models. Detailed discussion and citations of these cases can be found in Chapter 6.

53. This raises a host of significant issues regarding both the processes that lead workers to complain in the first instance and the relationship between complaints and underlying problems in the workplace. See Weil and Pyles (2006); Fine and Gordon (2010); and Weil (2008b, 2009, 2010) for detailed discussions of this issue.

54. Deterrence theory states that penalties should reflect the potential gains from failing to comply and the probability that noncompliance will be detected. A simplified model of enforcement provides a useful basis for understanding the components of setting an optimal penalty policy. Imagine that an agency in the Department of Labor is attempting to set a penalty level to induce compliance with a new law. Assume that the typical employer being regulated acts in a rational manner, balancing equally the benefits from complying with the law against not complying and facing some risk of being caught and penalized. If the government is seeking to bring the typical firm into compliance, it has two tools: inspections and fines. The government agency will need to set policy by seeking to change employer behavior, given that compliance with the new law is costly and that employers are choosing not to comply prior to its passage. This framework derives from Becker (1968) and Stigler (1970) and is laid out in greater detail by Polinsky and Shavell (2000). A useful summary of the deterrence literature can be found in Winter (2008) and Kleiner and Weil (2012). For early discussions regarding deterrence under workplace regulations, see Ashenfelter and Smith (1979) regarding the minimum wage standard of the Fair Labor Standards Act; Ehrenberg and Schumann (1982) regarding overtime provisions of that act; Smith (1979) regarding the Occupational Safety and Health Act; and Appleton and Baker (1984) regarding the Mine Safety and Health Act.

55. The politics surrounding mine health and safety have always been distinctive, leading to more stringent penalty mechanisms for MSHA than for its sister agency, OSHA, or, even more strikingly, the WHD. MSHA's penalty policies reflect periodic legislative and regulatory responses to crises that have shaken the mining industry over time. The legislative effort that led to passage of the Mine Safety and Health Act in 1969 began in response to a major mining disaster in Farmington, West Virginia,

that put the political coalition favoring its passage in a stronger position relative to industry opponents. This resulted in the original act including relatively stringent penalties and significant enforcement powers for the agency created by the legislation. National mining disasters and public awareness of the high incidence of black lung disease among miners led to major reform of the act in 1977. Even under Republican administrations, public outrage arising from deaths in the mines allowed further strengthening of the act. Most strikingly, the loss of nineteen miners in three successive accidents during the first five months of 2006 led Congress to introduce a wide-ranging set of changes, the Mine Improvement and New Emergency Response Act (MINER Act). In addition to strengthening penalty policies, it requires mine operators to adopt more extensive emergency response planning to allow evacuation of miners who may be trapped, or, if they cannot evacuate, places for them to retreat underground.

56. 30 U.S.C. 820(a); 30 C.F.R. 100.5(c), 100.4(c), 100.5(d).

57. See U.S. Department of Labor, Mine Safety and Health Administration (2011). The Department of Justice in December 2011 also reached a record settlement with Alpha Natural Resources (the company that purchased Massey Energy after the disaster). The settlement included corporate criminal liabilities for a record $209 million. Additional individual criminal prosecutions as well as civil litigation are still pending.

58. See Davitt McAteer and members of the Governor's Independent Review Commission, "The April 5, 2010, Explosion: A Failure of Basic Coal Mine Safety Practices," Report to the Governor of West Virginia, May 2011 (available at http://s3.document cloud.org/documents/96334/upperbigbranchreport.pdf).

59. An S&S violation is one where there exists a reasonable likelihood that the hazard will result in an injury or illness of a reasonably serious nature. In determining whether conditions or practices created by a violation could significantly and substantially contribute to the cause and effect of a mine safety or health hazard, the MSHA handbook notes that "inspectors must determine: whether there is an underlying violation of a mandatory health or safety standard; whether there is a discrete safety or health hazard—that is, a measure of danger to safety or health—contributed to by the violation; whether there is a reasonable likelihood that the hazard contributed to will result in an injury or illness; and whether there is a reasonable likelihood that the injury or illness in question will be of a reasonably serious nature" (U.S. Department of Labor, 2008, 18–19).

60. The history of the regulations providing for use of this authority is indicative of the highly contested nature of this enforcement procedure. The act authorizes the secretary of labor to establish the criteria for determining the presence of a pattern of violations. MSHA proposed a first POV regulation in 1980 (45 FR 54656). The proposal, which provided screening and pattern criteria and procedures for the issuing and termination of POV notices, was the subject of ongoing criticism regarding its complexity, vagueness, and breadth. It was ultimately withdrawn by the agency in

1985 (50 FR 5470). MSHA published a sector proposed rule in 1989 (54 FR 23156) with a revised procedure and criteria, addressing many of the critiques of the earlier proposal. It issued a final rule after numerous public hearings and commentaries in 1990 (ten years after the initial attempt and almost fourteen years after passage of the Federal Mine Safety and Health Act of 1977). The 1990 regulation provides for a decentralized process of screening for POVs and variable imposition of the annual screening requirement. The accidents at the Sago, Darby, and Aracoma mines in 2006 led to a reassessment of the program and efforts to centralize and more consistently quantify its procedures. The assistant secretary of MSHA, Joe Main, issued new proposed regulations in February 2011. Public comment on those procedures closed in August 2011. The final regulation was adopted on January 23, 2013, and went into effect on March 25, 2013. See "Pattern of Violations: Final Rule," 30 C.F.R. 104, RIN 1219–AB73 (available at http://www.msha.gov/REGS/FEDREG/FINAL/2013finl/2013-01250.pdf, accessed February 13, 2013).

61. See *Federal Register* 78, no. 15, January 23, 2013, 5057.

62. The number of contested citations and orders climbed markedly after the passage in 2006 of the MINER Act, which raised penalty levels. In November 2010, the Mine Safety and Health Review Commission that deals with contests faced a backlog of some 88,000 contested citations and orders. Under existing rules, these could not be included in the calculation of POV status.

63. See *Secretary of Labor v. Black Mag LLC,* OSHRC Docket 10-2043; see also U.S. Department of Labor, Occupational Safety and Health Administration, Region 1, "US Labor Department resolves OSHA citations against Black Mag LLC," News release 11-888-BOS/BOS 2011-233, June 29, 2011.

64. See Thornton, Gunningham, and Kagan (2005). A number of recent studies have attempted to assess the impact of perceptions of fairness, morality, and religion on compliance with tax laws and other social policies. These studies have generally found strong associations with perceptions of "tax morale" and compliance that help explain high rates of compliance (beyond what would be expected from an economically rational actor) in many areas. The important idea of this literature is that compliance behavior is dependent not only on the individual calculus of a regulated party, but also on how it perceives its actions relative to other socially relevant counterparts. The ripple effects of an enforcement system can be far more extensive if such perceptions are important and if an agency fashions its policies accordingly. See Torgler (2006) and Halla (2010) for two relevant papers.

10. Fixing Broken Windows

Epigraph: A more elaborate discussion is found in Kelling and Coles (1996). This chapter draws from Weil (2012a).

1. Once again the fairness notions are important here: work by Thornton, Gunningham, and Kagan (2005) and other political scientists and economists has shown that companies that comply with laws respond positively to signs of strong enforcement elsewhere in their industry because it provides greater confidence in the fairness of the system and allays worry that compliance in an environment of uneven enforcement could undermine precisely those who are obeying the law. But the same logic operates in reverse: perceptions that enforcement is lax will undermine incentives provided by fairness concerns for compliance.

2. See Freeman and Rogers (1999). The lack of knowledge of statutory rights under a variety of laws is also discussed in Morris (1989), Estlund (1992), Edwards (1993), DeChiara (1995), Sunstein (2001), and most recently Estlund (2011).

3. This point is developed in greater detail in Weil (2004) and Weil and Pyles (2006). See also Yaniv (2001).

4. Bernhardt, Milkman, et al. (2009).

5. For example, section 11(c) of the Occupational Safety and Health Act prohibits discharge or any form of retaliation against employees for exercising their rights under the act. OSHA also administers similar whistleblower protection for twenty-one statutes. Along with a number of statutes related to the workplace (e.g., the Federal Railroad Safety Act and the Surface Transportation Assistance Act, regulating safety in the railroad and trucking industries, respectively), this also includes whistleblower protections under the Sarbanes-Oxley Act, Clean Water Act, Safe Drinking Water Act, and other statutes. For a complete listing of whistleblower protection programs administered by OSHA, see http://www.whistleblowers.gov/index.html.

6. The percentage of complaints taken to employers versus through government agencies is reported in National Employment Law Project (2010); the 20% of employees who "either made a complaint in the last year or attempted to form a union" is reported in Bernhardt, Milkman, et al. (2009, 24). Since both estimates represent complaints across all types of problems taken through a government agency, the derived probability of a complaint represents complaint rates across all potentially applicable statutes (FLSA, Occupational Safety and Health Act, NLRA, policies relating to employment discrimination, etc.).

7. In order to create reasonably objective measures of underlying workplace conditions across industries, Weil and Pyles used lost workday injuries by industry for OSHA and a calculated rate of overtime violations per covered worker based on the Current Population Survey (CPS) for the FLSA. See Weil and Pyles (2006, 66–68) for details.

8. Complaint counts include all full and partial investigations, conciliations (complaints handled over the phone), and audits registered in 2001–2002 and 2007–2009 and closed (administratively completed) by third quarter 2010. Although most complaints filed in the 2007–2009 period would have been closed by 2010, a small

number of cases being contested or involving longer administrative activities would remain open and therefore not be included in complaint tallies. This means that the rate for the 2007–2009 period may represent an undercount. However, prior work suggests that the effect of open cases on complaint rate estimates is very small.

9. Table 10.1 uses a slightly different definition for counting complaints than used in Weil and Pyles (2006). It counts the number of complaints lodged with the Wage and Hour Division for violations of the Fair Labor Standards Act only, and not other statutes also overseen by that agency. In contrast, Weil and Pyles use a complaint measure also including other statutes administered by the WHD.

10. See in particular Osterman and Shulman (2011), Kalleberg (2011), and Bern- hardt, Milkman, et al. (2009).

11. See Fine and Gordon (2010) for a discussion of three cases of state and local part- nerships between community and workers organizations and government agencies.

12. This step has been advocated by a number of labor law scholars, such as Wiss- inger (2003) in regard to rights under the National Labor Relations Act and Estlund (2011) more generally.

13. In some cases, for example the Occupational Safety and Health Act, the re- quirement is built into the statute. In others, for example the Fair Labor Standards Act, the requirement arose from regulations issued after passage of the act.

14. State laws passed in Massachusetts and Illinois, for example, require that staff- ing agencies provide temporary workers with basic information about any job to which they are being sent, the wages offered, the name and address of the work site, whether a meal and transportation will be provided, and information about how to lodge complaints. See Massachusetts Temporary Worker Right to Know Act (M.G.L.A. 149 §159C) and the Illinois Day and Temporary Labor Services Act (820 ILCS 175/).

15. See the We Can Help campaign by the Wage and Hours Division of the Depart- ment of Labor (http://www.dol.gov/wecanhelp/). One of the criticisms by these groups was that the department was encouraging undocumented workers to exercise their rights because the Fair Labor Standards Act and other federal workplace policies cover all workers regardless of their immigration status. The sharp criticism of the We Can Help campaign led the Department of Labor to post the following public statement on its site as part of the campaign material: "Through Democratic and Republican administrations, the Department of Labor consistently has held that the country's minimum wage and overtime law protects workers regardless of their im- migration status. To argue otherwise diminishes the value of work in this country." See http://www.dol.gov/opa/media/press/whd/WHD20100890.htm.

16. See 75 Fed. Reg. 80410, December 22, 2010. The rule, supporting materials, and links to comments can be found at https://www.federalregister.gov/articles/2010 /12/22/2010-32019/proposed-rules-governing-notification-of-employee-rights-under -the-national-labor-relations-act#p-12. The proposed NLRB poster listing worker rights

can be found at http://www.nlrb.gov/poster. A statement by Mark Gaston Pearce, the chairman of the NLRB, regarding the current status of the posting can be found at http://www.nlrb.gov/news-outreach/news-releases/nlrb-chairman-mark-gaston -pearce-recent-decisions-regarding-employee-rig (accessed July 2, 2013).

17. Olson (1965) long ago established why it is difficult to overcome collective action problems, principally because individual incentives continue to dominate. This problem also highlights a central conundrum of much of workplace policy: it is individually focused but requires collective action to be effective (Weil 2004).

18. The role of unions in providing basic agency functions is discussed in Freeman and Medoff (1984), particularly in regard to personnel practices and benefits. Median voter models of union behavior predict that union leaders pursue policies reflective of more senior members of the unit. Alternatively, differences in the interests of union leaders and members may lead to divergence between the claims pressed by the union and what the typical worker might desire. The union may have incentives to "overuse" certain rights for strategic reasons unrelated to workplace regulation, for example as a source of pressure in collective bargaining or strikes (U.S. General Accounting Office 2000). However, union leader/ union member divergences in interests are likely moderated both through electoral processes and by the duty of fair representation claims that union members can file.

19. See in particular Weil (1991, 1992, 1996) for OSHA; Morantz (2011) for MSHA; Budd and Brey (2003) for FMLA; Butler and Worrall (1983) and Hirsch, Macpherson, and DuMond (1997) for workers' compensation; Blank and Card (1991) and Budd and McCall (1997) for unemployment insurance; and generally Weil (2004) and Fine and Gordon (2010).

20. See U.S. Department of Labor, Bureau of Labor Statistics (2013).

21. Labor laws include the Fair Labor Standards Act, the Labor Management Relations Act, the Railway Labor Act, and ERISA. Based on Annual Reports of the Director, Judicial Business of the United States Courts, table 4.4 (see http://www .uscourts.gov/uscourts/Statistics/JudicialFactsAndFigures/2010/Table404.pdf).

22. See *Circuit City Stores, Inc. v. Adams,* 532 U.S. 105 (2001). More recently, the Court upheld the primacy of the Federal Arbitration Act in *AT&T Mobility LLC v. Concepcion,* 584 F.3d 84 (2011).

23. The definitive study of worker centers remains Fine (2006). Theodore et al. (2008) have also undertaken detailed ethnographic and survey research looking at the structure and role of day labor markets in a number of different cities. Skerry (2008) offers a more skeptical view of the potential for this type of organization in immigrant communities to exert a significant role, however, given their legal and political vulnerability.

24. For example, Hellerstein, McInerney, and Neumark (2011) examine the spread of information about labor market conditions through local geographic and ethnic enclaves. Budd's findings (2010) that two-thirds of individuals under age forty have worked at least once in a unionized workplace is germane here. Of particular salience

are the attitudes that such exposure leaves individuals with regarding voice and exercise of rights in workplaces with and without unions.

25. Immigrants' ongoing ties between their country of origin and the country where they now reside are explored in a number of works, including Peggy Levitt's study (2001) of "transnational villagers." The work explores how immigration for many is a matter of continuing ties between two communities, rather than the one-way, momentous move of an earlier generation. This has profound impacts on the social networks and collective identities of people in those communities in both countries.

26. Eckstein and Nguyen (2010) examine the changing business and labor markets of workers in this industry. Sarah Maslin Nir, "Aided by Court Victory, Nail Salon Workers Rally," *New York Times,* April 11, 2012, A18.

27. For a detailed recent history, see Widdicombe (2011). This account is also drawn from Daniel Massey, "City Taxi Drivers' Organization Joins AFL-CIO," *Crain's New York Business,* October 20, 2011, http://www.crainsnewyork.com/article/20111020 /LABOR_UNIONS/ 111029995.

28. According to Lawrence and Kaufmann (2011), twelve of the twenty largest franchise systems in the United States have active independent franchisee associations. "Of the remaining eight (McDonald's, Ace Hardware, Marriott, Hilton, Re/Max, Coldwell Banker, and Health Mart, all have advisory councils comprised of franchisees" (285).

29. The following is an excerpt of the statement of the AAHOA to its members:

On behalf of our more than 9,000 members, last Friday, on October 17, 2008, AAHOA sent letters to the key executives at Accor, America's Best Value Inn, Best Western, Carlson, Choice, Hilton, IHG, La Quinta, Settle Inn & Suites/Guest House, Vista, and Wyndham. In the letters, AAHOA requested an opportunity to meet with them in the upcoming weeks to determine how best to proceed . . . We explained that since the franchise companies are dependent on its [*sic*] franchisees to withstand these uncertain times, and vice versa, we are all in this together. Given what is at stake, it is important to sit down together to discuss a plan of action that will protect the interests of all.

As part of this discussion, AAHOA stated that it will be identifying particular action items that it would like the franchise companies to implement, and AAHOA will also be interested in learning about other points that the franchise companies are already considering and implementing on an "as needed" basis, including:

- granting the franchisees 6–12 month extensions on their construction and/or renovation projects;
- postponing or suspending the introduction of any new amenities, programs, or systems until after the financial markets have stabilized and the industry is once again profitable;
- increasing the franchise companies' marketing efforts, both on a system-wide basis and at the local levels;
- decreasing the royalty fees for any franchisees who are encountering severe financial hardships; . . .

- protecting the existing franchisees by limiting the number of applications you approve for conversions or new hotels in their geographic areas, especially if there has been a downturn in reservations and occupancy rates in these areas;
- assigning key personnel to meet with each franchisee to discuss individual issues concerning their respective hotels, including potential inexpensive marketing opportunities, yield management, decreasing expenses, and operating the facilities in a more efficient and cost-productive manner; and
- in the event of an early termination (regardless of whether it is voluntary or involuntary), limiting the liquidated damages to no more than 6 months of royalty fees based on the amount of royalty fees the franchisee has paid in the immediately preceding 6 months.

See http://www.aahoa.com/Content/ContentFolders/Pressroom/AAHOANews/MemberAlert—WorkingWiththeFranchisors.pdf (accessed October 5, 2009).

30. There has been considerable controversy within the AAHOA regarding the standards themselves (which have been revised twice since 1998), including what party undertakes reviews of each brand (the AAHOA or the brand itself) and the consequences of failing to meet those standards. The current standards can be found at http://www.aahoa.com/Content/NavigationMenu/AboutUs/12Points/default.htm (accessed August 3, 2012).

31. The rule provides prospective purchasers of franchises with the information they need in order to weigh the risks and benefits of such an investment. It requires franchisors to provide all potential franchisees with a disclosure document containing specific items of information about the franchise. See "Disclosure Requirements and Prohibitions concerning Franchising," 16 C.F.R. 436, and "Disclosure Requirements and Prohibitions concerning Business Opportunities," 16 C.F.R. 437.

32. Of course, there are legal parameters regarding the role business associations can take in setting prices (that is, restrictions on price fixing). Within those boundaries, however, this discussion returns to one of the original concepts underlying the academic study of "industrial and labor relations": workplace wage, benefit, and working condition discussions are framed by industrial relations—that is, relations between firms in markets, including how prices are set—as well as around wages. David Brody, a labor historian, harkens to this older tradition in many essays, including a discussion of the evolution of unionism in the coal industry. "Payment by tonnage (to the individual coal miner) was the lynchpin of the entire labor-relations system in American coal mining . . . The tonnage rate was the cardinal datum of mine operation, and from its centrality we can extrapolate the leading characteristics of labor relations in coal-mining." See Brody (1993, 135 and chapter 4 generally).

33. This was necessary because farm workers are not covered by the National Labor Relations Act.

34. The original collective agreements covering growers, farm workers, and Campbell Soup and Vlasic Pickle were mediated by John Dunlop (described in Dunlop 1993, 34–36). Full disclosure: I currently serve as the chairman of the Dunlop Agricultural Commission, a tripartite body (with representatives from the growers, labor, and a neutral) that oversees dispute resolution under the agreements.

35. The CIW agreements are not collective bargaining agreements involving the individual growers, and are focused on providing additional wages to workers covered by them.

36. In the mid-1990s, a wave of public campaigns by student groups, labor unions, and worker and human right activists highlighted sweatshop conditions in garment factories and prominent footwear/apparel companies like Nike and Adidas. This led to the formation of a number different monitoring groups and efforts. In 1996 the U.S. Labor Department sponsored the Apparel Industry Partnership (AIP), in which U.S. apparel manufacturers, UNITE! (the labor union for U.S. apparel workers), the National Consumers League, and other religious and nonprofit organizations agreed to establish methods to monitor labor standards of international contractors. In November 1998, President Bill Clinton announced that an agreement reached among the parties on a monitoring mechanism represented a "historic step toward reducing sweatshop labor around the world and [that it] will give American consumers confidence that the clothes they buy are made under decent and humane working conditions." The AIP soon became the Fair Labor Association, which was incorporated formally in 1999 to carry out these activities. Other international monitoring groups such as Verité, COVERCO, and the Workers Rights Consortium formed around the same time.

37. See Keith Bradsher and Charles Duhigg, "Signs of Changes Taking Hold in Electronics Factories in China," *New York Times,* December 26, 2012 (http://www.nytimes.com/2012/12/27/business/signs-of-changes-taking-hold-in-electronics-factories-in-china.html, accessed January 15, 2013). Noteworthy is that the authors of the story also did some of the early stories that brought to light problems in the Apple supply chain initially.

38. See Steven Greenhouse and Jim Yardley, "As Walmart Moves Safety Vows, It's Seen as Obstacle to Change," *New York Times,* December 29, 2012, and Steven Greenhouse, "Retailers Split on Contrition after Collapse of Factories." *New York Times,* April 30, 2013.

39. Richard Locke and colleagues at MIT have intensively studied these developments in a variety of industries and the systems developed by many companies under them. See Locke, Amengual, and Mangla (2009) and Locke (2013) for assessments of these efforts. See James, Johnstone, et al. (2007) for a related discussion.

40. The emergence of multiple players in the monitoring space has been discussed in a number of papers written in the first decade of the twenty-first century. See in particular O'Rourke (2003) and Fung, O'Rourke, and Sabel (2001). A number of

research collaboratives are undertaking comparative studies, including the ILO's Regulating Decent Work initiative and the Stanford Just Supply Chain research network.

41. See Locke, Qin, and Brause (2007) and Locke and Romis (2007) on the benefits of such integration in the footwear and apparel industries. However, Locke, Distelhorst, et al. (2012) find more modest impacts of integrated approaches in the electronics industry.

42. In late 2006 the International Labour Organization called upon its member states to adopt a series of policies to strengthen and modernize labor inspectorates as a means of assuring implementation of fundamental workplace policies. In pursuing its broad Decent Work Agenda, the ILO's Governing Body Committee on Employment and Social Policy noted: "The main overarching strategic issue is that the quality of governance of the labour market is a major factor in distinguishing whether countries are successful or not in finding a development trajectory that leads to a sustainable reduction in poverty. Improved labour inspections and safe work management, as well as underpinning social protection at work, lead to a better quality product, higher productivity, a decline in the number of accidents and an increase in the motivation of the labour force." See International Labour Office (2006, 3). For discussion of the challenges facing international labor inspectorates, see Von Richthofen (2002); Lécuyer (2002); Piore and Schrank (2008); and Pires (2008).

43. Autor quoted in David Barboza and Charles Duhigg, "Pressure, Chinese and Foreign, Drives Changes at Foxconn," *New York Times,* February 20, 2012, B1, B2.

44. One of the promising aspects of the recent actions by Foxconn is the scale of its operations and its potential ability to affect the standards of other major competitors and in that way alter industry standards. But these efforts will still be affected by the final consumers' willingness to pay for better labor standards in international supply chains.

45. See Jacobs (1961, 31–32).

11. The Fissured Economy

Epigraphs: The Bituminous Coal Operators Association spokesman is quoted in Paul Nyden, "Coal Contracts: Shifting Mining Danger, Responsibility," *Sunday Gazette-Mail,* November 7, 1993, 1. Commenting on the same aspects of contracting in coal, Joseph Yablonski Jr., lawyer for seven widows of miners killed while working as contractors at the Island Creek mines, said, "Island Creek very carefully monitored everything that occurred on their coal lands and simultaneously disclaimed any responsibility for safety" (quoted in Nyden, "Small Mines Shunt Safety Concerns for Large Profits," *Charlestown Gazette,* December 19, 1993).

1. Estimated distribution of employment based on U.S. Department of Labor, Bureau of Labor Statistics, *Current Employment Statistics* for 2010 (http://www.bls .gov/ces/cesbtabs.htm); distribution of low-wage workers by Osterman and Shulman (2011) using Current Population Survey, Outgoing Rotation Group survey. Low-wage workers are defined by poverty level for a family of four (see Osterman and Shulman 2011, chapter 4).

2. See Houseman (2001). The survey defined contract workers as "individual who are employed by another organization to perform tasks or duties as specifically contracted by the organization. Contract workers may be used for carrying out administrative duties or providing business support . . . Contractors may also be used to perform activities that are core [to] the business's operations."

3. See Kalleberg and Marsden (2005).

4. Dey, Houseman, and Polivka (2010) use Current Employment Statistics (a monthly establishment survey overseen by the Bureau of Labor Statistics); the Economic Census (conducted every five years by the U.S Bureau of the Census of establishments in most industries); the Current Population Survey (CPS), a nationally representative survey of 60,000 households collected by the Bureau of the Census and the Bureau of Labor Statistics (BLS); the Contingent Worker Survey, a supplementary survey to the CPS; and the Occupational Employment Statistics program of the BLS, which generates employment and wage estimates based on a semiannual survey of 200,000 establishments. The paper shows that the estimates of levels of outsourcing vary considerably across these different surveys, as does the estimated rate of growth.

5. Dey, Houseman, and Polivka (2010): Economic Census estimates in table 1; distribution of industry assignments, based on the Contingent Worker Survey supplement to the CPS in table 3; growth in occupations in figure 7(a–f), based on the Occupational Employment Statistics.

6. The definition also states: "Persons who do not expect to continue in their jobs for personal reasons such as retirement or returning to school are not considered contingent workers, provided that they would have the option of continuing in the job were it not for these reasons." U.S. Bureau of the Census, Current Population Survey (CPS).

7. The CPS is a household survey conducted by the Bureau of the Census. It includes on a rotating basis the Contingent Work Supplement which asks respondents about the nature of their work relationship in these categories. The figures in the tables represent results from the February 1995 and 2005 surveys. The U.S. General Accountability Office uses these definitions in a 2006 report regarding misclassification. The figures presented here are based on the CPS Contingent Work Supplements as presented in that report.

8. These definitions are taken from U.S. General Accountability Office (2006). I do not include direct-hire temps (temporary workers hired directly by companies to

work for specified periods of time) or standard part-time workers since these are most likely to be engaged in more standard forms of employment relations, similar to standard full-time workers.

9. Among those nations with the fastest growth in part-time employment as a portion of total employment, Germany grew from 14.2% to 22.1%; Canada from 18.8% to 19.9%; and Italy from 10.5% to 16.7%. Temporary employment grew in Germany from 10.4% to 14.7%; in France from 12.3% to 15.3%; in Canada from 11.3% to 13.7%; and, most dramatically, in Italy from 7.2% to 13.4%. See Organization for Economic Cooperation and Development (2012), Statistical Annex, table E (incidence and composition of part-time employment) and table F (incidence of temporary employment).

10. This can be seen in the following table comparing the percentage increase between 1995 and 2011 in the incidence of the practices among women and the overall workforce among OECD nations.

	Women			All		
	Proportion of total employment			Proportion of total employment		
	1995	2011	% change	1995	2011	% change
Part-time employment	20.2	26	28.7	11.6	16.5	**42.2**
Temporary employment	11.3	12.5	10.6	10.6	12	**13.2**

Based on Organization for Economic Cooperation and Development (2012, tables E and F).

11. A great deal of what we know about workers and workplaces is based on household surveys administered by the Bureau of the Census and analyzed by the Bureau of Labor Statistics. But using household surveys to estimate the prevalence of fissured workplaces is problematic because workers may not be able to distinguish their legal employer from their supervisor from the party that determines daily work requirements. Employer-based surveys, also utilized extensively by the Bureau of Labor Statistics and the Bureau of the Census, may be more revealing in this regard, but also raise their own methodological complexities, as the discussion of the definition of "establishment" in Chapter 9 makes clear.

12. The comment was made during a mortgage refinancing that I was undertaking while writing this chapter, after I had described the book I was currently writing.

13. In a disclosure document presented to refinance customers, Title Source, a company that does this work for banks, describes the role of the "signing agent": "The signing agent joining you today is a representative of Title Source. The signing

agent does not work for your lender. Their role is to identify the documents that you will be signing, identify that the proper individuals are signing the necessary documents and witness the signatures for this transaction. Your signing agent is not able to give you any legal advice or explain the legal purpose of these documents. Your signing agent is **NOT** [caps, bold, and underline in original] allowed to answer questions regarding . . ." (and then lists a series of questions regarding interest rates, closing fees, duration of loan, lender processes, or the decision to sign a document). In short, the lawyer is present only to serve the lender's need for a lawyer to be present to witness the closing, and provides no services or benefits to the borrower.

14. This has long been a practice of law firms who historically would bill work at rates reflective of more specialized staff, but would staff that work with lower-cost (but internally provided) junior lawyers and paralegals.

15. A provocative discussion of the potential impact of LPOs is provided by Bruce MacEwen, drawing on Clayton Christensen's idea of the innovator's dilemma (Christensen 2006). See Bruce MacEwen, "Innovators at the Barricades," *Adam Smith, Esq.* (blog), July 10, 2010 (available at http://www.adamsmithesq.com/2010/07/innovators _at_the_barricades/, accessed February 18, 2013).

16. This three-level market breakdown appears on a number of law blog analyses of the changing legal market. See, for example, Jordan Furlong, "The Stratified Legal Market and Its Implications," *Law21* (blog), March 25, 2011 (available at http://www .law21.ca/2011/03/the-stratified-legal-market-and-its-implications/, accessed February 12, 2013).

17. It is interesting to compare this three-tiered classification of legal work with the three-tiered classification of coal extraction in the Massey Doctrine. In both cases, the strategic implication of the categorization is to contract out to the extent possible the commodity end of the work while retaining as much as possible of the specialized high-end legal work or coal extraction.

18. See LRSolutions, http://www.lrsolutions.com/expert.html (accessed February 9, 2013).

19. An example of the type of firm that is quickly emerging in the middle tier of the market is Axiom Global Inc. Axiom Global is a rapidly growing thirteen-year-old legal services company that provides corporate legal work for clients at a lower price point than the large "white shoe" firms it competes with. It received $28 million in additional equity funding from Carrick Capital Partners in February 2013. See Jennifer Smith, "Axiom Scores $28 Million Round of Funding," February 6, 2013, *Wall Street Journal Law Blog* (http://blogs.wsj.com/law/2013/02/06/axiom-scores-28 -million-round-of-funding/, accessed February 17, 2013).

20. On the continuing fall in law school applications, see Ethan Bronner, "Law Schools' Applications Fall as Costs Rise and Jobs Are Cut," *New York Times,* January 30, 2013 (available at http://www.nytimes.com/2013/01/31/education/law-schools-ap plications-fall-as-costs-rise-and-jobs-are-cut.html, accessed February 17, 2013). On the

changing distribution of legal salaries, see Catherine Rampell, "The Toppling of Top-Tier Lawyer Jobs," *New York Times,* July 16, 2012 (available at http://economix.blogs .nytimes.com/2012/07/16/the-toppling-of-top-tier-lawyer-jobs/, accessed July 3, 2013).

21. Commenting on this drop, James Leipold, the executive director of the Association for Legal Career Professionals, noted, "This drop in starting salaries, while expected, is surprising in its scope. Nearly all of the drop can be attributed to the continued erosion of private practice opportunities at the largest law firms." See "Median Private Practice Starting Salaries for the Class of 2011 Plunge as Private Practice Jobs Continue to Erode," NALP: The Association for Legal Career Professionals, July 12, 2012 (available at http://www.nalp.org/classof2011_salpressrel, accessed February 18, 2013).

22. Industry statistics and trends based on the Pew Research Annual Survey of Journalism (see Edmonds et al., 2012). The report looks at advertising revenues in detail on pages 8–12. Despite the flat level of revenues from circulation, the number of newspapers purchased annually declined, particularly on weekdays.

23. Based on statistics collected by the Newspaper Association of America and reported in Edmonds et al. (2012, 1).

24. The idea of a partial pay wall, where online users are given free access for a specified number of articles and then face a pay wall, was adopted by the *New York Times* and other papers in the past few years. The Pew Research Annual Survey of Journalism notes that private equity investors in the industry "tend to taken an aggressive approach to digital transition." See Edmonds et al. (2012, 17).

25. See ibid., 6.

26. Based on a census conducted by the American Society of News Editors, "ASNE Newsroom Census," April 2012.

27. Newspapers have always used stringers for specific kinds of reporting involving particular specialties, quirky news events, or feature areas that did not warrant full-time reporters. Journatic, in contrast, is a complete replacement of a former group of workers employed inside the organization—local news reporters.

28. From the home page of Journatic (http://www.journatic.com, accessed July 9, 2012).

29. It is not clear whether any of the writing of the stories actually occurs in the Philippines. In interviews, Timpone insists that the offshore writers only do data gathering and may write leads, but nothing beyond that.

30. See Anna Tarkov, "Journatic Worker Takes 'This American Life' inside Outsourced Journalism," *Poynter,* June 30, 2012, updated July 3, 2012 (http://www.poynter .org/latest-news/top-stories/179555/journatic-staffer-takes-this-american-life-inside -outsourced-journalism/, accessed July 9, 2012). Ryan Smith, the journalist who went public regarding his time writing for Journatic, similarly writes, "Journatic's greatest ruse has been to convince the world that the company and its workers barely exist." Ryan Smith, "My Adventures in Journatic's New Media Landscape of Outsourced Hyperlocal News," *The Guardian,* July 6, 2012 (http://www.guardian.co.uk/commen

tisfree/2012/jul/06/adventures-journatic-new-media-outsourced-hyperlocal-news, accessed July 14, 2012).

31. The Tribune Company, publisher of the *Chicago Tribune* and many other papers and an acknowledged customer of Journatic, announced in April 2012 that it had made "a strategic investment in Journatic, LLC . . . and that the two companies will have [a] significant operating relationship going forward." See http://journatic.com/news/provider-of-hyperlocal-content-will-expand-its-capabilities/ (accessed July 9, 2012).

32. The Ryan Tyler story aired on the National Public Radio program *This American Life* as one of several segments in a program titled "Switcheroo" that consisted of different stories about "people pretending to be people they're not." See http://www.thisamericanlife.org/radio-archives/episode/468/switcheroo (originally aired June 29, 2012).

33. Peter Frost and Ameet Sachdev, "Going Hyper: Media Companies Are Eager to Deliver Extremely Local News, but It's Proving to Be a Difficult Task," *Chicago Tribune,* July 22, 2012, 1, 4.

34. The "content farm" model did hit some difficulties in 2011 when Google's ranking protocol gave lower rankings to articles from acknowledged content farms (Edmonds et al. 2012, 19). However, the Journatic model is to embed the stories in established news outlets like the *Chicago Tribune,* subverting that problem.

35. Journatic also advertises on its home page that it is "also one of the largest producers of sponsored content, fueling the online marketing efforts for thousands of small and medium-sized businesses." Companies like Journatic have taken on the work traditionally done in part by in-house providers or marketing firms. Also, an industry has formed of outsourced companies that provide content for annual reports, etc., work once done by the company itself.

36. Nelson Schwartz, "Financial Giants Are Moving Jobs off Wall Street," *New York Times,* July 2, 2012, A1, A3.

37. In this example, companies would face a complicated balancing act regarding the "glue" keeping that keeps shedding employment from undermining a financial firm's core competency. On one hand, the potential savings from shedding a large number of mid-level jobs from the financial services firm would be significant. On the other, this must be balanced against the costs of shedding too much and potentially leaking investment information or compromising confidentiality. Since both are central to the core competencies of the firm, the methods used to ensure security among the companies that provide work for the lead financial company would be key components of the organizational arrangements used. The expansion of fissuring in the legal world, however, suggests that such arrangements can be developed.

38. The definitive study of income inequality in the United States is Picketty and Saez (2003). The authors have periodically updated their detailed estimates of income inequality and made them available to researchers and the public. For the most recent updates, see Saez (2013). See also Congressional Budget Office (2011).

39. Estimates from Mishel, Bivens, Gould, and Shierholz (2013).

40. Picketty and Saez show this redistribution back to the top of the income distribution: the share of income held by the top 10%–5% of the income distribution declined slightly, from 11.5% in 1980 to 11.0% in 2007, and even the top 5%–1% increased its share only modestly, from 13.0% in 1980 to 15.2% in 2007. See Picketty and Saez (2003) and Saez (2013).

41. Ibid.

42. See Mishel, Bivens, Gould, and Shierholz (2013).

43. During this period, Krugman notes that the United States went through a "great economic arc from high inequality to relative equality and back again" (2007, 5). Goldin and Margo (1992) discuss the opposite trend during the period between the Great Recession and the 1960s as "The Great Compression."

44. There is a very large literature on the drivers of wage changes in this period. For a general discussion, see Acemoglu (2002); Berman, Bound, and Griliches (1994); Berman, Bound, and Machin (1998); Bernard and Jensen (1997); Katz and Murphy (1992); Lee (1999).

45. Another change documented in recent work of Saez is that a large share of the gains to the top 1% of the income distribution came in the form of salary and other forms of payment to top executives. "The evidence suggests that top income earners today are not "rentiers" deriving their incomes from past wealth but rather are "working rich," highly paid employees or new entrepreneurs who have not yet accumulated fortunes comparable to those accumulated during the Gilded Age" (Saez 2013, 5).

46. See ibid. In a related vein, wage and salary income as a share of national income fell in 2010 to its all-time lowest level of 49.9% (for the first time falling below 50%), from a post–World War II high of close to 59% in 1970 (while employee benefits remained at relatively the same share of national income from 1970, about 12%). At the same time, corporate profits rose from about 8.5% of national income in 1970 to 14.2% in 2010. These figures are based on U.S. Department of Commerce, Bureau of Economic Analysis (2011). National income is the sum of employee, proprietor, rental, corporate, interest, and government income less the subsidies paid by government to any of those groups. Analysis of the percentage of gross domestic product shows the same trends: corporate profits after tax hit an all-time high as a percentage of GDP (over 10%), while the share of GDP going to wages and salary fell to an all-time low of 44%.

47. Kenneth Rogoff and Carmen Reinhart have objected that the term "Great Recession" itself is unhelpful since it implies that the recent recession is similar to typical downturns, just a particularly deep one. Instead, they refer to it as the "second great contraction" (the first being the Great Depression). See Reinhart and Rogoff (2009).

48. Empirical research on the relation of employment and output growth in the 1970s and 1980s tended to show lower employment response to increases in output than expected by macroeconomic models. There are multiple reasons this might be the case, including biases in the data used to estimate employment/output relationships; use of labor for other purposes during downturns that are not easily measured;

or the practice of firms keeping on labor (hoarding) even where it is not needed. In a sample of U.S. manufacturing establishments, Fay and Medoff (1985) found evidence that a significant percentage of workers were kept on despite downturns.

49. Annette Bernhardt, the author of the National Employment Law Project study, used data drawn from the Current Population Survey, a representative household survey that reports wages, hours, and occupations (coded into 366 occupational groups). The 366 occupations used in the analysis were grouped into the three wage categories based on a ranking of median wages in each occupation, from low to high. Employment declines during the recession cover the period from the first quarter of 2008 to the first quarter of 2010; employment growth in the recovery was calculated for the first quarter of 2010 until the first quarter of 2012. See National Employment Law Project (2012). See also Sum and McLaughlin (2011), which looks at similar issues at an earlier point in the recovery.

50. See Autor and Dorn (2009); Autor (2010); and Autor, Levy, and Murnane (2003). This analysis also goes back to the earlier explanations of the widening of the wage premium arising from college education (which has flattened in recent years) and for more advanced degrees. While the growth in demand for nonroutine, manual jobs has increased, so too has the supply of workers (in part drawn from the supply of workers who would have gone into routine, manual jobs previously). This accounts for continuing wage stagnation in these low-wage jobs. On the other hand, the growth in demand for nonroutine, abstract jobs continues to outpace the growth of college- and post-college- educated supply, pushing wages for those jobs upward. See also Levy and Murnane (2005) for an extended discussion of changes in skill requirements in the labor market. Goos, Manning, and Salomons (2009) show similar trends in job growth among the three occupational wage groupings in Europe.

51. This area is ripe with research questions, including the relative contribution of job polarization as posed by Autor and others versus fissuring as posed here on changes in the overall wage structure. Stay tuned.

12. A Path Forward

Epigraphs: Sarvadi, an industry attorney for logistics providers with Keller and Heckman, LLP, quoted in Bloomberg BNA, "California Warehouse Workers Allege Unsafe Working Conditions at Wal-Mart Warehouse," *Occupational Safety and Health Reporter* 42, no. 28, July 12, 2012, 628; Reynolds quoted in PBS *Frontline* episode "Anatomy of a Cell Tower Death" (originally aired on June 6, 2012) and three associated articles on the ProPublica site, all available via http://www.pbs.org/wgbh/pages/frontline/social-issues/cell-tower-deaths/anatomy-of-a-cell-tower-death/. Prophet quoted in Keith Bradsher and Charles Duhigg, "Signs of Changes Taking Hold in Electronics Factories in China," *New York Times,* December 26, 2012 (http://www.nytimes.com/2012/12/27/business/signs-of-changes-taking-hold-in-electronics-factories-in-china.html, accessed January 15, 2013).

References

Abernathy, Frederick, Kermit Baker, Kent Colton, and David Weil. 2012. *Bigger Isn't Necessarily Better: Lessons from the Harvard Home Builder Study.* Lanham, MD: Lexington Books.

Abernathy, Frederick, John T. Dunlop, Janice Hammond, and David Weil. 1999. *A Stitch in Time: Lean Retailing and the Transformation of Manufacturing—Lessons from the Apparel and Textile Industries.* New York: Oxford University Press.

Abernathy, Frederick, and Anthony Volpe. 2012. "Technology and Public Policy: The Preconditions of the Retail Revolution." In Gary Hamilton, Benjamin Senauer, and Misha Petrovic, eds., *How Retailers Are Reshaping the Global Economy.* New York: Oxford University Press.

Abraham, Katherine, and Susan Taylor. 1996. "Firms' Use of Outside Contractors: Theory and Evidence." *Journal of Labor Economics* 14, no. 3: 394–424.

Acemoglu, Daron. 2002. "Technical Change, Inequality, and the Labor Market. *Journal of Economic Literature* 40, no. 1: 7–72.

Adler, Paul. 2003. "Making the HR Outsourcing Decision." *Sloan Management Review* 45, no. 1: 53–60.

Alexander, Charlotte. 2012. "The Law and Economics of Peripheral Labor: A Poultry Industry Case Study." *Berkeley Journal of Employment and Labor Law* (forthcoming).

Appelbaum, Eileen, and Rose Batt. 2012. "A Primer on Private Equity at Work." *Challenge* 55, no. 5: 5–38.

Appelbaum, Eileen, Annette Bernhardt, and Richard Murnane, eds. 2003. *Low Wage America: How Employers Are Reshaping Opportunity in the Workplace.* New York: Russell Sage Foundation.

Arlen, Jennifer, and W. Bentley MacLeod. 2005. "Beyond Master-Servant: A Critique of Vicarious Liability." In *Exploring Tort Law,* edited by Stuart Madden. New York: Cambridge University Press, 111–142.

Appleton, William C., and Joe Baker. 1984. "The Effect of Unionization on Safety in Bituminous Deep Mines." *Journal of Labor Research* 4, no. 2: 139–47.

Ashenfelter, Orley, Henry Farber, and Michael Ransom. 2010. "Labor Market Monopsony." *Journal of Labor Economics* 28, no. 2: 203–210.

Ashenfelter, Orley, and Robert Smith. 1979. "Compliance with the Minimum Wage Law." *Journal of Political Economy* 87, no. 2: 333–350.

Autor, David. 2010. "The Polarization of Job Opportunities in the US Labor Market: Implications for Employment and Earnings." Center for American Progress / The Hamilton Project.

Autor, David, and David Dorn. 2009. "Inequality and Specialization: The Growth of Low-Skilled Service Employment in the United States." Cambridge, MA: National Bureau of Economic Research Working Paper 15150.

Autor, David, Frank Levy, and Richard J. Murnane. 2003. "The Skill Content of Recent Technological Change: An Empirical Exploration." *Quarterly Journal of Economics* 116, no. 4: 1449–1492.

Baker, George, and Thomas Hubbard. 2003. "Make versus Buy in Trucking: Asset Ownership, Job Design, and Information." *American Economic Review* 93, no. 3: 551–572.

Baldwin, Carliss, and Kim Clark. 1997. "Managing in an Age of Modularity." *Harvard Business Review* 75, no. 5: 84–93.

Barthélemy, Jérôme. 2001. "The Hidden Costs of IT Outsourcing." *MIT Sloan Management Review* 42, no. 3: 60–69.

Batt, Rosemary, David Holman, and Ursula Holtgrewe. 2009. "The Globalization of Service Work: Comparative Institutional Perspectives on Call Centers." *Industrial and Labor Relations Review* 62, no. 4: 453–487.

Batt, Rosemary, and Hiroatsu Nohara. 2009. "How Institutions and Business Strategies Affect Wages: A Cross National Study of Call Centers." *Industrial and Labor Relations Review* 62, no. 4: 533–552.

Bebchuk, Lucian, and Jesse Fried. 2004. *Pay without Performance: The Unfulfilled Promise of Executive Compensation.* Cambridge, MA: Harvard University Press.

Becker, Gary. 1964. *Human Capital: A Theoretical and Empirical Analysis with Special Reference to Education.* New York: Columbia University Press.

———. 1968. "Crime and Punishment: An Economic Approach." *Journal of Political Economy* 76, no. 1: 169–217.

Berle, Adolph, and Gardiner C. Means. 1932. *The Modern Corporation and Private Property.* New York: Harcourt, Brace and World.

Berlinski, Samuel. 2008. "Wages and Contracting Out: Does the Law of One Price Hold?" *British Journal of Industrial Relations* 46, no. 1: 59–75.

Berman, Eli, John Bound, and Zvi Griliches. 1994. "Changes in the Demand for Skilled Labor within US Manufacturing Industries: Evidence from the Annual Survey of Manufacturing." *Quarterly Journal of Economics* 109, no. 2: 367–397.

Berman, Eli, John Bound, and Stephen Machin. 1998. "Implications of Skill-Biased Technological Change: International Evidence." *Quarterly Journal of Economics* 113, no. 4: 1245–1279.

Bernard, Andrew, and J. Bradford Jensen. 1997. "Exporters, Skill-Upgrading, and the Wage Gap." *Journal of International Economics* 42, nos. 1–2: 3–31.

Bernhardt, Annette, Ruth Milkman, Nik Theodore, Douglas Heckathorn, Mirabei Auer, James DeFillipis, Ana Luz Gonzalez, Victor Narro, Jason Perelshteyn, Diana Polson, and Michael Spiller. 2009. *Broken Laws, Unprotected Workers: Violations of Employment in Labor Laws in America's Cities.* Center for Urban Economic Development, University of Illinois Chicago / National Employment Law Project / UCLA Institute for Research on Labor and Employment.

Bernstein, Peter. 1992. *Capital Ideas: The Improbable Origins of Modern Wall Street.* New York: The Free Press.

Bewley, Truman. 1999. *Why Wages Don't Fall during a Recession.* Cambridge, MA: Harvard University Press.

Blair, Margaret. 1995. *Ownership and Control: Rethinking Corporate Governance for the Twenty-First Century.* Washington, DC: Brookings Institution.

Blair, Roger D., and Francine Lafontaine. 2005. *The Economics of Franchising.* New York: Cambridge University Press.

Blanchflower, David, and Alex Bryson. 2010. "The Wage Impact of Trade Unions in the UK Public and Private Sectors." *Economica* 77, no. 305: 92–109.

Blank, Rebecca, and David Card. 1991. "Recent Trends in Insured and Uninsured Employment: Is There an Explanation?" *Quarterly Journal of Economics* 106, no. 4: 1157–1189.

Blinder, Alan. 2006. "Offshoring: The Next Industrial Revolution?" *Foreign Affairs* 85, no. 2: 113–128.

Bluestone, Barry, and Bennett Harrison. 1990. *The Great U-Turn: Corporate Restructuring and the Polarizing of America.* New York: Basic Books.

Boal, William, and Michael Ransom. 1997. "Monopsony in the Labor Market." *Journal of Economic Literature* 35, no. 1: 86–112.

Bobo, Kim. 2011. *Wage Theft in America: Why Millions of Americans Are Not Getting Paid and What We Can Do About It.* Rev. ed. New York: The New Press.

Boushey, Heather, Shawn Fremstad, Rachel Gragg, and Margy Waller. 2007. "Understanding Low-Wage Work in the United States." Center for Economic Policy and Research Policy Paper, March.

Bowles, Samuel. 1973. "Understanding Unequal Economic Opportunity." *American Economic Review* 63, no. 2: 346–356.

Bradach, Jeffrey. 1998. *Franchise Organizations.* Boston: Harvard Business School Press.

Brenner, Joël Glenn. 2000. *The Emperors of Chocolate: Inside the Secret World of Hershey and Mars.* New York: Broadway Books.

Bricker, Jesse, Arthur Kennickell, Kevin Moore, and John Sabelhaus. 2012.
    "Changes in U.S. Family Finances from 2007 to 2010: Evidence from the
    Survey of Consumer Finances." *Federal Reserve Bulletin* 98, no. 2: 1–80.
Brody, David. 1993. *In Labor's Cause: Main Themes on the History of the American
    Worker.* New York: Oxford University Press.
Brown, Charles, James Hamilton, and James Medoff. 1990. *Employers Large and
    Small.* Cambridge, MA: Harvard University Press.
Brown, Charles, and James Medoff. 1989. "The Employer Size-Wage Effect."
    Journal of Political Economy 97, no. 5: 1027–1059.
Brown, M., A. Falk, and Ernst Fehr. 2004. "Relational Contracts and the Nature of
    Market Interactions." *Econometrica* 72, no. 4: 747–780.
Brynjolfson, Eric, and Andrew McAfee. 2011. *Race against the Machine: How the
    Digital Revolution Is Accelerating Innovation, Driving Productivity, and Irrevers-
    ibly Transforming Employment and the Economy.* Lexington, MA: Digital
    Frontier Press.
Budd, John. 2010. "When Do U.S. Workers First Experience Unionization?
    Implications for Revitalizing the Labor Movement." *Industrial Relations* 49, no.
    2: 209–225.
Budd, John, and Angela Brey. 2003. "Unions and Family Leave: Early Experience
    under the Family Medical Leave Act." *Labor Studies Journal* 28, no. 3: 85–105.
Budd, John, and Brian McCall. 1997. "The Effect of Unions on the Receipt of
    Unemployment Insurance Benefits." *Industrial and Labor Relations Review* 50,
    no. 3: 478–492.
Buessing, Marric. 2013. "Vertical Integration in the Mining Industry: An Incom-
    plete Contracts Approach." Working paper, Boston University Department of
    Economics.
Buessing, Marric, and David Weil. 2013. "Health and Safety Consequences of
    Mine-Level Contracting and Vertical Integration." Working paper, Boston
    University School of Management / Department of Economics.
Butler, Richard, and John Worrall. 1983. "Workers' Compensation: Benefit and Injury
    Claims Rates in the Seventies." *Review of Economics and Statistics* 65: 580–589.
Camerer, Colin. 2003. *Behavioral Game Theory.* Princeton, NJ: Princeton Univer-
    sity Press.
Cappelli, Peter. 1999. "Career Jobs Are Dead." *California Management Review* 42,
    no. 1: 146–167.
Cappelli, Peter, and Monika Hamori. 2008. "Are Franchises Bad Employers?"
    Industrial and Labor Relations Review 61, no. 2: 147–162.
Card, David, and Alan Krueger. 1995. *Myth and Measurement: The New Economics of
    the Minimum Wage.* Princeton, NJ: Princeton University Press.
Carpenter, Jesse. 1972. *Competition and Collective Bargaining in the Needle Trades.*
    Ithaca, NY: New York State School of Labor and Industrial Relations.

Carré, Françoise, and Randall Wilson. 2004. "The Social and Economic Costs of Employee Misclassification in Construction." Report of the Construction Policy Research Center, Labor and Worklife Program, Harvard Law School and Harvard School of Public Health.

Chandler, Alfred D. 1977. *The Visible Hand: The Managerial Revolution in American Business.* Cambridge, MA: Harvard University Press.

————. 1980. *Giant Enterprise: Ford, General Motors, and the Automobile Industry.* New York: Arno Press.

————. 1990. *Scale and Scope: The Dynamics of Industrial Capitalism.* Cambridge, MA: Harvard University Press.

Chandler, Alfred D., and Richard Tedlow. 1985. *The Coming of Managerial Capitalism: A Casebook on the History of American Economic Institutions.* Homewood, IL: Irwin.

Christensen, Clayton. 2006. *The Innovator's Dilemma.* New York: Harper Business.

Cleeland, Nancy. 2009. "Dark and Bitter." *American Prospect,* October 2 (available at http://prospect.org/article/dark-and-bitter-0).

Cline, William. 1997. *Trade and Income Distribution.* Washington, DC: Institute for International Economics.

Coase, Ronald. 1937. "The Nature of the Firm." *Economica* 4: 386–405.

Cohan, William. 2009. *House of Cards: A Tale of Hubris and Wretched Excess on Wall Street.* New York: Doubleday.

Commons, John R. 1904. "The New York Building Trades." *Quarterly Journal of Economics* 18, no. 3: 409–436.

————. 1935. *History of Labor in the United States, 1896–1932.* Vol. 3. New York: Macmillan.

Computer Economics. 2000. *1999 Outsourcing Trends and Outsourcing Statistics.* Irvine, CA: Computer Economics Inc.

————. 2012. *2010/2011 Outsourcing Trends and Outsourcing Statistics.* Irvine, CA: Computer Economics Inc.

Congressional Budget Office. 2011. *Trends in the Distribution of Household Income between 1979 and 2007.* Washington, DC: Government Printing Office.

Cowie, Jefferson. 1999. *Capital Moves: RCA's Seventy-Year Quest for Cheap Labor.* Ithaca, NY: Cornell University Press.

Crandall, Grant, Sarah Starrett, and Douglas Parker. 1998. "Hiding behind the Corporate Veil: Employer Abuse of the Corporate Form to Avoid or Deny Workers' Collectively Bargained and Statutory Rights." *West Virginia Law Review* 100: 537–599.

Curry, James, and Martin Kenney. 2004. "The Organizational and Geographic Configuration of the Personal Computer Value Chain." In *Locating Global Advantage: Industry Dynamics in the International Economy,* edited by Martin Kenney and Richard Florida. Stanford, CA: Stanford University Press, 113–141.

Dalzell, Robert. 1987. *Enterprising Elite: The Boston Associates and the World They Made.* Cambridge, MA: Harvard University Press.

Davidov, Guy. 2004. "Joint Employer Status in Triangular Employment Relationships." *British Journal of Industrial Relations* 42: 727–746.

———. 2006. "The reports of my death are greatly exaggerated": "Employee" as a Viable (though Overly-Used) Legal Concept." In *Boundaries and Frontiers of Labour Law: Goals and Means in the Regulation of Work,* edited by Guy Davidov and Brian Langille. Oxford: Hart Publishing, 133–152.

Davidov, Guy, and Brian Langille. 2004. *Boundaries and Frontiers of Labour Law: Goals and Means in the Regulation of Work.* Oxford: Hart Publishing.

Davis, Gerald. 2009. *Managed by the Markets: How Finance Reshaped America.* New York: Oxford University Press.

———. 2013. "After the Corporation." *Politics and Society* (forthcoming).

Davis, Steven, John Haltiwanger, Ron Jarmin, Josh Lerner, and Javier Miranda. 2009. "Private Equity, Jobs, and Productivity." In *Globalization of Alternative Investments Working Papers: Global Impact of Private Equity 2009,* edited by A. Gurung and Josh Lerner. New York: World Economic Forum.

———. 2011. "Private Equity and Employment." Cambridge, MA: National Bureau of Economic Research Working Paper 17399.

DeChiara, Peter. 1995. "The Right to Know: An Argument for Informing Employees of Their Rights under the National Labor Relations Act." *Harvard Journal on Legislation* 32: 431–471.

Dey, Matthew, Susan Houseman, and Anne Polivka. 2010. "What Do We Know about Contracting Out in the United States? Evidence from Household and Establishment Surveys." In *Essay in Labor in the New Economy,* edited by Katherine Abraham, James Spletzer, and Michael Harper. Chicago: University of Chicago Press, 267–304.

Dobbin, Frank, and Erin Kelly. 2007. "How to Stop Harassment: Professional Construction of Legal Compliance in Organizations." *American Journal of Sociology* 112, no. 4: 1203–1243.

Dobbin, Frank, and John Sutton. 1998. "The Strength of a Weak State: The Rights Revolution and the Rise of Human Resources Management Divisions." *American Journal of Sociology* 104, no. 2: 441–476.

Doeringer, Peter, and Michael Piore. 1971. *Internal Labor Markets and Manpower Analysis.* Armonk, NY: M. E. Sharpe.

Dube, Arandajit, and Ethan Kaplan. 2010. "Does Outsourcing Reduce Wages in the Low-Wage Service Occupations? Evidence from Janitors and Guards." *Industrial and Labor Relations Review* 63, no. 2: 287–306.

Dunlop, John T. 1961. "The Industrial Relations System in Construction." In *The Structure of Collective Bargaining,* edited by Arnold Weber. Chicago: University of Chicago Press, 255–277.

———. 1993. *Industrial Relations Systems.* Rev. ed. Cambridge, MA: Harvard Business School Press Classic.

Eckstein, Susan, and Thanh-nghi Nguyen. 2010. "The Making and Transnationalization of an Ethnic Niche: Vietnamese Manicurists. Working paper, Department of Sociology, Boston University.

Edmonds, Rick, Emily Guskin, Tom Rosenstiel, and Amy Mitchell. 2012. *The State of the News Media 2012: An Annual Report on American Journalism.* Pew Research Center, Project on Excellence in Journalism, April 11.

Edwards, Richard. 1993. *Rights at Work: Employment Relations in the Post Union Era.* Washington, DC: Brookings Institution.

Ehrenberg, Ronald, and Paul Schumann. 1982. *Longer Hours or More Jobs? An Investigation of Amending Hours Legislation to Create Employment.* Ithaca, NY: ILR Press.

Ehrenreich, Barbara. 2008. *Nickel and Dimed: On (Not) Getting by in America.* New York: Holt.

Erickcek, George, Susan Houseman, and Arne Kalleberg. 2003. "The Effects of Temporary Services and Contracting Out on Low-Skilled Workers: Evidence from Auto Suppliers, Hospitals, and Public Schools." In *Low Wage America: How Employers Are Reshaping Opportunity in the Workplace,* edited by Eileen Appelbaum, Annette Bernhardt, and Richard Murnane. New York: Russell Sage Foundation, 368–406.

Erickson, Chris, and Daniel Mitchell. 2007. "Monopsony as a Metaphor for the Emerging Post-union Labor Market." *International Labor Review* 146, nos. 3–4: 163–187.

Estlund, Cynthia. 1992. "What Do Workers Want? Employee Interests, Public Interests, and Freedom of Expression under the National Labor Relations Act." *University of Pennsylvania Law Review* 140, no. 3: 921–1004.

———. 2005. "Rebuilding the Law of the Workplace in an Era of Self-Regulation." *Columbia Law Review* 105, no. 2: 319–404.

———. 2008. "Who Mops the Floors at the Fortune 500? Corporate Self-Regulation and the Low-Wage Workplace." *Lewis and Clark Law Review* 12, no. 3: 671–693.

———. 2010. *Regoverning the Workplace: From Self-Regulation to Co-regulation.* New Haven, CT: Yale University Press.

———. 2011. "Just the Facts: The Case for Workplace Transparency." *Stanford Law Review* 63: 351–407.

Eyster, James J., and Jan A. deRoos. 2009. *The Negotiation and Administration of Hotel Management Contracts.* 4th ed. New York: Pearson Custom Publishing.

Farber, Henry, and Kevin Hallock. 2009. "The Changing Relationship between Job Loss Announcements and Stock Prices: 1970–1999." *Labour Economics* 16, no. 1: 1–11.

Fay, Jon, and James Medoff. 1985. "Labor and Output over the Business Cycle: Some Direct Evidence." *American Economic Review* 75, no. 4: 638–655.

Federal Trade Commission. 1969. *Economic Report on Corporate Mergers*, 23. Washington, DC: Government Printing Office.

———. 2001. "Buying a Janitorial Services Franchise." Produced jointly with the Maryland Attorney General's Office. Washington, DC: Federal Trade Commission (available at http://www.ftc.gov/bcp/edu/pubs/consumer/invest/inv15.shtm #how, accessed December 18, 2011).

Feenstra, Robert. 1998. "Integration of Trade and Disintegration of Production in the Global Economy." *Journal of Economic Perspectives* 12, no. 4: 31–50.

Feenstra, Robert, and Gordon Hanson. 1999. "The Impact of Outsourcing and High-Technology Capital on Wages: Estimates for the United States." *Quarterly Journal of Economics* 114, no. 3: 907–940.

Fehr, Ernst, Lorenz Goette, and Christian Zehnder. 2009. "A Behavioral Account of the Labor Market: The Role of Fairness Concerns." *Annual Review of Economics* 1: 355–384.

Fehr, Ernst, and Klaus Schmidt. 1999. "A Theory of Fairness, Competition, and Cooperation." *American Economic Review* 114, no. 3: 177–181.

———. 2002. "Theories of Fairness and Reciprocity." In *Advances in Economics and Econometrics,* edited by Matthias Dewatripont, I. Hansen, and S. Turnovsly. New York: Cambridge University Press, 208–257.

———. 2007. "A Theory of Fairness, Competition, and Cooperation." *Quarterly Journal of Economics* 97, no. 2: 817–868.

Ferguson, Niall. 2008. *The Ascent of Money: A Financial History of the World.* New York: Penguin.

Fine, Janice. 2006. *Worker Centers: Organizing Communities at the Edge of the Dream.* Ithaca, NY: ILR Press / Cornell University Press.

Fine, Janice, and Jennifer Gordon. 2010. "Strengthening Labor Standards Enforcement through Partnerships with Workers' Organizations." *Politics and Society* 38, no. 4: 552–585.

Fishback, Price. 2007. "Seeking Security in the Postwar Era." In *Government and the American Economy: A New History,* edited by Price Fishback. Chicago: University of Chicago Press, 507–518.

Fishback, Price, and Shawn Kantor. 2000. *Prelude to the Welfare State: The Origins of Workers' Compensation.* Chicago: University of Chicago Press.

Foulkes, Fred. 1980. *Personnel Policies in Large Non-union Workplaces.* Englewood Cliffs, NJ: Prentice Hall.

Freeman, Richard. 2007. *America Works: Critical Thoughts on the Exceptional U.S. Labor Market.* New York: Russell Sage Foundation.

Freeman, Richard, and James Medoff. 1984. *What Do Unions Do?* New York: Basic Books.

Freeman, Richard, and Joel Rogers. 1999. *What Workers Want.* Ithaca, NY: ILR Press.

Friedman, Milton. 1970. "The Social Responsibility of Business Is to Increase Profits." *New York Times Magazine,* September 13.

Frydman, Carola, and Dirk Jenter. 2010. "Executive Compensation." *Annual Review of Financial Economics* 2, no. 1: 75–102.

Fung, Archon, Mary Graham, and David Weil. 2007. *Full Disclosure: Perils and Promise of Transparency.* New York: Cambridge University Press.

Fung, Archon, Dara O'Rourke, and Charles Sabel. 2001. "Realizing Labor Standards: How Transparency, Competition, and Sanctions Could Improve Working Conditions Worldwide." *Boston Review* 26, no. 1: 1–20.

Galbraith, John Kenneth. 1971. *The New Industrial State.* 2nd ed. Boston: Houghton Mifflin.

Gazel, Neil. 1990. *Beatrice: From Buildup through Breakup.* Urbana: University of Illinois Press.

Gereffi, Gary, John Humphrey, and Timothy Sturgeon. 2005. "The Governance of Global Value Chains." *Review of International Political Economy* 12, no. 1: 78–104.

Ghilarducci, Teresa. 2008. *When I'm Sixty-Four: The Plot against Pensions and the Plan to Save Them.* Princeton, NJ: Princeton University Press.

Gibson, John, and Steven Stillman. 2009. "Why Do Big Firms Pay Higher Wages? Evidence from an International Database." *Review of Economics and Statistics* 91, no. 1: 213–218.

Gilley, K. M, C. R. Greer, and A. A. Rasheed. 2004. "Human Resource Outsourcing and Organizational Performance in Manufacturing Firms." *Journal of Business Research* 57, no. 2: 232–240.

Glynn, Timothy. 2011. "Taking the Employer out of Employment Law? Accountability for Wage and Hour Violations in an Age of Enterprise Disaggregation." *Employee Rights and Employment Policy Journal* 15, no. 1: 101–135.

Goldin, Claudia. 1986. "Monitoring Costs and Occupational Segregation by Sex: A Historical Analysis." *Journal of Labor Economics* 4, no. 1: 1–27.

Goldin, Claudia, and Robert Margo. 1992. "The Great Compression: The Wage Structure in the United States at Mid-Century." *Quarterly Journal of Economics* 107, no. 1: 1–34.

Goldstein, Bruce, Marc Linder, Laurence Norton, and Catherine Ruckelshaus. 1999. "Enforcing Fair Labor Standards in the Modern American Sweatshop: Rediscovering the Statutory Definition of Employment." *UCLA Law Review* 46: 983–1106.

Gomory, Ralph, and William Baumol. 2000. *Global Trade and Conflicting National Interest.* Cambridge, MA: MIT Press.

Goos, Maarten, Alan Manning, and Anna Salomons. 2009. "The Polarization of the European Labor Market." *American Economic Review Papers and Proceedings* 99, no. 2: 58–63.

Gordon, David, Richard Edwards, and Michael Reich. 1982. *Segmented Work, Divided Workers: The Historical Transformation of Labor in the United States.* New York: Cambridge University Press.

Gordon, Jennifer. 2005. *Suburban Sweatshops: The Fight for Immigrant Rights.* Cambridge, MA: Belknap Press of Harvard University Press.

Greenhouse, Steven. 2008. *The Big Squeeze: Tough Times for the American Worker.* New York: Knopf.

Grossman, Gene, and Elhanan Helpman. 2005. "Outsourcing in a Global Economy." *Review of Economic Studies* 72, no. 1: 135–139.

Grossman, Sanford, and Oliver Hart. 1986. "The Costs and Benefits of Ownership: A Theory of Vertical and Lateral Integration." *Journal of Political Economy* 94, no. 4: 691–719.

Hacker, Jacob. 2006. *The Great Risk Shift: The Assault on American Jobs, Families, Health Care, and Retirement and How You Can Fight Back.* New York: Oxford University Press.

Halla, Martin. 2010. "Tax Morale and Compliance Behavior: First Evidence on a Causal Link." Working paper, Austrian Center for Labor Economics and the Analysis of the Welfare State.

Hallock, Kevin. 2009. "Job Loss and the Fraying of the Implicit Employment Contract." *Journal of Economic Perspectives* 23, no. 4: 69–93.

———. 2012. *Pay: Why People Earn What They Earn and What You Can Do Now to Make More.* New York: Cambridge University Press.

Hart, Bob. 1984. *The Economics of Non-wage Labor Costs.* London: George Allen and Unwin.

Hart, Oliver, and John Moore. 1990. "Property Rights and the Nature of the Firm." *Journal of Political Economy* 98, no. 6: 1119–1158.

Hayes, Robert, and William Abernathy. 1980. "Managing Our Way to Decline." *Harvard Business Review*, July–August, 67–77.

Hellerstein, Judith, Melissa McInerney, and David Neumark. 2011. "Neighbors and Coworkers: The Importance of Residential Labor Market Networks." *Journal of Labor Economics* 29, no. 4: 659–695.

Hirsch, Barry, David Macpherson, and Michael DuMond. 1997. "Workers' Compensation Recipiency in Union and Nonunion Workplaces." *Industrial and Labor Relations Review* 50, no. 2: 213–236.

Hollister, Matissa. 2004. "Does Firm Size Matter Anymore? The New Economy and Firm Size Wage Effect." *American Sociological Review* 69, no. 5: 659–676.

Houseman, Susan. 2001. "Why Employers Use Flexible Staffing Arrangements: Evidence from an Establishment Survey." *Industrial and Labor Relations Review* 55, no. 1: 149–170.

Hsiao, H. I., R. G. M. Kemp, J. G. A. J. van der Vorst, and S. W. F. (Onno) Omta. 2010. "A Classification of Logistic Outsourcing Levels and Their Impact on

Service Performance: Evidence from the Food Processing Industry." *International Journal of Production Economics* 124, no. 1: 75–86.

Hutchins, B. L., and A. Harrison. 1926. *A History of Factory Legislation.* 3rd ed. London: Frank Cass.

International Labour Office. 2006. *Strategies and Practices for Labour Inspection.* Governing Body, 297th Session, GB.297/ESP/3. Geneva: International Labour Office.

Investment Company Institute. 2012. *2012 Investment Company Fact Book.* 52nd ed. www.icifactbook.org.

Jacobs, Jane. 1961. *The Death and Life of Great American Cities.* New York: Vintage.

Jacoby, Neil. 1969. "The Conglomerate Corporation." *The Center Magazine* 2, 1–20.

Jacoby, Sandy. 1999. "Are Career Jobs Headed for Extinction?" *California Management Review* 42, no. 1: 123–145.

James, P., R. Johnstone, M. Quinlan, and D. Walters. 2007. "Regulating Supply Chains to Improve Health and Safety." *Industrial Law Journal* 36, no. 2: 163–187.

Jamieson, Dave. 2011. "The New Blue Collar: Temporary Work, Lasting Poverty, and the American Warehouse." 2011. *Huff Post Business,* December 20 (available at http://www.huffingtonpost.com/2011/12/20/new-blue-collar-temp-warehouses_n _1158490.html?view=print&comm_ref=false, accessed July 18, 2012).

Jensen, Michael, and William Meckling. 1976. "Theory of the Firm: Managerial Behavior, Agency Costs and Ownership Structure." *Journal of Financial Economics* 3, no. 2: 305–360.

Jensen, Michael, and Kevin Murphy. 1990. "Performance Pay and Top-Management Incentives." *Journal of Political Economy* 98, no. 2: 225–264.

Ji, MinWoong. 2010. "Impacts of Multi-unit Franchising on Workplace Compliance Behavior." Working paper, Boston University.

Ji, MinWoong, and David Weil. 2012. "Does Ownership Structure Influence Regulatory Behavior? The Impact of Franchisee Free-Riding on Labor Standards Compliance." Working paper, Boston University.

Jin, Ginger, and Philip Leslie. 2009. "Reputational Incentives for Restaurant Hygiene." *American Economic Journal: Microeconomics* 1, no. 1: 237–267.

Johnson, Simon, and James Kwak. 2011. *Thirteen Bankers: The Wall Street Takeover and the Next Financial Meltdown.* New York: Vintage.

Johnstone, R., C. Mayhew, and M. Quinlan. 2001. "Outsourcing Risk? The Regulation of Occupational Health and Safety Where Subcontractors Are Employed." *Comparative Labor Law and Policy Journal* 22, nos. 3–5: 351–394.

Joiner, Fred. 1942. "Incentive-Wage Plans and Collective Bargaining." *Bulletin of the United States Bureau of Labor Statistics,* no. 717. Washington, DC: Government Printing Office.

Jost, Micah Prieb Stoltzfus. 2011. "Independent Contractors, Employees, and Entrepreneurialism under the National Labor Relations Act: A Worker-by-Worker Approach." *Washington and Lee Law Review* 68, no. 1: 313–373.

Kahn, Shulamit. 1997. "Evidence of Nominal Wage Stickiness from Microdata." *American Economic Review* 87, no. 5: 993–1008.

Kahneman, Daniel. 2011. *Thinking, Fast and Slow.* New York: Farrar, Straus and Giroux.

Kahneman, Daniel, Jack Knetsch, and Richard Thaler. 1986. "Fairness as a Constraint on Profit Seeking: Entitlements in the Market." *American Economic Review* 76, no. 4: 728–741.

Kahneman, Daniel, and Amos Tversky. 1984. "Choices, Values, and Frames." *American Psychologist* 34, no.4: 341-350.

Kalleberg, Arne. 2011. *Good Jobs / Bad Jobs: The Rise of Polarized and Precarious Employment Systems in the United States, 1970s to 2000s.* New York: Russell Sage Foundation.

Kalleberg, Arne, and Peter Marsden. 2005. "Externalizing Organizational Activities: Where and How U.S. Establishments Use Employment Intermediaries." *Socio-Economic Review* 3, no. 3: 389–416.

Katz, Lawrence, and Kevin Murphy. 1992. "Changes in Relative Wages, 1963–1987: Supply and Demand Factors." *Quarterly Journal of Economics* 107, no. 1: 35–78.

Kaufmann, Stuart. 1986. *A Vision of Unity: The History of the Bakery and Confectionery Workers International Union.* Kensington, MD: Bakery, Confectionery, and Tobacco Workers International Union.

Kaufmann, Patrick J., and Francine Lafontaine. 1994. "Costs of Control: The Source of Economic Rents for McDonald's Franchisees." *Journal of Law and Economics* 37, no. 2: 417–453.

Keller, Kevin Lane. 2008. *Strategic Brand Management: Building, Measuring, and Managing Brand Equity.* 3rd ed. Upper Saddle River, NJ: Pearson / Prentice Hall.

Kelling, George, and Catherine Coles. 1996. *Fixing Broken Windows: Restoring Order and Reducing Crime in Our Communities.* New York: Martin Kessler Books / The Free Press.

Kelling, George, and James Q. Wilson. 1982. "The Police and Neighborhood Safety." *The Atlantic,* March, 29–38.

Kenney, Martin, and Richard Florida. 2004. *Locating Global Advantage: Industry Dynamics in the International Economy.* Stanford, CA: Stanford University Press.

Kerr, Clark. 1977. *Labor Markets and Wage Determination: The Balkanization of Labor Markets and Other Essays.* Berkeley: University of California Press, Institute of Industrial Relations.

Kleiner, Morris, and David Weil. 2012. "Evaluating the Efficacy of NLRA Remedies—Analysis and Comparison with Other Workplace Penalty Policies."

In *Research Handbook on the Economics of Labor and Employment Law,* edited by Cynthia Estlund and Michael Wachter. Cheltenham, UK: Edward Elgar, 209–247.

Kletzer, Lori. 2001. *Job Loss from Imports: Measuring the Costs.* Washington, DC: Institute for International Economics.

———. 2002. *Imports, Exports, and Jobs.* Kalamazoo, MI: Upjohn Institute for Employment Research.

Kochan, Thomas. 2005. *Restoring the American Dream: A Working Families' Agenda for America.* Cambridge, MA: MIT Press.

Koller, Frank. 2010. *Spark: Lessons from Lincoln Electric's Unique Guaranteed Employment Program.* New York: Public Affairs.

Krugman, Paul. 2007. *The Conscience of a Liberal.* New York: W. W. Norton.

Lafontaine, Francine, and Patrick J. Kaufmann. 1994. "The Evolution of Ownership Patterns in Franchise Systems." *Journal of Retailing* 70, no. 2: 97–113.

Lafontaine, Francine, and Kathryn L. Shaw. 1999. "The Dynamics of Franchise Contracting: Evidence from Panel Data." *Journal of Political Economy* 107, no. 5: 1041–1080.

———. 2005. "Targeting Managerial Control: Evidence from Franchising." *RAND Journal of Economics* 36, no. 1: 131–150.

Lawrence, Benjamin, and Patrick Kaufmann. 2011. "Identity in Franchise Systems: The Role of Franchisee Associations." *Journal of Retailing* 87, no. 3: 285–305.

Lazonick, William. 2010. "Innovative Business Models and Varieties of Capitalism: Financialization of the US Corporation." *Business History Review* 84, no. 4: 675–702.

Lécuyer, Normand. 2002. *New Forms of Labour Administration: Actors in Development.* Geneva: International Labour Office.

Lee, David. 1999. "Wage Inequality in the United States during the 1980s: Rising Dispersion or Falling Minimum Wage." *Quarterly Journal of Economics* 114, no. 3: 941–1024.

Lemann, Nicholas. 2012. "Transaction Man: Mormonism, Private Equity, and the Making of a Candidate." *The New Yorker,* October 1, 38–52.

Leonard, James. 2000. "Hot Goods Temporary Restraining Orders under the Fair Labor Standards Act in the Agricultural Sector of the Economy: A Manual for Legal Assistance Programs." Unpublished manuscript.

Lerner, Stephen, Jill Hurst, and Glenn Adler. 2008. "Fighting and Winning in the Outsourced Economy: Justice for Janitors at the University of Miami." In *The Gloves-Off Economy: Workplace Standards at the Bottom of America's Labor Market,* edited by Annette Bernhardt, Heather Boushey, Laura Dresser, and Chris Tilly. Champaign, IL: Labor and Employment Relations Association, 243–267.

Levinson, Marc. 2011. *The Great A&P and the Struggle for Small Business in America.* New York: Hill and Wang.

Levitt, Peggy. 2001. *The Transnational Villagers*. Berkeley: University of California Press.

Levy, Frank, and Richard J. Murnane. 2005. *The New Division of Labor*. Princeton, NJ: Princeton University Press.

Lewis, Michael. 2009. *Panic! The Story of Modern Financial Insanity*. New York: W. W. Norton.

———. 2010. *The Big Short: Inside the Doomsday Machine*. New York: W. W. Norton.

Liu, Peng. 2010. "Real Estate Investment Trusts: Performance, Recent Findings, and Future Directions." *Cornell Hospitality Quarterly* 51, no. 3: 415–428.

Livesay, Harold. 1975. *Andrew Carnegie and the Rise of Big Business*. Boston: Little, Brown.

Locke, Richard. 2013. *Improving Labor Rights in a Global Economy*. New York: Cambridge University Press.

Locke, Richard, Matthew Amengual, and Akshay Mangla. 2009. "Virtue out of Necessity? Compliance, Commitment and the Improvement of Labor Conditions in Global Supply Chains." *Politics and Society* 27, no. 2: 319–351.

Locke, Richard, Greg Distelhorst, Timea Pal, and Hiram Samel. 2012. "Production Goes Global, Standards Stay Local: Private Labor Regulation in the Global Electronics Industry." MIT Political Science Department Research Paper No. 2012–1.

Locke, Richard, Fei Qin, and Alberto Brause. 2007. "Does Monitoring Improve Labor Standards? Lessons from Nike." *Industrial and Labor Relations Review* 61, no. 1: 3–31.

Locke, Richard, and Monica Romis. 2007. "Improving Work Conditions in a Global Supply Chain." *Sloan Management Review* 48, no. 2: 54–62.

MacDuffie, John Paul, and Takahiro Fujimoto. 2010. "Why Dinosaurs Will Keep Ruling the Auto Industry: The Complexity Revolution." *Harvard Business Review* 88, no. 6: 23–25.

MacDuffie, John Paul, and Susan Helper. 2007. "Collaboration in Supply Chains: With and without Trust." In *The Firm as Collaborative Community*, edited by Charles Heckscher and Paul Adler. New York: Oxford University Press, 416–466.

Manning, Alan. 2003. *Monopsony in Motion: Imperfect Competition in Labor Markets*. Princeton, NJ: Princeton University Press.

Medoff, James, and Katherine Abraham. 1980. "Experience, Performance, and Earnings." *Quarterly Journal of Economics* 95, no. 4: 703–736.

Metcalf, David. 2008. "Why Has the British National Minimum Wage Had Little or No Impact?" *Journal of Industrial Relations* 50, no. 3: 489–511.

Milgrom, Paul. 1988. "Employment Contracts, Influence Activities, and Efficient Organization Design." *Journal of Political Economy* 96, no. 1: 42–60.

Milkman, Ruth. 2006. *LA Story: Immigrant Workers and the Future of the U.S. Labor Movement.* New York: Russell Sage Foundation.

Mines, Richard, and Jeffrey Avina. 1992. "Immigrants and Labor Standards: The Case of California Janitors." In *U.S.-Mexico Relations: Labor Market Interdependence,* edited by Jorge Bustamante, Clark Reynolds, and Raul Hinojosa-Ojeda. Stanford, CA: Stanford University Press.

Mishel, Lawrence, Josh Bivens, Elise Gould, and Heidi Shierholz. 2013. *The State of Working America.* 12th ed. Ithaca, NY: Cornell University Press.

Mookherjee, Dilip, and Masatoshi Tsumagari. 2004. "The Organization of Supplier Networks: Effects of Delegation and Intermediation." *Econometrica* 72, no. 4: 1179–1219.

Morantz, Alison. 2011. "Does Unionization Strengthen Regulatory Enforcement? An Empirical Study of the Mine Safety and Health Administration." *New York University Journal of Legislation and Public Policy* 14, no. 3: 697–727.

Moritz, Michael. 1984. *The Little Kingdom.* New York: William Morrow.

Morris, Charles. 1989. "NLRB Protection in the Nonunion Workplace: A Glimpse of the General Theory of Section 7 Conduct." *University of Pennsylvania Law Review* 137: 1673–1754.

National Employment Law Project. 2004. "Subcontracted Workers: The Outsourcing of Rights and Responsibilities." New York: National Employment Law Project, March.

———. 2010. "How Do Workers Make Complaints about Working Conditions? Findings from the 2008 Unregulated Work Survey." NELP Policy Paper, June (available at http://www.nelp.org/page/-/Justice/2010/ComplaintMethodsFact Sheet2010.pdf?nocdn=1, accessed December 14, 2011).

———. 2012. "The Low-Wage Recovery and Growing Inequality." Data brief (available at http://www.nelp.org/page/Job_Creation/LowWageRecovery2012 .pdf?nocdn=1, accessed September 3, 2012).

Oi, Walter. 1983. "The Fixed Employment Costs of Specialized Labor." In *The Measurement of Labor Costs,* edited by Jack Triplett. Chicago: University Chicago Press, 63–122.

Olson, Mancur. 1965. *The Logic of Collective Action: Public Goods and the Theory of Groups.* Cambridge, MA: Harvard University Press.

O'Neill, John, and Anna Mattila. 2006. "Strategic Hotel Development and Position: The Effect of Revenue Drivers on Profitability." *Cornell Hotel and Restaurant Administration Quarterly* 47, no. 2: 146–154.

———. 2010. "Hotel Brand Strategy." *Cornell Hospitality Quarterly* 51, no. 1: 27–34.

O'Neill, John, and Q. Xiao. 2006. "The Role of Brand Affiliation in Hotel Market Value." *Cornell Hotel and Restaurant Administration Quarterly* 47, no. 3: 210–223.

Organization for Economic Cooperation and Development. 2012. *Employment Outlook 2012.* Directorate of Employment, Labour and Social Affairs. Paris: OECD.

O'Rourke, Dara. 2003. "Outsourcing Regulation: Analyzing Nongovernmental Systems of Labor Standards and Monitoring." *Policy Studies Journal* 31, no. 1: 1–29.

Osterman, Paul, and Beth Shulman. 2011. *Good Jobs America: Making Work Better for Everyone.* New York: Russell Sage Foundation.

Ou, Charles, and Victoria Williams. 2009. "Lending to Small Businesses by Financial Institutions in the United States." In *Small Business in Focus: Finance; A Compendium of Research.* Washington, DC: Small Business Administration's Office of Advocacy, 9–38.

Perritt, Henry. 1988. "Should Some Independent Contractors Be Redefined as Employees under Labor Law?" *Villanova Law Review* 33, no. 6: 989–1041.

Perrow, Charles. 1984. *Normal Accidents: Living with High-Risk Technologies.* New York: Basic Books.

Pfeffer, Jeffrey. 1998. *The Human Equation: Building Profits by Putting People First.* Boston: Harvard Business School Press.

Picketty, Thomas, and Emmanuel Saez. 2003. "Income Inequality in the United States, 1913–1998." *Quarterly Journal of Economics* 118, no. 1: 1–39.

Piore, Michael, and Andrew Schrank. 2008. "Toward Managed Flexibility: The Revival of Labor Inspection in the Latin World." *International Labor Review* 147, no. l: 1–23.

Pires, Roberto. 2008. "Promoting Sustainable Compliance: Styles of Labor Inspection and Compliance Outcomes in Brazil." *International Labour Review* 147, nos. 2–3: 199–229.

Polinsky, A. Mitchell, and Steven Shavell. 2000. "The Economic Theory of Public Enforcement of Law." *Journal of Economic Literature* 38, no. 1:45–76.

Prahalad, C. K., and Gary Hamel. 1990. "The Core Competence of the Corporation." *Harvard Business Review,* May–June: 79–91.

Quinn, James Brian. 2000. "Outsourcing Innovation: The New Engine of Growth." *Sloan Management Review* 41, no. 4: 3–28.

Quinn, James Brian, T. Doorley, and P. C. Paquette. 1990. "Technology in Services: Rethinking Strategic Focus." *Sloan Management Review* 31, no. 2: 79–87.

Quinn, James Brian, and Frederick Hilmer. 1994. "Strategic Outsourcing." *Sloan Management Review* 35, no. 4: 43–55.

Ransom, Michael, and Ronald Oaxaca. 2010. "New Market Power Models and Sex Differences in Pay." *Journal of Labor Economics* 28, no. 2: 267–315.

Rebitzer, James. 1995. "Job Safety and Contract Workers in the Petrochemical Industry." *Industrial Relations* 34, no. 1: 40–57.

Rebitzer, James, and Lowell Taylor. 2011. "Extrinsic Rewards and Intrinsic Motives: Standard and Behavioral Approaches to Agency and Labor Markets." *Handbook of Labor Economics.* Amsterdam: Elsevier.

Reich, Michael, David Gordon, and Richard Edwards. 1973. "A Theory of Labor Market Segmentation." *American Economic Review* 63, no. 2: 359–365.

Reinhart, Carmen, and Kenneth Rogoff. 2009. *This Time Is Different: Eight Centuries of Financial Folly.* Princeton, NJ: Princeton University Press.

Rogers, Brishen. 2010. "Toward Third-Party Liability for Wage Theft." *Berkeley Journal of Employment and Labor Law* 30, no. 1: 1–64.

Rosen, Sherwin. 1988. "Implicit Contracts: A Survey." *Journal of Economic Literature* 25, no. 4: 1144–1175.

Ruckelshaus, Cathy. 2008. "Labor's Wage War." *Fordham Urban Law Journal* 35, no. 2: 373–404.

Saez, Emmanuel. 2013. "Striking It Richer: The Evolution of Top Incomes in the United States (Updated Data on Income Inequality Including 2011 Estimates)." Working paper, University of California at Berkeley (available at http://elsa.berkeley .edu/~saez/TabFig2011prel.xls).

Samuelson, Paul. 2004. "Where Ricardo and Mill Rebut and Confirm Arguments of Mainstream Economists Supporting Globalization." *Journal of Economic Perspectives* 18, no. 2: 135–146.

Schiller, Zach, and Sarah DeCarlo. 2010. "Wage Theft: Survey of the States." Report of Policy Matters Ohio, Cleveland, OH.

Seligman, Joel. 1985. "The SEC and Accounting: A Historical Perspective." *Journal of Comparative Business and Capital Market Law* 7: 241–266.

———. 1995. *The Transformation of Wall Street.* Boston: Northeastern University Press.

Shapiro, Carl, and Hal Varian. 1999. *Information Rules: A Strategic Guide to the Network Economy.* Boston: Harvard Business School Press.

Silverstein, Michael, and Neil Fiske. 2005. *Trading Up: Why Consumers Want New Luxury Goods—and How Companies Create Them.* New York: Portfolio Book.

Skerry, Peter. 2008. "Day Laborers and Dock Workers: Casual Labor Markets and Immigration Policy." *Society* 45, no. 1: 46–52.

Slichter, Sumner, James Healy, and Robert Livernash. 1960. *The Impact of Collective Bargaining on Management.* Washington, DC: Brookings Institution.

Smith, Robert. 1979. "The Impact of OSHA on Manufacturing Injury Rates." *Journal of Human Resources* 14, no. 1: 145–170.

Staiger, Douglas, Joanne Spetz, and Ciraran Phibbs. 2010. "Is There Monopsony in the Labor Market? Evidence from a Natural Experiment." *Journal of Labor Economics* 28, no. 2: 211–236.

Stark, Oded, and Walter Hyll. 2011. "On the Economic Architecture of the Workplace: Repercussions of Social Comparisons among Heterogeneous Workers." *Journal of Labor Economics* 29, no. 2: 349–375.

Stigler, George. 1970. "The Optimum Enforcement of Laws." *Journal of Political Economy* 78, no. 3: 526–536.

Stiglitz, Joseph. 2012. *The Price of Inequality: How Today's Divided Society Endangers Our Future*. New York: W. W. Norton.

Stone, Katherine. 2004. *From Widgets to Digits: Employment Regulation for the Changing Workplace*. New York: Cambridge University Press.

———. 2006. "Legal Protections for Atypical Employees: Employment Law for Workers without Workplaces and Employees without Employers." *Berkeley Journal of Employment and Labor Law* 27, no. 2: 251–281.

Sturgeon, Timothy, and Richard Florida. 2004. "Globalization, Deverticalization, and Employment in the Motor Vehicle Industry." In *Locating Global Advantage: Industry Dynamics in the International Economy,* edited by Martin Kenney and Richard Florida. Stanford, CA: Stanford University Press, 52–81.

Sum, Andrew, and Joseph McLaughlin. 2011. "Who Has Benefited from the Post–Great Recession Recovery?" Working paper, Center for Labor Market Studies, Northeastern University (July).

Sunstein, Cass, Daniel Kahnemann, David Schkade, and Ilana Ritov. "Predictably Incoherent Judgments." *Stanford Law Review* 54: 1153–1215.

Thaler, Richard, and Cass Sunstein. 2008. *Nudge: Improving Decisions about Health, Wealth, and Happiness*. New Haven: Yale University Press.

Theodore, Nik. 2010. "Realigning Labor: Toward a Framework for Collaboration between Labor Unions and Day Labor Worker Centers." Special report, Neighborhood Funders Group.

Theodore, Nik, Edwin Melendez, Abel Valenzuela Jr., and Ana Luz Gonzalez. 2008. "Day Labor and Workplace Abuses in the Residential Construction Industry: Conditions in the Washington, DC Region." In *The Gloves-Off Economy: Workplace Standards at the Bottom of America's Labor Market,* edited by Annette Bernhardt, Heather Boushey, Laura Dresser, and Chris Tilly. Champaign, IL: University of Illinois Press, 91–109.

Thornton, Dorothy, Neil Gunningham, and Robert Kagan. 2005. "General Deterrence and Corporate Environmental Behavior." *Law and Policy* 27, no. 2: 262–288.

Torgler, Benno. 2006. "The Importance of Faith: Tax Morale and Religiosity," *Journal of Economic Behavior and Organization* 61, no. 1: 81–109.

Tversky, Amos, and Daniel Kahneman. 1974. "Judgment under Uncertainty: Heuristics and Biases." *Science* 185, no. 4157: 1125–1131.

U.S. Department of Commerce, Bureau of Economic Analysis. 2011. *National Income and Product Accounts.* http://www.bea.gov/national/index.htm#gdp.

U.S. Department of Labor. 1998a. "Full Hot Goods Compliance Program Agreement." DOL Form FCPA(AB). CP1. Washington, DC: Wage and Hour Division, U.S. Department of Labor.

———. 1998b. "Protecting America's Garment Workers: A Monitoring Guide." Washington, DC: Department of Labor. October.

———. 2008. *MSHA Handbook Series.* Mine Safety and Health Administration. Handbook Number PH08-I-1. Washington, DC: Government Printing Office.

U.S. Department of Labor, Bureau of Labor Statistics. 1975. *Handbook of Labor Statistics.* Bulletin 1865. Washington, DC: Government Printing Office.

———. 1994. *Employment and Earnings,* vol. 41, January. Washington, DC: Government Printing Office.

———. 2003. *Employment and Earnings,* vol. 50, January. Washington, DC: Government Printing Office.

———. 2011. "Workplace Injuries and Illnesses—2010." USDL-11-1502. Released October 20.

———. 2013. "Union Members—2012" USDL-13-0105. Released January 23.

U.S. Department of Labor, Mine Safety and Health Administration. 2011. "Report of Investigation: Fatal Underground Mine Explosion, April 5, 2010—Upper Big Branch Mine–South, Performance Coal Company Montcoal, Raleigh County, West Virginia, ID No. 46–08436." December 6 (available at http://www.msha .gov/Fatals/2010/UBB/PerformanceCoalUBB.asp; downloaded January 15, 2012).

U.S. Department of Labor, Occupational Safety and Health Administration. 1990. *Phillips 66 Company Houston Chemical Complex Explosion and Fire: Implications for Safety and Health in the Petrochemical Industry.* Report to the President. Washington, DC: Government Printing Office.

U.S. General Accountability Office. 2006. *Employment Arrangements: Improved Outreach Could Help Ensure Proper Worker Classification.* GAO-06-656. Washington, DC: GAO.

———. 2009. *Employee Misclassification: Improved Coordination, Outreach and Targeting Could Better Ensure Detection and Prevention.* GAO-09-717. Washington, DC: GAO.

U.S. General Accounting Office. 2000. *Worker Protection: OSHA Inspections at Establishments Experiencing Labor Unrest.* GAO/HEHS-00–144. Washington, DC: GAO.

Von Richthofen, Wolfgang. 2002. *Labour Inspection: A Guide to the Profession.* Geneva: International Labour Office.

Webb, Sidney, and Beatrice Webb. 1897. *Industrial Democracy*. London: Macmillan.

Weil, David. 1991. "Enforcing OSHA: The Role of Labor Unions." *Industrial Relations* 30, no. 1: 20–36.

———. 1992. "Building Safety: The Role of Construction Unions in the Enforcement of OSHA." *Journal of Labor Research* 13, no. 1: 121–132.

———. 1996. "If OSHA Is So Bad, Why Is Compliance So Good?" *RAND Journal of Economics* 27, no. 3: 618–640.

———. 2004. "Individual Rights and Collective Agents: The Role of New Workplace Institutions in the Regulation of Labor Markets." In *Emerging Labor Market Institutions for the Twenty-First Century*, edited by Richard Freeman, Larry Mishel, and Joni Hersch. Chicago: University of Chicago Press, 13–44.

———. 2005a. "The Contemporary Industrial Relations System in Construction: Analysis, Observations, and Speculations." *Labor History* 46, no. 4: 447–471.

———. 2005b. "Public Enforcement / Private Monitoring: Evaluating a New Approach to Regulating the Minimum Wage." *Industrial and Labor Relations Review* 52, no. 2: 238–257.

———. 2008a. "Mighty Monolith or Fractured Federation? Business Opposition and the Enactment of Workplace Legislation." In *The Gloves-Off Economy: Workplace Standards at the Bottom of America's Labor Market*, edited by Annette Bernhardt, Heather Boushey, Laura Dresser, and Chris Tilly. Champaign, IL: Labor and Employment Relations Association, 287–314.

———. 2008b. "A Strategic Approach to Labor Inspection." *International Labor Review* 147, no. 4: 349–375.

——— 2009. "Rethinking the Regulation of Vulnerable Work in the USA: A Sector-Based Approach." *Journal of Industrial Relations* 51, no. 3: 411–430.

——— 2010. *Improving Workplace Conditions through Strategic Enforcement*. Report to the Wage and Hour Division. Washington, DC: U.S. Department of Labor.

———. 2012a. "Broken Windows, Vulnerable Workers, and the Future of Worker Representation." *The Forum* 10, no. 1 (available at http://www.degruyter.com/view/j/for.2012.10.issue-1/1540-8884.1493/1540-8884.1493.xml?format=INT).

——— 2012b. "Market Structure and Compliance: Why Janitorial Franchising Leads to Labor Standards Problems." Working paper, Boston University.

Weil, David, and Carlos Mallo. 2007. "Regulating Labor Standards via Supply Chains: Combining Public/Private Interventions to Improve Workplace Compliance." *British Journal of Industrial Relations* 45, no. 4: 805–828.

Weil, David, and Amanda Pyles. 2006. "Why Complain? Complaints, Compliance and the Problem of Enforcement in the U.S. Workplace." *Comparative Labor Law and Policy Journal* 27, no. 1: 59–92.

Wells, John Calhoun, Thomas Kochan, and Michal Smith. 1991. *Managing Workplace Safety and Health: The Case of Contract Labor in the U.S. Petrochemi-*

cal Industry. Report to the U.S. Department of Labor. Beaumont, TX: The John Gray Institute, Lamar University.

Widdicombe, Lizzie. 2011. "Thin Yellow Line: The Taxi-Driver's Advocate." *The New Yorker,* April 18, 72–77.

Williamson, Oliver. 1985. *The Economic Institutions of Capitalism.* New York: The Free Press.

Winter, Harold. 2008. *The Economics of Crime: An Introduction to Rational Crime Analysis.* London: Routledge.

Wissinger, G. Micah. 2003. "Informing Workers of the Right to Workplace Representation: Reasonably Moving from the Middle of the Highway to the Information Superhighway." *Chicago-Kent Law Review* 78: 331–356.

Womack, James, Daniel Jones, and Daniel Roos. 1991. *The Machine That Changed the World: The Story of Lean Production.* New York: Harper Perennial.

Woods, Rose. 2009. "Industry Output and Employment Projections to 2018." *Monthly Labor Review,* November, 52–81.

Yaniv, Gideon. 2001. "Minimum Wage Noncompliance and the Employment Decision." *Journal of Labor Economics* 19, no. 3: 596–603.

Zatz, Noah. 2010. " 'Who Is an Employee?' and Other Questions." Prepared for NLRB / George Washington University Symposium on "The National Labor Relations Act at 75: Its Legacy and Its Future." Manuscript (available at http://www .nlrb.gov/75th/Documents/Zatz.pdf).

Acknowledgments

It has been many years since I wrote a book without coauthors. I forgot what a lonely experience that can be. Fortunately, however, getting to that stage involved interacting and working with many people who have played diverse but essential roles in the course of research, thinking, and writing whom I wish to acknowledge and thank.

This book has roots in a series of projects, funded by the U.S. Department of Labor through a cooperative agreement with Mathematica Policy Research, to study patterns of compliance with workplace standards and the impact of enforcement in a variety of industries. In addition to a series of contracts with the Department of Labor, I have benefited for many years from the cooperation and insights of staff at the national, regional, and district offices of the department's Wage and Hour Division, where much of the research has focused. I am particularly grateful for the opportunity to work with Libby Hendrix, who continually provided unique perspectives on how a government agency can adapt to the challenges of a changing workplace. I am also deeply thankful to her predecessor, Rae Glass, whom I have had the good fortune to know and work with for more than a decade and who has provided deep insight into many aspects of the issues discussed in this book.

My gratitude also goes to the many talented national and field staff of the Wage and Hour Division I have met for their insights over the years of research. Discussions with others at the Department of Labor over the past few years, including Michael Felsen, Seth Harris, David Michaels, Raj Nayak, Doug Parker, Patricia Smith, Bill Spriggs, and Greg Wagner, have also been extremely informative and helpful. The comments in this book solely reflect my own analysis, perspectives, and conclusions and not the views or policies of the Department of Labor or the Wage and Hour Division.

I am grateful to the Russell Sage Foundation and program officer Aixa Citron for financial support and interest in this project. Assistance for the final push to complete this book arose from my appointment as a Jacob Wertheim Fellow of the Harvard

Law School Labor and Worklife Program in 2011–2012. I thank Elaine Bernard and Richard Freeman particularly in this regard.

This book also reflects the very able assistance and collaboration of a large and varied research team at Boston University over many years. Amanda Pyles Diab worked with me from the beginning of the Department of Labor project to its completion. Time and again I have benefited from Amanda's sharp mind, her assistance in analyzing large and ornery datasets, and her attention to detail, which is paramount in this type of research. My thanks to three Ph.D. students in economics at Boston University who undertook dissertation papers related to major themes in this book: Carlos Mallo, MinWoong Ji, and Marric Buessing. I also benefited from and enjoyed the energy, creativity, hard work, and tenacity of a group of highly talented undergraduate research assistants: Tucker DeVoe, Claire Gerson, Anne Klieve, Sam Kornstein, Jeff Li, Andrew Ryzhov, Ayumi Shimokawa, Huey Wu, and Jie Zheng. I particularly appreciate their good-humored willingness to suffer my long-winded digressions, anecdotes, and musings as I worked through many of the ideas contained in this book with them.

Many practitioners are active in improving the workplace, and, as I discuss in Part III of this book, many fruitful experiments are occurring at the state, federal, and international levels. I have learned enormously from discussions with many people who are doing innovative work in this area, including Nick Allen, Kim Bobo, Eric Frumin, Terri Gerstein, Joanne Goldstein, Janet Herold, Jon Hiatt, Sangheon Lee, Wilma Liebman, Cathy Ruckelshaus, Ray Scannell, Tony Sheldon, Damon Silvers, Baldemar Velasquez, Richard Whatman, Lee Wicker, and Nicholas Wilson.

I am also grateful to many colleagues for their critical insights at various points of this effort. The ideas have evolved over many years, and I have benefited from formal comments in seminars and conferences and from informal discussions in a variety of settings. In particular, I am grateful to Rose Batt, Elaine Bernard, Annette Bernhardt, Les Boden, Sean Cooney, Liz Day, Janice Fine, Richard Freeman, Archon Fung, Mary Graham, Susan Houseman, John Howe, Shulamit Kahn, Pat Kaufmann, Morris Kleiner, Ryan Knutson, Tom Kochan, Kevin Lang, Russell Lansbury, Peggy Levitt, Rick Locke, Ray Markey, Alex Mas, Bob McKersie, Joan Meyer, Alison Morantz, Paul Osterman, Michael Piore, Michael Quinlan, Jim Rebitzer, Andrew Schrank, Emily Spieler, Kathy Stone, and Noah Zatz. I offer particular thanks to Richard Freeman, Mary Graham, Paul Osterman, Michael Piore, Cathy Ruckelshaus, Amy Shapiro, Carla Weil, and anonymous referees who carefully read the entire manuscript and provided generous and constructive suggestions that helped shape the final draft of the book. As usual, Gregory D. Schetina Esq. provided wise counsel. My thanks to Michael Aronson at Harvard University Press for his enthusiasm and support for this book. I am also grateful to participants at seminars at Boston University, Columbia University, Cornell University, Georgetown University,

Harvard University, the International Labor Organization, MIT, Northeastern University, New York University, Rutgers University, Stanford University, UCLA, the University of Melbourne, the University of New South Wales, and the University of Sydney.

I have always been fond of the rabbinical admonition "Find yourself a teacher." Writing this book has made me reflect on my teachers and mentors—in both my academic and family life. Although I have learned so much from many colleagues as a student and academic over the years, several people stand out who profoundly affected the way I think about pursuing research and introduced me to various topics that underlie this book. The late John T. Dunlop gave me a deep appreciation that the phrase "wage determination" required understanding the intersection of product and labor markets, nested in real-world institutions. His example remains a lodestar to undertake the difficult but critical task of bridging academic and applied worlds. The late James L. Medoff taught me the importance of understanding the mosaic of empirical evidence in examining labor markets and employment relations. I continue to gain insights and inspiration from Frederick Abernathy and Nick Salvatore, who have been mentors and friends for a very long time.

Last but most important of all are thanks to my family. My parents, Nancy and Jerry Weil, straddle categories of teachers, role models, guides, and the most devoted cheering section I can imagine. My sisters, Carla and Lisa, have been buoyant and unwavering supporters of completing this book for the past few years, as have my daughters, Rachel and Alanna, whose emerging interests and efforts in improving the world in which they live give me continuing ambition to do the same. Finally, I will fondly remember writing drafts of this book in our home office late into the night with my back to my wife, Miriam, who sat at her desk simultaneously writing her doctoral dissertation. She has been an inspiration to me in so many ways for so long, and has patiently weathered the sometimes stormy moods that have accompanied writing this book.

I am deeply grateful for the assistance, comments, critiques, and insights from all of the above. But to return full circle to the loneliness of writing a book on your own, I am solely responsible for any errors that remain.

Index